The 21st Century Maritime Silk Road

This book explores the opportunities and challenges that both Europe and Asia face under the framework of the 21st Century Maritime Silk Road Initiative.

The 21st Century Maritime Silk Road Initiative (MSR Initiative), put forward by the Chinese government together with the Silk Road Economic Belt, reflects China's ambition and vision to shape the global economic and political order. The first step and priority under the MSR Initiative, according to documents issued by China, is to build three 'Blue Economic Passages' linking China with the rest of the world at sea, two of which will connect China with Europe. This initiative, however, still faces enormous challenges of geopolitical suspicion and security risks. This book seeks to assess these risks and their causes for the cooperation between the Eurasian countries under the framework of MSR and puts forward suggestions to deal with these risks in the interdisciplinary perspectives of international relations and international law.

Featuring a global team of contributors, this book will be of much interest to students of Asian politics, maritime security, international law and international relations.

Keyuan Zou is Harris Professor of International Law at the Lancashire Law School and Director of the Institute for International and Comparative Law, University of Central Lancashire, UK.

Shicun Wu is President of China's National Institute for South China Sea Studies, and a Deputy Director of the Collaborative Innovation Centre of South China Sea Studies, Nanjing University, China.

Qiang Ye is Research Associate, National Institute for South China Sea Studies, China. Currently, he is a PhD candidate at Lancashire Law School, University of Central Lancashire, UK.

Contemporary Issues in the South China Sea

Series Editors: Shicun Wu
National Institute for South China Sea Studies, China
Keyuan Zou
University of Central Lancashire, UK

The South China Sea involves a wide array of complex issues covering sovereignty over islands and reefs, maritime delimitation, maritime security, cooperation against piracy and terrorism, resource development and environmental protection, all of which require extensive research. The area's importance largely results from one-third of the world's shipping transiting through its waters and that it is believed to hold huge oil and gas reserves beneath its seabed. Several countries have made competing territorial claims over the South China Sea with such disputes being regarded as Asia's most potentially dangerous source of conflict. This series seeks to provide thoughtful consideration of these issues from a variety of interdisciplinary perspectives. It provides an opportunity for early career researchers as well as established scholars to publish theoretically informed monographs and edited volumes that engage with key issues in this region.

Also in the series

Major Law and Policy Issues in the South China Sea
European and American Perspectives
Edited by Yann-huei Song and Keyuan Zou

Assessing Maritime Disputes in East Asia
Political and Legal Perspectives
Edited by Barthélémy Courmont, Frédéric Lasserre and Éric Mottet

China's Policy towards the South China Sea
When Geopolitics Meets the Law of the Sea
Lingqun Li

The 21st Century Maritime Silk Road
Challenges and Opportunities for Asia and Europe
Edited by Keyuan Zou, Shicun Wu and Qiang Ye

The 21st Century Maritime Silk Road

Challenges and Opportunities for Asia and Europe

Edited by Keyuan Zou, Shicun Wu and Qiang Ye

Routledge
Taylor & Francis Group

LONDON AND NEW YORK

First published 2020
by Routledge
2 Park Square, Milton Park, Abingdon, Oxon OX14 4RN

and by Routledge
52 Vanderbilt Avenue, New York, NY 10017

Routledge is an imprint of the Taylor & Francis Group, an informa business

British Library Cataloguing-in-Publication Data
A catalogue record for this book is available from the British Library

Library of Congress Cataloging-in-Publication Data
A catalog record has been requested for this book

ISBN: 978-0-367-17945-8 (hbk)
ISBN: 978-0-429-05858-5 (ebk)

Typeset in Times New Roman
by Wearset Ltd, Boldon, Tyne and Wear

Printed and bound in Great Britain by
TJ International Ltd, Padstow, Cornwall

Contents

Illustrations

Figures

Tables

Editors and contributors

Editors

Keyuan Zou is Harris Professor of International Law at the Lancashire Law School of the University of Central Lancashire (UCLan), United Kingdom. He specialises in international law, in particular Law of the Sea and International Environmental Law. Before joining UCLan, he worked in Dalhousie University (Canada), Peking University (China), University of Hannover (Germany) and the National University of Singapore. He has published over 70 refereed English papers in over 30 international journals. His recent books include *Arbitration concerning the South China Sea: Philippines versus China* (2016), *Sustainable Development and the Law of the Sea* (2016), and *Global Commons and the Law of the Sea* (2018). He is a member of Editorial Boards for the *International Journal of Marine and Coastal Law, Ocean Development and International Law, Journal of International Wildlife Law and Policy, Copenhagen Journal of Asian Studies, Journal of Territorial and Maritime Studies, Marine Policy*, and *Chinese Journal of International Law*, as well as a member of the Advisory Boards of the *Global Journal of Comparative Law, Asian Pacific Journal of Ocean Law and Policy, Korean Journal of International and Comparative Law* and *China Oceans Law Review*.

Shicun Wu has a PhD in history and is President of China's National Institute for South China Sea Studies, Deputy Director of the Collaborative Innovation Center of South China Sea Studies, Nanjing University, a member of Foreign Policy Advisory Group of the Chinese Foreign Ministry, and Vice President of Bo'ao Forum for Asia Research and Training Institute. Dr Wu's research interests cover the history and geography of the South China Sea, maritime delimitation, maritime economy, international relations and regional security strategy. His main single-authored books include: *What One Needs to Know about the Disputes between China and the Philippines, What One Needs to Know about the South China Sea, Solving Disputes for Regional Cooperation and Development in the South China Sea: A Chinese Perspective, A Study on the South China Sea Disputes* and *The Origin and Development of the Nansha*

Disputes. His main edited books include: *Non-Traditional Security Issues and the South China Sea-Shaping a New Framework for Cooperation, Recent Developments in the South China Sea Dispute: the Prospect of a joint Development Regime, Securing the Safety of Navigation in East Asia: Legal and Political Dimensions, Maritime Security in the South China Sea, Selective Studies on World Famous Island Economic Bodies* and a collection of documents relating to South China Sea Issues.

Qiang Ye is Research Associate at the Research Center for Oceans Law and Policy of the National Institute for South China Sea Studies, China. Qiang Ye joined the National Institute for South China Sea Studies in 2013, where he received a Master of Law degree from Tsinghua University. His research interests focus on public international law, particularly international dispute settlements and the Law of the Sea. His major published works include: *Case Study on the Law of the Sea* (NPC Publishing 2016); *Interpretation and Application of Article 298 of the Law of the Sea Convention in Recent Annex VII Arbitrations: An Appraisal* (Ocean Development and International Law); 'Does China's Position Paper on the *South China Sea Arbitration* Constitute a Preliminary Objection?' (in: *Arbitration Concerning the South China Sea: Philippines versus China*, Ashgate Publishing 2016); 'China's Position Paper on the *South China Sea Arbitration*: Legal Implications under the Diplomatic Objections' (*Chinese Review of International Law*); 'China's "Nine-Dash Line" Claim: US Misunderstands' (*RSIS Commentary*); 'A Study on the Advisory Proceedings before the ITLOS as a Full Court' (*China Oceans Law Review*); and 'On the Legal Basis of the Advisory Jurisdiction of ITLOS as a Full Court' (*Peking University International and Comparative Law Review*).

Contributors

Henrik Andersen is currently Associate Professor in law at the Copenhagen Business School. He was previously a senior lecturer at the Lancashire Law School, UCLan. He has an interdisciplinary background with a BSc and an MSc in commercial law and business administration, from Copenhagen Business School, Denmark, where in 2008, he was awarded a PhD degree for his thesis 'EU Dumping Determinations and WTO Law'. He worked as an Associate Professor at Copenhagen Business School, where he also was a member of the Confucius Institute, until in 2014, he joined the Lancashire Law School. Henrik Andersen researches in international economic law with a special focus on World Trade Organization law, in particular antidumping and rule of law, and WTO dispute settlements. He has also, for a number of years, worked with Chinese law and rule of law and has recently focused on China's 'One Belt One Road' programme. Henrik Andersen has had a number of international publications and has been speaker and keynote speaker at numerous international conferences and international research seminars.

Vivian Louis Forbes is presently an Adjunct Research Professor, NISCSS, Haikou, China and Adjunct Professor, School of Earth and Environment, UWA. He was a Distinguished Research Fellow and Guest Professor, CIBOS and CICTSMR, Wuhan University (2013–2017) and Guest Professor, Xiamen Universities; Dalian Maritime University and Yunnan University, China. He was also a Visiting Research Fellow, Maritime Institute of Malaysia (1993–2018). His research interests are in the disciplines of cartography, marine political geography and maritime studies. He lectures in these topics and has published widely on these themes. The main focus of his research is on maritime boundary delimitation and geopolitical issues. He has specialised on Indian Ocean maritime affairs and international boundary issues of East, South and Southeast and Southwest Asia. He has presented a number of papers at conferences and seminars nationally and internationally and has conducted workshops on the cartographical concepts and geopolitical concerns in determining maritime boundaries. He is author of a number of books, atlases and journal articles, and has been consulted on matters relating to maritime and terrestrial boundaries. He appeared as a witness at the Joint Standing Committee on Treaties Sessions for the Australian Federal Senate, in relation to the delimitation of Australia's maritime boundaries with Indonesia in 1997 and East Timor in 2002. He has presented, on an annual basis (since 1995), workshops on maritime boundary and archival research issues at the Maritime Institute of Malaysia in Kuala Lumpur and other cities.

Erik Franckx is a full-time Research Professor, President of the Department of International and European Law, Faculty of Law and Criminology, Vrije Universiteit Brussels (V.U.B.). He also holds teaching assignments at Vesalius College (V.U.B.); Université Libre de Bruxelles; Brussels School of International Studies (University of Kent); Institute of European Studies (V.U.B.); Université Paris-Sorbonne Abu Dhabi, United Arab Emirates; and the University of Akureyri, Iceland. He is appointed by Belgium as an expert in marine scientific research for use in special arbitration under the 1982 United Nations Convention on the Law of the Sea (1982 Convention) (2004–present); expert in maritime boundary delimitation to the International Hydrographic Organization (2005–present); member of the Permanent Court of Arbitration (2006–present); arbitrator under the 1982 Convention (2014–present). He was an invited speaker at about 80 international conferences during 2006–2017 in the following countries: Canada, Chili, China (PRC), Germany, Greece, Greenland, Finland, France, Iceland, Italy, Japan, Latvia, Lebanon, Luxembourg, Malaysia, Netherlands, Norway, Poland, Portugal, Singapore, South Africa, South Korea, Spain, Russian Federation, Taiwan, Turkey, UK, USA and Vietnam. He served as a consultant to governments (foreign as well as the three levels of the Belgian structure, i.e. at federal, regional and community level), international, supra-national and non-governmental organisations. He is legal counsel on behalf of the Netherlands in the Arctic Sunrise Arbitration against the Russian Federation (2013–present). He has published widely in the area of the Law of the Sea (for a complete list, see www.vub.ac.be/IERE/efranen.html).

Christian Frier is a PhD student at the Department of Law of the University of Southern Denmark. His PhD project deals with the legal implications concerning the use of privately contracted armed security personnel on board Danish ships as protection against contemporary piracy. Other areas of interest include international trade law and transport law. Christian Frier has so far published a few articles within this area of research. Christian Frier is currently affiliated with a research project Policing the Sea (PolSEA), funded by the Danish Government (Independent Research Fund Denmark), dealing with 'policing functions' and the Law of the Sea. The project consists of a multi-level structure comprising a theoretical level focusing on methodological issues as well as case studies, including but not limited to piracy and the Arctic.

Jörn Axel Kämmerer has been a Professor (chair holder) at Bucerius Law School since 2000. He was a guest professor at Université Paris I (Panthéon-Sorbonne) from 2005 to 2007 (part-time) and at Seoul National University, Republic of Korea in 2007. He studied law at Tübingen University, Germany and Université d'Aix-en-Provence/Marseille III, France. Appointed Doctor of Law in 1993, with a thesis on the Antarctic System after the Madrid Protocol, he received a 'venia legend' (Habilitation) in Public Law, European Law and Public International Law in 2000 by Tübingen Law Faculty. His research focuses, *inter alia*, on market regulation, privatisation, as well as law and finance in both German public law and EU law. One of the Directors of the Institute on Company and Capital Markets Law (ICCML/IUKR) at Bucerius, he was appointed member of an advisory committee to the German Ministry of Finance on financial markets regulation in 2011. He is the author of a textbook on Constitutional Law and has made contributions to renowned legal commentaries, mostly on fundamental rights. With two colleagues, he conducted an interdisciplinary research project on the evolution of Public International Law (with financial assistance by the Deutsche Forschungsgemeinschaft). In 2016, he was elected Secretary-General of the Societas Iuris Publici Europaei (SIPE). Jörn Axel Kämmerer teaches in German and English and has given lectures or lecture series to academic institutions in various countries, including Australia, Brazil, Canada, China, Israel, Japan, New Zealand, Singapore and South Africa.

Sophia Kopela is Lecturer in Law at Lancaster University Law School. She holds an LLB from the University of Athens (Greece), an LLM in Public International Law from the University of Nottingham (UK) and a PhD in International Law of the Sea from Bristol University (UK). Her specialisation lies in the Law of the Sea, International Environmental Law and Public International Law. She has published articles in international journals and presented papers at international conferences in these fields. Her article *2007*

'Archipelagic Legislation of the Dominican Republic: An Assessment' was awarded the Gerard Mangone Prize for the best article in the *International Journal of Marine and Coastal Law* in 2009. She is the author of a mono-graph entitled *Dependent Archipelagos in the Law of the Sea* published by Martinus Nijhoff/Brill in 2013. She is also the book review editor of the *International Journal of Marine and Coastal Law*.

Lingqun Li is a research fellow at the China Center for Collaborative Studies of the South China Sea at Nanjing University. Dr Li obtained a PhD degree in Political Science from the University of Delaware, USA. Her research inter-ests include great-power relations in the South China Sea, maritime security in East and Southeast Asia, regional maritime cooperation in the South China Sea and other enclosed and semi-enclosed sea areas, and the development of domestic maritime governance system in China.

Fu-Kuo Liu is a research fellow at the Institute of International Relations (IIR), Taiwan Chengchi University and Professor at the International Doctorate Program in Asia Pacific Studies (IDAS), College of Social Science, Taiwan Chengchi University. He is also the Executive Director of the Taiwan Center for Security Studies. He leads the publication of a policy-oriented monthly and currently serves as chief editor of *Strategic & Security Analyses* (pub-lished monthly in Chinese) and a bimonthly *Strategic Vision* at IIR. He is also the CEO of the Association for Emerging Market Studies in Taiwan. Dr Liu was Chairman of the Research Division of American and European Studies, IIR; Chairman of the Research and Planning Committee at the Ministry of Foreign Affairs, Taiwan and a consultative adviser of the Mainland Affairs Council, Taiwan. He was visiting fellow at the Department of International Business, Economics, and Politics, Aoyama Gakuin University, Tokyo (2000); research associate, Asian Studies Program, School of Foreign Service, Georgetown University (2000–2001); visiting fellow, Center for Northeast Asian Policy Studies (CNAPS), the Brookings Institution (2006–2007); visit-ing fellow at the National Institute for the South China Sea Studies, China (2012); and visiting fellow at Department of Government and Public Admin-istration, University of Macau (2014). His research focuses on Asia Pacific security, Asian regionalism, national security and the South China Sea, peace process across the Taiwan Strait, US strategy in Asia, Asian maritime security and Taiwan foreign and security policy. He received a PhD in Politics from the University of Hull, UK.

Rafael Emmanuel Macatangay is Lecturer in Energy Economics, Centre for Energy, Petroleum and Mineral Law and Policy, conducts research and teaches postgraduate modules on energy market risk management, competi-tion and regulation in the energy sector, and natural resource policy. He has extensive professional experience in physical and financial markets for energy commodities, and has provided oral and written testimony in US regulatory proceedings on the prudence of energy portfolio optimisation decisions. His co-authored publication *The Role of Valuation and Bargaining in Optimising Transboundary Watercourse Treaty Regimes* pioneers the concept of treaty optimisation. He has a PhD from the University of Manchester, UK.

David M. Ong, LLB (Hons) and LLM International Law (with Dist.) (Hull), is Research Professor of International and Environmental Law at the Nottingham Law School, Nottingham Trent University, UK. His main research interests are in the Law of the Sea and International Environmental Law; he has published in the *American Journal of International Law* (1999) and the *European Journal of International Law* (2001). More recently, his research has focused on the interplay between international development finance and investment in natural resource infrastructure projects, as well as the social and environmental risks of such projects. He has published on these issues in the *Nordic Journal of International Law* (2010 and 2016) and the *International Journal of Law in Context* (2015). He has also co-edited three edited volumes of essays in each of these three sub-fields of international law. David's continuing research and publications in Law of the Sea issues affecting the East and Southeast Asian maritime regions is increasingly being recognised both in the UK and abroad. During May and June 2016, he was invited to present conference papers on these issues in Vietnam, South Korea, and at three conferences in China. His recent publications on South China Sea issues include: 'Specifying Procedural Obligations for Joint Development and Alternative Joint Development Models for the South China Sea', in: Wu Shicun and Nong Hong (eds.), *Recent Developments in the South China Sea Dispute: The Prospect of a Joint Development Regime*, Routledge (2014) Ch. 7, pp. 99–136; and 'A Bridge Too Far? Assessing the Prospects for International Environmental Law to Resolve the South China Sea Disputes', *International Journal of Minority & Group Rights* (2015).

Kim Østergaard, PhD, is a professor at the Law Department of the Copenhagen Business School, Denmark. In his research, Kim Østergaard deals with strategic contracting, contract law, transport law, including maritime law, and the methodological challenges in the intersection between law and economics. Kim Østergaard has so far published in total more than 80 articles and books in Danish or English. He is currently dealing with two major research projects. One of the research projects, funded by the Danish Government, comprises Policing the Sea (PolSEA). The other research project funded by the Lundbeck Foundation deals with the access and possibilities to use health data in research contracts. The findings of the latter project will be published as a book in Danish in autumn of 2019 and in English in 2020.

Volker Röben is Professor in Energy Law and Global Regulation at the University of Dundee, as well as a visiting professor at the China University of Political Science and Law, Beijing, and docent at the University of Turku. Prior to joining Dundee, he was a professor at Swansea University and a senior research fellow at the Max Planck Institute for Comparative Public Law and

International Law. He has held visiting professorships *inter alia* at the University of Chicago School of Law, served as a clerk to Justice Di Fabio of the German Constitutional Court, and advised the Energy Charter, the European Parliament, international organisations and national parliaments. Volker's research combines public international law, European Union law and the theory of global law, with several books and numerous articles published and a research monograph on the European Energy Union is in press with Cambridge University Press. He also serves on the board of the Max Planck Encyclopedia of Comparative Constitutional Law.

Lorenzo Schiano di Pepe is a Full Professor of European Union Law at the University of Genoa, Italy, currently teaching 'EU Law' and 'International and European Law of the Sea'. He is the scientific coordinator of a Jean Monnet module on 'European Union and the Law of the Sea' (www.eu-los. eu) and teaches 'Legal Aspects of Hydrography' at a Master's course programme in 'Marine Geomatics'. He holds degrees from the University of Genoa (*laurea cum laude*, 1997), the University of London (UCL) (LL.M. in International Business Law with merit, 1999), Georgetown University Law Center (LL.M. in International Legal Studies with distinction, 2000) and the University of Milan (PhD in International Law, 2004). He has authored or co-authored several monographs, book chapters, essays, articles, encyclopaedic entries and case notes in areas such as public international law, private international law, international and European environmental law, international and European transport law, European institutional law and Law of the Sea. He is on the scientific board of various scientific publications, including *European Papers* (www.europeanpapers.eu) and *Il diritto marittimo* and on the editorial board of *Diritto del commercio internazionale*. He is also on the scientific committee of the Institute for the Law of the Sea and International Marine Environmental Law (ISRIM), based in Bremen, Germany. He is a member, *inter alia*, of the European Society of International Law (ESIL), the Italian Society of International and European Union Law (SIDI), the Italian Society of Maritime Law (AIDIM) and the Italian Association of European Jurists (AIGE).

Shihui Yu is a lecturer at Dalian Maritime University (DMU) Law School. Her teaching covers tort law, maritime law and charterparties. She is a recipient of the DMU Annual Award for Excellence in Teaching several times (2007, 2012, 2013, 2014). She obtained a Master's degree in law from both Dalian Maritime University (2002) and Ghent University (2003). She was a visiting scholar at Tulane University Law School (USA) during 2015–2016. Her research interests include marine pollution, seafarers and other maritime-related issues. She published *Charterparties: English and Chinese Law* (DMU Press, 2014; in English) and co-edited other volumes, including *A Study of Maritime Torts* (2012), *ILO Regulations on Seafarers and China's Response* (2009). She is currently a part-time lawyer with the Goodwell Law Firm (Dalian, China).

Lei Zhang is Lecturer in Law at Qingdao University of Science and Technology, majoring in the Law of the Sea. She obtained a PhD degree from Zhejiang University in 2018. She was a visiting scholar at Walther Schücking Institute for International Law, Kiel University, Germany (2016–2017). She published 'Cooperation on Climate Change in the South China Sea Region under the "Maritime Silk Road Framework"' in *Southeast Asian Studies*, and was given the 2nd Scholarship of Collaborative Innovation Center of South China Sea Studies. In 2017, a co-authored paper 'Implementing the London Dumping Convention in East Asia' was published in the *Asia Pacific Journal of Ocean Law and Policy*.

Renping Zhang is Director of the Centre for International Maritime Convention Studies at Dalian Maritime University of China. Professor Zhang has been engaged in maritime education and the study of maritime conventions for over 30 years, and his main research and study areas include maritime communication, maritime safety, maritime security, marine environment protection. Professor Zhang has published several books on maritime conventions and their implementations in China, and some papers on maritime safety and security-related areas. Professor Zhang used to work in the Chinese Embassy in London, responsible for the matters of the International Maritime Organization (IMO), International Maritime Satellite Organization (IMSO) and the International Oil Pollution and Compensation Funds (IOPC Funds), mainly dealing with IMO's Assembly Council, Maritime Safety Committee, the Marine Environment Protection Committee and the Legal Committee.

Acknowledgements

It is acknowledged that the contributing chapters of this edited volume generate from two international symposia, respectively convened in Preston, UK: the International Symposium on 'Maritime Silk Road: Challenges and Opportunities for Asia and Europe', jointly organised by the Institute for International and Comparative Law/Confucius Institute, University of Central Lancashire, UK and the National Institute for South China Sea Studies, China (4–5 May 2017); and the International Symposium on 'Maritime Security and the Belt and Road Initiative: European Perspectives' jointly organised by the Institute for International and Comparative Law and Confucius Institute, University of Central Lancashire (10 May 2018) under a research project on 'Belt and Road Initiative: Challenges and Opportunities for Asia and Europe' funded by the University of Central Lancashire (UCLan) through its Confucius Institute and partially by the National Institute for South China Sea Studies in China. The editors express their sincere appreciation to the two funding institutions, particularly Ms Feixia Yu, Director of the UCLan Confucius Institute for her involvement in the successful execution of the research project. Meanwhile, the editors express their sincere gratitude to all the contributors whose contributions are essential to make the volume a reality.

The editors also express their sincere appreciation to Routledge, particularly Mr Andrew Humphrys for his constant support of publishing the Book Series on *Contemporary Issues in the South China Sea*, including this book.

1 Introduction

Keyuan Zou, Shicun Wu and Qiang Ye

Introduction

The 'One Belt, One Road' Initiative launched by Chinese President Xi Jinping in the year 2013, is providing new impetus and practical paths for intra- and inter-regional connectivity. The Initiative focuses on cooperation between China and countries along the land-based 'Silk Road Economic Belt' and the ocean's '21st-Century Maritime Silk Road', which is essentially shipping lanes from China to Europe. The promotion of policy coordination and strategic integration within the framework of the Initiative is China's key policy towards Europe. The fact that the demographic coverage between the European Union (EU) and China accounts for 64 per cent of the world's population and 30 per cent of global Gross Domestic Product (GDP), will make the cooperation among the Asian and European partners more beneficial. In addition to the mutual benefit for Asian and European countries, the Initiative may be more beneficial for the UK, particularly after its formal Brexit.

Undoubtedly, however, the Initiative faces enormous challenges of geopolitical suspicion and security risks. Despite reshaping the geoeconomic landscape of the Initiative, doubts remain that China is trying to realise its geopolitical objectives through the Maritime Silk Road Initiative. On the other hand, the regions along the Road are full of geopolitical conflict zones with traditional and non-traditional security challenges. Therefore, it is necessary to develop a risk assessment for the Initiative, which given its long-term and large scale cooperation with so many countries and regions involved, it has elicited a strong response from not only China's neighbouring countries and regions, but the entire international community.

In order to cope with these issues from the academic perspective, the Institute for International and Comparative Law of the University of Central Lancashire, UK and the China National Institute for South China Sea Studies have jointly undertaken a research project on the Maritime Silk Road. Part of those research outputs was successfully presented at the International Symposium on 'Maritime Silk Road: Challenges and Opportunities for Asia and Europe', on 4–5 May 2017 (Preston, UK). By bringing global experts together in discussion, the Symposium explored various issues concerning the opportunities and challenges that both Europe and Asia face, including sea lanes and maritime connectivity, safety of navigation, non-traditional security threats, sustainable development and marine environment protection.

Contents and structure

This book includes papers selected from the above Symposium and constitutes four parts. Part I focuses on the Asia-Europe maritime cooperation and handles challenges arising from the cooperation under the framework of the Initiative. In Chapter 2, Jörn Axel Kämmerer discusses an EU perspective on the Maritime Silk Road. He concludes that, by erecting a structure that connects a multitude of States, markets and jurisdictions, the architects of the Maritime Silk Road will need to price in tensions, incompatibilities and clashes – as well as mutual mis-perceptions – between legal and political systems. While laying the foundations is a matter of public international law, the interior fittings must also be adjusted to EU law – that is, to an intermediate order that is neither national nor international. Although third-state actors cannot formally invoke the free movement of goods and the freedom to provide services in the Union, secondary Union law, especially the rules providing for a non-discriminating public tendering procedure, are actually conceived in a way that they also benefit non-Union players. These provisions are derived from the market freedoms and the underlying concept of unobstructed competition, constituent pillars of that order that China cannot expect to be waived for the sake of building the Maritime Silk Road. Moreover, the EU is unlikely to hail the Maritime Silk Road if they feel that it turns on China's interests only; that Chinese unilateralism drives a wedge between the Member States and between the latter and the Union; that the access of European companies to Chinese markets, especially service markets, remains limited; and that no reciprocity can be expected as regards access to land use rights, concessions or shares of port management companies.

In Chapter 3, Erik Franckx discusses the Northern Sea Route in the context of China's Maritime Silk Road Initiative, and tries to answer the question of whether the Initiative also encompasses a maritime leg running north of the Silk Road Economic Belt, i.e. a maritime waterway making use of the sea route running north of the Eurasian continent, the so-called Northeast Passage, including the Russian Northern Sea Route.

In Chapter 4, Renping Zhang and Shihui Yu examine the challenge of Maritime Silk Road to port connectivity. They conclude that the connectivity of the Initiative will: tap market potential; promote investment and consumption; create demands and job opportunities; enhance people-to-people and cultural exchanges in the countries along the Maritime Silk Road; and mutual learning among the peoples of the relevant countries, enabling them to understand, trust and respect each other and live in harmony, peace and prosperity. On the other hand, challenges exist where the Maritime Silk Road extends and ports connect across Asia and Europe. The challenges to Maritime Silk Road and port connectivity may include, but not be limited to, those of political factors, economic factors, legal and policy factors, cultural factors, technological factors, maritime security factors and environmental factors.

Part II addresses the traditional and non-traditional security issues of sea lanes of communication (SLOCs). In Chapter 5, Fu-Kuo Liu analyses how the Maritime Silk Road Initiative will change the geopolitical configuration in the Indo-Pacific region. He concludes that with dramatic efforts in place, China through the Maritime Silk Road Initiative, making more cooperative partners along maritime routes, will push through transformation of the geostrategic landscape in the Indo-Pacific. While the Initiative has been gradually implemented, assurance of SLOCs becomes pivotal. Undoubtedly, uncertainties and suspicions of China's grand efforts remain to be challenging. A new doubt about China's assertive effort of reshaping international norms may obscure its rightful goal of the Initiative. The upcoming negotiation on the Code of Conduct (CoC) however, would definitely be considered the progress the region has been long awaiting. It is critically important for China to make the Maritime Silk Road Initiative useful and credible to regional peace in the South China Sea.

Vivian Louis Forbes discusses the SLOCs security from the perspective of geography and its implications on the Belt and Road Initiative (BRI), in Chapter 6. He suggests that a major component and concern of the BRI is the utilisation of the concept of SLOCs, namely, the maritime trade routes employed by ships. In addition to the traditional shipping lanes, there exist potential new routes, for example, weather permitting, via the Arctic Ocean. From the European perspective, cargo shipped from the ports of East Asia via the Polar Silk Road would take a relatively shorter duration than using the routes through the South East Asian seas. However, the SLOCs via the geographical choke points, for example, the Straits of Malacca and Singapore, the Bab-el Mandeb, Strait of Hormuz and Strait of Gibraltar have experienced, and still report, a fair share of problems in the context of maritime security, especially regarding acts of piracy and terrorism. Ensuring safety of the ships and the cargoes they carry, the personnel and the commercial value of the ships is of prime concern to operators and governments of the littoral states. Whereas, freedom of navigation and innocent passage are rights that apply to all commercial shipping, a 'legal grey area' exists for ships engaged in scientific research and other activities. This chapter highlights the problem areas, examines the issues and offers an analysis of maritime security.

Keyuan Zou and Qiang Ye, in Chapter 7, examine the SLOCs security in the South China Sea and its implications on the Maritime Silk Road. The security of SLOCs in the South China Sea still remains an issue in the sense that territorial and maritime disputes between/among multiple claimants in the region, and the geopolitical competition between China and countries outside the region, may constitute threats to the safety of navigation in the South China Sea. While the United States has believed that its Freedom of Navigation Operation Programs (FONOPs) are there to enforce rules of law at the sea, legal analysis better supports China's position that the US FONOPs in the South China Sea are offensive to its sovereignty. Moreover, the adverse effect on the process of peaceful settlement of territorial issues and maritime disputes, as well as to the security of SLOCs in the South China Sea region, cannot be ignored.

In Chapter 8, Christian Frier and Kim Østergaard examine the Polar Code's suitability as legal protection against negative externalities in the Arctic in the context of the 'Polar Silk Road'. The Polar Code is the latest example of a source of law, which relates to the commercial activities in the Arctic, aimed at raising the standard of maritime activities in the Arctic by introducing mandatory minimum requirements for the industry. The suitability of the Polar Code as legal protection, however, depends largely on the states' ability to ensure compliance and enforcement, whether it be the flag State itself or foreign states. This will be a task that is imposed on the coastal states to the extent allowed by the Law of the Sea.

Part III addresses the environmental security and fishery cooperation. In Chapter 9, Lorenzo Schiano di Pepe focuses on the Climate Law and its implications of the Maritime Silk Road Initiative. He addresses some implications of the Initiative from the perspective of its possible contribution to climate change patterns, given the fact that the bunker oil usually burnt by merchant ships produces a number of polluting substances, including carbon dioxide. From a legal standpoint, the issue of vessel-generated greenhouse gas emissions sits at the crossroads of two different regimes, namely the United Nations Framework Convention on Climate Change (UNFCCC) and its subsequent developments, including the so-called Paris Agreement of 2015, on the one hand, and the body of rules adopted under the auspices of the International Maritime Organization (IMO), on the other. The interaction between two such normative systems and the approach adopted by the European Union (EU) with regard to carbon dioxide emitted by ships is critically examined.

In Chapter 10, Lei Zhang addresses the environmental security in the South China Sea region. She concludes that environmental issues are the common threat to South China Sea states, which creates a driving force for the South China Sea states' cooperation in order to not only protect the common interests but also maintain regional peace and stability. Although efforts are made at bilateral, regional and inter-regional levels, environmental cooperation still needs to be more effective to achieve a balance between environment and economic development, without being tilted towards fast economic growth. Only if the political leaders address environmental problems as security matters, will environmental conservation be at the top of a country's agenda and they might be more willing to enhance environmental cooperation. The Maritime Silk Road is a chance for China and ASEAN states to deepen trust and strengthen the foundation for cooperation, which will be a new driving force for environmental cooperation in the South China Sea region. In addition, not only joint development but joint protection in the disputed areas might be a better choice for the disputed states.

In Chapter 11, Sophia Kopela addresses the protection of marine environment in the South China Sea in the aftermath of the Philippines/China arbitration. She concludes that protection of the marine environment in the South China Sea requires urgency, ambition and innovative perspectives. As noted by the Tribunal in the *South China Sea Arbitration*, the states are already bound by international obligations to protect the environment and to cooperate as enshrined in international instruments such as the Law of the Sea Convention, and customary international law. These obligations apply both within and beyond national jurisdiction but also regardless of which state has sovereign rights and jurisdiction in these maritime areas. Joint management/protection solutions reflect the ecosystem approach, which does not recognise maritime boundaries and different types of maritime jurisdiction, but also the history of the South China Sea as an area of long coexistence and interaction of nations. This communal regime beyond sovereignty claims can be re-established with an emphasis on sustainable management and protection of the South China Sea. An innovative joint-management regime would demonstrate leadership and ambition to create a pioneering prototype of sustainable management of the seas with people and the marine environment at its centre. Any such solution would require strong political will, reconsideration of foreign and national policy and progressive and innovative thinking, but it might be the only solution for the creation of a peaceful sea of harmonious coexistence, collaboration and effective management, which would implement and facilitate the Maritime Silk Road Initiative.

Volker Röben and Rafael Emmanuel Macatangay, in Chapter 12, discuss the conciliation for marine transboundary energy resources from a law and economics approach. The 1982 UN Convention on the Law of the Sea assigns the right to exploit resources exclusively to one or other coastal state. However, much of the world's marine energy resources, such as oil, gas and renewables, straddle jurisdictional lines. There is a huge risk to the efficient, equitable, legally certain and ultimately secure exploitation of marine transboundary energy resources. The peril arising from the national assignment of the exclusive right to exploit such resources is pervasive, yet remains barely discussed methodically in the literature on the Law of the Sea, international economic law or cognate disciplines. The objective in this chapter is to characterise axioms of rationality underpinning international conciliation for the governance of marine transboundary energy resources. It takes the successful conclusion of the first ever conciliation between Timor-Leste and Australia relating to the Greater Sunrise Gas field as a reference. The analytical foundations are the advance of social welfare, the instrumentality of contract and the integration of legal concepts and economic analysis. The findings of this chapter produce interdisciplinary insights for the formulation of general principles guiding, not only the judicious administration of marine transboundary energy resources through unitisation agreements, but also future efforts at international conciliation to reach such agreements in the likely event of misunderstandings among coastal states over actual or potential resources. Such agreements will, long term, be self-enforcing and help de-fuse tensions between riparian states.

In Chapter 13, Lingqun Li examines the possible fishery cooperation in the South China Sea. Fishery cooperation in the South China Sea is in urgent need, as the region is facing serious challenges of marine environmental degradation and overexploitation of fisheries resources. She has identified two useful elements for decision makers to consider when formulating fisheries cooperation in the South China Sea. First, bilateral approach is the dominant approach in existing cooperative efforts in fisheries management between China and its maritime neighbours. Bilateral approach is pragmatic to lower the threshold of negotiation. It also helps to reduce sensitivity and complexity of the issues in question. The second element, drawn from the Mediterranean experience, is the establishment of a regional framework or mechanism, which as a basic regular venue, pulls together all parties in the region to consult with each other and share concerns with regard to fisheries management. With the Declaration on the Conduct of Parties in the South China Sea (DOC) implementation process progressing smoothly and China and ASEAN making a major breakthrough on the issue of a legally binding COC, the ASEAN is granting the opportunity and responsibility to take the lead in promoting concrete cooperation in regional fisheries co-management and regional marine governance in general.

Part IV discusses handling financial and trade issues. In Chapter 14, David Ong focuses on the Asian Infrastructure Investment Bank (AIIB) and examines whether it will finance environmentally sustainable infrastructure along the Maritime Silk Road. This chapter begins by observing that the Chinese Maritime Silk Road Initiative relies on the development of major infrastructure designed to facilitate the growth of related maritime industries along the route of the Silk Road. This infrastructure is in turn dependent on the usual mix of public and private investment finance that characterises much of the world's major infrastructure projects today. In this regard, the AIIB represents a new and potentially useful source of international finance for direct and indirect support for proposed infrastructure projects along the Maritime Silk Road. The chapter focuses on AIIB decisions to support such infrastructure projects in light of the AIIB international investment finance decision-making procedures and the Environmental and Social Framework. Specifically, it examines whether the environmental sustainability objectives, principles, procedures and standards within this framework are (or will be) effectively applied within such proposed projects along the Maritime Silk Road.

In Chapter 15, Henrik Andersen makes a comparative analysis of the overall principles guiding the Maritime Silk Road of China's 'One Belt, One Road' (OBOR) programme and the rules and principles of the World Trade Organization (WTO). Both the WTO and OBOR aim at trade facilitation but via different means. Where the WTO is based on non-discrimination principles, transparency and market access in a multilateral setting, where disputes are settled in the WTO Dispute Settlement System, the Maritime Silk Road is based on bilateral agreements, flexibility with a dialogue-based approach to disputes. The chapter discusses overlaps between the OBOR principles and WTO law and it is assessed whether they complement each other from a WTO perspective. OBOR investments are important contributors to trade facilitation and seem to complement the WTO trade facilitation rules. However, there are two sides to the coin; where harmony is achieved on the one side, it opens up for the use of the unfair trading rules on the other.

Conclusion

The 21st Century Maritime Silk Road is a historic opportunity for further China-Europe maritime cooperation, as both sides have much to share and more to build in terms of vision, policies and security, making it possible for a new line in the already-thriving exchanges across the continent. To ensure the success of the Initiative, the chapters in this book put forward many constructive suggestions for overcoming obstacles in Maritime Silk Road cooperation, from different perspectives.

China held the 'Belt and Road Forum for International Cooperation' in Beijing in mid-May 2017, and released a document entitled *Vision for Maritime Cooperation under the Belt and Road Initiative*, to synchronise development plans and promote joint actions among countries along the 21st Century Maritime Silk Road. During the editing process of this book, we were also pleased to witness that the relationship between China and European countries has been continuing to deepen – the latest events include the French President Emmanuel Macron's visit and the UK Prime Minister Theresa May's visit to China in 2018 – although Europe still faces some uncertainties with Brexit and EU reforms.

Just as the title of our edited book indicates, there are opportunities and challenges. It is expected, on the one hand, that the Initiative has huge potential in promoting economic development in the participating regions. The Initiative has potential in promoting orderly and free flow of economic factors, highly efficient allocation of resources and deep integration of markets; encouraging the countries along the Road to achieve economic policy coordination and carry out broader and more in-depth regional cooperation of higher standards; and jointly creating an open, inclusive and balanced regional economic cooperation architecture that will promote economic development in all the concerning countries. On the other hand, we have to realise that doubts and distrust still remain in some European countries in regard to the real intention of China to put forward the Initiative and whether it is really a win-win plan for both Asia and Europe. The debates are still going on.

We do hope that this edited book can contribute itself to the continuing studies on the 21st Century Maritime Silk Road, as well as on the maritime cooperation between Asia including China and Europe.

Part I

The Maritime Silk Road and the challenges to Asia–Europe cooperation

2 An EU perspective on the Maritime Silk Road

Legal issues

Jörn Axel Kämmerer

Introduction

The focus of this chapter will not be so much on China as on the western terminus of what is referred to as the Maritime Silk Road (MSR): Europe or, to be precise, the European Union (EU). At the tenth Asia-Europe Meeting in October 2014, the political leaders purportedly agreed that 'the beginning and the end of these routes are the EU and China'.[1] The dictum that history does not repeat itself is not entirely true, at least in this respect: a regular maritime trade route for silk and other products (Roman glass, for example) was already in operation as early as the 1st century, when most of Europe had been unified under the yoke of the Roman Empire. Whereas that early precursor of the MSR was a mere supply chain that neither Roman nor Chinese authorities were formally involved in, its modern counterpart, to which silk matters fairly little for that matter, is a governmental issue in more than one respect – (1) It was initiated by the Chinese government. (2) Its implementation may require the conclusion of various international agreements. Moreover (3), as a highly integrated concept that involves not only transport of goods but also the nodal points or hubs of the maritime transportation network (the 'beads in the string') and the transport-related services provided there, it will have to be adjusted to applicable procedural law – unless the procedural law will be aligned to the MSR.

This is not the place to assess whether and to what extent the MSR may contribute to a transformation of sovereignty where a more traditional, centristic Chinese perception of international relations starts shining through.[2] As regards Europe, sovereign equality has undergone a fundamental metamorphosis insofar as even core functions of States have already been conferred upon the European Union, an entity that operates beyond the binary categories of State and non-State and whose law is neither national nor international. Thus, the Union has been given the exclusive competence for the 'common commercial policy' (Article 3 (1) lit. e TFEU), which means that no international trade agreements may be concluded with third States without its involvement. Other competencies are shared ones, accessible for both the Member States and – provided that it complies with the principle of subsidiarity (Art. 5 (3) TEU), which in legal practice is not taken overly serious – the Union. Shared competencies that are, or may become, relevant to maritime waterways encompass matters such as trans-European networks (Art. 4 (2) lit. h TFEU), transport (Art. 4 (2) lit. g TFEU) but also the internal market as such (Art. 4 (2) lit. a TFEU), which by definition is 'an area without internal frontiers in which the free movement of goods, persons, services and capital is ensured ...' (Art. 26 (2) TFEU). The abundant secondary EU law aiming to implement the free movement of goods and services and fair competition includes provisions that apply to ports and other transport hubs. Against this backdrop, the key role of the EU in setting up the Western branch of the MSR seems to have been ultimately acknowledged by the Chinese government after its initial reluctance to enter into negotiations with Brussels.[3] An 'EU-China Connectivity Platform'[4] was successfully established in September 2015 as a forum for consultation and information on the MSR, for coordination, identification of investment opportunities and, last but not least, explanation of the relevant EU rules and regulations – some of which will be elaborated upon later.

The EU itself appears to cautiously embrace the MSR project but has not positioned itself very firmly and no legal acts relating to it have been adopted so far. The Union has left no doubt that it regards OBOR as a project involving reciprocity and that it expects a higher degree of permeability of Chinese markets for European market actors in return for Chinese investment in Europe.[5] Its 'wait and see' approach may also be accounted for by the need for concretion of the MSR concept: only when the sectors, or policies, affected by the MSR have been clearly identified, will the EU be in a position to assess whether, where and to what extent (considering the principle of subsidiarity) it is permitted to act. Trade and competition, including matters of State aid, are the exclusive competence of the Union; competences relating to the internal market and trans-European networks are shared with the Member States. This distribution of powers also applies to the – probably indispensable – conclusion of international treaties. Where an international partner is desirous of a 'lump-sum' agreement that covers all matters touched upon, including international trade, the price it will have to pay is that of having to conclude a 'mixed agreement' with both the Union and its Member States, which means that 28 (or 27, respectively, after Brexit) ratifications[6] will then be required. We should add that the EU as a whole will be supportive of OBOR and the MSR only if China renounces approaching individual Member States in search of bilateral agreements[7] – irrespective of whether the EU is exclusively competent or not. State-to-State bilateralism, for which there is evidence in the construction of the terrestrial OBOR branch, undermines European integration and cohesion[8] and may ultimately counter China's intention to link itself to an already integrated continental market.

This chapter is going to touch upon a handful of rather technical but sometimes intricate legal questions that the implementation of the MSR in Europe is likely to address. One is whether, and how, it could fit into the trans-European networks and the European motorways of the sea concept as a whole. Insofar as China envisages a comprehensive or inclusive port management, a glance at the legislative provisions governing concessions and other exclusive rights and at the latest legislative acts of the EU on the provision of port services ('Port

Package') is indispensable. Finally, any assistance provided by a Member State – but not the Union – entailing financial benefit is under suspicion of being classified as unlawful State aid, which is why the applicable provisions must be dutifully assessed.

Trans-European networks: connecting the MSR to the European 'motorways of the sea'

One of the EU 'policies' – or of the 'matters' that the Union is competent for – touched upon by the MSR, relates to 'trans-European networks'. Even though it officially is a shared competence according to Article 4 (2) lit. h TFEU, the transnational linking of infrastructure must first and foremost be regarded as a task of the Union by virtue of its nature. Article 171 TFEU specifies that in order to achieve the objective to establish trans-European networks, the Union shall deploy three types of activities: establishment of guidelines, implementation of measures that ensure the interoperability of networks and financial support of projects of common interest, in turn supported by Member States.

The EU wants trans-European networks to be interoperable, multimodal and open for connection to the networks of third countries. This includes the promotion of maritime transport and what is known as European 'motorways of the sea' (Art. 8 of Reg. 1315/2013, hereinafter referred to as the TEN-T [Trans-European Transport Networks] Regulation 2013).[9] In the guidelines adopted by the European Parliament and the Council on 29 April 2004,[10] which aimed to enhance the interoperability of different infrastructures by the year 2020, those 'motorways of the sea' made their first appearance: Art. 12a (1)

> The trans-European network of motorways of the sea is intended to concentrate flows of freight on sea-based logistical routes in such a way as to improve existing maritime links or to establish new viable, regular and frequent maritime links for the transport of goods between Member States so as to reduce road congestion and/or improve access to peripheral and island regions and States. Motorways of the sea should not exclude the combined transport of persons and goods, provided that freight is predominant.

A more comprehensive definition can be found in Article 21 of the TEN-T Regulation 2013. The aim behind the concept is to rationalise the transport and the handling of goods, including terminal infrastructure, roll-on/roll-off facilities, etc. In spite of some striking similarities between the trans-European network of motorways and the MSR concept, the latter appears to be conceived as a supply chain for China rather than a polycentric web. Even so, as far as its European branches are concerned, the MSR will both build upon and need to be adjusted to the 'motorways of the sea', both as a concept and an established network; the legal and political prerogative to conclude a Treaty that would involve them. On the other hand, China will profit from an infrastructure that is already in place[11] – even though the implementation of the five motorway systems proposed by the

Commission has advanced only little, so far. The shipping business has held various motorways of the sea conferences in recent years, the latest of them in Liverpool in 2016. The MSR approach may be a catalyst to their completion and thus ultimately benefit both sides. Moreover, investors in those 'motorways' are eligible for financial support by the Union – on the basis of a transparent, fair and non-discriminatory tendering procedure. The TEN-T Regulation 2013 provides for support of connection of infrastructure networks, including motorways of the sea, by the EU and its cooperation seeking to promote the interoperability with third countries (Art. 8). While the EU welcomes interconnection and some measures are eligible for financial support by the EU even in third States, third-country ports and projects aiming to facilitate maritime transport and the promotion of motorways of the sea with third countries are exempt from this (Art. 8 (1) lit. e, (2) lit. d). Yet, the pros inherent in the motorways of the seas concept seem to outweigh the cons for China: even though it will not be completely free to fix the shipping paths in Europe and agreements on interconnection can be indispensable, it will benefit from synergy and from building upon an already extant network.

Managing the hubs: how to cope with EU harbour legislation

Public tendering for concessions, purchases and land lease

Chinese operators seeking to 'run' European ports must beware that any attribution of rights or assets by the State and its authorities is limited by the freedom to provide services and the freedom of establishment. A single-handed sale or lease of land, any conferral of an exclusive right is usually unlawful, because it deprives potential European competitors of their chances – except where an open, transparent and non-discriminatory tendering procedure has been conducted. This obligation stems from primary law and has only recently been specified by secondary law for the granting of concessions.[12] It applies (with only few exception), irrespective of whether a port authority traditionally resorts to concessions, as in parts of Western and Southern Europe, contracts on the lease of limited land. The duration of a concession (and of associated contracts) must also be limited: once 30 years or so have passed, another call for bids will usually have to be issued and the cards reshuffled (see Art. 18 of the Concessions Directive).

For China, this has some undesired but also some welcome implications. On the one hand, it means that, in implementing the MSR, a Chinese 'walk it alone' is legally impossible. If Chinese actors want more than just an improvement of transport logistics, if they aim to create port infrastructure or have existing facilities allocated to Chinese companies and/or their European partners, or where they seek a port-related concession, concluding treaties with the EU and its Member States is not enough and may not be rewarding at all. China, which is known to shun public procurement procedures, cannot completely evade pesky tendering competition on the regional or local level. Bidding is Union-wide and involves potential bidders from EU Member States (and beyond). On the other hand, the standard of non-discrimination that has been established by secondary Union legislation might benefit Chinese undertakings at least in the areas of public concessions and procurement, considering that EU primary law awards them no such rights.

Incidentally, authorities that oppose China's plan might decide to desist from inviting bidders at all if they take the tasks into their own hands ('internal operators'[13]), but this is unlikely to work with larger ports; moreover, such a decision cannot discharge the authority from respecting the prohibition of State aid. In any case, the not always predictable outcome of a tendering procedure has to be built into China's MSR equation as a variable. This is illustrated by the fact that, even though COSCO had operated Piraeus port for years, Chinese bidders were unsuccessful in their attempt to win the concession to run the second largest port of Greece, Thessaloniki in 2017.[14]

Regulation of the provision of port-related services (Port Package III)

In early 2017, the EU promulgated a legislative act on the provision of services in maritime ports, an act a trifle euphemistically referred to as the 'Port Package'. After several attempts (Port Package I and II) had failed in 2003 and 2006, respectively,[15] the Union was ultimately successful on the third attempt. The act, which eventually took the legislative hurdles between December 2016 and January 2017, aims to enhance fair competition between service providers – and thus the free movement of services and the freedom of establishment – in European ports. Its adoption as early as in the first reading may come as a surprise considering the controversies that had unfolded; but at a closer look, it only obviates that the original, ambitious draft submitted by the Commission had been stripped off most of the controversial topics, which means that not much was left that the political actors could have disagreed on. All this led to a rather tame compromise – a 'port parcel', as the EP's rapporteur himself purportedly dubbed it.

Port Package III, in official terms Regulation (EU) 2017/352 of 17 February, establishing a framework for the provision of port services and common rules on the financial transparency of ports,[16] endeavours, *inter alia*, to establish a framework for the provision of specific port services (such as bunkering, cargo-handling, mooring, pilotage, etc.). Their providers have to comply with minimum requirements as regards their qualification, professional capacity, equipment, social standards, etc. Especially where land or waterside space is scarce, the competent authority or managing body may limit the number of port service providers on the basis of a non-discriminatory and transparent selection procedure that shall be open to all interested parties. This will be followed by the allocation of rights, land or waterside space to individual providers, which is subject to virtually the same criteria (but not covered by the Port Package itself).

In sum, Port Package III reaches not much beyond what primary law requires anyway: access of EU-based operators to all European ports, which can be denied only where an overwhelming public interest or concern so requires. In handling goods in European ports, China and its undertakings will have to take account of the EU approach, which favours not only competition but also deconcentration. In offering port services, they will need to comply with the Port Package standards and, where appropriate, with the rules applying to concessions. In sum, whereas the new legal provisions will render the access to port services markets in the EU neither easier nor more complicated, they can be expected to mar China's preferred 'all in one' strategy.

Financial assistance for waterways and ports: the EU rulebooks on State aid

Maybe the greatest hazard of all those that lurk behind any involvement in EU ports – as a port operator or port service provider – and even, albeit to a lesser extent, establishment of any other navigational infrastructure stems from the prohibition of State aid, enshrined in Art. 107 TFEU. Competition law within the internal market, to which State aid law belongs, falls within the exclusive powers of the Union (Art. 3 (2) lit. b TFEU). The benefit accruing to the company ('undertaking') must be notified to the European Commission for scrutiny. If the Commission finds that it fulfils the State aid criteria, the aid must not be disbursed until, or unless, that authority has waived the prohibition in accordance with Article 107 (3) TFEU. State aid encompasses all sorts of financial advantages which a Member State confers upon undertaking and which the latter provides no market-adequate *quid pro quo* for in return:[17] non-repayable grants, interest-free loans, favourable operating conditions, privileged treatment, etc., but also direct sale of port assets where public tendering would have been a means to determine the fair market price. In March 2015, the European Commission held that a set of selective benefits (mainly tax exemptions) that the Greek government had awarded the Chinese COSCO Group as the operator of parts of Piraeus harbour constituted illegal State aid and had to be claimed back from COSCO.[18] This does not mean that Chinese investors are not welcome in EU ports – neither the privatisation of the port nor the purchase of shares by COSCO[19] had been challenged – but that there are legal limits to rolling out the red carpet for them. That portent should be taken serious by Chinese actors, especially as no distinction is made in EU law between public and private investment.

State aid may become a legal trap for investors in more than one respect. If an authority erroneously holds that the support it lends a company is not State aid and does not make a notification to the Commission, the entire investment will have to be wound up. Misjudgements can easily occur because the distinction between selective aid and general fiscal, infrastructural or maintenance measures is as demanding as assessment of the market-adequacy of a benefit, the cross-border effect of a distortion of trade and, last but not least, the relevant market. Maritime ports may compete not only with each other but also, for example, with airports, and companies established there.[20] Ports that are run by, or as, public authorities are by no means exempt from the interdiction of State aid.[21] However, topographic, demographic and geological differences between EU ports and the diverging legal systems governing them must not be sidestepped. For example, the indistinctive qualification of dredging services as State aid would be inappropriate, insofar as ports located on sandy shores or estuaries may require it much more than ports on rocky shores.

To complicate things, State aid can in some circumstances be justified. This includes aid to promote the execution of an important project of common European interest – such as trans-European networks, including motorways of the sea –, which the EU may declare compatible with the internal market (Art. 107 (3) lit. b Var. 1 TFEU). Accordingly, the 2004 guidelines,[22] in Article 12a (4), stipulate that aid can be provided for 'projects of common interest of the trans-European network of motorways of the sea', which shall involve both the public and the private sectors, that it shall be granted from the national budgets and can be supplemented by aid from the Union on the basis of a public tendering procedure. The EU, which is not bound to the legal limits imposed on State aid, may, on a subsidiary basis, provide financial support for infrastructure and facilities. On a more general scale, the granting of Union aid for Trans-European Network is governed by a Regulation adopted in 2007.[23] In 2014, the Innovation and Networks Executive Agency (INEA) took the place of the former Trans-European Transport Network Executive Agency (TEN-T EA). It has since been charged with the implementation of various programmes relating to the financing of TEN-T, including one that strikingly was named after the first person to navigate the seas between Europa and East Asia since antiquity: the Marco Polo II programme,[24] which adds to the more general TEN-T programme, also administered by that authority. Moreover, investors may profit from various EU funds (structural funds, cohesion funds). It is worthwhile to clarify that in most cases, funding will not be required for the waterway as such but for ports and the facilities established there, such as terminals or for port services.

In 2015, the European Commission proposed an amendment to a 'group exemption regulation' already in force, with a view to establishing, *inter alia*, rules governing investment aid for maritime ports. Until recently, the legislative project had little progress, due to its lack of consistency, but the Commission eventually managed to enact it in June 2017.[25]

In sum, State aid law, which no Chinese investor can sidestep, entails both a chance and a source of uncertainty. Notification to the Commission is essential, except where it has been waived through a group exemption, such as the one that has now been enacted for maritime ports. Even so, many details of these provisions require clarification and explanation; moreover, the waiver only applies where the financial support remains below the upper ceilings defined therein. In other terms, investment will probably be accelerated but not necessarily facilitated insofar as in some respect, the investors will remain burdened with the hazard of an erroneous judgement.

The MSR and Brexit

By the time the MSR is implemented, the UK will probably have already exited the EU. If Brexit will be 'hard' or 'soft' is still hard to predict and none of the approximately five basic exit scenarios is completely unlikely. The 'softest' form of Brexit would be to leave the EU but to remain in the European Economic Area (EEA), alongside Norway, Iceland and Liechtenstein. This form would only pay lip service to the outcome of the British referendum because all EEA members are subject to the four freedoms of the internal market and hence the free movement of persons must be accepted. Unless the parties (i.e. the EU-28 and the three non-EU (EFTA) members) decide to amend the EEA Treaty to provide room for a more customised application of the freedoms,[26] the UK will have to strive for an individual treaty of association with 'EEA minus' features – in other terms, a treaty according to which all freedoms apply – except for the free movement of natural persons.[27] Considering that the TFEU does not distinguish between natural and legal persons and that the free movement of services and freedom of establishment, granted to both, also encompasses financial services, which from an UK perspective should not be barred, the conceptual pillars that such a model could rest upon are highly unclear. Moreover, this model is unlikely to get the consent of the EU, which is desirous to discourage States from 'cream skimming' when it comes to the core features of the internal market. At least it would find a way to be compensated (financially or elsewhere) by the UK for conferring on it the privilege to lawfully interfere with the free flow of workforce. Whether the UK is ready to pay the requested price is an open question. A treaty would also be required for the 'Turkish' option – according to which the UK and the EU would form a customs union without a factor mobility for services, workforce and capital – and the 'Swiss' option, which does not provide for a common customs area but emulates at least some characteristics of the internal market through multiple agreements on individual matters. The UK will find none of them very attractive as long as the free movement of persons is included, as in the agreements with Switzerland, but financial services are not dealt with, as in both cases. There are various reasons why a 'hard', unbuffered, Brexit – option number five – remains the most likely scenario.[28] One of them is that the perspectives opened by the latter four options for a divorce from the Union that really enhances the independence of the UK are rather dissatisfying. Second, the Brexiteers, who often fail to apprehend the importance of 'services' in the concept of the internal market, might cling too much to their unrealistic expectations. Third, the EU is reluctant to give in to what it considers as cherry-picking and which, from its perspective, will trigger false and dangerous compromises. The fourth and maybe most crucial reason why the Brexit will become hard rather than soft is elapsing time: if, since two years after Theresa May's notification of the British intention to withdraw, no agreement on future relations – an agreement that requires the consent of the European Parliament (Art. 50 (2) TEU) – between the UK and the EU has entered into force, the EU membership of the EU will end and EU law will cease to apply to, and in, Britain without further ado. The European Council[29] may extend that period (now, at time of writing, extended to October 2019) but only unanimously so, which implies that any Member State has a right of veto (Art. 50 (3) TEU).

If Brexit happens in such a way that the UK is barred from the internal market, then the legal provisions on 'motorways of the sea' and all secondary EU law relating to harbours and waterways will cease to be legal points of reference for – or hurdles to – connecting the UK to the MSR.[30] At first glance, this may appear advantageous for both the UK and China, considering, for instance, that the European Commission will no longer be able to scrutinise measures that would have qualified as State aid under EU law before, and to intervene where the State has failed to notify the Commission of it.[31] Yet, it must be doubted that a lifting of legal constraints that comes with Brexit would be sufficient to induce China to move the Western terminus of the MSR to the UK, because in this case, China would not gain what it aspires to in the first place, namely convenient access to the European internal market. Moreover, a re-routing of the MSR through the Mediterranean and the Gulf of Vizcaya instead of short-cutting through continental Europe would reduce some of the expected logistic benefits. After all, if the Brexit negotiations lead to no agreement and/or to isolation of the UK from the Internal Market, the creation of a turn-off from the Mediterranean route towards the UK (which would follow the line of an EU maritime motorway, anyway) may be worth considering.

Conclusion

Silk is a delicate and sensitive tissue, and as an issue, the MSR is quite as sensitive and delicate. As is the case with many big and ambitious projects, the devil is in the detail, and we have no reason to expect the MSR to be the exception to that rule. Erecting a structure that connects a multitude of States, markets and jurisdictions, the architects of the MSR will need to price in tensions, incompatibilities and clashes – as well as mutual misperceptions[32] – between legal and political systems. While laying the foundations is a matter of public international law, the interior fittings must also be adjusted to EU Law – that is, to an intermediate order that is neither national nor international. Although third-State actors cannot formally invoke the free movement of goods and the freedom to provide services in the Union, secondary Union law, especially the rules providing for a non-discriminating public tendering procedure, are actually conceived in a way that they benefit non-Union players as well. These provisions are derived from the market freedoms and the underlying concept of unobstructed competition, constituent pillars of that order that China cannot expect to be waived for the sake of building the MSR. Moreover, the EU is unlikely to hail the MSR if they feel that it turns on China's interests only, that Chinese unilateralism drives a wedge between the Member States and between the latter and the Union, that the access of European companies to Chinese markets, especially service markets, remains limited and no reciprocity can be expected as regards access to land use rights, concessions or shares of port management companies. In any event, an MSR is truly a road and not just another shipping route when it has dual carriageways and more than just a single destination. Cautious optimism may be justified against the backdrop of some legal developments that have been taking place beyond the realm of EU law: considering that on the one hand, China became a member of the EBRD in 2016, and that many EU States have joined the AIIB on the other,[33] the financing of infrastructural projects has become somewhat intertwined. The successful conclusion of a MoU between the EBRD and the Chinese Silk Road Fund in June 2016[34] may be seen as a good omen for future institutional cooperation between China and the EU on the MSR and all the legal issues relating to it.

Notes

1 Michał Makocki, The EU Level: 'Belt and Road' Initiative Slowly Coming to Terms with the EU Rules-based Approach, in: van der Putten *et al.* (eds.), *Europe and China's New Silk Roads*, 2015, p. 67, 68, www.clingendael.nl/sites/default/files/ Europe_and_Chinas_New_Silk_Roads_0.pdf (accessed 18 July 2017).
2 See Secretary of State Markus Ederer, *China's Belt and Road Initiative in Context*, Speech of 5 November 2016, www.auswaertiges-amt.de/DE/Infoservice/Presse/ Reden/2016/161109_StS_E_China.html. (accessed 18 July 2017).
3 Michał Makocki, *op. cit.* (n. 1), at p. 68.
4 European Union, High Representative of the Union for the Foreign Affairs and Security Policy, Joint Communication to the EP and the Council: Elements for a new EU strategy on China, JOIN(2016) 30 final, 22 June 2016, p. 9 *et seq*, http://europa. eu/rapid/press-release_MEMO-16-2258_en.htm (accessed 22 June 2016).
5 European Union, High Representative of the Union for the Foreign Affairs and Security Policy, Joint Communication to the EP and the Council: Elements for a new EU strategy on China, JOIN(2016) 30 final, 22 June 2016, p. 10.
6 The EU-27 plus the EU itself.
7 Francesco Saverio Montesano and Maaike Okano-Heijmans, Economic Diplomacy in EU-China Relations: Why Europe Needs its Own 'OBOR', *Clingendael Policy Brief*, June 2016, p. 4, 5, www.clingendael.nl/sites/default/files/Policy%20Brief%20Economic% 20Diplomacy%20in%20EU%E2%80%93China%20relations%20-%20June%202016. pdf (accessed 18 July 2017).
8 See Francesco Saverio Montesano and Maaike Okano-Heijmans, *ibid.*
9 Reg. (EU) No 1315/2013 of 11 December 2013 on Union guidelines for the develop-ment of the trans-European network […], OJ L 348 of 20 December 2013, p. 1. – Also see European Commission, Motorways of the Sea: Detailed Implementation Plan, 2015, https://ec.europa.eu/inea/sites/inea/files/motorways-of-the-sea-dip-june-2016.pdf (accessed 18 July 2017); Regulation (EU) No 1315/2013 […] of 11 December 2013 on Union guidelines for the development of the trans-European transport network and repealing Decision No 661/2010/EU, OJ L 348 of 20 December 2013, p. 1.
10 Decision No 884/2004/EC of the EP and the Council of 29 April 2004 amending Decision No 1692/96/EC on Community guidelines for the development of the trans-European transport network, OJ L 167 of 30 April 2004, p. 1.
11 Fraser Cameron, The Maritime Silk Road – An EU Perspective, in: *World Commerce Review*, June 2015, p. 2(4), www.worldcommercereview.com/html/cameron-the-maritime-silk-road--an-eu-perspective.html (accessed 18 July 2017).
12 Directive 2014/23/EU of the EP and the Council of 26 February 2014 on the award of concession contracts, OJ L 94 of 28 March 2014, p. 1.

13 See Art. 8 Regulation (EU) 2017/352 […] of 15 February 2017 establishing a framework for the provision of port services and common rules on the financial transparency of ports, OJ L 57 of 3 March 2017, p. 1.

14 Kerin Hope, *Greece to Sell Stake in Thessaloniki Port Operator to German-led Consortium*, 25 April 2017, www.ft.com/content/7221b849-5627-369c-8337-ce541f 44f11a.

15 See Thomas Schmidt-Kötters, in: Martin Heidenhain (ed.), *European State Aid Law* (Munich: Beck, 2010), § 18, para. 125.

16 OJ No. L 57 of 3 March 2017, p. 1.

17 For details and exceptions where services in the general economic interest (SGI) are provided, see 'Opinion of Advocate General Léger' of 14 January 2003 on Case C-280/00, Altmark Trans, ECLI:EU:C:2002:188.

18 Commission Decision (EU) 2015/1827 of 23 March 2015 on State aid SA 28876 (12/C) (ex CP 202/09) implemented by Greece for Piraeus Container Terminal SA & COSCO Pacific Limited, OJ L 269 of 15 October 2015, p. 93.

19 On the background, see Frans-Paul van der Putten and Minke Meijnders, *China, Europe and the Maritime Silk Road*, Clingendael Report, March 2015, p. 9 *et seq.*, www.clingendael.nl/sites/default/files/China_Maritime_Silk_Road.pdf (accessed 18 July 2017).

20 See Michael Gayger, *Infrastrukturförderung zwischen EU-Beihilfenrecht und mitgliedstaatlicher Wirtschaftspolitik* (Berlin: Duncker & Humblot, 2016), p. 126 *et seq.*

21 Art. 106 (1) TFEU; see also Recitals no. 5 and 7 of the Commission Directive 2006/11/EC of 16 December 2006 on the transparency of financial relations between Member States and public undertakings as well as on financial transparency within certain undertakings, OJ L 318 of 17 November 2006, p. 17.

22 See above (n. 10).

23 No. 680/2007 […] of 20 June 2007 laying down general rules for the granting of community aid in the field of the trans-European transport and energy networks, OJ L 162 of 22 June 2007, p. 1.

24 For details, see https://ec.europa.eu/inea/. On the Marco Polo II Programme, see Regulation (EC) No 1692/2006 […] of 24 October 2006 establishing the second 'Marco Polo' programme for the granting of Community financial assistance to improve the environmental performance of the freight transport system (Marco Polo II) and repealing Regulation (EC) No 1382/2003, OJ L 328 of 14 November 2011, p. 1.

25 Commission Regulation (EU) 2017/1084 of 14 June 2017 amending Regulation (EU) No 651/2014 as regards aid for port and airport infrastructure, notification thresholds for aid for culture and heritage conservation and for aid for sport and multifunctional recreational infrastructures, and regional operating aid schemes for outermost regions and amending Regulation (EU) No 702/2014 as regards the calculation of eligible costs, OJ L 156 of 20 June 2017, p. 1. Art. 56b of the amended Regulation refers to aid for maritime ports.

26 See for instance, Carl Baudenbacher, After Brexit: EEA Plus as a Solution for the UK?, *Neue Zeitschrift für Kartellrecht [NZKart]*, 2016, p. 498 *et seq.*

27 See Matthias Lehmann and Dirk Zetzsche, Brexit and the Consequences for Commercial and Financial Relations between the UK and the EU, *European Business Law Review (EBLR)* 27 (2016), 999 (1001); Andreas Kokkinis, The Impact of Brexit on the Legal Framework for Cross-Border Corporate Activity, *EBLR* 27 (2016), 959 (966).

28 Tusk: Only Alternative to Hard Brexit Is No Brexit, *EU Observer*, 13 October 2016, https://euobserver.com/tickers/135498 (accessed 18 July 2017).

29 The heads of State and Government (Art. 15 TEU).

30 See Andrew Dinsmore and Richard Aitkens, Jurisdiction, Enforcement and the Conflict of Laws in Cross-Border Commercial Disputes: What Are the Legal Consequences of Brexit?, *EBLR* 27 (2016), 903 (905).

31 For more information, see Richard Whish, Brexit and EU Competition Policy, *Journal of European Competition Law and Practice* 7 (2016), 297 *et seq.*; Ulrich Soltész, Das künftige EU-Beihilferecht und der Brexit – Folgen, künftige Modelle und Vorwirkungen, *Europäische Zeitschrift für Wirtschaftsrecht (EuZW)* 2016, 846 *et seq.*

32 On how language and its graphic codification convey differences in legal perceptions between the EU and China and mutual comprehension of these differences matters to the desired establishment of commercial and legal ties, see Bernhard Großfeld, Neue Seidenstraße [New Silk Road], *Zeitschrift für Vergleichende Rechtswissenschaft (ZVglRWiss)* 103 (2004), 395 *et seq.*

33 www.ebrd.com/news/2016/china-becomes-ebrd-member-as-suma-chakrabarti-visits-beijing.html. The following EU Member States are also (non-regional) AIIB members: Austria, Denmark, Finland, France, Germany, Italy, Luxembourg, Malta, Netherlands, Norway, Poland, Portugal, Sweden and the UK (www.aiib.org/en/about-aiib/governance/members-of-bank/).

34 www.ebrd.com/news/2016/ebrd-silk-road-fund-agree-to-cooperate.html (all pages accessed 18 July 2017).

3 The Northern Sea Route in the context of China's Maritime Silk Road Initiative

Erik Franckx

Introduction

When China launched its grand Silk Road Initiative in 2013, a well-orchestrated diplomatic effort spread the news *urbi et orbi*. The initiative itself might have generated traction rather quickly, but the same could certainly not be said about its concrete content, for it was not until 2015 that the initiative started to take shape in the real world through the approval of concrete projects, the creation of institutions and the actual spending of money.[1]

During the early period, this particular initiative also attracted many different denominations.[2] What, nevertheless, transpired from the very beginning was that the initiative would have a maritime component. This chapter intends to discern the role, if any, that the Northeast Passage, i.e. the maritime route connecting the Atlantic Ocean and the Pacific Ocean by making use of the maritime waters lying north of the Eurasian Continent, plays within the framework of this broader initiative.[3]

In order to answer the question whether OBOR also has a northern maritime component, this chapter starts by briefly describing the origin of this particular Chinese initiative as well as assessing the original Russian interest in it. The Northern Sea Route, i.e. that part of the Northeast Passage between Novaia Zemlia in the west and the Bering Strait in the east,[4] and more particular its opening up for international navigation, which really started in 2010, is addressed here, as well as the Chinese interest in it. The link between these two initiatives of the present decade, one by China and the other by the Russian Federation as described in the second and third parts, respectively, will form the central question of this chapter. Finally, some conclusions are drawn that will try to characterise the relationship between China's OBOR and the Russian Federation's Northern Sea Route, past as well as present, with even some attempted predictions as to the future.

The OBOR initiative

It will be clear by now that the Maritime Silk Road is part of a larger initiative, namely the OBOR, which in essence started out as a land-based idea. The latter is clearly demonstrated by the origins of this initiative, which are to be found in a speech of President Xi Jinping, given on 7 September 2013, at the Nazarbayev University in Astana, Kazakhstan, a land-locked country, where he referred to the building of 'an economic belt along the Silk Road'.[5]

At first Russia was not very enthusiastic about this Chinese initiative, as it did have its own Eurasian Economic Union project. But on the occasion of the visit of the Chinese President to the Victory Day Parade in Moscow on 9 May 2015, where most Western leaders were absent because of the crisis in the Ukraine, both Presidents issued a joint declaration. In this declaration, both presidents confirmed that they would unite the Russian Eurasian Economic Union project and the Chinese Silk Road Economic Belt Initiative.[6] At the 20th Prime Ministers' Regular Meeting between the two countries, held in Beijing on 17 December 2015, Li and Medvedev reaffirmed that their countries would work together to join both projects.[7] The changed Russian attitude corresponded with a more general shift in policy in this country around that time, away from Europe and towards Asia, in which this joining of both projects fitted perfectly.[8]

OBOR contains two clearly distinguished routes, namely the Silk Road Economic Belt to the north, and a 21st Century Maritime Silk Road to the south. Given the flexible nature of the initiative when it was first developed, it should come as no surprise that its graphical representation also lacked uniformity. Whether Moscow was included in the line depicting the Silk Road Economic Belt, for instance, was far from uniform. On the other hand, one thing all these early graphical representations of the OBOR initiative seemed to have in common, was that there was no maritime component located north of the Silk Road Economic Belt.

The Northern Sea Route

After the existence of the Northeast Passage had been demonstrated, Imperial Russia had sent several expeditions to the area during the 18th century in order to further map and develop this novel route.[9] When the Soviets came to power, the crucial importance of the maritime route between the White Sea in the west and the Bering Strait in the east had been duly stressed by means of the establishment of the Main Administration of the Northern Sea Route in 1932. This high-level body was tasked to develop this route, to equip it, keep it in good repair and secure the safety of navigation on it.[10] This route was however for a long time of national interest only. Its opening up to international navigation had been suggested, it is true, at different times during the Soviet period, but never really applied in practice.

For a first such occasion, one has to go back in time to the start of the shipping season up north in 1967, when the then Minister of Merchant Marine, Victor Bekayev, suggested that foreign cargo could be transported on Soviet vessels along the route.[11] But is has been submitted that this offer was later tacitly withdrawn as the Soviet Union did not want to give the impression to their Arab allies that they were offering an alternative route in the wake of the

Suez canal crisis.[12] On 1 October 1987, Michael Gorbachev, at that time President of the Soviet Union, gave a much clearer signal at the occasion of a speech delivered in Murmansk: 'Depending on the evolution of the normalization of international relations we could open the Northern Sea Route for foreign shipping subject to the use of our icebreaker pilotage'.[13] It took two more years before the first hard currency was generated as a result of Gorbachev's initiative, namely when goods were shipped from Hamburg to Osaka on board a Soviet registered vessel through the Northern Sea Route.[14] This then prompted the Soviet government to enact specific legislation to regulate shipping in the Northern Sea Route, which became operational as of 1 June 1991. Together with some further enactments adopted in 1996, this legal framework remained operational for a good number of years, mainly because very few ships ever made use of this route.[15]

These slow developments noticeably gained momentum during the shipping season of 2010. As remarked by a privileged observer at that time: '[W]hen the future history of the Arctic will be written, 2010 will be marked off as the breakthrough year for commercial shipping along the Northern Sea'.[16] These early developments in foreign shipping along the Northeast Passage in general, and the Northern Sea Route more particularly, and especially its use by foreign skippers for through passage between the Atlantic and the Pacific, have been followed rather closely by the present author, as reflected in a number of publications spanning the period 2010–2012.[17] As a result of this flurry of foreign use of the Northern Sea Route, the Russian Federation has overhauled its applicable legislation, which became operational in time to be applied to the shipping season 2013.[18] These amendments initially did not have a negative impact on the further growth of the number of foreign vessels making use of the Northern Sea Route during the shipping season in 2013, even though it needs to be admitted that the tonnage transported stagnated[19] and that it still only represented 0.08 per cent of the number of ships and 0.14 per cent of the amount of tonnage that passed through the Suez canal that year.[20]

Climate change in the Arctic, if not the direct cause, has certainly helped to bring about the developments just described. A joint assessment effort of this phenomenon, undertaken around the turn of the century by the Arctic Council and the International Arctic Science Committee,[21] involving more than 300 scientists, experts and members of the indigenous communities,[22] came to a key finding that reduced sea ice is very likely to increase marine transport and access to resources.[23] These findings in turn triggered the Artic Council, together with PAME (Protection of the Marine Environment), to publish an Arctic Marine Shipping Assessment Report in 2009,[24] indicating that the Northeast Passage would profit most in this respect.[25]

China has witnessed these developments, not only as an interested observer, but also as an active (in)direct participant from the early days. Indeed, right from the year 2010, when the use of the Northeast Passage and the Northern Sea Route for transit passage started to pick up, that country has played an active role. During a first phase, ports of China served as destination of the transited goods and later also as ports of departure, especially since this country started to send ships flying its own flag, or the flag of Hong Kong, in transit through this route.

This chapter now attempts to give an overview of this concrete involvement of China in the use of this 'northern maritime route'. The use of this generic term, not usually encountered in the literature, is on purpose for a few reasons. First, the Northeast Passage and Northern Sea Route are not synonyms.[26] The Northeast Passage links the Atlantic and Pacific Oceans, while the Northern Sea Route, which for all practical purposes can be considered to form part of the Northeast Passage at present,[27] only stretches from Novaia Zemlia in the west, more specifically the western entrances of Matochkin Shar, Karskie Vorota and Iugorskii Shar and the meridian starting at Cape Zhelaniia, i.e. the northernmost point of Novaia Zemlia, to the Bering Strait in the east; more specifically the meridian starting at Cape Dezhneva, and bounded in the north by the 200 nautical mile limit of the Russian exclusive economic zone in the area.[28] This means that cargo shipped from the port of Zeebrugge in Belgium and unloaded in Dalian (called here 'example A') will use both routes, whereas a cargo leaving from the port of Murmansk in Russia to be unloaded in Dalian ('example B') will only use the Northern Sea Route.[29] Second, when used here, destinational shipping indicates that either the port of departure or the port of destination is located in the Russian Federation, while transit passage implies that neither the port of departure nor the port of destination are located within the Russian Federation. This may seem straightforward, but unfortunately, many grey areas remain. The two examples A and B given above already indicate that not all crossings of the Northern Sea Route are to be qualified 'transit passage' as understood here, even though, when looking at the issue from a mere Russian perspective, to label them as such, makes sense.[30] How do we qualify moreover a variant of example A, where the ship makes a port call at the Russian port of Sabetta to load some more cargo before discharging the whole cargo at the port of Dalian? Similarly, what do we think of a variant of example B, where the port of departure is Sabetta, rather than Murmansk, or even Pevek, both located inside the water area of the Northern Sea route? Because such voyages will have used only a part, whether large or small, of the Northern Sea Route, are they to be included in the present overview?[31]

Another preliminary caveat that needs to be taken into consideration concerns the data. This is somewhat related to the grey areas just referred to, because the two main sources normally relied upon, namely the Center for High North Logistics[32] and the Administration of the Northern Sea Route,[33] tend to use different definitions, as alluded to above.[34] Given the fact that these two sources span different time periods,[35] provide different kinds of information[36] and that even within one and the same source not always the same basic information is provided during the years covered,[37] it should not be a surprise that the data provided by these two sources does not always correspond and that gaps do exist, leading some authors to conclude quite frankly: 'We do not know what exactly is happening at the N[orthern]S[ea]R[oute]'.[38] The present author[39] relies mostly on the information provided by the CHNL, press reports, occasional reports provided by shipping companies or other people directly involved in the use of the Northern Sea Route, as well as the specialised literature. If information provided by these different sources turns out to be contradictory, a value judgement by the author indicates, to the best of his abilities, what seems to him to be the most reliable source under the given circumstances.

2010

The first foreign ship ever, not visiting a Russian port when making use of the Northeast Passage for commercial purposes, left Norway with the destination China in 2010.[40] It concerned the Nordic Barents, an ice-strengthened bulk carrier flying the flag of Panama and belonging to Nordic Bulk Carriers,[41] delivering a cargo of about 40,000 tonnes of iron ore concentrate[42] from the Sydvaranger mine near Kirkeness to the port of Lianyungang.[43]

During the same year, other ships with destination China made use of the Northern Sea Route, but not the Northeast Passage *stricto sensu*, as they did not connect the Atlantic with the Pacific. These ships instead started their journey in the Russian port of Murmansk and subsequently crossed the Northern Sea Route from west to east. It concerned first of all the Baltica, an ice-strengthened Aframax tanker of 117,000 DWT flying the flag of Liberia and belonging to the Russian Sovcomflot Group, which became the first high tonnage tanker to make the passage delivering 70,000 tonnes of gas condensate to the port of Ningbo.[44]

A second voyage leaving from Murmansk with the destination China that year was undertaken by the Monchegorsk, an ice-strengthened cargo vessel flying the Russian flag and owned by the mining company Norkilsk. Special about this voyage was that the ship made a port call at the Russian port of Dudinka.[45] It became the first cargo vessel to make a round-trip through the Northern Sea Route without icebreaker assistance. The vessel delivered metal to the port of Shanghai and returned with consumer goods for the Russian port of Dundinka.[46]

2011

During the 2011 shipping season, no transit passages through the Northeast Passage were made from or to China. However, four ships sailed the Northern Sea Route, all transporting gas condensate from the Novatek company to China. The first to open the season was the Perseverance, a Belgium owned Panamax tanker flying the flag of Singapore, which made use of a new route north of the New Siberian Islands allowing vessels with draughts of over 12 meters.[47] This ship was the first ever to make three crossings during one and the same season. It first sailed between the Russian port of Vitino in the western extremity of the White Sea and the Chinese port of Ningbo, where it delivered its cargo of about 60,000 tonnes gas condensate. From there it set sail for the Republic of Korea to pick up a load of naphtha to deliver to France. It finally sailed back to Vitino to pick up another load of gas condensate of about 61,000 tonnes and delivered it to the Chinese port of Huizhou, close to Hong Kong.[48] Also the vessels Marilee, flying the flag of Norway,[49] Palva, flying the flag of Finland, and Affinity, flying the flag of Singapore, all left the port of Vitino and delivered between roughly 59,000 and 60,000 tonnes of gas condensate to the port of Huizhou during 2011.[50]

Another major commodity transported through the Northern Sea Route to China during the shipping season 2011 was iron ore concentrate exported from the port of Murmansk. Four vessels were involved in this traffic. The first was the Sanko Odyssey, at that time the most modern bulk carrier with ice class in the world, flying the flag of Liberia,[51] breaking another record as this Panamax vessel, with a cargo of about 66,000 tonnes, was the largest bulk carrier to transit the Northern Sea Route.[52] Two smaller 23,000 deadweight bulk carriers, both flying the flag of Russia and belonging to the Murmansk Shipping Company, namely the Mikael Ktuzov and Dmitriy Pozharskiy,[53] also sailed the Northern Sea Route that year, delivering their cargo of iron ore to Jingtang.[54]

2012

It seems appropriate to start the shipping season 2012 with the transit passage of the first ship flying the flag of China, namely the Xuelong. This is said to be the 'world's largest non-nuclear icebreaker'.[55] And even though this crossing disqualifies for present purposes,[56] it nevertheless deserves special mention because it was not only the first Chinese vessel ever to sail the Northern Sea Route[57] but at the same time, it deserves to be stressed that, as a government vessel, it complied with all the regulations of the Russian Federation while making the crossing.[58] Being an icebreaker itself, the Xuelong was nevertheless escorted by the Russian icebreaker Vaygach.[59] It made the crossing from east to west, leaving Shanghai for Reykjavik, and came back, after a short visit to Akureyri, via a route close to the North Pole.[60]

During this shipping season, only one transit passage through the Northeast Passage apparently occurred according to the CHNL. It allegedly concerned the Nordic Barents, the same foreign-flagged vessel that made the first commercial crossing ever 2 years earlier, this time delivering iron from Qinhuangdao to Rotterdam, the Netherlands.[61] It seems, however, highly doubtful whether this particular transit ever took place. Indeed, Mr Mads Boye Petersen, the Managing Director of Nordic Bulk Carriers, did not include this particular crossing in an exhaustive list of transits made by his company's vessels during the period 2010–2013, that he presented at the occasion of a workshop on safe ship operations in the Arctic, held in 2014.[62] Also a list compiled by Rosatomflot, listing the transits of the Northern Sea Route in 2012, does not mention this particular passage.[63]

What is certain, on the other hand, is that five more iron ore crossings by two different vessels belonging to Nordic Bulk Carriers took place between Murmansk and Huanghua along the Northern Sea Route that year.[64] It concerned first of all the Nordic Odyssey, flying the flag of Panama, sailing first from Murmansk to Huanghua in July with a cargo of about 67,500 tonnes, returning the next month in ballast to pick another load of 66,000 tonnes and delivering it to the same Chinese port in September. Second, the Nordic Orion, flying the flag of Panama, needs to mentioned. This ship made five runs along the Northern Sea Route that year connecting the same two ports. It arrived in ballast in Murmansk to pick up about 66,000 tonnes a first time, and repeated that feat a second time with about 63,000 tonnes, before returning a third time in ballast to Murmansk. Finally, the trip of the STT Harmony, a chemical and product tanker, flying the flag of the Marshal Islands, needs to be mentioned as this ship also used the Northern Sea Route that year to transport a cargo of about 61,000 tonnes of gas condensate from Murmansk to Zhenjiang.[65]

2013

After 4 years of steady increase of the number of transit passages, 2013 was the last year before a serious drop in such passages would occur.[66] The amount of cargo that passed through the Northern Sea Route already stagnated, as a slight decrease had to be noted in comparison with the year before.[67] During this last year of general expansion, it has been remarked, about 20 per cent of all the transited cargo either departed or arrived in Chinese ports.[68]

As already announced during the month of March that year,[69] 2013 was special for China because it was the first time that a commercial vessel flying the flag of Hong Kong made a transit voyage through the Northeast Passage, namely the Yong Sheng.[70] This is a general cargo vessel, which transports fluid and solid goods in, respectively, barrels and crates, rather than by means of inter-modal containers.[71] According to the statistical information provided by the CHNL, this vessel transported about 16,500 tonnes of general cargo between the ports of Busan, the Republic of Korea, and Rotterdam, the Netherlands.[72] On the bases of this information, the transit by the Yong Sheng of the Northeast Passage appears of no direct interest here, for China served neither as port of departure nor as port of destination of the transported cargo. However, a detailed analysis of this particular voyage by two Chinese scholars[73] allows one to better interpret this data and to enclose this voyage in the present listing. Indeed, according to the additional information provided by this Chinese source, the vessel left from the port of Dalian in China,[74] with a cargo of about 14,500 tonnes of rolled steel.[75] It subsequently set sail for the port of Taicang, where an additional 2199 tonnes were loaded, as well as '155 pieces of large facility'.[76] The Yong Sheng then set sail to the port of Busan in the Republic of Korea, where it bunkered,[77] before continuing its voyage to the port of Rotterdam in the Netherlands.[78] On the basis of this additional information, it appears therefore justified to conclude that the trip of the Yong Sheng did have China as port of departure and consequently deserves it place in this enumeration.

A second transit passage through the Northeast Passage that year, which related to China, was the voyage of the Nordic Bothnia, flying the flag of

Panama and belonging to Nordic Bulk Carriers, which made one transit that year.[79] The ship transported about 42,000 tonnes of general cargo between the port of Xingang and the port of Amsterdam in the Netherlands.

The other voyages that year involving China all concerned the Northern Sea Route and involved the transport of iron ore from the Russian port of Murmansk.[80] The first full use of the Northern Sea Route in 2013 concerned the voyage of the Nordic Orion, a ship that already crossed the Northern Sea Route the year before,[81] delivering 66,000 tonnes to the port of Lanshan.[82] The second such vessel was the Nordic Odyssey, which had also crossed the Northern Sea Route in 2012.[83] This ship made the transit of the Northern Sea Route twice in 2013: it first sailed in ballast from the port of Beilun to Murmansk, to pick up about 70,000 tonnes of iron ore, and subsequently sailed back to the port of Qingdao to deliver its cargo.[84] The third, and last vessel to be listed here concerns the NS Yakutia, a bulk carrier flying the flag of Liberia and belonging to the Sovcomflot Group, delivering about 67,000 tonnes of iron ore to the port of Lanshan.[85]

During the year of 2013, the import of Russian gas condensate to PRC via the Northern Sea Route, a kind of shipment that had been steadily present during all the previous years, suddenly dried up. This has been explained by the fact that the Russian Federation during the summer of that year started to operate a new such processing plant at Ust-Luga, in the Baltic Sea.[86]

Finally, it could be added that Chinese goods were also carried over part of the Northern Sea Route during 2013,[87] but these are not included here.

2014

The shipping season 2014 was characterised by a sharp decline in the number of transit passages, a trend that persisted in 2015.[88] With 77 per cent less cargo shipped through the Northern Sea Route compared with the year before, this marked downturn has been explained in part by the fact that 200,000 tonnes of iron ore left port of Murmansk in 2014 when compared with 2013, because the producer was 'not able to agree on prices with its customers and freighters' according to the Head of the ANSR.[89] As this figure amounts *grosso modo* to the totality of iron ore exported in 2013, all of which had China as the destination,[90] one can infer that not so much cargo was destined for China during 2014.

Such assumptions are important in this overview, because the statistical information provided for 2013 does exceptionally not provide the ports of departure and arrival.[91] What is certain, however, is that no Chinese flagged vessels passed through the Northern Sea Route,[92] and consequently neither through the Northeast Passage, during that year[93] and that the only bulk carrier that made use of the Northeast Passage in 2013, moreover, sailed between Japan and Finland.[94] Whether any of the tankers that crossed the Northern Sea Route that year carried any cargo to or from China is less easy to ascertain. However, in view of the 2013 experience, when no such transits involved China,[95] it would consequently seem plausible to conclude that the Chinese involvement in the 2014 shipping season was minimal at best, or possibly even non-existent.

Even though, strictly speaking, it could be added that 2014, which appeared rather irrelevant for China as far as the use of the Northern Sea Route and the Northeast Passage were concerned, was nevertheless a historic year when looked at from the perspective of the Northwest Passage. Indeed, for the first time, a crossing without icebreaker assistance was made by a Canadian flagged vessel, the Nunavik, which used the Northwest Passage to deliver a cargo of 23,000 tonnes of nickel concentrate from a Chinese owned mine near Deception Bay, Canada, to the port of Bayuquan.[96]

2015

The sharp decline in the use of the Northeast Passage and the Northern Sea Route for transit passage, which started in 2014,[97] continued in 2015.[98] However, totally contrary to the 2014 shipping season, China's involvement in 2015 was very significant, as the Yong Sheng made two voyages through the Northeast Passage accounting for more than 75 per cent of the total volume of cargo that passed through the Northern Sea Route in transit that year.[99]

Of these two voyages by the Yong Sheng, the vessel that made the historic transit passage of the Northeast Passage in 2013,[100] the first one is important, for it concerned a shipment of steel coils, project and windmill towers and blades, loaded in Shanghai and delivered to the port of Varberg, Sweden.[101] As in 2013, the Yong Sheng received icebreaker assistance. At the same time, it is interest-ing to note that when it sailed back that year with cargo, for the port of Busan, the Republic of Korea, the vessel was able to do so without any icebreaker assistance.[102]

A second transit through the Northeast Passage to be mentioned is the Libe-rian flagged Valparaiso, like the Yong Sheng a general cargo vessel, which loaded a cargo of windmill equipment in the ports of Taicang and Xingang, part of the larger Tianjin port area, with destination of Gdansk, Poland.[103]

The third passage that year only concerns the Northern Sea Route, when the Kogoriak, an icebreaker tug flying the flag of Russia, sailed without icebreaker assistance from Murmansk to the port of Shanghai, without cargo.

As in 2013, finally, it could be added that the Northern Sea Route was partly sailed in 2015 when the Yury Arshenevsky, belonging to the Murmansk Ship-ping Company and flying the flag of Russia, made a round trip in 2 months from the port of Sabetta to Shanghai, in order to fetch a drilling installation.[104] As the client could not wait for the extra 2 months the trip would have taken if use had been made of the Suez Canal, the decision was taken to use the shorter route instead.[105]

2016

If about the same number of vessels made a transit passage as in 2015,[106] the amount of cargo transported in 2016 increased 5.5 times when compared with the previous year.[107] China actively participated in this increase through its state-owned COSCO

Company. It was not only the first time that a foreign-flagged operator sent more than three vessels through the Northern Sea Route during one and the same season,[108] it was also a primer for that same company to send five of its vessels up north that year.[109]

The first of its vessels to make a transit passage of the Northeast Passage was the Yong Sheng, which already made such transits in 2013 and 2015. A first round trip was apparently made between Shanghai and Glasgow, UK. What is certain is that the vessel delivered a cargo of about 13,500 tonnes of steel and ore in bulk.[110] What is less certain is that the ship also returned to Dalian taking the same route, because this return voyage does not appear in the statistics of the CHNL. The Executive Vice President of the COSCO Company nevertheless affirmed at the Arctic Circle conference, held in early October that year, that the ship came back using the same route.[111] The latter is moreover confirmed by a more detailed analysis of the 2016 shipping season by the Head of the CHNL's Information Office in Murmansk, which does list this return voyage of the Yong Sheng.[112] It should be noted that this particular entry does not mention the cargo type, the amount of cargo transported or the entrance and leaving dates of the Northern Sea Route. It consequently also does not mention, as the only ship of all those making a transit that year, the number of days spent on the Northern Sea Route.[113] On the other hand, it appears from this list that the vessel did not need icebreaker assistance on its return voyage.[114]

A second such voyage through the Northeast Passage was undertaken by the Tian Xi, a multipurpose heavy lift vessel for the carrying of general cargo flying the flag of Hong Kong. The vessel loaded about 30,000 tonnes of paper pulp at the port of Kotka, Finland, and delivered its cargo to Qingdao.[115]

The other three vessels of the COSCO Company, all semi-submersible heavy load carriers, used the Northeast Passage in one way, taking the route through the Suez Canal on the other leg. They consequently all sailed the Northeast Passage that year, and thus the whole Northern Sea Route as well, but what all these vessels had in common, was that they delivered cargo from China to the port of Sabetta, Russia. That is probably why none of them figures in the list of the CHNL as transit passages.[116] Two of them, both flying the flag of China, delivered their cargo on a westbound passage. The Xia Zhi Yuan 6 left the port of Tianjin to deliver parts of the Yamal LNG project, and then continued its voyage with a port call at Zeebrugge, Belgium, before returning.[117] The Xiang Yun Kou left the port of Qingdao to deliver three modules of the Yamal LNG project. The third vessel, the Xiang He Kou, flying the flag of Hong Kong,[118] delivered its cargo on an eastbound voyage.

Also two non-COSCO vessels were active that year north of the Eurasian continent, which either had ports in China as place of departure or destination. The first one concerns the BBC Lima, a general cargo vessel flying the flag of Germany, which made a transit through the Northeast Passage departing from Shanghai and delivering 369 tonnes of general cargo to Bremerhaven, Germany.[119] The second vessel was the Inzhener Trubin, which had already made partial use of the Northern Sea Route in 2013,[120] now sailed the whole route in ballast from Arkhangelsk to Qingdao.

Of all the vessels making transit passages in 2016 mentioned above, probably only the BBC Lima was allowed to sail the Northern Sea Route without ice-breaker assistance.[121]

Evaluation

A number of tendencies can be discerned from the analysis of China's involvement in the use of the Northeast Passage and the Northern Sea Route so far, while always keeping in mind that the information relied upon has its flaws.

First, this country was involved from the very beginning of the opening up of the Northern Sea Route by the Russian Federation. Indeed, the very first real cargo transit passage of the Northeast Passage, not calling at a Russian port, was destined for China in 2010.[122]

Second, it is clear that the interest of China concerned, foremost, minerals. Some of these transits went through the Northeast Passage either east or west-bound, it is true, but these are by far outweighed tonnage-wise by the destinational shipping making use of the Northern Sea Route to reach China, namely the cargoes of eastbound Russian minerals, mostly iron ore concentrate and gas condensate. In 2010, for instance, after the transit of the Baltica,[123] an agreement was concluded between the Sovcomflot Group and the China National Petroleum Corporation to use the vessels of the Sovcomflot Group to ship hydrocarbons to China.[124] The transport of gas condensate, however, stopped in 2013, when the Russian Federation opened a new facility at Ust-Luga in the Baltic Sea.[125] At the same time, occasional return voyages from the Taimyr Peninsula to China, involving consumer goods on the way back, were noticed.[126]

Third, very little container cargo has so far been transported via this route to or from China, even though this country, through the COSCO Company, seems lately to have developed an interest in increasing its general cargo traffic by means of ice-strengthened vessels, despite the general decline of interest by others in the use of this route. An agreement concluded in September 2012 between the COSCO Company and the Russian authorities[127] apparently paved the way for the first voyage by the Yong Sheng in 2013, which has been described as 'the beginning of ... Chinese expansion on the N[orthern]S[ea] R[oute]'.[128] With the exception of 2014, this ship has been making transit passages using the Northeast Passage every year since. At the same time, research has indicated that besides the COSCO Company, the other Chinese shipping companies show no real interest.[129]

Fourth, with very few exceptions,[130] all passages described above required icebreaker assistance. Moreover, all ships flying the flag of mainland China or Hong Kong, with cargo to or from China, made use of icebreaker assistance.[131] The fees to be paid for this service remain an unpredictable element in the equation at present, especially since the year 2011, when these fees determined by law became no longer compulsory but only represented a maximum amount that could be charged.[132] Practice reveals that these fees are thus negotiable. In order to stay competitive, these rates will probably relate to the Suez Canal charges, as

in the case of the Yong Sheng, where they were set a little higher, but not sufficient to make the use of the Northern Sea Route unattractive from a commercial
point of view.[133] It has been stated, however, that these competitive prices are
not sufficient to cover the real costs of companies such as Rosatomflot in charge
of rendering these services.[134]

Finally, even though one can discuss whether these voyages have to be considered as transit passages of the Northern Sea Route,[135] China has been actively
involved since 2015 in sending equipment for the Yamal LNG project to the port
of Sabetta. Besides the COSCO Company, some other Chinese shipping companies seemed at least interested in becoming involved in these particular shipments along the Northern Sea Route,[136] despite their overall lack of interest to
use this route in general.[137] The latter nicely links this part with the next, which
will look for interrelationships between the OBOR initiative and the Northern
Sea Route developments just described.

The link: the Yamal LNG project

It will be clear that interest of China in the Northeast Passage and the Northern
Sea Route was substantial from the very beginning in 2010 until the shipping
season 2014, when it totally disappeared, as evidenced by the practice during
that year.[138] This might seem surprising at first sight, since China and the Russian
Federation had signed a joint statement in May 2014, in which they included the
improvement of the transit of Chinese goods through the Northern Sea Route as
a point of action.[139] However, these political intentions were probably unable to
bend the underlying political and economic realities.

The political crisis in Ukraine earlier that year led to the 2014 February
revolution, which resulted in the ousting of the President Yanukovych and his
government, followed by the annexation of the Crimea less than a month later. If
these political developments foremost concerned the relationship between
Europe and the Russian Federation, and can probably help to explain in part the
lack of interest of European shippers in the Northern Sea Route that year, this
nevertheless also had an indirect, be it with opposite effect as will be seen, on
the relationship between China and the Russian Federation. It is consequently, in
the first place, underlying economic realities that helps to explain the waning
Chinese interest in 2014. The low oil prices and the sharp fall in commodity
prices of raw materials had started to outweigh the advantages of using the
Northern Sea Route in western eyes since 2013.[140] These economic factors might
help to explain why China could not negotiate an agreeable tariff for transporting iron ore from Russian through the Northern Sea Route in 2014.[141]

The political crisis in Ukraine also seems to have played a key role in the
changing interrelationship between China and the Russian Federation. Indeed, as
the Russian-Ukrainian crisis was already inflaming during the last months of
2013, China decided to sign a memorandum purchasing 20 per cent of the
Novatek shares in the Yamal LNG project, while the Russian company would
sign a contract to guarantee a 15-year supply of LNG to China.[142] This deal was

finalised in January 2014, making CNODC, a subsidiary of China National Petroleum Corporation, a 20 per cent shareholder in the Yamal LNG project.[143] During the same month, the two governments furthermore concluded a specific agreement on cooperation in the field of the realisation of the Yamal LNG project.[144]

Later that year, the Deputy Prime Minister Dmitry Rogozin, in charge of the defence industry, stated:

> Our Chinese partners got interested in it. We do not rule out that there may be interests related to the economic development of the Silk Road. We proposed them to participate in such projects of building railways to transport cargos to the ports of the N[orthern]S[ea]R[oute]. In fact, we can say now that this is not just the economic Silk Road but the cool Silk Road.[145]

One had to wait until March 2016 before a transaction was finalised through which the Chinese Silk Road Fund acquired a 9.9 per cent equity stake in the Yamal LNG project.[146] In light of the circumstances, this decision by China has been described to be 'as significant economically as it was politically'.[147]

Since then, we see that China has been very present, certainly when compared with other international players, on the Northeast Passage and the Northern Sea Route, *inter alia* through its state-owned COSCO Company, steadily increasing the number of its vessels up north. Part of these voyages, it should be noted, related directly to the Yamal LNG project, as they concerned the shipments of equipment from China to the Russian port of Sabetta.

Conclusions

The time has come now to try to answer the main research question addressed by this contribution, namely whether the OBOR initiative today contains a new northern maritime leg, the 'cool Silk Road' as suggested by a high Russian official in 2015.[148]

A study trying to answer this particular question in 2013 concluded rather straightforwardly that the 'Arctic shipping routes will not become a new silk road for China'.[149] This categorical statement was founded on the economic reality that, at that time, only 2.9 per cent of China's international trade concerned Northern Europe, the region that would profit most from the opening up of the Northeast Passage. Moreover, during the next couple of decades, this trade with Europe was destined to decline rather than to increase. Finally, the author also argues that the general shallowness of the Arctic Ocean, especially of the continental shelf located in front of the Eurasian continent, would run counter to the general trend in the shipping industry to build ever bigger ships in order to take advantage of the economies of scale. The only positive development envisaged by the author at that time was that future 'destinational transport, delivering supplies into the Arctic for its increasing economic activity and transporting the region's natural resources to markets in East Asia'.[150]

In view of the developments that have taken place since November 2013, when this study by Humpert was written, it seems clear that the candid submission that the Arctic will not offer a new maritime Silk Road needs to be somewhat adjusted. Since then, the highest governmental authorities of China and the Russian Federation have expressed their joint intention to link the OBOR and the Eurasian Economic Union project in 2015. As the Ukrainian crisis deepened, the linking of both initiatives fitted nicely in the policy swing towards the east of the Russian Federation, as already explained above.[151] It should be stressed, however, that the official linking in 2015 did not directly relate to the Northern Sea Route, as it could have concerned the land Silk Road as well. Some authors even considered the Silk Road initiative to constitute a potential threat to the further development of the Northern Sea Route, as China had much more to gain from the route over land in economic terms.[152]

If these political statements initially remained rather vague and devoid of any real initiatives on the ground,[153] in practice the first indications of such rapprochement are of rather recent nature. It was indeed only in 2016 that China decided to invest in Eurasian Economic Union project through its Chinese Silk Road Fund and as it turned out, the Yamal LNG project was selected.[154] This investment by China certainly builds further on the 2015 participation this country acquired in the Novatek Company, including an agreed delivery of LNG during 15 years,[155] which by necessity will need to use part of the Northern Sea Route either west or eastbound.

This seems to indicate that the link between the OBOR and the Northern Sea Route remains at present still a rather tenuous one. Through the investment of the Silk Road Fund, the notions of Silk Road and Northern Sea Route seem to have been formally linked, but in reality, it will only support the LNG project that has come under threat because of Western sanctions in the wake of the Ukrainian crisis.[156] The use of the Northern Sea Route that this particular investment will trigger is rather destinational shipping instead of transit passage,[157] which seems to have been the primary objective of the OBOR initiative.

It must finally be admitted that one Chinese company, namely the COSCO Company, has against all odds kept a presence and interest in the area at a time when most other non-Russian shippers have put the (further) use of the Northern Sea Route on ice.[158] Whether this will be sufficient to demonstrate the transit use of the Northeast Passage, and thus the concrete linkage between the Silk Road project and the Norther Sea Route, only the future will be able to tell.

At the official level, the OBOR and the Eurasian Economic Union projects have been linked by now, but this has not yet been done between the OBOR and the Northern Sea Route. Given the present political context, the time seems ripe for such an official formalisation in the not too distant future.

Notes

1 Alice Ekman *et al.* (eds.), *Three Years of China's New Silk Roads: From Words to (Re)action?* (Paris: Ifri, 2017), p. 7, www.ifri.org/en/publications/etudes-de-lifri/three-years-chinas-new-silk-roads-words-reaction#sthash.dp7cdQtL.dpbs.

2 *Ibid.*, such as 'Silk Road Economic Belt', '21st Century Maritime Silk Road', 'One Belt, One Road', 'Belt and Road Initiative'. The present contribution will use 'OBOR', which is the abbreviation of 'One Belt, One Road', to denominate the initiative as a whole.

3 The *status iuris* of this contribution is 4 May 2017.

4 For a more exact definition, see *infra* (n. 28) and accompanying text.

5 Michelle Witte, Xi Jinping Calls for Regional Cooperation Via New Silk Road, *The Astana Times*, 11 September 2013, http://astanatimes.com/2013/09/xi-jinping-calls-for-regional-cooperation-via-new-silk-road/.

6 Alexander Gabuev, Russia–China Talks: Silk Road Leads to Eurasia, *Russia Beyond the Headlines*, 15 May 2015, www.rbth.com/international/2015/05/15/russia-china_talks_silk_road_leads_to_eurasia_46031.html).

7 China, Russia Sign over 30 Deals During Medvedev Visit, *Xinhuanet*, 17 December 2015, http://news.xinhuanet.com/english/2015-12/17/c_134928157_2.htm.

8 For more details on this change in Russian policy, see Tatiana Kastouéva-Jean, Russian Perceptions of OBOR: From Threat to Opportunity, in: Alice Ekman *et al.* (eds.), *Three Years of China's New Silk Roads: From Words to (Re)action?* (Paris: Ifri, 2017), p. 41–49, www.ifri.org/en/publications/etudes-de-lifri/three-years-chinas-new-silk-roads-words-reaction#sthash.dp7cdQtL.dpbs.

9 N. D. Koroleva, V. Iu. Markov and A. P. Ushakov, *Pravovoi rezhim sudochodstva v Rossiiskoi Arktike* [Legal Regime of Navigation in the Russian Arctic] (Moscow: Soiuzmorniiproekt, 1995), p. 4 and 61 (Russian and English version).

10 M. Y. Zinger, *Osnovnye zakony po krayinemy Severy* [Basic Laws for the Extreme North] (Leningrad: Izdetel'stvo glavnogo upravlenii Severnogo morskogo puti, 1935), p. 14 (English translation by the author). For the text of the enactment itself, see p. 86.

11 Terence Armstrong, *The Northern Sea Route in 1967*, Inter-Nord, vol. 11, 1970, p. 123, 123.

12 Terence Armstrong, *The Northern Sea Route in 1968–70*, Inter-Nord, vol. 12, 1972, p. 118, 119.

13 Mikhail Gorbachev, Speech at the Ceremonial Meeting on the Occasion of the Presentation of the Order of Lenin and the Gold Star Medal to the City of Murmansk, Izvestiia, 1 October 1987, at 1, 3 (trans by the author).

14 G. Ovchinnikov, *Za valiutu cherez Severnyi Ledovityi* [Through the Arctic Ocean Against Hard Currency], Izvestiia, 9 September 1989, p. 1 (translation by the author).

15 For an overview of this legislation as applicable of 2010, see Erik Franckx, The Legal Regime of Navigation in the Russian Arctic, *Journal of Transnational Law and Policy* 18(2) (2010), 327–342.

16 Thomas Nilsen, 'The Future History of the Arctic is Now', *Barents Observer*, 2 September 2010, http://barentsobserver.com/en/sections/opinion/future-history-arctic-now.

17 See Erik Franckx and Laura Boone, New Developments in the Arctic: Protecting the Marine Environment from Increased Shipping, in: Myron H. Nordquist *et al.* (eds.), *The Law of the Sea Convention: US Accession and Globalization* (Leiden: Martinus Nijhoff Publishers, 2012), p. 178–205 (shipping season 2010); Erik Franckx, The Shape of Things to Come: The Russian Federation and the Northern Sea Route in 2011, *The Yearbook of Polar Law* 5 (2013), 255–269 (shipping season 2011); and Erik Franckx, Global Warming and Its Impact on Arctic Navigation: The Northern Sea Route Shipping Season 2012, in: Adam Weintrit (ed.), *Marine Navigation and Safety of Sea Transportation: Navigational Problems* (Leiden: CRC Press, 2013), pp. 173–179 (shipping season 2012).

18 For an overview, see Erik Franckx, The 'New' Arctic Passages and the 'Old' Law of the Sea, in: Henrik Ringbom (ed.), *Jurisdiction over Ships: Post-UNCLOS Developments in the Law of the Sea* (Leiden: Brill, 2015), pp. 194–216.

19   See *infra* (n. 67) and accompanying text.

20   *Ibid.*, p. 206.

21   Carolyn Symon (ed.), *Arctic Climate Impact Assessment* (Cambridge: Cambridge University Press, 2005), 1042.

22   *Ibid.*, p. iii.

23   Susan Joy Hassol (ed.), *Impacts of Warming Arctic: Arctic Climate Impact Assessment* (Cambridge: Cambridge University Press, 2004), pp. 82–84. This is a synthesis report, which was released one year ahead of the full-fledged report mentioned, *supra* (n. 21).

24   Arctic Council, *Arctic Marine Shipping Assessment 2009 Report* (Second Printing), *sine loco*, Arctic Council, 2009, 189, https://arctic-council.org/filearchive/amsa2009report.pdf.

25   Compare *ibid.*, pp. 32 and 114 with pp. 33 and 119, concerning the Northwest and Northeast Passages, respectively. Similar indications can also be found in the Arctic Climate Impact Assessment. See Hassol, *supra* (n. 23), pp. 85 and 83 concerning the Northwest and Northeast Passages, respectively.

26   Erik Franckx and Laura Boone, The Northeast Passage and the Northern Sea Route: Unity in Division?, in: Sungjae Choo (ed.), *The 18th International Seminar on Sea Names: Asian and European Perspectives* (7–9 March 2012, Brussels, Belgium), p. 63–69, http://gsdemo194.giantsoft.co.kr/files/2012_18th/04_Erik.pdf.

27   One could, in theory, envisage the use the Northeast Passage without sailing the Northern Sea Route, namely if a route were to be followed north of the Russian exclusive economic zone, and thus outside of area of application of the Northern Sea Route, as described below (see *infra* n. 29 and accompanying text). Under present ice conditions, however, this is not a feasible alternative for commercial shipping today.

28   For a map depicting the water area of the Northern Sea Route, see www.nsra.ru/en/ofitsialnaya_informatsiya/granici_smp.html. Recent maps included in western publications are sometimes misleading as they give the impression that the northern limit of the Northern Sea Route area stretches in fact to the North Pole where both meridians starting in Cape Zhelaniia and Cape Dezhneva merge, *quod non*. See for instance Arild Moe, The Northern Sea Route: Smooth Sailing Ahead?, *Strategic Analysis* 38(6) (2014), 784, 785, Figure 1. As the legend indicates, this is a reproduction of a map drawn up by Claes Lykke Ragner, of the Fridtjof Nansen Institute, in 2012. If at that time there might have been some justification, certainly in Russian circles, in prolonging the western and eastern legs of this zone to the North Pole, this definitively changed in 2013 by means of the introduction of a sharper definition of the concept Northern Sea Route in Russian domestic legislation (as explained in Franckx, *supra* n. 18, p. 212). The same map, but this time in a 2015 version, relied upon by Moe in a more recent and co-authored publication (Arild Moe and Lawson Brigham, Organization and Management Challenges of Russia's Icebreaker Fleet, *Geographical Review* 107(1) (2017), 48, 49, Figure 1) correctly reflects this new reality.

29   Making a similar distinction, see Frédéric Lasserre *et al.*, Polar Seaways? Maritime Transport in the Arctic: An Analysis of Shipowners' Intentions I, *Journal of Transport Geography* 57 (2016), 105, 106, Table 1.

30   As explained in more detail *infra* (n. 135).

31   As the research question, which this contribution tries to answer, concerns the possible existence of a northern leg of the OBOR, linking Europe to Asia, one is inclined to leave partial uses of the Northern Sea Route out of the picture. But the importance of the Yamal LNG project, as will be discussed in Part IV, and the particular role played by the port of Sabetta in these developments, has pleaded in favour of at least drawing attention to these voyages. A similar approach has been taken with respect of the port of Dudinka, given the interest the PRC has in the Norilsk area and the natural resources it contains.

32 Hereinafter CHNL. For further information on this organisation, see www.arctic-lio.com/.

33 Hereinafter ANSR. For further information on this body, see www.nsra.ru/en/home.html.

34 See also *infra* (n. 135).

35 The CHNL covers the years 2011–2016, www.arctic-lio.com/nsr_transits; the NSRA the years 2013–2016, www.nsra.ru/en/rassmotrenie_zayavleniy/perechen_zayavlenii.html.

36 If the CHNL focuses on transit passages and information related thereto, the ANSR rather lists the applications to sail the Northern Sea Route (see *supra* n. 34) as well as the permissions, www.nsra.ru/en/rassmotrenie_zayavleniy/razresheniya.html and refusals, www.nsra.ru/en/rassmotrenie_zayavleniy/otkazu.html.

37 For a convenient table listing these differences, spanning the period 2011–2016, see Yiru Zhang, Qiang Meng and Liye Zhang, Is the Northern Sea Route Attractive to Shipping Companies? Some Insights from Recent Ship Traffic Data, *Marine Policy* 73 (2016), 53, 54, Table 1. For 2016, two more fields of information were added: The deadweight tonnage of the vessels as well as the entry point of Iugorskii Shar, as one of the vessels used this strait to enter the Northern Sea Route that year.

38 Yiru Zhang and Qiang Meng, Current Ship Traffic Analysis at Northern Sea Route, paper presented at the 95th Annual Meeting of Transportation Research Board, 2016, p. 3, http://docs.trb.org/prp/16-1187.pdf. These authors tried to include a third source in their assessment, namely port call data obtained through a commercial provider. However, the reliance on this additional source of information only seemed to add to the confusion by adding yet another layer of information, which sometimes confirmed, sometimes contradicted other sources, or simply did not provide any information where some was expected (*ibid.*, pp. 9–11). The authors conclude themselves (*ibid.*, p. 11):

> Moreover, the discrepancies between transit data and port call data should be addressed with great cautions. We may need to consult corresponding ship operators for confirmation. Another issue puzzled us is that there are thousands of entries yearly that recorded port calls at various Russian Arctic ports. However, these activities were not classified as N[orthern]S[ea]R[oute] transits and thus were not included in transit data. We wonder what the criteria are for a shipping activity to be counted towards a N[orthern]S[ea]R[oute] transit. Overall, the recordkeeping of transit data should be standardised, and the criteria should be disclosed.

In a kind of follow-up article, these statements are somewhat softened, but the essence of the concerns nevertheless is still there. See Zhang, Meng and Zhang, *supra* (n. 37), pp. 53 ('we know little about what exactly is happening at N[orthern] S[ea]R[oute]'), 57–58 and 58 ('Moreover, the discrepancies between transit data and port call data should be addressed with great cautions. It is good to consult corresponding ship operators for confirmation'), respectively.

39 See the sources listed *supra* (n. 17), where a similar approach was adopted.

40 This clearly distinguished it from the transit of the Northeast Passage by the French flagged vessel *Astrolabe* in 1991: the *Astrolabe*, which was an ice-strengthened French research vessel, was certainly not used for commercial purposes at that time. In fact, it was not even allowed to conduct marine scientific research as a prior condition imposed by the Soviets. The vessel did make an obligatory port call in Murmansk before it was allowed to proceed to the Northern Sea Route. About this historical voyage, which occurred moreover at the time of the aborted coup of 19–21 August of that year by the conservatives in Moscow, see in more detail Erik Franckx, The Soviet Maritime Arctic, Summer 1991: A Western Account, *Journal of Transnational Law and Policy* 1(1) (1992), 131–149.

41 Thomas Nilsen, 'MV Nordic Barents' Makes Historic Voyage, *Barents Observer*, 26 August 2010, http://barentsobserver.com/en/sections/murmansk-obl/mv-nordic-barents-makes-historic-voyage.

42 Felix H. Tschudi, New Frontiers: The Northern Sea Route, PowerPoint presentation used at the occasion of the Cefor Centennial Conference, Oslo, 7 April 2011, slide 15, www.cefor.no/Documents/News/CC%202011%20Felix%20Tschudi.pdf and Mikhail Belkin, Rosatomflot: The Traffic Regime on the Northern Sea Route Today and in the Future, PowerPoint presentation posted on the official website of Rosatomflot, slide 8, http://rosatomflot.ru/rosatomflot.pdf. See also M/V Nordic Barents Set to Take on Northern Sea Route, GCaptain, 27 August 2010, https://gcaptain.com/nordic-barents-northern-route/.

43 Tschudi Arctic Transit AS, Northern Sea Route: Faster Transportation between Europe and the Far East, www.jus.uio.no/nifs/forskning/arrangementer/gjesteforelesninger-seminarer/sjorett/materiell/sjorettsem-transport-nordostpassasjen.pdf; Tschudi, Historic Sea Route Opens Through the Arctic to China, www.tschudiarctic.com/page/208/Northern_Sea_Route_Project_2010.

44 SFC Baltica Completes her Arctic Voyage, TankerOperator, 14 September 2010, www.tankeroperator.com/news/scf-baltica-completes-her-arctic-voyage/2172.aspx.

45 It is not entirely clear where exactly the cargo of non-ferrous metal was loaded, because other sources describe this voyage rather as a round trip between the ports of Dudinka and Shanghai. See, for instance Tschudi, *supra* (n. 42), slide 35. If the entire Russian cargo were indeed loaded at Dudinka, this would imply that the ship only sailed part of the Northern Sea Route, unless one adopts a broad definition of what to understand by a crossing of the Northern Sea Route (see *infra* n. 135).

46 Thomas Nilsen, Norilsk-Nickel Shipment Arrived in Shanghai, *Barents Observer*, http://barentsobserver.com/en/sections/articles/norilsk-nickel-shipment-arrived-shanghai; and by the same author, First Ever Round-trip Voyage Without Icebreaker, *Barents Observer*, 17 November 2010, http://barentsobserver.com/en/sections/business/first-ever-round-trip-voyage-without-icebreaker.

47 NOVATEK Sends Tanker 'Perseverance' via Northern Sea Route, http://worldmaritimenews.com/archives/39177/novatek-sends-tanker-perseverance-via-northern-sea-route/; Record Number of Vessels in Transit on Northern Sea Route, http://worldmaritimenews.com/archives/40275/record-number-of-vessels-in-transit-on-northern-sea-route/.

48 CHNL, Statistics 2011, *supra* (n. 35).

49 Marinvest's MT Marilee Completes Northern Sea Route Passage, http://worldmaritimenews.com/archives/34503/marinvests-mt-marilee-completes-northern-sea-route-passage/.

50 Nikolai Monko, Northern Sea Route Administration, Summary of the Navigation 2011; Legislation and Administrative Procedures Regulating the Navigation Along the Northern Sea Route, PowerPoint presentation, www.chnl.no/publish_files/Nikolay_Monko.

51 Trude Pettersen, Record Number of Bulk Carriers Through Northern Sea Route, *Barents Observer*, 14 June 2012, http://barentsobserver.com/en/business/record-number-bulk-carriers-through-northern-sea-route.

52 Arctic Bulk, Another First for Arctic Bulk, www.arcticbulk.com/article/431/Another_First_for_Arctic_Bulk.

53 Trude Pettersen, Japanese Bulk Carrier Sets Record on Northern Sea Route, *Barents Observer*, 26 August 2011, http://barentsobserver.com/en/articles/japanese-bulk-carrier-sets-record-northern-sea-route.

54 CHNL, Statistics 2011, *supra* (n. 35), which exceptionally does not provide any tonnage of the goods transported. As a footnote here, because only part Northern Sea Route was sailed; mention can also be made of the Russian flagged vessel *Zapolyarniy*, which made a journey that same year from the port of Dudinka on the

Yenisei river, i.e. in the middle of the Kara Sea, with a cargo of copper and nickel to China and came back to Dudinka the same season after having loaded a cargo of containers in Shanghai.

55 Paul McLeary, The Arctic: China Opens a New Strategic Front, *World Politics Review*, 19 May 2010, www.worldpoliticsreview.com/articles/5558/the-arctic-china-opens-a-new-strategic-front.

56 Like the *Astrolabe* (*supra* n. 40) the *Xuelong* is a research vessel belonging to the Polar Research Institute of the PRC. It was consequently not used for commercial purposes.

57 Olya Gayazova, China's Rights in the Marine Arctic, *International Journal of Marine and Coastal Law* 28(1) (2013), 61, 78.

58 *Ibid.*, p. 74. This appears to be according to an established policy of the government of China. See Olga V. Alexeeva and Frédéric Lasserre, Le Dragon des Neiges: les stratégies de la Chine en Arctique, *Perspectives chinoises* 3 (2012), 67, 71, where further reference can be found to a Chinese source. The active lobbying by the PRC to become an observer in the Arctic Council, which finally occurred in 2013 despite the initial negative attitude of the Russian Federation, has been directly linked to this policy of not challenging Russian interests in the Arctic, even though, as a rising maritime power, this country might well have good reasons to do so. On this relationship, see Tom Røseth, Russia's China Policy in the Arctic, *Strategic Analysis* 38(6) (2014), 841–859 in general, and pp. 844–848 (Arctic Council) and 850–854 (Northern Sea Route) more specifically.

59 Wang Qian, Breaking the Ice, *China Daily*, 30 September 2012, www.chinadaily.com.cn/sunday/2012-09/30/content_15793745.htm.

60 Trude Pettersen, Chinese Icebreaker Concludes Arctic Voyage, *Barents Observer*, 27 September 2012, http://barentsobserver.com/en/arctic/chinese-icebreaker-concludes-arctic-voyage-27-09; Xuelong to Sail Through Future Central Route, 23 August 2012, http://arcticportal.org/aplibrary/news/827-xuelong-to-sail-through-future-central-route.

61 CHNL, Statistics 2012, *supra* (n. 36). This information is relied upon by Malte Humpert, Quick Winter Transit of Northern Sea Route by Russian Icebreaker, *High North News*, 8 January 2016, www.highnorthnews.com/quick-winter-transit-of-northern-sea-route-by-russian-icebreaker-vaygach/.

62 Mads Boye Petersen, Managing Director of Nordic Bulk Carriers, PowerPoint presented at a Workshop on Safe Ship Operations in the Arctic Ocean, held at IMO Headquarters, London, UK, 28 February 2014, www.imo.org/en/MediaCentre/Hot-Topics/polar/Pages/Arctic-Safe-Ship-Operations-Workshop-(2014).aspx. It is interesting to note in this respect that this particular voyage was not mentioned by the Managing Director of the CHNL, Bjørn Gunnarsson, NSR Transit Voyages in 2011 and 2012 (YTD), https://weathernews.com/TFMS/topics/seminar/2012/pdf/16th/NSR/4_NSR_Transit_Voyages.pdf). This particular entry in the list of the CHNL (CHNL, Statistics 2012, *supra* n. 36), is furthermore deficient, in that it indicates China as the flag State of the *Nordic Barents*.

63 As reprinted in Scott R. Stephenson *et al.*, Marine Accessibility along Russia's Northern Sea Route, *Polar Geography* 37(2) (2014), 111, 114.

64 This information is based on CHNL, Statistics 2012, *supra* (n. 49), and confirmed by Pettersen, *supra* (n. 62), slide 3, implying that all the transits of that company in 2012 concerned the transport of iron ore between Murmansk and Huanghua. It does not totally correspond with the listing of Rosatomflot, which moreover does not mentioned the ballast crossings. As reproduced in Stephenson *et al.*, *supra* (n. 63), p. 114.

65 CHNL, Statistics 2012, *supra* (n. 35). This trip also shows up in the statistics of Rosatomflot, as included in a presentation made by Mikko Niini, President of Aker Arctic Technology Inc. at the occasion of the 8th Arctic Passion Seminar, Helsinki,

14 March 2013, slide 11, http://akerarctic.fi/sites/default/files/page/fields/field_attachments/02_niini_1_0.pdf.

66 See *infra* (n. 88) and accompanying text.

67 Moe, *supra* (n. 28), p. 787, Figure 2.

68 Malte Humpert, Arctic Shipping: An Analysis of the 2013 Northern Sea Route Season, Akureyri, Northern Research Forum, 2014, p. 2, http://arcticyearbook.com/images/Arcticles_2014/BN/Humpert_AY2014_FINAL.pdf.

69 Trude Pettersen, China Starts Commercial Use of Northern Sea Route, *Barents Observer*, 14 March 2013, http://barentsobserver.com/en/arctic/2013/03/china-starts-commercial-use-northern-sea-route-14-03.

70 Port of Rotterdam Sees Arrival of First Commercial Ship via Northern Sea Route, GCaptain, 11 September 2013, http://gcaptain.com/port-of-rotterdam-sees-arrival-of-first-ship-via-northern-sea-route/.

71 Humpert, *supra* (n. 68), p. 4.

72 CHNL, Statistics 2013, *supra* (n. 35). This also seems to be the way that Humpert interpreted this information. See Humpert, *supra* (n. 68), p. 4, Map 4, depicting the general cargo transits of the Northern Sea Route in 2013.

73 Hui Zhao and Hao Hu, Study on Economic Evaluation of the Northern Sea Route: Taking the Voyage of *Yong Sheng* as an Example, *Transportation Research Record* 2549 (2016), 78–85.

74 This fact was also related in the Western press. See Trude Pettersen, China to Release Guidebook on Arctic shipping, *Barents Observer*, 20 June 2014, http://barentsobserver.com/en/arctic/2014/06/china-release-guidebook-arctic-shipping-20-06. But it could still have been interpreted as meaning that the ship sailed to the port of Busan in ballast to pick up its cargo there, as apparently suggested by the CHNL statistics for 2013.

75 Zhao and Hu, *supra* (n. 73), p. 80.

76 *Ibid.*

77 *Ibid.*, p. 81, Figure 3.

78 CHNL, Statistics 2013, *supra* (n. 35).

79 Petersen, *supra* (n. 62), slide 3.

80 In fact, all of the iron ore transported through the Northern Sea Route that year was delivered to the PRC. Humpert, *supra* (n. 68), map on p. 3. The same was true in 2011 and 2012. Moe, *supra* (n. 28), p. 791.

81 See *supra* (n. 65) and accompanying text.

82 CHNL, Statistics 2013, *supra* (n. 35).

83 See *supra* (n. 65) and accompanying text.

84 CHNL, Statistics 2013, *supra* (n. 35). The *Nordic Odyssey* made a third crossing of the Northern Sea Route that year, which was a transit of the Northeast Passage as well this time, as the ship transported coal between Vancouver, Canada, and Pori, Finland.

85 *Ibid.*

86 Moe, *supra* (n. 28), pp. 789–791.

87 Russian Bulker Transits NSR Arrives Tianjin, China, MarineLink, 2 September 2013, www.marinelink.com/news/transits-russian-arrives358207.aspx. It concerns the *Inzhener Trubin*, a general cargo vessel flying the Russian flag, which was to deliver the products of domestic Russian enterprises to the PRC, and import Chinese goods on the return voyage. It should be noted that this transport of Chinese goods, be it only over part of the Northern Sea Route, does not show in the listing of the CHNL as a transport involving the PRC (CHNL, Statistics 2013, *supra* (n. 36) because the port of departure mentioned here is Kamchatksky.

88 PAME, Northern Sea Route Shipping Statistics, https://pame.is/index.php/projects/arctic-marine-shipping/older-projects/northern-sea-route-shipping-statistics. Here statistics of transit passages can be found for the period 2011–2015.

89 As reported by Trude Pettersen, Northern Sea Route Traffic Plummeted, *Barents Observer*, 16 December 2014, http://barentsobserver.com/en/arctic/2014/12/northern-sea-route-traffic-plummeted-16-12.

90 See *supra* (n. 80).

91 CHNL, Statistics 2013, *supra* (n. 35). See also *supra* (n. 37) and the further reference to be found there.

92 It appears that such a trip was actually planned by the COSCO Company, but that, according to this company, the Russian authorities refused this. Leah Beveridge *et al.*, Interest of Asian Shipping Companies in Navigating the Arctic, *Polar Science* 10(3) (2016), 404, 412, Appendix 1. This information is confirmed by the data provided by the ANSR. The COSCO Company requested permission that year for the *Xiang Yun Kou*, a ship which would later sail the Northern Sea Route (see *infra* n. 118 and the text following that note), but was refused access in 2014 because of a lack of completed surveys for the years 2012, 2013 and 2014, www.nsra.ru/en/rass-motrenie_zayavleniy/otkazu.html?year=2014.

93 CHNL, Statistics 2014, *supra* (n. 35).

94 New Ice Class Bulk Carrier Will Have a Dramatic Impact on Fuel Costs and Emissions, Ship & Bunker, 29 October 2014, https://shipandbunker.com/news/world/259495-new-ice-class-bulk-carrier-will-have-a-dramatic-impact-on-fuel-costs-and-emissions.

95 Humpert, *supra* (n. 68), pp. 2–3 and map on p. 3.

96 Peter Farquhar, A Cargo Ship Just Completed a Historic Trip Through the Northwest Passage, *Business Insider*, 2 October 2014, www.businessinsider.com/a-cargo-ship-just-completed-a-historic-trip-through-the-northwest-passage-2014-10?IR=T.

97 See *supra* (n. 88) and accompanying text.

98 If one looks at the number of ships making transit passages, roughly double the number of ships made such passage in 2014, and four times as much in 2013 when compared with 2015. PAME, *supra* (n. 88). If the quantity of cargo is taken as yardstick, an 86 per cent drop has been noted in the specialised press for 2015. Trude Pettersen, Declining Interest in Use of Northern Sea Route, *Barents Observer*, 18 March 2016, https://thebarentsobserver.com/en/industry/2016/03/declining-interest-use-northern-sea-route.

99 Alte Staalesen, New Low for Northern Sea Route, *Barents Observer*, 15 February 2016, https://thebarentsobserver.com/en/industry/2016/02/historical-low-northern-sea-route).

100 See *supra* (n. 70–78) and accompanying text.

101 CHNL, Statistics 2015, *supra* (n. 35).

102 *Ibid.*

103 For a video showing the entering of the Valparaiso in its port of destination that year, while providing some basic information, see www.youtube.com/watch?v=zH98N7fjJ8U.

104 Alte Staalesen, Vessel Sails 11,000 Miles along Northern Sea Route to Pick Up Oil Rig, *Barents Observer*, 18 November 2015, https://thebarentsobserver.com/en/arctic/2015/11/vessel-sails-11000-miles-along-northern-sea-route-pick-oil-rig.

105 'Yuri Arshenevskiy' Delivered the Boring Rig for the Yamal SPG Project, *Arctic Info*, 17 November 2015, www.arctic-info.com/news/17-11-2015/-yuri-arshenevskiy–delivered-the-boring-rig-for-the-yamal-spg-project/).

106 One more transit passage occurred in 2016 when compared with 2015. Compare CHNL, Statistics 2015 and 2016, *supra* (n. 35).

107 Malte Humpert, Shipping Traffic on Northern Sea Route Grows by 30 Percent, *High North News*, 23 January 2017, www.highnorthnews.com/shipping-traffic-on-northern-sea-route-grows-by-30-percent/.

108 Malte Humpert, China's COSCO Shipping Company Expands Activities on Northern Sea Route, *High North News*, 30 September 2016, www.highnorthnews.com/chinas-cosco-shipping-company-expands-activities-on-northern-sea-route/.

109 Alte Staalesen, COSCO Sends Five Vessels Through Northern Sea Route, *Barents Observer*, 10 October 2016, https://thebarentsobserver.com/en/arctic-industry-and-energy/2016/10/cosco-sends-five-vessels-through-northern-sea-route.

110 CHNL, Statistics 2016, *supra* (n. 35).

111 Staalesen, *supra* (n. 109), affirming that the vessel made a two-way passage through the Northeast Passage. See also Humpert, *supra* (n. 108), where it is further specified that the ship left the port of Tianjin to arrive in Sheerness after port calls in Hamburg and Bremerhaven, Germany. Before returning to Dalian, the ship made a port call at Zeebrugge, Belgium. The nature of the cargo on the return voyage is, however, not specified.

112 Sergey Balmasov, Detailed SOF of the 2016 Season at the NSR: Ship Movements Based on AIS Data, PowerPoint presentation used at the occasion of the Arctic Shipping Forum 2017, Helsinki, 25 April 2017, slide 21, http://arctic-lio.com/docs/25_04_17_Helsinki.pdf. A more detailed analysis of this particular return voyage is moreover to be found on slide 30. It is interesting to note that, despite the addition of one more transit passage entry when compared to the general list to be found on their website (CHNL, Statistics 2016, *supra* n. 35) both listings contain 19 transits in total! This similarity in the total number of transits despite the fact that the list of Balmasov adds one more entry of particular importance here, is to be explained by the fact that the general list does not contain a number 5 entry, as it jumps from 4 to 6.

113 Balmasov, *supra* (n. 112), slide 21.

114 *Ibid.*

115 CHNL, Statistics 2016, *supra* (n. 35). According to Humpert, *supra* (n. 108), the vessel departed from Rauma, Finland, and first made a port call in Kotka in the Gulf of Finland before heading for Qingdao.

116 The information in this paragraph is based on Humpert, *supra* (n. 108), unless otherwise indicated.

117 See the comment attached to a picture of the vessel when it visited the port of the Zeebrugge that year, www.ship-hunters.be/SHDB/pict_ot_month_p01.php.

118 As this is the third vessel, besides the Yong Sheng and the Tian XI, flying the flag of Hong Kong that used the Northern Sea Route that year, the detailed report by the Head of the CHNL's Information Office seems incorrect as it only lists two such vessels. See Balmasov, *supra* (n. 112), slide 12.

119 CHNL, Statistics 2016, *supra* (n. 35).

120 See *supra* (n. 87).

121 Only with respect to the passages of the *Xiang He Kou* and the *Xiang Yun Kou* no particular information is available in the sources consulted above, but taking into account their low ice class, the nature of these vessels and their cargo, it seems reasonable to assume that icebreakers escorted them.

122 See *supra* (n. 40) and accompanying text.

123 See *supra* (n. 44) and accompanying text.

124 Sovcomflot Group and China National Petroleum Corporation Become Strategic Partners, 22 November 2010, www.scf-group.ru/en/press_office/press_releases/item1726.html. See also: Nong Hong, The Melting Arctic and its Impact on China's Maritime Transport, *Research in Transportation Economics* 35(1) (2012), 50, 52; Olga V. Alexeeva and Frédéric Lasserre, La Chine en Arctique: stratégie raisonnée ou approche pragmatique?, *Études internationales* 44(1) (2013), 25–41 and by the same authors, *supra* (n. 58), p. 74; Linyan Huang, Frédéric Lasserre and Olga Alexeeva, Is China's Interest for the Arctic Driven by Arctic Shipping Potential?, *Asian Geographer* 32(1) (2015), 59, 65.

125 See *supra* (n. 86) and accompanying text.

126 As in 2010 (see *supra* n. 46 and accompanying text) and in 2011 (see *supra* n. 55).

127 Huang *et al.*, *supra* (n. 124), p. 66.

128 Nataliya Marchenko, Northern Sea Route: Modern State and Challenges, in: Proceedings of the ASME 2014 33rd International Conference on Ocean, Offshore and Arctic Engineering, 8–13 June, 2014, San Francisco, CA, USA, (New York: ASME, 2014), p. 1, 6.

129 *Huang, Lasserre and Alexeeva, supra* note 124, p. 65.

130 See *supra* (n. 121) and accompanying text.

131 The exceptional voyage of the *Yong Sheng* in 2015, when this vessel was allowed to sail the Northern Sea Route without icebreaker assistance, did not involve the PRC as port of departure or destination. See *supra* (n. 102) and accompanying text. The return voyage of that same vessel in 2016 to the port of Dalian remains uncertain in this respect as information about cargo is lacking (see *supra* n. 113 and accompanying text).

132 Moe, *supra* (n. 28), p. 793.

133 Zhao and Hu, *supra* (n. 73), p. 83.

134 Moe, *supra* (n. 28), pp. 793–794.

135 At least according to the ANSR, transit passages of the Northern Sea Route include all voyages that have sailed its most difficult eastern leg. Voyages from the Ob bay eastward thus are considered a crossing, but those going west are not so considered. As explained by Moe, *supra* (n. 28), p. 787. The shipping from the Yamal LNG project direction the PRC can thus be considered a crossing of the Northern Sea Route under this definition adopted by the ANSR.

136 Frédéric Lasserre, China's Interest in Arctic Shipping, China Policy Institute: Analysis, 12 March 2015, https://cpianalysis.org/2015/03/12/chinas-interest-for-the-arctic-and-arctic-shipping/.

137 See *supra* (n. 129) and accompanying text.

138 See *supra* (n. 92–95) and accompanying text.

139 Joint Statement of the Russian Federation and the People's Republic of China on a New Stage in the Comprehensive Partnership and Strategic Cooperation, 20 May 2014, under Point II, http://kremlin.ru/supplement/1642.

140 Or to use the words of a western user of the Northern Sea Route of the first hour, Felix Tschudi: 'The economic calculations have changed since 2013 and the benefits of the N[orthern]S[ea]R[oute] as a shortcut have largely been lost'. As quoted by Malte Humpert, Is Northern Sea Route Shipping in a Deep Freeze?, *High North News*, 6 June 2016, www.newsdeeply.com/arctic/articles/2016/06/06/is-northern-sea-route-shipping-in-a-deep-freeze.

141 See *supra* (n. 89) and accompanying text.

142 Aurélie Bros and Tatiana A. Mitrova, Yamal LNG: An Economic Project Under Political Pressure, *Fondation pour la Recherche Stratégique* 17(2 August 2016), p. 4.

143 NOVATEK closes sale of 20% interest in Yamal LNG to CNPC, 14 January 2014, http://novatek.ru/en/investors/events/archive/index.php?id_4=826&afrom_4=01.01. 2014&ato_4=31.12.2014&from_4=5.

144 Moe, *supra* (n. 28), p. 791.

145 Statement in the Russian Arctic Commission, as reprinted in Northern Sea Route Operational All Year Round, Arctic Sea Ice Blog, 11 December 2015, http://neven1. typepad.com/blog/2015/12/northern-sea-route-operational-all-year-round.html.

146 Bros and Mitrova, *supra* (n. 142), p. 14.

147 Kastouéva-Jean, *supra* (n. 8), p. 44.

148 See *supra* (n. 145) and accompanying text.

149 Malte Humpert, The Future of Arctic Shipping: A New Silk Road for China? (Washington, DC: The Arctic Institute, 2013), p. 15, www.thearcticinstitute.org/the-future-of-arctic-shipping-new-silk/.

150 *Ibid.*

151 See *supra* (n. 6–8) and accompanying text.

152 Mia Bennett, China's Silk Road Plans Could Challenge Northern Sea Route, *Cryopolitics*, 29 December 2014, https://cryopolitics.com/2014/12/29/chinas-silk-road-plans-could-challenge-northern-sea-route/). See also Lawson W. Brigham, Future Perspective: The Maritime Arctic in 2050, *Fletcher Forum of World Affairs* 39(1) (2015), p. 109, 113, pointing at the strong competition of the Silk Road rail connection between Asia and Europe in this respect.

153 Gabuev, *supra* (n. 6).

154 See *supra* (n. 146) and accompanying text.

155 See *supra* (n. 142) and accompanying text.

156 Bros and Mitrova, *supra* (n. 142), pp. 10–16.

157 As admitted by Humpert when answering the question, whether the Arctic will host a new Silk Road in the future, in the negative. See *supra* (n. 150) and accompanying text.

158 It is, in this respect, interesting to note that scholars of the PRC often seem to be somewhat more optimistic about the economic viability of the Northern Sea Route when compared with the assessment made by their western colleagues. For an example in point, see for instance Frédéric Lasserre, Case Studies of Shipping along Arctic Routes: Analysis and Profitability Perspectives for the Container Sector, *Transportation Research Part A* 66 (2014), 144–161, and a comment on this article by Nuo Wang *et al.*, Comments on 'Case Studies of Shipping along Arctic Routes. Analysis and Profitability Perspectives for the Container Sector' [Transp. Res. Part A: Policy Pract. 66 (2014) 144–161], *Transportation Research Part A*, 94 (2016) 699–702.

4 The challenge to the Maritime Silk Road and port connectivity

Renping Zhang and Shihui Yu

Introduction

The Silk Road Economic Belt links China with Europe through Central and Western Asia, while the 21st Century Maritime Silk Road connects China with Southeast Asia, Africa, Europe, Oceania and America. The Belt and the Road comprise the Belt and Road Initiative (BRI) and becomes a roadmap showing how China wants to further integrate itself into the world economy. President Xi Jinping emphasised, in his keynote speech on 'Building the Community of Common Destiny of Mankind' at the United Nations Office in Geneva in January 2017, that China remains unchanged in its commitment to pursuing common development. The BRI aims to achieve a win-win and shared development, and will be jointly built through consultation to meet the interests of all, and efforts to integrate the development of the countries along the Belt and the Road.

China actively promotes the BRI, and plays a proactive role in maritime connectivity through the 21st Century Maritime Silk Road (MSR). The MSR aims to promote the port connectivity, establish and strengthen partnerships among the countries along the Road, set up all-dimensional, multi-tiered and composite connectivity networks, and realise diversified, independent, balanced and sustainable development in the countries along the MSR.

In line with the priorities of the MSR, China continues to deepen maritime cooperation by fostering closer ties with countries along the MSR. Maritime cooperation between China and Europe is focused on building a Blue Economic Passage from China to the Indian Ocean further to the Mediterranean Sea, by linking the China Indo-China Peninsula Economic Corridor, running westward from the South China Sea, to the Indian Ocean, into the Mediterranean Sea.

Another shipping route of MSR, referred to the Ice Silk Road, is seasonally operative that connects China and north Europe via the Arctic Ocean. The Arctic route as one of the three major maritime transport channels is brought up in *Vision for Maritime Cooperation under the Belt and Road Initiative.*[1] With the construction of the Arctic route in China and Russia, China's regional port pattern may change gradually. The ports of Shanghai, Dalian and others become important ports for the Arctic route. The northeastern route near Russia is the shortest route for many parts in China to Europe. It is estimated that sailing from port of Shanghai to the north of Europe, the North Sea, the Baltic Sea and other ports is 25 to 55 per cent shorter than the traditional route. The development of the Arctic route is a slow process, thus the impact of the Arctic route on national port and national trade pattern is a slow process as well. However, stakeholders should be prepared in advance.[2]

Maritime Silk Road and port connectivity

Shipping routes between China and Europe

The MSR between China and Europe is the western route, which starts from China to the Malacca Strait, and further crosses the Indian Ocean to the Red Sea, transits through Suez Canal, into the Mediterranean Sea, and connects ports in Asia and Europe.[3] The MSR network covers most of vital international shipping routes. These vital international shipping lanes constitute the cargo transport corridor at sea between the ports within the region, and connects the separated ports together, which forms the related nodes and shipping network.

China COSCO Shipping Corporation Limited plays an essential role in the MSR. COSCO Shipping proactively participates in the MSR to explore new shipping routes. The COSCO Shipping fleet covers more than 160 countries and regions with its international voyages, connecting over 1500 ports worldwide. COSCO Shipping deploys more than 260 container ships with the capacity of 1.7 million TEUs, covering nearly 200 main shipping routes along the MSR countries and regions.[4]

As the largest container liner in China, COSCO Shipping Lines operates container ships in four major shipping routes between Asia and Europe, i.e. Asia and North Europe, Asia and Mediterranean, India/Middle East and North Europe, India/Middle East and Mediterranean. Based on the container liner routes of COSCO Shipping in 2018, the liner routes between China and North Europe along the MSR are identified, while the COSCO Shipping Lines also provides regular shipping services between Asia and Mediterranean.[5]

Port connectivity between China and Europe

The status quo of port development in China and Europe

Since the implementation of the MSR, its impact is obvious on various aspects of shipping and port sectors. Port container throughput measures the flow of containers from land to sea transport modes and vice versa, in twenty-foot equivalent units (TEUs), a standard-size container. Transshipment is counted as two lifts at the intermediate port and includes empty units.

There are many ports along the MSR, where the seaborne trade is quite frequent and the shipping market has great potential for development. Lloyd's List announced top 100 ports in August 2018, among which 54 in Asia and 19 in Europe.[6] 'Top 10' container ports of 2018 are shown in Table 4.1.

Table 4.1 Top 10 container ports in 2018

Rank	Port	Country
1	Shanghai	China
2	Singapore	Singapore
3	Shenzhen	China
4	Ningbo-Zhoushan	China
5	Hong Kong	China
6	Pusan	Republic of Korea
7	Guangzhou	China
8	Qingdao	China
9	Dubai	United Arabic Emirates
10	Tianjin	China

Source: Lloyd's List, August 2018, https://lloydslist.maritimeintelligence.informa.com/one-hundred-container-ports-2018/.

In 2015, the Chinese government issued *Vision and Actions on Jointly Building Silk Road Economic Belt and 21st century Maritime Silk Road*, in which it is committed to focusing on strengthening the port construction of coastal cities in China, including ports of Shanghai, Tianjin, Ningbo-Zhoushan, Guangzhou, Shenzhen, Zhanjiang, Shantou, Qingdao, Yantai, Dalian, Fuzhou, Xiamen, Quanzhou, Haikou and Sanya, and supporting Fujian Province to become a hub of the 21st Century Maritime Silk Road.

With the MSR implementation, the infrastructure of those coastal ports are further improved to a new level. For example, the world's largest container automated terminal, 'Shanghai International Shipping Center Yangshan Deep-water Port Fourth Project', completed its successful trial operation in December 2017. The throughput capacity in the short term is designed for up to 4 million TEUs per year, the long-term throughput capacity will reach 6.3 million TEUs per year, which meets the need of multiple large container ships berthing at the same time. Use is made of auto mated equipment and control systems for the first time. Computer-controlled bridge cranes are used for the loading and unloading, and unmanned automated-guided transport vehicles are utilised to carry the containers.[7] Numerous berths and reasonable distribution provides a firm foundation for the MSR development.

In Europe, port infrastructure is well equipped. European ports play a crucial role in MSR port connectivity. European countries and China make great efforts in cooperation for investment and operations in European ports. COSCO Shipping invests in and operates ten terminals in European ports, including Greece, Turkey, the Netherlands, Belgium, Spain and Italy, as well as the ports in Egypt, UAE, Singapore and Korea.[8]

Maritime transport hubs

A maritime transport hub is a place where two or more transportation lines are intersected. At the junction of water and rail, ports are a significant portion of the transport hub and provide a crucial interface between land and sea. Many transportation activities are conducted in hub ports. Nowadays, more than 90 per cent of the transport of goods are accomplished by water transport and ports.

According to Lloyd's List of top 100 container ports in 2018,[9] the ports of Shanghai, Shenzhen, Hong Kong, Singapore, Hambantota, Colombo, Piraeus, Rotterdam, Hamburg and Felixstowe have formed the function of hub ports, which can be developed into a core port network. More investment should be put into the construction of hub ports to develop into a perfect port network layout. For the top ten ports of 2018, Shanghai ranks top, followed by Singapore, Shenzhen, Ningbo-Zhoushan, Hong Kong, Busan, Guangzhou, Qingdao, Dubai and Tianjin.[10]

The port performance is assessed in several aspects, including the port infrastructure, shipping connectivity and logistics performance index. The port infrastructure means the most basic infrastructure used to realise the function of port. It is the foundation for the development of a port. Being an indispensable part of the port logistics system, the port infrastructure is composed of the port logistic infrastructure and its equipment, including channels, collecting and distributing, berth and wharf. MSR advocates speeding up the improvement of coastal port infrastructure, encouraging the countries in the region to reach a consensus in port layout, as well as promoting infrastructure construction in wharf, channel, collecting and distributing system, and so on. Thus the connectivity between the coastal economic belt and port cities along the route becomes possible and efficient. Good port infrastructure lays solid foundations for implementing the connectivity along MSR.

The quality of the port infrastructure is used to measure the overall performance of port facilities. Scores range from 1 (port infrastructure considered extremely underdeveloped) to 7 (port infrastructure considered efficient by international standards). The Liner Shipping Connectivity Index captures how well countries are connected to global shipping networks. It is computed by the United Nations Conference on Trade and Development (UNCTAD), based on five components of the maritime transport sector: number of ships, their container-carrying capacity, maximum vessel size, number of services and number of companies that deploy container ships in a country's ports. The Liner Shipping Connectivity Index has relations with the liner alliance. With the reorganisation of the liner alliance, a new shipping alliance has been formed by the 2M Alliance, Ocean Union, a new alliance which began its operation in April 2017. As the shipping companies are concerned about the loss caused by the delay of ships, they attach importance to the ports where most delays occur. Therefore, many shipping companies began to invest in terminals. The impact of the new alliance on the route is mainly larger shipping delivery, but fewer routes.[11]

The Logistics Performance Index score reflects on perceptions of a country's logistics. The index ranges from 1 to 5, with a higher score representing better performance. The Logistics Performance Index (LPI) analyses countries through six indicators:

1   The efficiency of customs and border management clearance
2   The quality of trade- and transport-related infrastructure
3   The ease of arranging competitively priced international shipments
4   The competence and quality of logistics services
5   The ability to track and trace consignments
6   The frequency with which shipments reach consignees within the scheduled or expected delivery time.

The components are chosen based on theoretical and empirical research and on the practical experience of the logistics professionals involved in international freight forwarding.[12,13]

Challenges to Maritime Silk Road and port connectivity

It is envisaged that challenges to MSR and port connectivity may include, but not be limited to, political, economic, legal and policy, cultural, technological, maritime security and environmental factors.

Political factors

With the development of economic globalisation, the scale of foreign direct investment of Chinese enterprises to ports has been expanding, and political risk has become the main factor that restricts foreign direct investment. Political challenge therefore has great impact on the port investment projects.

Political instability

Territorial disputes between relevant countries pose a threat to economic cooperation. East Asia, South Asia and Southeast Asia have complicated border issues and there are territorial disputes among various countries. China has settled border issues with 12 neighbouring countries. While issues at sea are relatively complicated, and there exist disputes over maritime sovereignty and islands with neighbouring countries in the South China Sea, these disputes form an obstacle and bring the challenge and risk for deepening economic cooperation along the MSR.

The South China Sea is one of the most vital shipping lanes along the MSR. An estimated US$5 trillion worth of global trade passes through the South China Sea every year.[14] The South China Sea disputes involve both island and maritime claims among several sovereign states within the region, namely China, Malaysia, the Philippines, Vietnam, etc.

Piracy and armed robbery at sea

Piracy is defined in Article 101 of the 1982 UNCLOS, and Armed Robbery is defined by IMO Assembly Resolution A.1025 (26).[15] Piracy and armed robbery at sea is an organised and persistent criminal activity prevalent in many parts of the world. Attackers are often aggressive and subject their victims to violence and ill treatment. Ships have been hijacked, either for a ransom payment for the release of captive seafarers, theft of cargo or both. The complicated issues of piracy and armed robbery have brought great threats to the shipping activities of the MSR.

Piracy and armed robbery at sea most often occurs in the areas of western Indian Ocean, the Gulf of Guinea, and Southeast Asia. Piracy nowadays takes place in a number of waters along the MSR, including the Strait of Malacca. The increasing threat posed by piracy has also caused concern in the Indian Ocean, since most of its shipping trade routes pass through the Gulf of Aden. Navies from China, Russia and other countries have joined international efforts by deploying warships in the Indian Ocean to combat piracy.

A total of 156 incidents of piracy and armed robbery against ships were reported in the first 9 months of 2018, and the figure is broken down as 107 vessels boarded; 32 attempted attacks; 13 vessels fired upon; 4 vessels hijacked.[16] A total of 64 incidents of piracy and armed robbery against ships were reported by the ReCAAP in Asia during January to September 2018. Of the 64 incidents, three were incidents of piracy and 61 were incidents of armed robbery against ships. Compared with January–September 2017, there was a 3 per cent increase in total number of incidents reported during January to September 2018.[17] Piracy and armed robbery occurs most often in African regions; Southeast Asia is second in the number of incidents of piracy and armed robbery and the Indian sub-continent is also victim to piracy and armed robbery. The incidents of piracy and armed robbery by region indicate that MSR between China and Europe is under threat in Southeast Asia, the Indian Ocean and in the Gulf of Aden.

Economic factors

Global seaborne trade was doing well in 2017, supported by the upswing in world economy. Global maritime trade has expanded at 4 per cent, and global containerised trade has increased by 6.4 per cent. While prospects for seaborne trade are positive, as UNCTAD projected volume increases of 4 per cent in 2018, UNCTAD forecasts a 3.8 per cent compound annual growth rate between 2018 and 2023.[18]

The economic developments in China are of acute relevance to shipping, as China remains at the centre of shipping activity in 2017 and accounts for nearly half of seaborne trade growth recorded during the year. Developing countries continue to account for most global seaborne trade flows, both in terms of exports and imports, and shipped 60 per cent of world merchandise trade by sea. Developed countries have witnessed their share of both types of traffic decline over the years, now representing about one-third of world seaborne imports and exports.[19]

The international seaborne trade between China and European countries along the MSR is increasing. The sustainable economic developments of China need a lot of mineral, oil and other resources, as well as technology. While the European countries along the MSR are also in need of China's technology, capital and market, the relations between China and European countries along the MSR are getting closer.

Legal and policy factors

The MSR is committed to the connectivity of the Euro-Asia continent and related oceans and seas. While China is dedicated to strengthening the cooperation and sharing the fruits of development, the risk may exist in different legal systems and policies in individual countries where conflicts could occur. In the process of overseas port investment and construction, China should understand and prevent a series of policy and legal risks that may arise in the whole process of investment, construction and operation, therefore avoiding investment loss and financial waste due to the change of the national policy of the host country or the legal systems with which the investors are unfamiliar.

Legal challenges

Overseas port construction is considered a commercial activity. If the investor violates the basic laws of the host country, the host country's own legal system will inevitably take measures to restrict, punish or even stop the commercial behaviour of the investors, thus causing a series of political and economic losses. The legal challenges include three main factors to be considered.

Challenge of anti-monopoly law. The construction of overseas maritime ports is often aimed at obtaining the monopolisation of the port. Therefore, it is necessary to avoid being suspected of monopolising by the host country during the process of investment and construction. The host country can start anti-monopoly investigation and measures, strictly control investment behaviour or take anti-monopoly tax and other measures to limit the scope of the capital investment.

Challenge of labour law. Overseas companies would inevitably like to employ a large number of local labour force in the process of constructing a maritime port, which may be subject to strict foreign labour laws. If enterprises neglect the specific ethnic, gender and other issues during employment in the host country, or pay no special attention to treatment and welfare protection for employees, it would violate relevant laws of equality and face risks of penalties and strikes.

Challenge of environment law. The construction and operation of overseas ports not only involve the implementation of the project, but also the handling of dry bulk cargo, which can easily lead to environmental pollution problems. Once the investing enterprises do not meet the standards set by local environment law, it would face legal proceedings, or be forced to suspend or even close their projects. For example, Sri Lanka announced in early 2015, the suspending of the construction of the port city in Port Colombo, the reason being that they believe the port project would cause harm to the environment, which violates its environment law and regulation.

Policy challenges

In the construction of the sea ports, the host country may apply special laws to supervise the investing enterprises, on the basis of factors such as policy changes. The emergence of such risks is often difficult to predict. The policy challenges also have three main factors to consider.

Unstable domestic policy. The unstable environment of the host country's domestic policy is bound to have a serious impact on the construction of a sea port. Policy communication is an important part of the Five Links of the MSR, so we must be cautious of implicit policy risks of infrastructure construction. Once the host country imposes nationalisation and other measures on foreign enterprises out of the needs of state and public interests, the port enterprises will face difficulties in recourse to the judiciary or arbitral institutions.

Excessive administrative discretion power. The host country may give legislature and executive authorities comparatively large discretion power through the enactment of the law. In the case of Chinese enterprises investing in overseas ports, if certain interests of the host country are involved, a situation not clearly defined by the law may lead to the abuse of discretionary power by the local administration.

Temporary law amendment. When the existing law is not sufficient to regulate the construction of China's port investment, the host country may amend the law to carry out strong monitoring of investment. This legislation is unpredictable, so it is difficult for investors to predict possible legal changes.

Cultural factors

The MSR between China and Europe connects European coastal countries from the Mediterranean to Northern Europe, involving different religions, cultures and customs. It would affect international multimodal transport and increase logistical costs if little is known of the religion and culture.

Those enterprises having investment and joint venture cooperation in Europe should be fully aware of the unique religion and culture when trading with the countries along the MSR, in order to avoid unnecessary misunderstanding.

Religion and culture may have very important impacts on economic trade cooperation and cultural exchanges. Some countries along the MSR are multi-religious, multi-ethnic gathering areas, including three major religions of Buddhism, Christianity and Islam. For effective implementation of MSR, it is necessary to take systematic and in-depth consideration of these religions and cultural factors and develop corresponding cross-cultural conflict risk management plans.

Technological factors

The Secretary-General of the International Maritime Organization (IMO), Mr Ki-tack Lim once proposed that it would be a big challenge for the shipping industry to maintain sustainable development while meeting the demands of safety construction and environmental performance at the same time.[20] It not only requires sound management mechanisms but also needs to be supported by new technologies. In the digital era of industry, the efficiency in the maritime sector and the environment protection mainly rely on new technologies, which give rise to a great potential of opportunities to shipping. However, new opportunities are always accompanied with new challenges with regard to profits, security, the impact on the environment, international trade and the potential cost of industry, and the influence of these technologies for the shipping and maritime industry.

Over the last 25 years, automation has entered into the operations of container terminals and today almost 30 terminals worldwide have installed automated handling and/or transportation of containers through centralised control systems. Automation in terminals and its application bring huge benefits such as cost-savings, well planned operations and high efficient performance. In some terminals, a risk-avoiding approach and a partly automated concept are introduced to an automated stacking yard, and a control system for the scheduling of manually operated transportation equipment between ship-to-shore (STS) cranes and the stack area.[21]

The following challenges may be identified in port terminal automation:

- Automation is significantly more expensive than a manual terminal which requires a highly strong financial and technological strength.
- Automated terminals lack flexibility. Their physical layout is difficult to change once fixed unless it is an automated straddle carrier solution, and it is fixed for the long term. Decisions have to be made at the design stage to evaluate the terminal's needs for decades ahead. The activities of the terminal and the needs of its customers may change over time.
- The processes carried out by a terminal are not necessarily stable and homogenous. They may be volatile and change over time. Automation confers a high degree of repetition and predictability.
- In some locations, union resistance may make it difficult to achieve the full extent of headcount reduction that automation in theory offers.
- Automation is a highly bespoke process, which varies from terminal to terminal. Management and software of the automated equipment is key, as is the way that it integrates with all other systems on the terminal.
- Automation does not necessarily result in faster handling and higher service levels.
- Automation projects carry greater risk and are harder to implement, whereas manual terminals are tried and tested before operation.[22]
- Different countries have different shipping rules and they will need to be amended to allow robot ships to sail.[23]

The Internet, computing, big data and other emerging technologies promote the arrival of the tide of information; meanwhile, an industrial revolution is also brewing. For the shipping industry, the latest successful trial of the world's first fully autonomous ferry conducted by Rolls-Royce and the Finferries indicates that maritime autonomous surface ships (MASS) have a greater impact on the shipping industry.[24] It is undeniable that the MASS has presented an infinite vision towards the future of the shipping industry and the port terminals. However, there are still many obstacles before the implementation.

Information sharing factor

Information sharing is a crucial process in group decision making. Port and terminal managements favour teams with heterogeneous members, hoping that the knowledge from different domains and experiences will lead to better solutions. The initiative of information connectivity will contribute to establish a scientific design mechanism extending to a wider range with higher level application. It will achieve the integration and market allocation of resources in large space, promote the orderly free flow of economic elements, the efficient allocation of resources and fundamentally promote resource conservation, consumption reduction, efficiency development and environmental protection. With the development of the MSR, the relevant ports, which act as an important carrier linking to freight business, logistics warehousing and information services, become a key node of the MSR. At the same time, the requirements of relevant port information, monitoring, logistics docking, port management, security and other capabilities will be stricter.

The construction of a cross-border electronic highway is insufficient to upgrade a regional electronic information exchange network. Traditional trade barriers would give rise to the inadequacy of information-sharing among the countries, which will impede the development of a transparent, opening, equal, and diversified market mechanism, causing concerns such as market malfunction, imbalanced competitions, unfair treatment and abnormal market development.

Maritime security factors

The 21st Century Maritime Silk Road covers several international vital shipping lanes from China extending to the north, south, east and west. The north shipping lane goes through Korea and Japan, crossing the Bering Strait, reaching Russia and Far East areas and finally arriving at the Arctic Ocean. The south vital shipping route passes through Indonesia and reaches Australia. The east shipping lane heads to the Panama Canal splitting to north America and Latin America. The west shipping lane is an important one, which starts from China's eastern costal ports to Europe, passing through the South China Sea, the Malacca Strait, the Lombok Strait, linking to the Northern Indian Ocean, the Persian Gulf, the Red Sea, the Gulf of Aden, Mediterranean Sea and up to South and West Europe.

Among these international vital shipping lanes, the western lane plays an important role in connection with Asia and Europe for the development of MSR, with enormous potential, but the risks of maritime security should not be ignored.

Maritime cyber security

The port connectivity can only be meaningful if major countries and regions around the world are involved in the global maritime transportation network. One of the most important challenges to the maritime industry is maritime cyber security. Many ports in the world are highly automated and the terminal operations rely on computerised information and communication technologies, which may be vulnerable to cyber-based attacks. The invasion and disturbing of the cyber system of ports and ships would finally result in threatening the safe, security and efficient operations of ships and ports, as well as the cooperation among the member countries. One of the victims of maritime cyber-attacks suffered a great loss in 2011, where the commercial shipping line suffered from a cyber-attack. A serious problem is that the protection measures are insufficient to address the actual domain and size of the threats.[25]

Port security

The IMO provides support, assistance and guidance to Member Governments on matters relating to the implementation of the International Convention for the Safety of Life at Sea (SOLAS), 1974, as amended, the International Ship and Port Facility Security Code (ISPS Code).[26] The ISPS Code was adopted under SOLAS 1974 through Chapter XI-2 on Special Measures to enhance maritime security. The ISPS Code, which is a mandatory instrument for all countries party to the Convention, is the IMO's main legislative framework to address maritime security-related matters. The ISPS Code entered into force on 1 July 2004 and has since formed the basis for a comprehensive mandatory security regime for international shipping. The Code is divided into two sections, Part A and Part B. Mandatory Part A outlines detailed maritime and port security-related requirements, which SOLAS contracting governments, port authorities and shipping companies must adhere to, in order to be in compliance with the Code. Part B of the Code provides a series of recommended guidelines on how to meet the requirements and obligations set out within the provisions of Part A.

The main objectives of the ISPS Code include:

• Establishment of an international framework that fosters cooperation between Contracting Governments, Government agencies, local administrations and the shipping and port industries, in assessing and detecting potential security threats to ships or port facilities used for international trade, so as to implement preventive security measures against such threats

- Determining the respective roles and responsibilities of all parties concerned with safeguarding maritime security in ports and on board ships, at the national, regional and international levels
- To ensure that there is early and efficient collation and exchange of maritime security-related information, at national, regional and international levels
- To provide a methodology for ship and port security assessments, which facilitates the development of ship, company and port facility security plans and procedures, which must be utilised to respond to ships' or ports' varying security levels
- To ensure that adequate and proportionate maritime security measures are in place on board ships and in ports.[27]

Environmental factors

Among the risks with which the modern ports are faced, the port environment is the most common concern. As a convergence point connecting the land and the sea, the environment of water, land and the air of ports are closely related to the advancement of MSR initiative and the common destiny of the countries to which particular attention should be paid.

Poor environmental quality would directly reduce the port's operational efficiency and threats the operators and stevedores' health and security. Poor management of port operations can create many risks to the environment, such as the lack of adequate berthing space and the inadequate area for ships to steer during the discharge process as well as the disordered traffic rules, which may lead to unnecessary traffic accidents and the spread or leakage of the goods. Moreover, the irregular cargo storage would lead to cargo spill or hampering the operation of emergency equipment.[28]

Water pollution is also a big issue, as there are so many pollution sources. Examples are the discharge of oily water and waste water, the surface water containing pollutants and sediment, accidental leakage from pipelines, sewage leakage from cruise ships in the drainage process. Due to the leaking of a large number of toxic substances, the quality of water could possibly decline in a very short period of time.

Air pollutants are of international concern. Annex VI of MARPOL convention has stringent requirements to control air pollution from ships. The air pollution from ships mainly include the nitrogen oxides, which are embodied in diesel engine exhaust gas, while the sulphur oxides rise from burning sulphur containing fuel, marine ozone-depleting substances and particulate matter (PM) from the burning wastes. Mishandling fluorine, which can be emitted from equipment such as ice-makers, air conditioning, refrigerators, etc. on board the ship, destroys the ozone. Incinerators are used for toxic gas on board but although it reduces the direct contamination of the ship, it increases the air pollution.

Conclusions and suggestions

The MSR is inclusive, seeking common ground while reserving differences and drawing on each other's strengths, so that all countries can coexist in peace for common prosperity. The MSR aims to promote the connectivity of Asia and Europe, through cooperation and coordination, mutual beneficiary and win-win mechanisms, in terms of the maritime transport and port connectivity.

Shipping is indispensable to the world, as 90 per cent of global trade is carried by maritime transport. The seaborne trade is frequent and the shipping market has great potential for development. The COSCO Shipping company operates container fleets in four major shipping routes between Asia and Europe, mainly between China and Northern Europe, China and Mediterranean. Among the top 100 ports announced in August 2018, there are 54 Asian ports and 19 European ports. The shipping along the MSR connects the ports in China and Europe. The port performance is assessed in the aspects of the port infrastructure, shipping connectivity and the Logistics Performance Index.

Challenges to the MSR and port connectivity exist in aspects of political and economic situations, different national legal regimes, diversified cultures, advancing technology, maritime security and environment. Technological developments and emerging issues in the maritime industry along the MSR may bring together advancing technology and challenges. Examples include maritime cyber-attacks and vulnerability in maritime technology interface. More specific is the maritime autonomous surface ships (MASS), as the IMO is conducting the regulatory scoping exercise in the use of MASS, which may bring potential benefits and challenges.

The Belt and Road Initiative has become the preferred platform for international cooperation with the most prospects through providing public goods. China and European countries should cooperate to effectively implement the MSR. As of May 2017, China has entered into bilateral maritime transport agreements with 36 countries, including the EU and established 31 platforms of logistics information sharing globally.[29] The protocol of the amendment to the maritime transport agreement between China and the EU was signed in December 2018, to apply to Croatia.[30]

The MSR is a driving force to lead a new era of inclusive globalisation. China–EU cooperation has reached an unprecedented high level and share more converging interests. China and the EU should strengthen bilateral economic and trade cooperation, which conforms to the common interests of both sides and complies with the trend of the globalisation. Both China and the EU are accelerating structural reform to boost social and economic development; China's investment in the EU is of mutual beneficial. China and the EU should support economic globalisation and trade and investment facilitation and liberalisation, and resist various forms of protectionism.[31]

In consideration of the legal and policy challenges that might have adverse impacts on the MSR and the port connectivity, the authors would like to bring forward the following suggestions: first, efforts should be made to harmonise various laws and regulations in the regions along the MSR. Although each of the MSR countries has different laws and policies, it is still possible to achieve uniformity of domestic laws regarding international economy, trade and shipping, since some of the MSR countries share common and similar culture and history background. For this purpose, the regional international organisations which would promote the unification of laws in certain fields should be established, and the academic cooperation which would accelerate the draft of new rules common to MSR countries should also be encouraged. Second, more attention should be given to international customs and usages than domestic laws. International customs include those recognised by the industries in certain regions beyond the boundary of sovereign states. For disputes arising under port construction activities, international customs, which are stable and less vulnerable to political changes than domestic rules, would provide better solutions to some extent. Third, priority shall be given to arbitration as an appropriate dispute resolution mechanism in relation to MSR and the port connectivity. Unlike the judges, the arbitrators who often possess the expertise in the industries would be more likely to apply the recognised customs and usages. Therefore, it is helpful to avoid the legal risks by referring the disputes in relation to MSR and the port activity to arbitration. Finally, to quote China's Vice Foreign Minister, 'the Belt and Road has never been considered the construction project of China, it is a common roadmap that all parties are involved to participate in, to share the interest, to undertake the risks'.[32]

Notes

1 *Vision for Maritime Cooperation under the Belt and Road Initiative*, www.yidaiyilu. gov.cn/wcm.files/upload/CMSydylgw/201706/201706200153032.pdf.
2 Arctic Waterways, http://dz.china.com.cn/sd/gfgz/2017-07-06/52806.html.
3 Camille Brugier, China's Way: The New Silk Road, European Union Institute for Security Studies, May 2014, www.iss.europa.eu/uploads/media/Brief_14_New_Silk_Road.pdf.
4 COSCO Shipping Speeds Up Global Resources Network via One Belt, One Road, *China Water Transport Newspaper*, 16 November 2018.
5 COSCO Shipping Lines, Europe Routes, http://lines.coscoshipping.com/home/Services/route/12, visited in December 2018.
6 Top 100 Container Ports, *Lloyd's List*, August 2018, https://lloydslist.maritime intelligence.informa.com/.
7 China's Biggest Unmanned Port Is Open by the End of the Year with the World Highest Throughput, 15 August 2017, www.yidaiyilu.gov.cn/xwzx/dfdt/23484.htm.
8 *Supra* (n. 6).
9 *Ibid.*
10 *Ibid.*
11 Xie Wenqing *et al.*, *The Impact of the New Shipping Alliance on the Strategic Development of Global Port Operators*, Shanghai Research Centre for International Shipping, 23 August 2017, http://mp.weixin.qq.com/s/5I9ECzbE28WxNc78IZqJRA.
12 World Bank, *Connecting to Compete, Trade Logistics in the Global Economy* 2018, p. 8.
13 *Supra* (n. 12), pp. 11–13.
14 Anthony Fensom, $5 Trillion Meltdown: What If China Shuts Down the South China Sea?, *The National Interest*. For details, see Chapter 7 of this book.

15 ICC-IMB, Piracy and Armed Robbery against Ships, Report for January to September 2018, p. 3.

16 *Supra* (n. 15), p. 27.

17 ReCAAP, Piracy and Armed Robbery against Ships in Asia, 3rd Quarter Report, January–September 2018, p. 5, www.recaap.org/resources/ck/files/reports/quarterly/ReCAAP%20ISC%203rd%20Quarter%202018%20Report.pdf.

18 UNCTAD, *Review of Maritime Transport 2018*, p. XI.

19 *Ibid.*, p. 4.

20 Leaders for Sustainable Shipping, www.imo.org/en/MediaCentre/WhatsNew/Pages/default.aspx.

21 Armin Wieschemann, Terminal Automation Challenges in Systems Integration, *Port Technology Journal*, Germany, May 2016, p. 79.

22 *Ibid.*

23 Could Computers Captain the World's Cargo Ships?, 18 August 2014, www.bbc.com/future/story/20140818-robot-ships-poised-to-set-sail.

24 World's First Fully Autonomous Ferry, Rolls-Royce, www.rolls-royce.com/products-and-services/marine/news-and-events/svan-2018.aspx.

25 Maritime Cyber Security, IMO MSC 97/4, 17 August 2016, www.imo.org/en.

26 *Ibid.*

27 SOLAS XI-2 and ISPS Code, www.imo.org/en.

28 Li Youming, Management of Environmental Risks in Foreign Ports, *China Surveying and Design* [in Chinese], 4 (2000), 43–44.

29 BRI in 2017, 12 January 2018, www.yidaiyilu.gov.cn/xwzx/gnxw/43662.htm.

30 China and EU Sign Maritime Agreement Amended Protocol, 23 December 2018, www.chinanews.com/cj/2018/12-23/8710204.shtml.

31 B&R Initiative benefits China and Europe, https://eng.yidaiyilu.gov.cn/ghsl/wksl/11518.htm.

32 Speech of Vice Foreign Minister Le Yucheng at the first meeting of the BRI Summit Consultative Committee, 21 December 2018, www.fmprc.gov.cn/web/wjbxw_673019/t1623909.shtml.

Part II
Sea lanes of communication and navigational safety

5 Maritime Silk Road Initiative changing geopolitical configuration in the Indo-Pacific

Fu-Kuo Liu

Introduction

Focusing on the new impetus to elevate national development, China boldly launched an ambitious grand strategy, 'One Belt, One Road' (OBOR) in 2013. Although it began with a series of rather vague ideas and concepts, official efforts with following elaborations have gradually made it more comprehensive and substantial. Over the last couple of years, OBOR has progressed to a more realistic approach and has transformed into the Belt and Road Initiative (BRI). Although BRI presents a new driving force for economic cooperation by facilitating infrastructure projects, concerns have been raised by some countries in the international community that BRI may hide China's strategic ambition searching to transform the existing global order in a new era.[1]

Just as many experts have observed, BRI is at the centre of China's strategies that aim to transform Asian order and China itself. While BRI was, according to the Chinese official view, put forward in line with a political belief to promote peace, development, cooperation so as to have a win-win outcome for all, BRI has far-reaching strategic implications with a global impact.[2] For example, over the last few years, China and its partners have substantially developed and strengthened bilateral ties and enhanced regional cooperation through investment in infrastructure projects under the BRI framework. Since 2013, China has made impressive efforts by investing $50 billion in countries along the route of the BRI. 'A total of 56 economic and trade cooperation zones have already been built by Chinese businesses in Belt and Road countries, generating nearly $1.1 billion in tax revenue and creating 180,000 local jobs'.[3]

Among those infrastructure projects, port connectivity plays an important role in terms of international transportation network and shipping lanes being critical to regional cooperation. Thus, the 21st Century Maritime Silk Road (MSR) Initiative, as a constituent part of BRI, has been focusing on economic cooperation by encouraging collaboration of infrastructure building and facilitation of communication, and elevating China's global maritime influence by enhancing networks of connectivity and communication with countries along the MSR.

In terms of maritime influence, MSR has been increasing China's geostrategic influence in the Indo-Pacific region and Eurasia, and will potentially reshape the world economic pattern. Traditionally, the Indo-Pacific region is important because the sea lanes of communication (SLOCs) in this region connect the largest energy exporting countries and the world's largest economies, including the USA and China. Through the new efforts of the MSR, China can take advantage of the infrastructures and SLOCs to import energy from the Middle East and Africa, and export its industrial outputs to global markets. Thus beyond the economic level, BRI has provided China with an unprecedented opportunity for political and strategic advance.

While the MSR facilitates connectivity and communication networks all along the route, it could at the same time help assure the safety of SLOCs in the Indo-Pacific region. Through the cooperation frameworks, the MSR not just promotes individual national interests, but also brings about regional security and mutual prosperity in the Indo-Pacific. More importantly, the MSR is also an effort to maintain free trade and globalisation. The debate between globalisation and de-globalisation has been growing since US President Donald Trump put forward his famous 'America First' strategy.[4] The MSR is clearly in a position to push forward 'inclusive globalisation'.[5] On the other hand, however, it may lead to strategic concerns with China's possible dominance in this region. For example, India and Japan have jointly launched a new initiative: the Asia-Africa Growth Corridor (AAGC), which is regarded as a joint effort between the two countries to counterbalance China's BRI influence,[6] by relying on four pillars: enhanced capacity and skills; quality infrastructure and institutional connectivity; development and cooperation projects; and people-to-people partnership.[7]

It is important to examine how significant and what profound implications China's BRI will bring about in the coming years. This chapter explores to what extent the MSR will change the geopolitical structure in the Indo-Pacific and how it may enhance the safety of SLOCs.

Potential strategic implications of the Maritime Silk Road Initiative: an overview

Being part of the BRI, the MSR is defined as a grand trade and infrastructure plan along the sea lanes of communication connecting China through South East Asia, South Asia, Middle East, Africa and finally to Europe. By new efforts of facilitating trade and infrastructure cooperation, the MSR would further tighten bilateral links between China and related countries, and could also establish further networks of regional cooperation. It would definitely help China enhance its influence and collaborate with its partners. As is opined on BRI,

[i]t is aimed at further strengthening the Chinese role in economic integration with these nations and playing a larger role in global political affairs. As and when the infrastructure is ready, the Chinese are not only looking to push its indigenous technologies but also find means to export its surplus manufacturing.[8]

From the economic perspective, all infrastructure projects would not only generate more business thereafter, but also undoubtedly help expand China's strategic ambition one way or another. While the current US policy tends towards anti-globalisation and isolationism, China rises as a new champion of globalisation through the MSR.[9] The MSR will also redefine China's peace image and the usefulness of soft power, if those proposed projects proceed smoothly.

From a geopolitical perspective, the MSR is connected to maritime security where the safety of SLOCs along the Indian Ocean and the Pacific Ocean is essential to the success of the MSR. Given the fact that the unresolved territorial and maritime disputes in the Indo-Pacific endanger regional stability, maritime security and energy security, peace and security have become a major desire of regional countries, especially those countries adjacent to the South China Sea, who are increasingly concerned with China's assertive expansion. As a result of its entangling territorial disputes and fast strategic advance, China is risking its credential for peace in South East Asia and South Asia. The image of assertiveness has stalled China's attempt to lead regional integration and somewhat crippled its peaceful rise. Nevertheless, in the long term, as the MSR is put forward with a strong economic incentive with a focus on economic cooperation between regional countries, the strategic suspicion is likely to be offset and geopolitical structure in the Indo-Pacific will be reshaped.

Indo-Pacific strategic configuration and the importance of maritime security

As a single 'strategic system', which is increasingly formed through economic transactions, energy supply, diplomatic manipulation and big power strategic competition, the Indo-Pacific region represents a new articulation of geographic significance. Maritime security and sea lane protection have been at the core of the Indo-Pacific strategy initiated by the USA. During the 12th East Asian Summit, the US President Donald Trump emphasised the concept of the Indo-Pacific with more strategic implications, but the details were rather insufficient and remain to be developed.[10] The then US Secretary of State, Rex Tillerson, articulated that from the strategic perspective, the USA would elevate its engagement with democratic allies, including Australia, Japan and India, for a free and open Indo-Pacific.[11] China and India have, in particular, generated major momentum for the emergence of the Indo-Pacific era. When China steps up its overall efforts on the maritime domain, including trade, energy, transportation and strategic advance, its vision on maritime strategy has been observed as a key point.

Presently, China is rapidly increasing its dependence upon oil from the Middle East, while the United States and others are gradually reducing such dependence. Roughly 85 per cent of the oil that China imports passes through the Straits of Malacca.[12] Not only would the Straits be critical to the persistent development of China, but also the Indian Ocean is strategically pivotal to its energy supply and overall prosperity. As a state of energy scarcity, China's increasing dependence on maritime shipments through the Indian Ocean indicates its importance to China. Undeniably, to protect its energy supply, trade and national interests, China is driven by strategic transformation to step up capabilities of military presence and of power projection in the Indian Ocean. China may for now have doubts about the emergence of an Indo-Pacific strategic system, while India, Australia, the United States and Japan have publicly advocated their strategic advance to deter China's expansion. Although the Chinese government has not yet responded formally to the idea of the Indo-Pacific, its latest grand strategy – the MSR, has reflected just what the Indo-Pacific strategy aims to target.

In the same vein, Indian Prime Minister Narendra Modi chants for an 'Act East' policy, the US then President Barack Obama pushed through its rebalance to Asia strategy (though President Donald Trump does not have a clear maritime strategy of this kind yet), and India and Japan advocate a new partnership for the AAGC.[13] All of China's MSR, India's Act East policy and the US rebalance to Asia, reflect big power competition for influence in the Indo-Pacific. In March 2015, the US Navy released 'A Cooperative Strategy for 21st Century Sea Power' for the first time emphasising the strategic idea of the Indo-Asia-Pacific. This implies that the US military will calculate the importance of this strategic shift and endorse the concept and increasing significance of the Indo-Pacific. The United States has recognised that 'the economic importance, security interests, and geography of this vast maritime region dictate a growing reliance on naval forces to protect US interests and maintain an enduring commitment to the stability of the region'.[14] Increasing dependence upon the transportation routes of the Indian Ocean indicates that security stakes has considerably risen.

According to the new strategy, the United States will deploy 60 per cent of its naval forces in the Asia-Pacific region by 2020 to cope with new challenges. Presented with the new strategic situation, the United States will not only enhance its warfighting advantages in-theatre, it 'improves interoperability, more integrated operations, and increasingly complex exercises and training', but will also enhance partnerships with regional players through 'expanded maritime security operations, shared maritime domain awareness, and longer multilateral engagements'.[15] Against the strategic environment of the Indo-Pacific region, the US Navy and Marine Corps have strengthened their forward deployment in the region. The deployment of the US Marine Corps to Darwin, Australia reflects exactly that the strategic consideration is related to the Indo-Pacific. Under the US rebalance to Asia strategy, overall deployment was aligned with the Indo-Pacific 'strategic arc'.

The importance of maritime security centres on the concept of the Indo-Pacific. The economic development of China and India has further accelerated the increase in energy demand, which definitely heightens their dependence on maritime security for energy supply and trade flows. The countries concerned, i.e. the United States, India, Australia, Indonesia and Japan, have all responded to the strategic importance of the Indo-Pacific. Therefore, it is almost inevitable that all related countries will try to strengthen their naval control on the sea lanes from the Indian Ocean through to the Pacific Ocean. Today, in the context of the Indo-Pacific, the region witnesses three aspects of developments: first, booming trade flows and increasing energy demands identify critical importance of the region; second, Chinese naval forces try to stretch out its reach into the Indian Ocean to protect its increasing interests and gain access to the supply of energy resources; third, by deploying naval forces into the Indian Ocean, China would lift up its weight in competing for strategic space with India, Japan and the United States.

A pivotal place in the Indo-Pacific strategy is the South China Sea. On a global level, the maritime strategy competition between China and the United States in the West Pacific seems inevitable. In April 2018, the US government gave a clear definition of the 'free and open' Indo-Pacific. On defining 'free', the United States wants all nations in the region to be free from coercion. 'They can pursue in a sovereign manner the paths they choose in the region ... and become progressively more free'.[16] By 'open', the United States means 'open sea lines of communication and open airways'. It is clear that the interpretation of the Indo-Pacific strategy aims at China's recent assertiveness in the South China Sea and aggressiveness in pushing the process of BRI. It offers policy rationale on which recent US conducts of Freedom of Navigation Operations (FONOPs) in the South China Sea are based. As BRI is further developed, the Indo-Pacific strategy is accelerated in accordance, as a way to balance Chinese increasing influence. Under the new circumstances, competition between the MSR and Indo-Pacific strategy will be intensified and lead to transforming geopolitical structure.

At the regional level, peace and stability in the South China Sea are the real interests of all littoral countries. In the past decade, although tensions occurred from time to time, China had been working with all parties concerned to manage disputes and maintain overall peace, stability and cooperation, by introducing the 'dual-track' approach.[17] With intensified international pressure on China's militarisation of artificial islands in the Spratly Islands, China and ASEAN countries have managed to progress the negotiation of the Code of Conduct (COC) by reaching consensus on a single draft negotiating text, in August 2018.[18] In general, the progressing negotiation presents a positive political will among the parties concerned and indicates that China and ASEAN countries are able to manage regional disputes on their own.

Changing strategic configuration of the Indo-Pacific through the Maritime Silk Road Initiative

As an effect of China's rise, the Indo-Pacific has become the central ground of the big powers' strategic competition, i.e., the United States, China and India. Accelerated by strong economic and energy incentives, the progress of China's long-term development depends much on the security of SLOCs in the Indo-Pacific. As discussed previously, for decades, the United States together with

India controls most important choke points along the SLOCs connecting the India Ocean and the Pacific Ocean. Today, China's fast growing economy relies more and more on energy supply lines and maritime trading routes in the Indo-Pacific. For this reason, China envisions greater strategic vulnerability on SLOCs and thus has broadened its scope of strategic preparation by directly engaging with regional partners and concretised bilateral cooperation on infrastructure projects relating to energy supply lines. Building closer relationships to ensure energy supply, China has enhanced its direct involvement in economic development in Pakistan, Myanmar and Bangladesh.

Before the MSR formally launched, China had already focused on investing in establishing strategic strong-footing in the littoral states of the Indian Ocean, described by the US government in 2005, as the Chinese aggressive 'string of pearls' strategy.[19] Although the Chinese government has never officially admitted to such a strategic effort, it does not rule out such Chinese effort by economic, diplomatic, political and military means. After decades of groundwork in the surrounding areas of the Indian Ocean, China was well prepared to launch BRI/MSR with more comprehensive and strategic features from which it developed regional projects. There would be at least four important strategic implications of MSR for the region: expanding China's influence by building stronger economic ties with trading partners and safeguarding SLOCs connecting these partners; shifting strategic configuration; and helping ease tensions concerning regional territorial and maritime disputes.

The first strategic implication is that China is rising and has more influence on the future trend of global markets. While the traditional world markets are shrinking, China is on high demand for exploring overseas markets to help its over-supplied markets and industries with excessive production capacity. While the global markets do not grow at the speed of China's domestic demand, and production is gradually reaching the point of saturation, increasing pressure from domestic market and society is pushing China to explore new overseas markets. With advocating and implementing the MSR, China could effectively ease domestic economic pressure, especially for those infrastructure-related industries. Politically, it is critical to the survival of the Chinese Communist Party, as continuing slowdown of economic growth may cause negative repercussion that threatens social stability in China.

By exporting its excessive supply–market momentum, China would connect its economy further to the world markets. Along the MSR, China could build a new economic alliance that relies on Eurasia, rather than the existing US-led global economic institutions. By building stronger financial ties with its trading partners, China would be further accelerating internationalisation of its currency-RMB and try to boost its role as a regional economic hub. To reinforce BRI progress, China established the Asia Infrastructure and Investment Bank (AIIB) and Silk Road Fund, and helped create the BRIC Development Bank (New Development Bank), and Shanghai Cooperation Organization Development Bank. It is clear that, through launching ambitious projects and new financial agencies, China could extend its multiple influences far beyond the domain of pure economic policy.

The second strategic implication regards a response from China to an increasing reality of critical shipping lanes. Since 2015, China has continuously invested in Djibouti, including infrastructure projects, and strengthened its military presence in the Eastern Part of Africa. By enhancing its investment in Djibouti, China could connect Asia and Middle East with Africa. In 2017, there were already at least eight projects confirmed in the region.[20] Thus, the MSR currently carries a huge amount of strategic significance. This is how the MSR could play a significant role in the shift of strategic relevance in the Indo-Pacific today. It accompanies the larger strategic landscape as China rises. With the MSR in place, China is gaining stronger ability to transform strategic structure along the maritime routes from Asia, Africa to Europe. As a result, China's soft power looms large by engaging in collaboration with partners for regional development.

The third strategic implication concerns the United States rebalance to Asia strategy, under the then President Obama, which attempted to define China as a critical regional player in Asia rather than a global one. Although it was not designed specifically to contain China, it came in to deter China's advance beyond its national borders. Naturally, the Chinese understanding of rebalance to Asia is that the United States was purposely to confine China's role in the global arena. Therefore, China felt that if it does not respond to it with proactive strategy, its national development would then be continuously confined and obstructed at the regional level. As such, China initiated BRI and the MSR to re-engage with new partners and regenerate new momentum for facilitating regional cooperation as a way to break through the strategic confinement and progress with its own ambition. Pushing for the BRI project, China could develop its own strategic sphere of interest and liberate its geostrategic limitation.

In light of challenging existing predominant maritime powers in the Indian Ocean, China needs to tie up relationships with regional countries, in order to ensure their common interest. The MSR would give China a proactive advantage, it has long awaited, to shift strategic configuration in its favour. By strengthening protection of sea lanes in the Indo-Pacific and deepening infrastructure cooperation with littoral states, China would ensure its trade and energy supply going through safely. This indicates how China lays a foundation on establishing the centrepiece of the BRI: the 'China-Myanmar economic corridor'.[21] Based on the original idea of connectivity and energy supply, the economic corridor would not only provide sufficient assistance for Myanmar's national development, but also ensure energy supply for China through the shore of the Bay of Bengal. Of course, it is helping China fulfil an important strategic desire for direct access to the Indian Ocean. Especially, China's new role, e.g., in the case of regional humanitarian crisis, shows its determination to remove all obstacles that the major project would encounter. In considering possible obstacles to construction of the 'economic corridor', China stepped into the trouble spot of the Rohingya crisis, and proposed a 'three stage plan' to tackle the crisis between Myanmar, Bangladesh and Rokhine State.[22] While the United Nations' report on violence inflicted on Rohingya Muslims and other minorities by Myanmar's security forces came out in August 2018, China took a different position from others from shelving off punishment on Myanmar.[23] It appears that China has extensive investment, trade and energy interest in Myanmar. By protecting Myanmar from international intervention, China would not only ensure its interest and development of BRI, but also further strengthen the bilateral relation with Myanmar.

Regarding the fourth strategic implication, we know that China entangles with its neighbours in territorial disputes in the South China Sea, the tension swirls up and this could hamper any possible cooperation initiated by China. Since the Philippines pushed for international arbitration in 2013, the situation on the ground has become very tense and has resulted in distrust and increasing hostility between the parties concerned and China. Although, after the arbitral tribunal gave the final award in July 2016, tensions in the South China Sea quietened down. However, it has not changed the status quo or added any new value to the situation. Thereafter, individual claimants of the South China Sea have maintained their national policies and stand with no significant change. After President Rodrigo Duterte of the Philippines visited China in October 2016, prolonged tension between China and the Philippines dramatically turned to a new direction. The immediate political effect to the South China Sea tension, is that the region now follows through the pace of bilateral rapprochement. ASEAN countries are gradually tilting towards China and seeking more cooperation. It is important for China to realise that first, general feeling in South East Asia is now hope for peace and more cooperation on economic development; second, President Duterte's realistic policy approach may be only short term; and third, South East Asian countries remain to be suspicious and anxious about China's long-term intention.

It appears that the resumption of the bilateral relations between China and the Philippines remains fragile, as the Philippines' new policy towards China is completely driven by President Duterte himself. Over the last few years, mass media in the Philippines consistently reflects hesitant views on Duterte's pro-China policy.[24] Also, with his controversial actions against drug criminals, he is under serious political pressure at home and abroad. Particularly, the majority of Filipinos and civil servants are accustomed to the long-term alliance with the United States and frequently doubt the pro-China policy. It is doubtful that Manila's current course of pro-China policy would sustain development. If current South China Sea peace is built on such a volatile Philippine policy, it will not be sustainable in the future.

From a political perspective, there is no existing applicable solution to territorial disputes in the South China Sea. As pointed out above, over the last decade or so, many difficult hurdles that claimants have been confronted with, e.g., internal legal restriction, sovereignty insistence, nationalism sentiment, international law and UNCLOS, and power politics, have blocked chances of flexibility for a compromise. What China has done in the South China Sea may have been portrayed as creating a more negative image than a positive one, e.g., Huangyan Island (Scarborough Shoal) and Ren Ai Reef (Second Thomas Shoal) incidents against the Philippines in 2012; the oil rig HD-981 incident against Vietnam in 2014; and land reclamation in the Spratly Islands in 2015. While China is pushing for more strategic leverage in the South China Sea, it is adding more security concerns for ASEAN members, which will not be helpful to China–ASEAN relations.

In implementing the MSR in South East Asia, there are two sets of challenges: shelving territorial disputes and exploring cooperation with regional partners for common interest. For now, it remains a big challenge for China to progress the MSR convincingly in the region, when the South China Sea disputes are still disturbing the regional order. At the G7 2017 Foreign Ministers' meeting, it ended with a joint communiqué indicating that the final award by the arbitral tribunal on the South China Sea in July 2016 should be considered as 'a useful base for further efforts to peacefully solve disputes in the South China Sea'.[25] G7 foreign ministers also stressed their opposition to the militarisation of disputed features in the South China Sea. Obviously, in the global diplomatic context, China's reclamation efforts in the South China Sea and disregard of the arbitral award have been repeatedly disapproved of.

On the occasion of the 2015 ASEAN–China Expo, Zhang Gaoli, China's Vice Premier, said that

China is willing to work with ASEAN countries to comprehensively and effectively implement the Declaration on the Conduct of Parties in the South China Sea (DOC), and accelerate consultations on formulating a COC for the South China Sea, in order to jointly maintain peace and stability.[26]

There is no doubt that the South China Sea dispute would be the most difficult obstacle for China to implement the Maritime Silk Road Initiative. With tensions still in the region, regarding China's militarisation of artificial islands in the South China Sea, members of ASEAN countries have further increased their concerns with China's strategic advance. While the Philippines' arbitration case was concluded in July 2016 and clearly not in favour of Chinese interest, the final award was immediately rejected by China and has since not been implemented. It is conceivable that the suspicion of China's grand project in the region remains high. Under the overarching structure of the MSR, China is encouraging cooperation on trade, economic, cultural exchanges, but does not directly refer to the solution of territorial disputes in the South China Sea. That is the reason why many countries in South East Asia do not want to be differentiated from the main development China is now advocating, but at the same time, they would like to keep a certain distance from China's security and diplomatic advance and call for strong unity inside the ASEAN countries to withstand potential risks.

From the Chinese perspective, the MSR could serve as a fine diplomatic tool to help cultivate friendly ground, or keep away from political differences and for finding a solution to the territorial disputes in the South China Sea. During the first Belt and Road Summit held in Beijing in May 2017, Xi Jinping emphasised that BRI was a 'brand of cooperation' of an open and inclusive nature and it meant to facilitate a win-win result.[27] Although he did not specifically indicate issues in the South China Sea, it becomes more likely that under current circumstances China would seek for more cooperation with neighbouring countries.

To implement the MSR, China needs to avoid pushing too hard and aggressively in the region, as China's assertive presentation in the region only dampens its hope for a successful MSR.[28] Thus, China would have to identify a fine balance between the protection of the South China Sea's sovereign rights and the implementation of the Initiative.

Although China will not give up what it has progressed in the South China Sea, in August 2015, Minister of Foreign Affairs, Wang Yi, announced at the occasion of Foreign Ministers' Meeting of East Asian Summit and ASEAN Regional Forum, that China had completed land reclamation work and moved onto the second phase of building facilities for public goods.[29] For the region, Wang's articulation sent out a positive message, which may have softened regional concerns about China's expansive action.

As such, the BRI may well serve the best interest in building partnerships and preventing regional tension. China and ASEAN members would need to maintain regional stability and peace. Under the framework of the BRI, China would have to connect with the ASEAN Economic Community (AEC) Blueprint 2025, to strengthen a base of common interest.[30] It would be critical that China expands the scope of its bilateral cooperation with individual ASEAN members. It may help not only deepen their economic and industrial ties, but also reduce tension in the South China Sea. Ideally, regional focuses would thus be shifted away from regional tension to BRI for more cooperation, as sovereign disputes would not be solved in the foreseeable future. When the Declaration on the Conduct of Parties in the South China Sea (DOC) was agreed upon by China and ASEAN countries in November 2002, regional concerns with China began to diminish and facilitation of bilateral economic cooperation leading to the ASEAN-China Free Trade agreement charged the main thrust of regional diplomacy. During the 20th ASEAN-China Summit held in Manila in November 2017, leaders endorsed the Framework of the Code of Conduct in the South China Sea adopted by the Foreign Ministers of ASEAN member states and China, though some may have been reluctant. They also committed to substantive negotiation on the text and formally tasked the Joint Working Group and the Senior Official Meeting on the DOC to be responsible for drafting the COC from early 2018 onwards.[31] Now, only if China and the ASEAN countries replicate previous positive experiences and seal the deal on COC with good faith in the near future, can they clear the political stumbling block for implementing the BRI.

Conclusion

The MSR is a fresh incentive in terms of geostrategic and geoeconomic transformation. Although the Indo-Pacific will be reinforced by further development of energy security and global economic transactions, the MSR will boost China's strategic competence in the Indo-Pacific and regional geopolitical areas. Certainly, now dominated by the United States and India, the Indo-Pacific strategic configuration is on the way to be increasingly shared by the United States, India, Japan and China. When China launched the ambitious BRI, the strategic configuration in the Indo-Pacific gradually tilted in China's favour.

While the MSR is being gradually implemented, safeguarding the SLOCs in the Indo-Pacific has become a critical issue to the success of the BRI. The basic concept of the MSR focuses on promoting trade and facilitating cooperation on infrastructure and economic development. While regional tension remains high in the uncertainty of the South China Sea, how much would the MSR work to encourage cooperation between China and other claimants? From a geostrategic perspective, the initiative as planned by the Chinese government would carry significant strategic implications for the region. Even though swirling tensions in the South China Sea seem to be refraining from settling territorial disputes for the time being, it may not stop countries in the region from continuously deepening their economic engagement with China. In fact, over the last few years, while the tension was rising between China and other claimants in the South China Sea, the increasing degree of their dependence on Chinese markets does not see a slowdown. With the proposition of shelving territorial disputes and working on joint development, it may give China more favourable leverage to win support from the regions within its initiated Maritime Silk Road.

Notes

1 Michael Clauss, Why Europe and the US Cannot Afford to Ignore China's Belt and Road, *South China Morning Post*, 16 June 2017, www.scmp.com/comment/insight-opinion/article/2098527/why-europe-and-us-cannot-afford-ignore-chinas-belt-and-road.
2 Commentary: China's 'Belt and Road' Initiative Delivering Benefits to World, *Xinhua*, 15 April 2017, http://news.xinhuanet.com/english/2017-04/15/c_136210956.htm.
3 China's Investment along Belt and Road Booms, The State Council, 19 April 2017, http://english.gov.cn/state_council/ministries/2017/04/19/content_281475631160170.htm.
4 Remarks of President Donald J. Trump – As Prepared for Delivery Inaugural Address, The Whitehouse, 20 January, 2017, www.whitehouse.gov/inaugural-address.
5 Weidong Liu and Michael Dunford, Inclusive Globalization: Unpacking China's Belt and Road Initiative, *Area Development and Policy* 1(3) (2016).
6 Dipanjan Roy Chaudhury, India, Japan Come Up with AAGC to Counter China's OBOR, *The Economic Times*, 26 May 2017, https://economictimes.indiatimes.com/news/economy/policy/india-japan-come-up-with-aagc-to-counter-chinas-obor/articleshow/58846673.cms.
7 Asia Africa Growth Corridor: Partnership for Sustainable and Innovative Development – A Vision Document, African Development Bank Meeting, Ahmedabad, India, 22–26 May 2017, www.eria.org/Asia-Africa-Growth-Corridor-Document.pdf.
8 Hemant Chandak, China's Grand Project – One Belt One Road, Swarajya, 18 July 2015, http://swarajyamag.com/world/chinas-grand-project-one-belt-one-road/.
9 28 Heads of State Confirm Attendance at China's Belt and Road Summit Next Month, *South China Morning Post*, 18 April 2017, www.scmp.com/news/china/diplomacy-defence/article/2088478/28-heads-state-confirm-attendance-chinas-belt-and-road.
10 Demetri Sevastopulo, Trump Gives Glimpse of 'Indo-Pacific' Strategy to Counter China, *Financial Times*, 11 November 2017, www.ft.com/stream/6dcdaee0-65f3-3358-a4da-810083e187ad.

11 US Elevated Its Ties with India for Free, Open Indo-Pacific: Rex Tillerson, *The Economic Times*, 13 December 2017, https://economictimes.indiatimes.com/news/defence/us-elevated-its-ties-with-india-for-free-open-indo-pacific-rex-tillerson/articleshow/62052518.cms.

12 China is Hooked on Mideast Oil, Which Helps Build a Good Case for a Petroyaun, *FAILAKA*, 24 January 2014, http://failaka.com/china-is-hooked-on-mideast-oil/; see also Michael Lelyveld, China Ignores Risks as Oil Imports Rise, Radio Free Asia, 6 February 2017, www.rfa.org/english/commentaries/energy_watch/china-ignores-risks-as-oil-imports-rise-02062017103809.html.

13 Maulik Pathak, India–Japan Partnership to Play Key Role in Asia–Africa Corridor, *Livemint*, 25 May 2017, www.livemint.com/Politics/gfSbaVJjfHuoUKPTMxrU8L/IndiaJapan-partnership-to-play-key-role-in-AsiaAfrica-corr.html.

14 A Cooperative Strategy for 21st Century Sea Power, US Navy, March 2015, www.navy.mil/local/maritime/150227-CS21R-Final.pdf.

15 *Ibid.* p. 14.

16 Briefing on the Indo-Pacific Strategy, Alex N. Wong, Deputy Assistant Secretary, Bureau of East Asian and Pacific Affairs, Washington DC, 2 April 2018, www.state.gov/r/pa/prs/ps/2018/04/280134.htm.

17 Why Dual-Track Approach Most Effective to Solve South China Sea Disputes?, *Xinhua Net*, 6 July 2016, www.chinadaily.com.cn/world/2016-07/06/content_25992241.htm.

18 Charissa Yong, Asean, China Agree on Text to Negotiate Code of Conduct in South China Sea, *Strait Times*, 2 August 2018, www.straitstimes.com/politics/asean-china-agree-on-text-to-negotiate-code-of-conduct-in-south-china-sea.

19 The US informal official document used the term. China Builds Up Strategic Sea Lanes, *The Washington Times*, 17 January 2005, www.washingtontimes.com/news/2005/jan/17/20050117-115550-1929r/.

20 Elizabeth Shim, China Rapidly Expands Port, Military Base in Djibouti, UPI, 18 April 2017, www.upi.com/Top_News/World-News/2017/04/18/China-rapidly-expands-port-military-base-in-Djibouti/8261492533611/.

21 China Plans Economic Corridor with Myanmar for Access to Indian Ocean, NDTV, 21 November 2017, www.ndtv.com/world-news/china-plans-economic-corridor-with-myanmar-for-access-to-indian-ocean-1778361.

22 Sarah Zheng, China and Myanmar Talk Infrastructure as Rohingya Crisis Rages, *South China Morning Post*, 20 November 2017, www.scmp.com/news/china/diplomacy-defence/article/2120759/china-and-myanmar-talk-infrastructure-rohingya-crisis.

23 Ben Blanchard, China Says Pressure Unhelpful in Resolving Rohingya Issue, Reuters, 28 August 2018, www.reuters.com/article/us-myanmar-rohingya-china/china-says-pressure-unhelpful-in-resolving-rohingya-issue-idUSKCN1LD0NB.

24 Narciso Reyes Jr., The Fatal Flaw in Duterte's China Policy: Philippine Daily Inquirer Columnist, *The Strait Times*, 29 March 2017, www.straitstimes.com/asia/se-asia/the-fatal-flaw-in-dutertes-china-policy-philippine-daily-inquirer-columnist.

25 Joint communiqué, G7 Foreign Ministers' Meeting, Lucca, 10–11 April 2017, www.g7italy.it/sites/default/files/documents/G7_FMM_Joint_Communique.pdf; Patricia Lourdes Viray, G7 Ministers Call for Implementation of Hague Ruling on South China Sea, *Philstar*, 19 April 2017, www.philstar.com/headlines/2017/04/19/1691830/g7-ministers-call-implementation-hague-ruling-south-china-sea.

26 China Vows More ASEAN Maritime Cooperation, *Xinhua Finance*, 18 September 2015, http://en.xinfinance.com/html/OBAOR/Policy/2015/143799.shtml.

27 Xi Elaborates on Inspiration behind Belt and Road Initiative, *Xinhuanet*, 15 May 2017, http://news.xinhuanet.com/english/2017-05/15/c_136285408.htm.

28 Feng Zhang, Beijing's Master Plan for the South China Sea, *Foreign Policy*, 23 June 2015, http://foreignpolicy.com/2015/06/23/south_china_sea_beijing_retreat_new_strategy/.

29 Wang Yi on the South China Sea Issue At the ASEAN Regional Forum, Ministry of Foreign Affairs, 6 August 2015, www.fmprc.gov.cn/mfa_eng/zxxx_662805/t1287277. shtml.
30 Zhao Hong, How Asean's Vision Can Live with China's Belt and Road Initiative, *The Strait Times*, 30 March 2017, www.straitstimes.com/opinion/how-aseans-vision-can-jive-with-chinas-belt-and-road-initiative.
31 Partnering for Change, Engaging the World, Chairman's Statement of the 20th ASEAN–China Summit, ASEAN Secretariat, 13 November 2017, Manila, the Philippines, http://asean.org/storage/2017/11/FINAL-Chairmans-Statement-of-the-20th-ASEAN-China-Summit-13-Nov-2017-Manila1.pdf.

6 Maritime security and sea lanes of communication

Geopolitical perspective on the Belt and Road Initiative

Vivian Louis Forbes

Introduction

In an optimistic observation, the World Trade Organization (WTO) noted, on 18 May 2018, that a strong rate of trade was likely to continue, while slowing during the second quarter of 2018.[1] The international shipping industry is responsible for the carriage of around 90 per cent of world trade. Shipping is the life blood of the global economy. Without the benefit of the shipping industry, inter-continental trade, the bulk transportation of raw materials and the import/export of affordable food and manufactured goods, would simply not be possible. However, the industry is exposed to cyber-attack threats and terrorism, with severe repercussions.[2] The primary aim of this chapter is to discuss security of sea lanes along the Belt and Road Initiative.

Seaborne trade continues to expand, bringing benefits for consumers across the world through competitive freight costs. Thanks to the growing efficiency of shipping as a mode of transport and increased economic liberalisation, the prospects for the industry's further growth continue to be strong, notwithstanding, the geopolitical issues linked to economic policies that arise periodically. Indeed, it does not take much to shatter the optimism, as days and weeks progress during the year, as witnessed on the morning of 28 July 2018. Reports issued in the international electronic and print media on this day stated that the Government of Saudi Arabia announced a temporary halt on oil shipments via Bab-el-Mandeb – the narrow strait that separates Eritrea and Djibouti from Yemen – with immediate effect following reports that two oil tankers owned by Bahri (Saudi National Shipping Company) were attacked by Yemen's Houthi militia surfaced during the preceding days; however, fortunately there were no injuries or spills as a result of the incident.[3]

A disruption in the flow of oil, natural gas and general cargo movement through this geographical constriction, as indeed, through any of the international straits, such as the Strait of Hormuz, Straits of Malacca and Singapore, will naturally leave a significant impact on the shipping markets, as some other Middle East nations have expressed concern with Kuwait indicating a potential halt in flow. Iraq will continue exports as normal: it sells its oil on a free-on-board basis, thereby passing the transportation risk onto the buyer.[4]

There are over 50,000 merchant ships trading internationally, transporting every type of cargo and commodity. The world fleet is registered in over 150 nations, and manned by over a 1.6 million seafarers, of which 780,000 are officers and the remainder are ratings of virtually every nationality. The five largest supply countries for seafarers are: China, the Philippines, the Russian Federation and Ukraine. The Philippines is the biggest supplier of ratings and China is the biggest supplier of officers. The future outlook indicates that the industry and relevant stakeholders should not expect there to be an abundant supply of qualified and competent seafarers without concerted efforts and measures to address key human-resource issues – such as health, welfare and punctual payment of salary, through promotion of careers at sea, enhancement of maritime education and training worldwide, addressing the retention of seafarers.[5]

Ships are technically sophisticated, high value assets (larger hi-tech vessels can cost over US$200 million to build), and the operation of merchant ships generates an estimated annual income of over half a trillion US dollars in freight rates.[6] The maritime industry is heavily reliant on electronic commerce (e-business) in many of its daily business transactions that includes record-keeping, human-resources' data, loading and discharging of cargo and location of containers on the docks, on land transportation and on ships. The industry is exposed to cyber-attack threats with severe repercussions. Businesses are using cutting-edge techniques to stop cyber criminals breaching their networks; however, many enterprises are still not effectively protected. Governments have introduced legislation to counter such attacks. Implementation of enacted legislation and international conventions may not presently, appear to be effective.[7]

Acts of armed robbery at sea, hijacking of ships, terrorism and actual and potential cyber-attack on aids to navigation in the second decade of the 21st century are still evident and pose problems to the marine transportation and port infrastructure. Some historical examples, in relative terms, include the attack on the Spanish destroyer Marquis de la Ensenada in the port of Santander, on 3 October 1981, by a suspected ETA bomb; the hijacking of the passenger cruise ship, mv Achille Lauro, in the Mediterranean Sea, during 7–10 October 1985, allegedly by Palestinian militants; and, on the USSN Cole off the port of Aden, on the morning of 12 October 2000, Al-Qaeda organisation claimed responsibility for the attack on this naval vessel while it was being refuelled in Aden Harbour, Yemen (see Appendix I).[8]

The French-flagged vessel, mv Limburg (later re-named Maritime Jewel), was attacked on 6 October 2002 while it was some distance offshore of Al-Mukkallah, Yemen. It was carrying about 397,000 barrels of crude oil that was loaded in Iran and destined for Malaysia. The ship made a stop at this port to load an additional volume of oil. Allegedly, Al-Qaeda suicide bombers rammed an explosive-laden dinghy into the starboard side of the tanker. Upon detonation of explosive and impact of the boat, the tanker caught fire and approximately 90,000 barrels of oil leaked into the Gulf of Aden.[9] These are just four incidents that demonstrated how terrorist attacks at sea in the vicinity of an important trade route, for ideological and political gains. Such attacks have been devastating just as those in the air and on the land.

In the light of attacks on ships, potential attacks on port infrastructure and disruption of supply chain, the need to ensure sea lanes are open and free to be utilised and ships are unimpeded and protected from possible cyber-hackers and terrorism. The Government of China's attempts to create a suite of political and institutional instruments with which China can commence to reorganise global value chains and make its mark on the rules governing the global economy is underpinned by an initiative announced by the President of China in October 2013.[10]

China's Belt and Road Initiative

The Belt and Road Initiative (BRI) or One Belt, One Road (OBOR) objective is to enable the Government of China to influence the rules governing the global economy, and it may be argued also a 'blue-water navy' that is capable to respond to any eventuality in the East and South China Seas as well as the Indian Ocean basin and points beyond. Since the initial proposal of the global concept by China in October 2013, it has received positive responses from many countries around the world; and route network for the maritime silk-road has become more distinct, argue Xinhua and The Baltic Exchange in their latest International Shipping Centre Development Index report. Indeed, the PLA(N) the naval unit of the Peoples' Liberation Army, has demonstrated its rapid responses to crisis in Libya, the Middle East countries and in cooperating with naval units of other nations to combat acts of piracy in the Gulf of Aden and off the coast of Somalia in the Arabian Sea.[11]

The BRI has a land and a sea component, known, respectively, as the Silk Road Economic Belt and the 21st Century Maritime Silk Road. Unlike the original Silk Road, however, the new project is not predominantly about transportation infrastructure but about economic integration.[12] These projects are grand concepts to aid economic development for all who wish to participate. The AIIB (Asian Investment and Infrastructure Bank) will assist in fostering the economics of the schemes. The initiative reaches out to Europe and nations of the Middle East and Africa.[13]

Sea Lanes of Communication (SLOCs)

The security of sea lanes (also referred to sea lines) of communication (SLOCs) is vital to the functioning of the global economy. Maximising the economic security of maritime trade thus necessitates the maximisation of security within and amongst all five basic elements in the trading process – cargoes, ports and infrastructure, seafarers, ships and SLOCs. For example, according to the International Maritime Bureau (IMB) at least 40 VLCCs (Very Large Crude Carriers) had completed voyages from ports in the Persian Gulf to ports in the Mediterranean and North Europe since during the period, January to June 2018, while 14 additional vessels were in transit on this same route, at the time of compiling this study. Of these 54 ships, 17 were loaded at ports in Saudi Arabia.[14]

According to statistics on shipping routes of various liner (cargo carrying) companies, the nine major shipping companies have opened more shipping routes between Asia, Southeast Asia and South Asia. In 2018, this route and that of the Asia–Europe route each represented about 30 per cent of the total shipping trade. There is huge potential for development of the China-Southeast Asia and China-South Asia routes in the future. The major shipping companies operating along these routes are COSCO of China; EVA of Taiwan; American President Line (APL) of the USA; Mitsui OSK of Japan; DAF of France and MAERSK of Denmark. Generally speaking, the quality of port infrastructure of sampled ports of countries or regions along the Maritime Silk Road has been relatively stable.[15]

Maritime security

Economic and security needs are among the most basic desires listed in Maslow's hierarchy of requirements.[16] The concept of maritime security is concerned with the prevention of intentional damage to ship and cargo through sabotage, subversion or terrorism. It encompasses activities that occur at port infrastructure, on board ships and in the vicinity of ships at anchor or in port, at sea especially in restricted spaces, such as straits and even at shore-based facilities such as offices, warehouses and logistics chains.[17]

The Australian Government's Maritime Border Command (Border Force), for example, identifies eight maritime security threats, namely: marine pollution, prohibited exports and imports, compromise to biosecurity, illegal maritime arrivals, illegal exploitation of natural resources, illegal activity in protected areas, piracy, armed robbery or violence at sea and maritime terrorism.[18]

The concept of marine security is concerned with the protection of the natural marine environment that includes the inland water, the coastal zone, the sea and its seabed and the marine biotic resources contained therein.[19]

All nations, and in particular, coastal and island states, have a strong reliance on seaborne trade. The ability of ships to navigate without substantial restriction around the world is a critical issue. It is vital to all states in their interest that the guarantees in the 1982 *United Nations Convention on the Law of the Sea* (the 1982 Convention) providing the freedom of navigation (FON) are retained, upheld and respected by all States. The unlawful restriction of the SLOCs between nations could have a devastating effect of the economies of many States, either directly or indirectly, and on the international market.

There is substantial likelihood of instability in the regimes of innocent passage, transit passage and archipelagic sea lanes passage (ASL) based on the contrary practice of some States. Since 1982, there are ample examples that navigation freedom cannot be taken for granted. There is general contention that the innocent passage regime would not remain stable; transit passage through international straits could not be guaranteed; and archipelagic sea lane passage would not remain stable. State practice, with respect to maritime zones and freedom of navigation has been legally challenging and varied. It is not in this brief to argue the merit of the practices.[20]

Given the assertion of jurisdiction by coastal and island States beyond the ambit of the 1982 *Law of the Sea Convention*, it appears to be motivated most commonly by the desire to improve maritime security, as most of the restrictions relate to the activities of warships, and, to a lesser extent, military aircraft. Most coastal States also accrue substantial benefit from the FON, so have not, to date, been over zealous in asserting their security regimes. An exception would be North Korea. There has been some tension with China with respect to transits through the Taiwan Straits and of US Naval ships operating in the South China Sea.[21]

Developments in the Law Of The Sea to-date, while requiring monitoring, also do not suggest that the navigational regimes are being fatally undermined. The 1982 Convention says very little as to what level of force may be imposed by a State in order to uphold its rights and jurisdiction at sea. However, the 1982 Convention notes that the exercise of jurisdiction should be by a warship or other marked government vessel. As the 1982 Convention does not deal with the issue, it is necessary to apply older principles of international law.[22]

Acts of piracy

A study of the acts of piracy during the modern era, in the context of the Straits of Malacca and Singapore, was undertaken by Beckman *et al*.[23] The authors stated that between 1984 and 1994, these waters were among seven other 'hotspots' in the Northeast and Southeast Asian seas. During 1982, there were 83 incidents recorded in these seas out of 106 reported worldwide. Within Singapore's territorial waters, 14 cases of 'sea robbery' were recorded by the Police Coast Guard of Singapore. The authors' opined that piracy by its very nature both a transboundary and an international problem. Forbes and Sakhuja discoursed that acts of piracy, hijacking and other maritime violence should be considered to be a crime under international law and thus demand a concerted effort at the international level with effective support from coastal states' administrators and law enforcement agencies.[24]

Richardson presented evidence that Al-Qaeda's objective to disrupt the seaborne trading, which is the foundation of the model global economy. In his book, he opines that this terrorist group of strong ideological motives would use a crude nuclear device or radiological bomb to do so if it could obtain one.[25] The device would then be placed in a position and by remote control activated to detonate in a port-city, geographical constriction – the narrowest portion of a strait or waterway that plays a key role in international trade. Richardson's report of 2006, demonstrates that extremist groups such as Al-Qaeda and Hezbollah, have also sought to exploit vulnerabilities in shipping, ports and the container supply chain in Asia, Europe, the Middle East and North America. These groups have allegedly, or admitted responsibility, for attacking the naval vessels that protect the vital SLOCs.

The maritime industry has witnessed the perceived threats and actual acts of armed robbery and piracy in the seas of Southeast Asia, the Gulf of Aden and off the west coast of Africa. Piracy has become more virulent. Maritime terrorism continues to threaten the security of regional ports and seas. Ong-Webb suggested that the only way to deal with piracy and marine terrorism is to confront and fight them through effective policies and laws and their enforcement. However, he argues that in the context of the immediacies of these threats, the current limitations of international law, as well as the current deficiencies within current enforcement measures due to the handicap of regional politics, one possible way forward in dealing with piracy and maritime terrorism, particularly in the Southeast Asian region, is to couple them.[26] In this way, extreme cases of piracy could be reclassified by international law and conventions as acts of maritime terrorism. This would intensify the current overall threat of piracy into a significant security issue.

The historical and contemporary perspectives of piracy in the context of Asia was discussed in a volume edited by Kleinen and Osseweijer, which was an important contribution to the literature on piracy in Asian seas, as indeed have many authors have done in the past two decades.[27] Kusmuk and Forbes offered an analysis of the acts of piracy that occurred in the north-western sector of the Indian Ocean basin, in particular, the Gulf of Aden and off the coast of Somalia. This study also discussed the cultural and social impacts that acts of piracy had on the families of the pirates.[28]

The first six months of 2018 witnessed a significant rise in the number of recorded acts of armed robbery and piracy and incidents in the Gulf of Guinea region compared with the same period in 2017 – with Nigeria topping the list.[29] The second quarterly report from the ICC International Maritime Bureau (IMB) illustrated an increase in global piracy, with 107 incidents recorded in the first six months of 2018 compared with 87 in the same period in 2017.

Most alarming is the increase in the number of incidents recorded in the Gulf of Guinea region, off the West African coast, which had risen from 16 in the first half of 2017 to 46 so far by June 2018 – with 31 incidents recorded in Nigerian waters alone. Pirates and robbers were armed with guns in almost half of the Nigerian incidents and vessels were fired upon in eight of them. On the positive side – the IMB reported that the number of crew kidnappings has decreased from 41 by the second quarter in 2017 to 25 in 2018. However, all 25 crew kidnappings reported in 2018 year were from six incidents in the Gulf of Guinea, emphasising even further the higher risks in this region.[30]

An oil tanker with 19 crew members on board, most of them national from Georgia, had been missing in waters off West Africa frequently plied by pirates, and no word was heard from it for a week. Officials commented on 23 August 2018, that communication was lost with the Panama-registered Pantelena on 14 August 2018, when it was near the port of Libreville in Gabon. The ship is owned by Greece's Lotus Shipping Company and was *en route* from Lome to Libreville. The Georgian crew agency Ialkani and the Georgian government said 17 Georgians were aboard the tanker, along with two Russians. While piracy has decreased worldwide, it has increased recently in the Gulf of Guinea, with more than 100 incidents of ship seizures, crew abductions, and robberies reported. Piracy in previous decades thrived off the East African coast, where Somali pirates ply the waters.[31] Ships in the Gulf of Guinea were the target of a series of piracy-related incidents last year, according to a report in January by the International Maritime Bureau, which highlighted the waters off West Africa as an area of growing concern. Apparently ten incidents of kidnapping involving 65 crew members took place in or around Nigerian waters during 2017, while seven vessels were fired on in the Gulf of Guinea.[32]

A positive development is also that the IMB reports of fewer piracy and armed robbery incidents in piracy hotspots other than the Gulf of Guinea. No incidents were recorded off the coast of Somalia in the second quarter of 2018 and, while the number of incidents reported by vessels at berth/anchorage in Indonesia and Bangladesh remains high, the situation in the Philippines has improved.[33] Abductions of crew from vessels in the Sulu-Celebes Seas and waters off Eastern Sabah have also improved, with no such successful incidents recorded in the first half of 2018. According to the Regional Cooperation Agreement on Combating Piracy and Armed Robbery against Ships in Asia (ReCAAP), the first six months of 2018 saw the lowest number of piracy and armed robbery incidents in Asia at that time of the year for the past ten years.[34]

The effect of piracy on crew and their safety continues to be a cause for concern and transiting the seas off the coast of West African remains particularly challenging. The shipping industry and ships' officers must therefore ensure that crews of vessels operating in piracy hotspots remain vigilant and closely monitor the situation by staying in close contact with relevant regional authorities. A risk assessment should be conducted prior to entering a risk area and the relevant preventive measures adopted, taking reference from the BMP5 as well as regional guides such as the Guidelines for Owners, Operators and Masters for Protection Against Piracy and Armed Robbery in the Gulf of Guinea Region and Regional Guide to Counter Piracy and Armed Robbery Against Ships in Asia.[35]

Such experts, however, fail to realise that the popular perception that the international community has eliminated sea piracy is far from true. Not only has piracy never been eradicated, but the number of pirate attacks on ships has also tripled in the past decade-putting piracy at its highest level in modern history. Contrary to the stereotype, today's pirates are often trained fighters aboard speedboats equipped with satellite phones and global positioning systems and armed with automatic weapons, antitank missiles and grenades.

Counter terrorism: international conventions and protocols

The basic problem met when looking for ways to regulate conduct, and especially criminal conduct, on board an aircraft or ship, or otherwise, is one of jurisdiction. There are three different concepts to consider in dealing with the nature of criminal jurisdiction. They are:

1   Prescriptive jurisdiction: the power of a State to make legal rules
2   Enforcement jurisdiction: the power of a State to enforce legal rules by executive action

3   Judicial jurisdiction: the power of the Courts of a State to apply legal rules
    and punish their contravention.

There are at least 12 universal counter-terrorism treaties – seven Conventions, three International Conventions and two Protocols. A brief commentary is offered for selected conventions pertinent to this discussion. A list of international conventions and protocols relating to the suppression of terrorist violence and hijacking of ships and aircraft is appended at Annex II.[36]

The International Convention against the Taking of Hostages (Hostage Convention) of 17 December 1979, entered into force on 3 June 1983. Hostage-taking is an alarming manifestation of international terrorism, which disrupts the internal peace and security of states and seizes control of policy and action away from the government. It is a violation of the hostages' fundamental rights. Hostages are typically innocent civilians, for example seafarers, who have, at best, tenuous connections with the terrorists' (or pirates') aims or grievances.[37]

The impetus for *The International Convention for the Suppression of Unlawful Acts against the Safety of Marine Navigation* (Rome Convention) of 10 March 1988 was the seizure, on 7 October 1985, of the Italian cruise ship Achille Lauro in international waters off the coast of Egypt by four members of the Palestine Liberation Front (PLF). The Rome Convention entered into force on 1 March 1992. The rationale for the 'Rome Protocol' provides for the *Suppression of Unlawful Acts against the Safety of Fixed Platforms located on the Continental Shelf*, 1988 was for the obvious danger to the increasing number of fixed offshore platforms, used mainly by the oil and gas industries.[38]

The *International Convention for the Suppression of Financing of Terrorism* (Financing Terrorism) adopted on 9 December 1999, entered into force on 10 April 2002. Previous conventions dealt with tangible terrorist crimes, such as hijacking, hostage-taking and placing of bombs (plastic explosives) in public places – shopping centres, ferries, on trains and railway stations. The purpose of this convention is to help prevent terrorism by cutting off the funds which terrorists need in order to carry out their criminal acts. The Convention deals with matters that are at least once removed from terrorist acts, the provisions in earlier conventions about being an accomplice to terrorist acts not having been intended to cover financing. The Convention offences are therefore principal, not subsidiary, offences.[39]

The *International Ship and Port Facility Security Code* (ISPS Code) is a comprehensive set of measures to enhance the security of ships and port facilities. It was developed in response to the perceived threats to ships and port facilities in the wake of the 9/11 attacks in the United States.[40] The IMO, by introducing the ISPS Code, presented a prompt response to actual and potential terrorist attacks on ships during the late-1990s and especially in the wake of the 11 September 2001 attacks on US soil, the bombing of the French tanker Limburgh and the USSN Cole in the Gulf of Aden. The ISPS Code entered into force in 2004. The ISPS Code was an amendment to the *Safety of Life at Sea (SOLAS) Convention* (1974/1988) on minimal security for ports, ships and government agencies.[41]

The ISPS Code prescribed responsibilities to governments, shipping companies, shipboard personnel and port/facility personnel to detect security threats and adopt preventative measures against security incidents affecting ships or port facilities used in international trade.[42]

The *Container Security Initiative* (CSI) was launched in 2002 by the US Bureau of Customs and Border Protection (CBP). Its purpose was to increase security for container cargo shipped to the ports of the United States.[43] The US-initiated *Proliferation Security Initiative* (PSI), launched in 2003, is a global effort that aims to stop trafficking of weapons of mass destruction (WMD), their delivery systems and related materials to and from states and non-states actors of proliferation concern.[44]

The IMO had been perceived to be late and somewhat slow in considering appropriate regulation in reacting to cyber-security. In 2014, the IMO consulted its membership on what the maritime cyber-security code should contain. In 2016, IMO issued an interim cyber-security risk management guidelines, which was broad in content and, some may argue, in hindsight, was not particularly maritime specific.[45]

In 2017, the IMO amended two of its general security management codes to explicitly include cyber-security. The ISPS and *International Security Management Code* (ISM) infer how port and ship operators should undertake risk management processes. Operators should be at least conscious of cyber risks and make cyber-security an integral part of the processes.[46]

The cyber-specific amendments to the ISPS and ISM do not enter into force until 1 January 2021. Thus the maritime industry, by mid-2018, appears to be ill-equipped to deal with future challenges, such as the cyber-security of fully autonomous vessels.[47] Development of forceful maritime cyber-security regulations may be sluggish, costly and possibly a painful process. This is discerning after news of some contemporary attacks.

Rising concerns for maritime transportation

Cyber operations raise complex legal questions. The answers will in part depend on whether the particular cyber event takes place during an armed conflict or in peacetime, and humanitarian assistance can of course be conducted in both of those contexts. However, some characteristics of cyber activity render the traditional distinction between those states of affairs decidedly less clear, which necessarily clouds the issue of which legal regime applies. To add to the complexity, there is disagreement between strategically important States as to the rules that apply and, even, as to the approach to adopt in determining such rules. The seminar will seek to explain some of these differences of approach, and will show how they reflect perspectives that pre-date the cyber age. The Tallinn Manual process, in which the speaker participated, will be assessed.[48] The Reports issued by the UN General Assembly-mandated Groups of Governmental Experts will be considered and an initiative from Russia, China and certain other States for a Code of Conduct will be mentioned. The 'Internet of Things' also presents challenges in the peacetime context that will receive appropriate mention.[49] The exploitation of the Internet of Things to secure national security goals raises complex questions about the relationship between privacy rights and collective security.

Modern bridge navigation systems and advanced ships technologies could be vulnerable to a cyber-attack. There are rising concern that ships do not have sufficient cyber protection. Automatic Identification Systems (AIS) are used for tracking and identification by vessel traffic services, which exchange data with ports, coast guards and nearby vessels. The location of each ship can be obtained by clicking on the icon: the red target represents the position of an oil tanker at that instance in time; the green target is cargo-carrying ship; and, the brown-coloured icon is the position of boat engaged in fishing operations.

AIS systems supplement marine radars, which is a primary method of collision avoidance for waterborne traffic. A ship's position, course and speed are displayed on ECDIS (Electronic Chart and Display and Information System). ECDIS charts for navigation are updated off the internet, and if the system is hacked and false information is downloaded it could create a major casualty.[50]

Marine communication between ships or with the shore was carried out with the help of onboard systems through shore stations and even satellites. While ship-to-ship communication was brought about by very high frequency radio, digital selective calling (DSC) came up with digitally remote control commands to transmit or receive distress alert, urgent or safety calls or routine priority messages. DSC controllers can now be integrated with the VHF radio in accord with the SOLAS Convention.

Satellite services, as opposed to terrestrial communication systems, need the help of geostationary satellites for transmitting and receiving signals, where the range of shore stations cannot reach. These marine communication services are provided by two multinational organisations. One gives the scope of two-way communications, whereas the other has a system that is limited to reception of signals from emergency position and places with no facilities of two way marine communications, indicating the position of radio beacons. For international operational requirements, the Global Maritime Distress Management System has divided the world in four sub-areas. Different radio communication systems are required by the vessel to be carried on board ships, depending on the area of operation of that particular vessel. Given the threat of cyber-attacks ship personnel are urged to place a greater reliance on usage of radio telephone.[51]

Fewer ship personnel, larger ships and the increased reliance on automation (SMART SHIPS) have been cited in recent reports as contributing to the risk of cyber-attacks, which could cause a collision, grounding or losses. The interconnectivity of activities could greatly impact the entire maritime industry. Additionally, remote access to the control of a ship, terminal activity and container data could cause severe business interruption costs. Another risk factor is the ever-increasing amount of different systems available to ships. Firewalls are unable to adequately provide protection because doing so would interfere with communication between other ships' systems. Cyber risk may be in its infancy;[52]

however, ships and ports could become enticing targets for hackers in the future. Shipping Companies must simulate potential scenarios and identify mitigation strategies, as attacks on particular electronic navigation systems could lead to a total loss of a ship or even involve several vessels from one company.

Maritime cyber-attacks

Cyber-attacks are continuously evolving into smarter, relentless and unforgiving incidents. They are forcing businesses into conjuring a three-part defence mechanism: prevent, detect and respond. The likes of worms, viruses and data breaches have advanced rapidly in the past 25 years, thus becoming increasingly sophisticated. A Network is critical to the operation of a ship as it is to shore-based operations and any business. It is imperative that networks systems do not expose other systems to cyber-attacks. However, shipboard computer networks usually lack boundary protection measures and segmentation of networks. Such networks are among the most common cyber vulnerabilities on board existing ships. Some guidelines to help maintain maritime cyber security include the Network employed.[53]

Malware is any malicious content which is designed to access, gain control and damage systems. These damages to systems require: risk management regime; secure configuration; managing user privileges; employees' education and awareness; incident management; constant monitoring; and removable media controls.[54]

The maritime industry has experienced several attacks since June 2017. Shipping companies are largely unprotected from potential cyber-attacks even after the June 2017, when the Petya ransomware attacked the Maersk Shipping Company, whose container shipping, oil tanker and tug boat operations were crippled by computer outages, which allegedly slashed the company's profits by up to US$300 million. A financial disaster of this magnitude sent shockwaves through the maritime industry, and shipping companies are increasingly concerned about the lack of effective security on their vessels. The current IT defences are not effective in repelling cyber-attacks.[55]

Shipping companies have become increasingly reliant on inter-connectivity between IT and Operational Technology (OT) to automate operations on ships. However, the higher number of systems connected to the Internet has heightened the risk of cyber-attacks, the effects of which can be devastating, as witnessed by Maersk Shipping Company.

The latest victim, on 25 July 2018, was the Chinese shipping company COSCO, according to media reports. The company's network applications in the United States and other countries, for example, Argentina, Brazil, Canada, Chile, Panama, Peru and Uruguay were affected and suffered failure. However, the company's ships were not affected and continued operating as normal and, by 30 July 2018, the operations were back to normal mode.[56]

Ship- and shore-operations are cyber-connected. If shore-based and ship-based IT systems are linked it could open the flood gates to shipping companies, leaving them highly susceptible to an attack. Vessels do not need to be attacked directly but an attack can arrive via the company's shore-based IT systems and very easily penetrate the ship's critical OT systems.

Ships are increasingly using systems that rely on digitisation, integration and automation. As a result, security of data and other sensitive information has become a major concern of maritime. Training and awareness of appropriate company policies and procedures may provide an effective response to cyber incidents.

A significant regional threat

The presence of the so-called Islamic State (IS) in the Philippines continues to be a significant threat in this region. After Marawi, IS fighters have been reported as still active in the southern part of the country. Jolo and Maguindanao are likely to be the next IS stronghold. On 22 March 2018, exactly five months after the Philippine government liberated Marawi, *An-Naba*, the self-proclaimed Islamic State's (IS) official statement, reported a clash between Abu Sayyaf (ASG) fighters and the Armed Forces of the Philippines (AFP) in the island of Jolo. Since the failure of the 'Marawi project', the pro-IS groups that escaped from Marawi City or were outside the operational zone, have been regrouping. This has led to a new development with fighters from the former four pro-IS areas being reorganised into two, now based in Jolo and Maguindanao.[57]

Given the circumstances, the security apparatus in the Philippines and neighbouring countries should be more vigilant, as violence is likely to escalate. Keeping track of the jihadists' movements is imperative in curbing another Marawi. Particularly important to focus on is the extensive jihadi networks of Amin Baco and Abu Dar, both in the Philippines and in Malaysia and Indonesia.[58]

EUNAVFOR (the European Union Naval Force engaged in the Arabian Sea) informed that the oil tanker that was attacked on 3 March 2018, off Hodeidah, Yemen, was the merchant tanker Abqaiq, a Kingdom of Saudi Arabia flagged vessel. Combined Maritime Forces and EUNAVFOR confirmed that the incident was related to the ongoing conflict in Yemen. The tanker was sailing in international waters off Hodeidah. Houthi rebels in Yemen attacked the Saudi Arabian oil tanker. The Houthis said that this attack was made to avenge a Saudi aerial assault on Hodeidah; the only Yemeni port that Houthis control. A Saudi-coalition warship escorted the tanker, but it is possible that fuel might be leaking.[59]

Conclusion

Most disturbingly, the scourges of piracy and terrorism are increasingly intertwined: piracy on the high seas is becoming a key tactic of terrorist groups. Unlike the pirates of old, whose sole objective was quick commercial gain, many of today's pirates are maritime terrorists with an ideological bent and a broad political agenda. This nexus of piracy and terrorism is especially dangerous for energy markets: most of the world's oil and gas is shipped through the world's most piracy-infested waters.

The pace of overall technology development has been unprecedently fast in the past few years and more developments are looming in the forthcoming years to make the smart shipping concept a reality. However, the 'smart era' escalates cyber security risks; last year shipping industry reported the first significant cyber incidents, which rang the bell for this new kind of threats. Certainly, with the sheer amount of data getting generated globally across the shipping industry, cyber security is one the major issues that needs to be addressed.

The event, organised by SAFETY4SEA, brought together global experts who focused on the recent and future cyber challenges that shipping faces amid digital transformation. The presentations, which were given in two sessions, provided a comprehensive review of current cyber threats and outlook for effective 'cyber hygiene', examining both the theoretical framework and lessons learned from response to cyber-attacks that have been recorded.

Greater coordination of regional governments' policy should be tabled. There is no global best practice in maritime governance, only a set of references based on common challenges and tested options. Maritime security challenges presently exist along the west coast of the African continent; in offshore Somalia in the Indo-Pacific basins, including the South China sea; as well as piracy. The potential consequences of not following industry best practices in the context of actual and potential acts of armed robbery and piracy may be severe. The AGCS reported that grounding and ships sinking were the primary loss of vessels in 2014.

The success of maritime governance depends a great deal on securing the representation of and contributions from, non-state actors such as the maritime industries, fisheries groups, scientific communities, NGOs, think-tanks and local communities. The IMO's Maritime Safety Committee (MSC) is currently considering a proposal to develop cyber security guidelines that will protect and enhance the safety of cyber systems used by ports, vessels and marine facilities.

Major attacks, such as NotPetya, which caused around $3bn of economic losses, have created a renewed urgency in tackling the threats posed to vessels and the supply chain, as well as increasing interest in cyber business interruption insurance. The current lack of incident reporting masks the true picture in shipping when it comes to cyber risk. New regulations such as the European Union's Network and Information Security Directive will change that and also exacerbate the fall-out from any cyber failure.

Appendix I

Ship bombings (Table 6.1)

Table 6.1 Ship bombings

Date	Incident	Location	Actors
19 Sep. 1915	SS *Athinai* (fire/incendiary bombs)	North Atlantic	Conspiracy
25 Nov. 1940	SS *Patria* (sinking)	Haifa	Haganah
20 Feb. 1944	sf *Hydro* (plastic explosives)	Rjukan	Nor. Resist
16 Jan. 1945	SS *Donau* (saboteurs placed limpet mine)	Drobak	Saboteurs
2 Apr. 1947	HMT *Ocean Vigour* (bomb detonated)	Famagusta	Palyam
6 Sep. 1990	RFA Fort Victoria (bomb detonated)	Belfast	Prov IRA
8 Apr. 1961	SS *Dara* (allegedly an explosive device)	Persian Gulf	Dhofar R
2 May 1964	USNS *Card*	Saigon	Viet Cong
2 Jun. 1969	USNS *Noxubee*	Cua Viet	Viet Cong
3 Mar. 1973	SS *Royal Ulsterman* (sunk sabotage op.)	Beirut	?
22 Aug. 1975	ARA Santisima Trinidad (D2)	Porto Belgrano	ERP
23 Jan. 1977	SS *Lucona* (insurance fraud)	Indian Ocean	Fraud
27 Aug. 1979	Boat (on board was Earl Mountbatten)	Mullaghmore	IRA
1981–1982	Shipping in Lough Foyle	Co. Lon'derry	IRA
10 Jul. 1985	mv *Rainbow Warrior* Greenpeace	Auckland	Fr. Intell.
15 Feb. 1988	mv *Sol Phryne* (Al Awda)	Limassol	PLO
19 Apr. 1995	SLNS Sooraya and Ranasuru (bomb detonated)	Trincomalee	LTTE
12 Oct. 2000	USNS *Cole*	Aden	Al-Qaeda
6 Oct. 2002	mv *Limburg* (oil tanker)	G. of Aden	Al-Qaeda
27 Feb. 2004	mv *SuperFerry* 14 (terrorist attack)	Manila bay	AbuSayyaf
24 Apr. 2004	USNS *Firebolt*	Bahrain	Suicide
27 Jul. 2010	VLCC mv M. *Star* (explosion)	Persian Gulf	Suicide

Appendix II

Counter terrorism: international conventions and protocols

These instruments form part of the international community's legal response to help prevent terrorist acts and bring to justice those who commit them.

- Convention on Offences and Certain Other Acts Committed on Board Aircraft (Tokyo, 1963)
- Convention for the Suppression of Unlawful Seizure of Aircraft (The Hague, 1970)
- Convention for the Suppression of Unlawful Acts against the Safety of Civil Aviation (Sabotage) (Montreal, 1971)

- Protocol for the Suppression of Unlawful Acts of Violence at Airports Serving International Civil Aviation (Montreal, 1988)
- Convention on the Physical Protection of Nuclear Material (Vienna, 1980)
- International Convention against the Taking of Hostages (New York, 1979)
- Convention on the Prevention and Punishment of Crimes against Internationally Protected Persons, including Diplomatic Agents (New York, 1973)
- International Convention for the Suppression of Terrorist Bombings (New York, 1997)
- International Convention for the Suppression of the Financing of Terrorism (New York, 1999)
- International Convention for the Marking of Plastic Explosives for the Purposes of Detection (Montreal, 1991)
- Convention for the Suppression of Unlawful Acts Against the Safety of Maritime Navigation (Rome, 1988)
- Protocol for the Suppression of Unlawful Acts against the Safety of Fixed Platforms Located on the Continental Shelf (Rome, 1988)
- International Convention for the Suppression of Acts of Nuclear Terrorism (New York 2005)
- 2005 Amendment to the Convention on the Physical Protection of Nuclear Material
- Protocol of 2005 to the Convention for the Suppression of Unlawful Acts against the Safety of Maritime Navigation
- Protocol of 2005 to the Protocol for the Suppression of Unlawful Acts against the Safety of Fixed Platforms located on the Continental Shelf
- The Convention on the Suppression of Unlawful Acts Relating to International Civil Aviation
- The Protocol Supplementary to the Convention for the Suppression of Unlawful Seizure of Aircraft

Notes

1 World Trade Organization's World Trade Outlook Indicator (WTOI) released 17 May 2018, Finance. See also, Nazery Khalid, The Role of the Indian Ocean in Facilitating Global Maritime Trade, 2007, pp. 95–105.
2 See V. L. Forbes, The Global Maritime Industry Remains Unprepared for Future Cybersecurity Challenges, *Associate Paper, Future Directions International*, Online version, 21 August 2018. In this paper, I argue that the shipping industry is still some way unprotected from the threat of cyber-attack. Dennis Rumley *et al.* (eds.), Securing Sea Lanes of Communication in the Indian Ocean Region, in: *The Security of Sea Lanes of Communication in the Indian Ocean Region*, (Indian Ocean Region Group, MIMA, 2007), pp. 5–25. Swaran Singh, The Emerging Centrality of SLOCs in China's Maritime Strategy, in: Rumley *et al.* (eds.), *ibid.*, pp. 59 72.
3 BAHRI Announce Temporary Halt to Oil Shipment, *BBC World News*, 28 July 2018.
4 A slightest hint of a terrorist attack to the oil transportation industry tends to send the financial market in a spin and cause a rise in the price of crude oil. Consider the events of 1970–1985 in the Middle East region. See, for example, Consistently Higher Oil Prices…, *Offshore*, www.offshore-mag.com, 5 September 2018.

5 The ILO and IMO websites offer statistics on seafarers, their education, training and general concerns on work conditions at sea and in port.

6 For daily rate of oil prices, fluctuations in pricing, etc., see https://oilprice.com/.

7 See V. L. Forbes, The Global Maritime Industry Remains Unprepared for Future Cybersecurity Challenges, *Associate Paper, Future Directions International*, Online. 21 August 2018. A. J. A. Fernandez-Rodera, *International Legal Dimension of Terrorism* (Leiden: Brill, 2016).

8 Brief account of the *Achille Lauro* incident is available at: https://it.wikipedia.org/ wiki/Dirottamento. For the attack on USSN Cole: www.history.navy.mil/.../terrorist-attack-on-uss.

9 BBC World News, Guantanamo Prisoner al-Darbi Admits MV *Limburgh* Attack, 2014, www.bbc.com/news/world-us-canada-276277556 (accessed 28 July 2018). Seshadri Vasan, Re-Visiting the Attacks on USSN *Cole* and MV Limburgh. *Academia*, www.academia.edu/3196191/Revisiting (accessed 28 July 2018).

10 President Xi Jinping of the PRC announces his initiative of the Maritime Silk Road. Also see V. L. Forbes, Securing Shipments of Uranium and Nuclear Waste in the Indian Ocean, 2007, p. 124–141; and Dennis Rumley and Timothy Doyle, The Uranium Trade in the Indian Ocean Region, 2007, p. 106–123.

11 Natasha Kusmuk and Vivian Louis Forbes, The Scourge of Piracy, Measures and Wider Implications, *Occasional Paper* 2(1) (May 2016), Kuala Lumpur: MIMA; G. G. Ong-Webb, *Ships Can Be dangerous Too: Coupling Piracy and Maritime Terrorism in Southeast Asia's Maritime Security Framework*, (Singapore: ISEAS, 2004).

12 The other Economic Roads planned by China are from Urumqi to the port of Gwadar and from Xi'an via Kunming to Mandalay and the port of Sittwe, Myanmar. The Maritime Silk Road (Route) traverses the Malacca Strait to Kolkata, Colombo and ports further westward. Maritime Silk Road: Critical Routes in Maritime Channels, *Finance*, 18 July 2018.

13 See V. L. Forbes, China's Arctic Policy and 'Polar Silk Route/Road', *Diplomatic Voice* 2 (2018) p. 5–7; and V. L. Forbes and Liu Zhenhua (Kara,) Ensuring and Enhancing Safety of Navigation in the Arctic Ocean: A Reflective Essay *MIMA Bulletin* 22(1) (2015), 18–31.

14 For statistics and maritime issues, see also the International Maritime Bureau (IMB).

15 See also SAFETY4SEA Online News daily Service that offers all manner of ship-related topics.

16 A. H. Maslow, A Theory of Human Motivation, *Psychological Review* 50(4) (1943), 370 396; and A. H. Maslow, *Motivation and Personality* (New York: Harper and Row, 1954).

17 Rumley, Chaturvedi and Yasin Mat Taib (eds.), Securing Sea lanes of Communication in the Indian Ocean Region, in: *The Security of Sea Lanes of Communication in the Indian Ocean Region* (Indian Ocean Region Group, MIMA, 2007), p. 5–25.

18 The Australian Border Force webpages offers a section on maritime security issues: www.homeaffairs.gov.au/australian-border-force-; Lin K-C. and A. V. Gertner, Maritime Security in the Asia-Pacific, *Chatham House Research Paper*, July 2015.

19 Marine security relates to the natural marine environment. For example the ADMIRALTY Maritime Security Charts contain safety-critical information to assist bridge crews in the planning of safe passages through high risk areas. All information has been gathered by the UKHO through work with NATO and other government organisations, ensuring each chart has the most accurate, up-to-date and verified information available. See also V. L. Forbes, For Australian and Indian Perspectives on Maritime Security, in: D. Gopal and D. Rumley, *India-Australia Issues and Opportunities* (New Delhi: South Asian Publishers, 2004), Ch. 5, pp. 107–140.

20 Joshua Ho, *Securing the Seas as a Medium of Transportation in Southeast Asia*, 2007; Stuart Kaye, Freedom of Navigation in the Indo-Pacific Region, Papers in *Australian Maritime Affairs*, No. 22, Sea Power Centre, Australia, 2008, p. 56.

21 Nong Hong *Understanding the Freedom of Navigation Doctrine and the China-US Relations in the South China Sea, Institute for China-America Studies*, May 2017; Mark Valencia, US Makes Up Some Lost Diplomatic Ground over South China Sea, *The Diplomat*, 31 July, 2018; Carl Thayer, South China Sea: Australia and Freedom of Navigation, *Thayer Consultancy Background Brief*, 3 March 2018. Thayer and Valencia and many other authors have been regular contributors to the media on this topic. US Dept of Defense, FON Report for FY 2016.

22 See, for example, Stuart Kaye, Freedom of navigation, Surveillance and Security: Legal issues Surrounding the …, University of Wollongong *Research Online*, 2005; Part 3 of the 1982 *UN Law of the Sea Convention*; and J. W. Houck, *The United States and Freedom of Navigation in the South China Sea* 13(3) (2014); M. A. Becker, *The Shifting Public Order of the Oceans: Freedom of Navigation and the Interdiction of Ships at Sea* 46(1) (2005).

23 R. Beckman, C. R. Grundy-Warr and V. L. Forbes, Acts of Piracy in the Malacca and Singapore Straits, *Maritime Briefing* 1(4) (1994), International Boundaries Research Unit, Durham, 1994, 37 pp.

24 V. L. Forbes and Vijay Sakhuja, Challenging Acts of Marine Trans-Boundary Transgressions in the Indian Ocean Region, *MIMA Issue Paper* 1(2) (2004), 23.

25 Michael Ricardson, *Maritime-Related Terrorism: Al-Qaeda, Hezbollah, What Next from the International Jihadist Network?* (Singapore: ISEAS, 2006).

26 G. G. Ong-Webb, *Piracy, Maritime Terrorism and Securing the Malacca Straits* (Singapore: ISEAS/IIAS, 2006), p. 266; A. J. Young, *Contemporary Maritime Piracy in Southeast Asia: History, Causes and Remedies* (Singapore: IIAS, 2007).

27 John Kleinen and Manon Osseweijer (eds.), *Pirates, Ports and Coasts in Asia: Historical and Contemporary Perspectives* (Singapore: ISEAS, 2010).

28 See also V. L. Forbes, Continuing Menace: Acts of Piracy and Armed Robbery, *MIMA Bulletin* 11(1) (2004), 37–40; V. L. Forbes and Tomoko Ishihara, Efforts to Combat Armed Robbery and Piracy: Timely Policy Change of Japanese Government, *MIMA Bulletin* 16(1) (2009), 27–40; Kusmuk and Forbes, The Scourge of Piracy: Measures and Wider Implications, *MIMA Occasional Paper* 2(1) (2016), 152.

29 GARD West Africa Remains a Piracy Hotspot, *Hellenic Shipping News*, www.gard.no/web/updates/content/25933544/westafrica (accessed 28 July 2018).

30 *BBC World News* Online.

31 GARD see (n. 29).

32 IMB Piracy Report of 20 July 2018 shows persistent piracy risk in the Gulf of Guinea.

33 IMB Piracy Reports are available at www.icc-ccs.org.

34 ReCAAP *Report Half-Yearly Report January–June 2018*, https:// www.recaap.org.

35 GARD see (n. 29).

36 IMO website contains the International Conventions pertaining to criminal conduct in commercial aircraft and on board ships.

37 See IMO website for the text of the Hostage Convention and other available literature.

38 IMO website contains the Rome Convention.

39 IMO website for the Suppression of Financing, www.imo.org.

40 IMO website for ISPS Code, www.imo.org.

41 IMO website and SOLAS, www.imo.org.

42 ISPS Code (ISPS Code, Part A 1.2.1), www.imo.org/en/ourwork.

43 Vijay Sakhuja, *Container Security Initiatives: A South Asian Perspective*, 2007, pp. 182–195. Refer to CSI website, https:// www.cbp.gov/border.

44 For details, view PSI website, www.state.gov/t/isn.

45 Cyber security – see NATO advice of today.

46 ISPS Code and TSM Code.

47 David Rider, 10 March 2018, Maritime Cyber Security, www.maritime-executive.com/blog/cyber-security-at-sea-the-real-threats#gs.

48 *THE TALLINN Manual*; EU cyber security, https://ec.europa.eu/digital-single-market/en/cyber-security.
49 For the Australian example, refer to the Threat Report, Australian Cyber Security Centre, 2017.
50 ECDIS system and potential problems. V. L. Forbes, ECDIS: More Than an Aid to Navigation, *Proceedings of the International ECDIS Conference*, Singapore, 1998, pp. 42–48. V. L. Forbes, ECDIS and Potential Legal Implications: Proceeding with Caution, *The Hydrographic Journal* 111 (2004), 3–11.
51 Reverting to the use of radio telephone at sea. See IMO website.
52 Cyber risk in its infancy. Cyber-Threats Aboard Ships: A Sensitive Theme. Capt. Gunter Schutze, *Opinion*, 19 July 2018. Max Bobys, A Case for Maritime Cyber Security Capability, *Hudson Analytix*, 7 June 2017.
53 *Cyber Security Considerations for Oil and Gas Industry* offers an insight to the vulnerabilities of cyber-crime, *SAFETY4SEA* online version, 30 August 2018.
54 See, for example, Abrams, M. D. and Weiss, Joe. Malicious Control System Cyber Security Attack Case Study – Maroochy Water Services, Australia, *Annual Computer Security Applications*, December 2008.
55 *BBC World News* (June 2017) and *Ship Technology* (8 November 2017) relating to the Maersk Shipping Line cyber-attacks.
56 *BBC World News* 26 July 2018 and *World Maritime News*, COSCO Shipping Lines Back to Normal After Attack, 30 July 2018.
57 Michael Richardson, *A Time Bomb for Global Trade: Maritime-Related Terrorism in an Age of Weapons of Mass Destruction* (Singapore: ISEAS, 2004), 157 pp. Terrorist attacks in the Philippines and region. Council of Europe Treaty Series, No. 196 *Council of Europe Convention on the Prevention of Terrorism* 2008.
58 The *Safety and Shipping Review of 2017* by Allianz offers valuable insight into the shipping industry.
59 EUNAVFOR operations off Yemen and within the Arabian Sea and Persian Gulf.

7 SLOCs security in the South China Sea

Enhancing or hindering the Maritime Silk Road?

Keyuan Zou and Qiang Ye

Introduction

The 21st Century Maritime Silk Road (MSR) Initiative, which was put forward together with the Silk Road Economic Belt by the Chinese government in 2013, has provided new impetus and practical paths for intra- and inter-regional cooperation. By proposing full connectivity in policy coordination, facilities, unimpeded trade, financial integration and a people-to-people bond as its five cooperation priorities, the Initiative aims to strengthen global cooperation through more substantial, convenient and profitable connectivity.[1] Five years on, over 100 countries and international organisations have supported and become involved in this initiative. Important resolutions passed by the UN General Assembly and Security Council contain reference to it.[2] The vision of the Belt and Road Initiative (BRI) has become a reality.

In line with the priorities of the MSR, three 'Blue Economic Passages' are closely related to maritime cooperation. First, efforts will be made to build the China-Indian Ocean-Africa-Mediterranean Sea Blue Economic Passage, by linking the China-Indochina Peninsula Economic Corridor, running westward from the South China Sea to the Indian Ocean, and connecting the China-Pakistan Economic Corridor (CPEC) and the Bangladesh-China-India-Myanmar Economic Corridor (BCIM-EC). Second, efforts will also be made to jointly build the Blue Economic Passage of China-Oceania-South Pacific, travelling southward from the South China Sea into the Pacific Ocean. Third, another Blue Economic Passage is also envisioned, leading up to Europe via the Arctic Ocean.[3] According to this plan, issued by the Chinese government, the South China Sea region, as a pivot for at least two Blue Economic Passages, will play an important role for the success of MSR.

The South China Sea is a marginal sea to the Pacific Ocean that forms a semi-enclosed sea under the 1982 United Nations Convention on the Law of the Sea ('Convention', 'UNCLOS' or 'LOSC'),[4] between the South East Asian countries and China, through its unique properties and geography. The South China Sea's unique geographic properties make it important in the sense of global trade and communications. There are important sea lanes of communications (SLOCs), which are vital for the adjacent countries in East Asia and also for the rest of the world. More than half of the world's merchant fleet capacity sails through the Straits of Malacca, Sunda and Lombok and the South China Sea.[5] More than 10,000 vessels of greater than 10,000 deadweight move southward through the South China Sea annually, with well over 8000 proceeding in the opposite direction.[6] In addition, the South China Sea also connects the rich oil fields of the Middle East with the East Asian 'tiger economies' and is a vital part of the global economy. For example, in 2016, it is estimated that 80 per cent of China's crude oil imports is transported through the South China Sea.[7] This means that this small sea is an important transportation route for energy, unfinished and finished goods. With an extensive coastline, China is a major trading and ship-owning country, with a growing trading interest under the MSR Initiative. This gives China a strong vested interest in securing the SLOCs in the South China Sea. Thus China reiterated in the *Vision for Maritime Cooperation under the Belt and Road Initiative* the importance of '[c]ooperation on maritime navigation security' and that 'China will shoulder its due international obligations, participate in bilateral and multilateral maritime navigation security and crisis-control mechanisms, and work with all parties to combat non-traditional security issues such as crimes on the sea'.[8]

The security of SLOCs in the South China Sea, however, still remains an issue in the sense that territorial and maritime disputes between/among multiple claimants in the region, and the geopolitical competition between China and countries outside the region, may constitute threats to the safety of navigation in the South China Sea.

The South China Sea dispute and its impact on the SLOCs security in the region

There are three layers of disputes in the South China Sea. The first and most fundamental are the overlapping claims of sovereignty to the geographic features between/among littoral states; the second are the overlapping claims to the maritime zones generated either from the islands or from the surrounding coasts of the littoral states, which are basically in terms of sovereign rights and jurisdiction as stipulated under the LOSC; and the third one are the disputes in relation to the use of the oceans, including conflicting uses of marine resources and development between/among littoral states, the use of sea lanes and the conduct of military activities in the name of the freedom of navigation between littoral states and user states. These disputes are entangled with one another, thus making the South China Sea disputes the most complicated of all territorial and maritime disputes in the world.[9]

A pending dispute related to territorial sovereignty or maritime rights may pose severe dangers to the safety of navigation in the disputed area. Blockades have historically been used in wartime,[10] e.g. the United States imposed a 'quarantine' around Cuba during the October 1962 Cuban Missile Crisis.[11] During the 1982 Falklands/Malvinas War, the UK declared a 200-nautical-mile military exclusion zone around the islands.[12]

The South China Sea dispute, observed from the situation in recent years, has not reached a degree that 'the continuance of [the dispute] is likely to endanger the maintenance of international peace and security'.[13] Nevertheless, the South China Sea has long been regarded as one of the most dynamic and controversial regions in the world and has been causing potential challenges to the security of SLOCs in the region. Moreover, the South China Sea issue involves a number of countries, and it is not an easy task to ultimately resolve it. In order to mitigate the disputes and safeguard the security of navigation and stability of the region, the countries concerned have been working together to enter into provisional arrangements of a practical and cooperative nature by negotiations.[14]

On the other hand, the exchanges of views between China and other claimants in relation to their disputes have so far pertained to responding to incidents at sea in the disputed areas and promoting measures to prevent conflicts, reduce frictions, maintain stability in the region and promote measures of cooperation. The 'dual-track' approach – disputes should be resolved peacefully through negotiation between the parties directly concerned, and China and ASEAN countries should work together to maintain peace and stability in the South China Sea – was first initiated by Brunei and supported by China.[15] This approach complies with the Declaration on the Conduct of Parties in the South China Sea (DOC) and principles of the UN Charter, and serves the common interests and desire of countries in the region.

Safeguarding the security of SLOCs in the South China Sea after the South China Sea Arbitration

The *South China Sea Arbitration* case initiated by the Philippines in 2013 and filed by a final award in 2016 has touched upon the navigational issues by the Philippine Submissions No. 9–15, in which the Philippines requests the arbitral tribunal to rule that China violated the Convention by interfering with the exercise of the Philippines' sovereign rights and jurisdiction, by interfering with the Philippines' *freedom of navigation* and by conducting construction and fishing activities that harm the marine environment.[16]

This arbitration, however, neither facilitates the ultimate settlement of dispute between China and the Philippines, nor touches upon the core issue which endangers the freedom of navigation in the South China Sea.

1 The ineffectiveness of the arbitration to resolve disputes concerning navigational rights

For the submissions put forward by the Philippines in relation to navigational rights and safety, essentially, China argues that the essence of the submissions for arbitration is land territorial matters regarding some islands and reefs in the Nansha Islands (Spratlys), which are beyond the scope of UNCLOS, and maritime delimitation issues, which have been excluded by China in its 2006 optional exceptions declaration,[17] made under Article 298 of UNCLOS from compulsory procedures entailing binding decisions under Section 2 of Part XV.[18] As a result, China made it clear from the outset that it would neither accept nor participate in the arbitral proceedings as the disputes presented by the Philippines were outside the jurisdiction of the Tribunal. On 12 July 2016, the final award was issued by the Tribunal. The Chinese government immediately stated that the award was null and void and had no binding force.[19]

As a general rule, China considers that States should be able to choose the means of settling a dispute, rather than being forced to face compulsory adjudication by an international court or tribunal. China considers negotiation and conciliation to be the most appropriate means for settling disputes involving its 'core interests', which include issues of sovereignty and territorial integrity. In most cases, therefore, when China enters into a treaty, it will opt out of any provision referring to dispute settlement under international courts or tribunals.[20]

In the meantime,

> [t]he Chinese government will continue to abide by international law and basic norms governing international relations, as enshrined in the Charter of the United Nations, including the principles of respecting state sovereignty and territorial integrity and peaceful settlement of disputes, and continue to work with states directly concerned to resolve the relevant disputes in the South China Sea through negotiations and consultations on the basis of respecting historical facts and in accordance with international law, so as to maintain peace and stability in the South China Sea.[21]

The mutual understanding between China and other disputed parties to settle relevant disputes through negotiation has also been reaffirmed in a regional multilateral instrument. In 2002, China and ASEAN countries signed the DOC, which, in Article 4, explicitly states that:

> the Parties concerned undertake to resolve their territorial and jurisdictional disputes by peaceful means ... through friendly consultations and negotiations by sovereign states directly concerned, in accordance with universally recognized principles of international law, including the 1982 UN Convention on the Law of the Sea.[22]

2 The positive trend towards a final dispute resolution

The election of Rodrigo Duterte qualitatively altered the political dynamics of the South China Sea disputes, while China and other disputant countries of the South China Sea are making active efforts to resume bilateral consultation as well as to promote cooperation at sea. The main feature of the dispute settlement in the South China Sea after the Arbitration can be described as 'back on the right track'.[23] Since the second half of 2016, the relationship between China and the Philippines has experienced a positive shift from open hostility to exchanges of goodwill, informal contacts and meetings between the leaders of both countries.[24] Sensitive issues concerning the South China Sea have been agreed to be brought to the negotiation table.[25] China and the Philippines also signed the *Memorandum of Understanding between the China Coast Guard and the Philippine Coast Guard on the Establishment of a Joint Coast Guard Committee on Maritime Cooperation* during President Duterte's visit in October 2016,[26] which laid a foundation for bilateral cooperation of two countries' Coast Guards.

In November 2017, China and the Philippines reaffirmed that the two sides will address,

> territorial and jurisdictional disputes by peaceful means, without resorting to the threat or use of force, through friendly consultations and negotiations by sovereign states directly concerned, in accordance with universally recognized principles of international law, including the Charter of the United Nations and the 1982 UNCLOS.

In addition, the two sides also 'agree to strengthen maritime cooperation in areas such as marine environmental protection, disaster risk reduction, including possible cooperation in marine scientific research'.[27]

Following the example of China and the Philippines, China and Vietnam agreed to make good use of the border negotiation mechanism between the two governments and seek a fundamental and long-term solution to the maritime disputes in the South China Sea. To achieve this, both sides agreed to conduct follow-up works of the joint inspection in waters outside the Beibu Gulf.[28] Concerning the cooperation at sea, the two sides agreed to promote the efforts of the working group on cooperation for development at sea and step up joint projects in less-sensitive fields.[29] Before that, the two countries' Coast Guards also signed a memorandum of understanding and held their first working meeting in August 2016.

On 20–21 November 2018, Chinese President Xi Jinping paid a State Visit to the Philippines, during which China and the Philippines,

> reaffirmed the importance of maintaining and promoting regional peace and stability, freedom of navigation in and over-flight above the South China Sea

and

> stay committed to addressing disputes by peaceful means, without resorting to the threat or use of force, through friendly consultations and negotiations by sovereign states directly concerned, and in accordance with universally recognized principles of international law, including the Charter of the [UN] and the [LOS Convention].[30]

More importantly, both sides agreed to 'exercise self-restraint in the conduct of activities in the South China Sea that would complicate or escalate disputes and affect peace and stability', and noted that 'the importance of confidence-building measures to increase mutual trust and confidence'. In this regard, China and the Philippines agreed to

> maximize and strengthen the on-going coast guard, defense and military dialogue and liaison mechanisms, with a view to facilitating quick responses to situations on the ground and contributing to the enhancement of mutual trust and confidence between their coast guards and defense agencies.[31]

The two governments signed the *Memorandum of Understanding on Cooperation on Oil and Gas Development*, and agreed to discuss maritime cooperation including maritime oil and gas exploration, sustainable use of mineral, energy and other marine resources.[32] Between December 13th and 14th, in the same year, China and Vietnam each assigned two naval vessels to participate in the 25th joint patrol in the Beibu Gulf, during which the fleet sailed for nearly 30 hours and they made information exchange on hydrological meteorology, sea and air conditions, formation course and speed, enhancing mutual maritime communications and resource sharing.[33]

Keeping peace and stability in the South China Sea

The relationship between China and ASEAN countries on the issue of the South China Sea has seen several positive trends since the last quarter of 2016. A series of new consensuses have been made by the parties concerned, such as promoting cooperation, and speeding up consultations on the Code of Conduct (COC) in the South China Sea. These positive trends have created a good climate for regional peace as well as for the SLOCs security.

China and ASEAN countries have reached consensus on further implementing the DOC and accelerating the COC consultation, which has borne fruitful results. With regard to the implementation of DOC, progress has been made via 'early harvest' measures. In July 2016, China and ten ASEAN countries issued: *the Joint Statement by the Foreign Ministers of ASEAN Member States and China on the Full and Effective Implementation of the Declaration on the Conduct of Parties in the South China Sea (DOC)*, which stressed that all parties shall resolve their disputes 'by peaceful means … through friendly consultations and negotiations by sovereign states directly concerned'.[34] In September 2016, at the 19th China-ASEAN Summit, leaders from China and ASEAN countries reviewed and approved the: *Guidelines for Hotline Communications among Senior Officials of the Ministries of Foreign Affairs of China and ASEAN Member States in Response to Maritime Emergencies*, and issued the *Joint Statement on the Application of the Code for Unplanned Encounters at Sea in the South China Sea*.[35] These two important documents provided an institutional mechanism for China and ASEAN countries to manage and control contingencies in the South China Sea so as to avoid the emergence or escalation of maritime conflicts.

In 2017, the implementation of the DOC has seen a new breakthrough. On 31 October 2017, China and six ASEAN countries, including Thailand, the Philippines, Cambodia, Myanmar, Laos and Brunei, held the first multilateral joint maritime search and rescue drill at waters off Zhanjiang, China.[36] On the 20th ASEAN-China Summit held in November, the *Leaders' Declaration for a Decade of Coastal and Marine Environmental Protection in the South China Sea (2017–2027)* was also formally adopted.[37] Despite various obstacles and difficulties, the consultation and negotiation of COC has made remarkable achievements. In August 2017, Foreign Ministers of China and ASEAN countries formally adopted the framework of the COC.[38] On the 20th ASEAN-China Summit held in Manila in November 2017, leaders collectively announced that the substantive negotiations on the text of the COC would commence in early 2018.[39]

The year 2018 marked the 15th anniversary of the establishment of the China-ASEAN strategic partnership, and joint efforts have made to push for greater development in East Asian regional cooperation by the two sides. On 2 August, the Minister for Foreign Affairs of Singapore, Vivian Balakrishnan, said ASEAN Member States and China have arrived at a single draft negotiating text of COC, which will be a living document and the basis of future COC negotiations.[40] Between 22 and 28 October, the navies of China and 10 ASEAN countries held the first joint maritime exercise in Zhanjiang, which aimed mainly at advancing defense cooperation and maritime security between China and ASEAN, as well as the application of *The Code for Unplanned Encounters at Sea*.[41]

However, given that the South China Sea has become primarily a crux of China-US competition in the Asia-Pacific, the uncertainties in this region still exist and will be closely related to how the United States behave in the future.

Differences and frictions between China and the United States related to navigational rights in the South China Sea

Without any maritime territorial claims to the South China Sea, the United States has maintained that freedom of navigation is at the heart of the country's maritime policy. It considers the freedom of navigation in the so-called 'international waters', including exclusive economic zones (EEZ), to be an unalienable right of all countries and will continue to pursue national interests in the South China Sea based on this stance.[42] On the other hand, to offset China's westward focus – the Belt and Road Initiative and Cooperation, the US seeks to create a global alliance strategy with the aim to maintain a balance of power in Eurasia,[43] and declares to 'maintain a forward military presence capable of deterring and, if necessary, defeating any adversary'.[44] Thus the Freedom of Navigation Operation Programs (FONOPs) has become a useful tool for these strategic aims. During the period of the Donald Trump Administration, the differences between the two sides not only led to diplomatic arguments and battles of public opinion, but also led to the escalation of regional tensions and risk to navigational safety. It is necessary to evaluate the merits of differences between the two sides.

Regime of navigation under the LOSC

The Law of the Sea Convention has been based on the fundamental principle of *mare liberum*, for the last five centuries. Although some States have sought to establish sovereignty over the high seas in order to monopolise trade and fishing, these attempts have failed in favour of the establishment of *mare liberum*, the freedom of the seas, for the benefit of every State.[45] At present, the navigational rights of vessels are mainly governed by the LOSC, though there are relevant treaties in this respect adopted under the auspices of the International Maritime Organization (IMO).[46] The LOSC today provides the legal framework with respect to navigational rights binding on all State parties and non-parties, including the US, be it through ratification, unilateral declaration or simply as reflecting customary international law.[47] The LOSC has made the legal arrangements for navigational rights of vessels in accordance with different sea zones – internal waters, territorial sea, straits used for international navigation, archipelagic waters, the EEZ, the continental shelf, and the high seas and the international seabed (the 'Area') – established under the Convention. Since internal waters are part of the territory of a coastal State, no freedom of navigation is granted there and any navigational rights are subject to the regulation of the coastal State.

Territorial sea is also part of the territory of the coastal State which owns the full sovereignty over it. However, due to the expeditiousness of navigation, the right of innocent passage is reserved for foreign vessels under the guarantee of international law. In addition, the coastal State should give appropriate publicity to any danger to navigation, of which it has knowledge, within its territorial sea.[48] On the other hand, the coastal State may adopt laws and regulations on, *inter alia*, the safety of navigation and the regulation of maritime traffic and the protection of navigational aids and facilities and other facilities or installations, in conformity with the provisions of the Convention and other rules of international law, relating to innocent passage through the territorial sea. Furthermore, the coastal State may take necessary steps in its territorial sea to prevent passage that is not innocent.[49]

For navigational safety reasons, the coastal State may, where necessary, having regard to the safety of navigation, require foreign ships exercising the right of innocent passage through its territorial sea to use such sea lanes and traffic separation schemes as it may designate or prescribe for the regulation of the passage of ships. In particular, tankers, nuclear-powered ships and ships carrying nuclear or other inherently dangerous or noxious substances or materials may be required to confine their passage to such sea lanes. In the designation of sea lanes and the prescription of traffic separation schemes, the coastal State should take into account:

1   The recommendations of the competent international organisation
2   Any channels customarily used for international navigation
3   The special characteristics of particular ships and channels
4   The density of traffic.[50]

The coastal State should clearly indicate such sea lanes and traffic separation schemes on charts to which due publicity should be given.[51] Foreign nuclear-powered ships and ships carrying nuclear or other inherently dangerous or noxious substances should, when exercising the right of innocent passage through the territorial sea, carry documents and observe special precautionary measures established for such ships by international agreements.

As to the navigation in the EEZ, the LOSC provides a legal regime similar to that in the high seas.[52] However, since it is an area within national jurisdiction, the coastal State may have the right to lay down necessary laws and regulations relating to navigation safety and marine environmental protection. In this respect, the coastal State may well be aware that its laws and regulations should not hamper the smooth navigation of foreign vessels in and through its EEZ. On the other hand, foreign vessels are obliged to have due regard to the rights and duties of the coastal State and should comply with the laws and regulations adopted by the coastal State in accordance with the LOSC and other applicable rules of international law.[53]

Navigation in the straits used for international navigation was hotly debated during the UNCLOS III. Finally, the LOSC adopted the 'transit passage' for foreign vessels passing through the straits used for international navigation. The other sea area within national jurisdiction, which foreign vessels enjoy navigational rights, is the archipelagic waters. As for the high seas, all States enjoy the freedom of navigation.

China's policy on the navigational issues in the South China Sea

In spite of the existence of unresolved disputes in related areas in the South China Sea, China has repeatedly upheld the freedom of navigation and over-flight enjoyed by all States under international law, and stayed ready to work with other coastal States and the international community to ensure the safety of and the unimpeded access to the international shipping lanes in the South China Sea.[54]

The South China Sea is home to a number of important sea lanes, which are among the main navigation routes for China's foreign trade and energy import. Ensuring freedom of navigation and over-flight and safety of sea lanes in the South China Sea is crucial to China. Over the years, China has worked with ASEAN Member States to ensure unimpeded access to and safety of the sea lanes in the South China Sea and made important contribution to this collective endeavour. The freedom of navigation and over-flight enjoyed by all states in the South China Sea under international law has never been a problem.

China has actively provided international public goods and made every effort to provide services, such as navigation and navigational aids, search and rescue, as well as sea conditions and meteorological forecast, through capacity building in various areas, so as to uphold and promote the safety of sea lanes in the South China Sea. China maintains that, when exercising freedom of navigation and over-flight in the South China Sea, relevant parties shall fully respect the sovereignty and security interests of coastal states and abide by the laws and regulations enacted by coastal states in accordance with the LOS Convention and other rules of international law.[55]

FONOPs as a major threat to the security of SLOCs in the South China Sea

The US FONOPs have been conducted globally since 1979, and US-China tensions in the South China Sea are nothing new, particularly regarding issues of surveillance in EEZs. However, the recent FONOPs conducted during the Trump Administration are clearly a response to China's land reclamation activities in the Nansha Islands (Spratlys).[56]

By January 2019, according to media reports, at least nine FONOPs had been conducted against China's presence in the South China Sea during the two years' presidency of Donald Trump.[57] This figure has more than doubled to that during the eight years of Obama Administration. According to the *Annual Freedom of Navigation Report* (Fiscal Year 2017) published by the US Department of Defense, six 'excessive maritime claims' by China were challenged by US forces during the period from 1 October 2016 to 30 September 2017. It is worth noting that 'multiple challenges' were conducted against each 'excessive maritime claim'.[58] These challenges focus on the legality of enclosing dependent archipelagos with straight baselines in the Xisha Islands (*Paracel* Islands), the entitlement of territorial sea enjoyed by the Meiji Jiao (Mischief Reef) and the right of innocent passage of warships.

Straight baselines in the Xisha Islands (Paracel Islands)

In May 1996, China designated straight baselines for the Xisha Islands, in their entirety, by joining several islands and reefs, including Zhongjian (Triton) Island, which was involved in the USS Stethem and the USS Chafee Incidents. China pointed out that the US warships 'entered China's territorial sea off the Xisha Islands without China's approval'.[59]

These incidents refer to the issue whether or not the use of straight baselines to enclose dependent archipelagos is authorised by international law. This issue is also mentioned in the Award of the *South China Sea Arbitration* case. The Tribunal concluded that it did not think it consistent with the LOSC or customary international law, but did not explain its rationale in detail.[60]

The Convention confers State Parties with the right to establish their baselines either through the 'normal baseline' prescribed by Article 5, or through the 'straight baseline' provided by Article 7 of the Convention.[61] According to these provisions, Article 3 of the *Law of the People's Republic of China on the Territorial Sea and the Contiguous Zone* prescribes that '[t]he method of straight baselines composed of all the straight lines joining the adjacent base points shall be employed in drawing the baselines of the territorial sea of the People's Republic of China'.[62]

The Tribunal, however, believes that: Article 7 provides for the application of straight baselines only '[i]n localities where the coastline is deeply indented and cut into, or if there is a fringe of islands along the coast in its immediate vicinity'. These conditions do not include the situation of an offshore archipelago.[63]

The problem is that Article 46 defines an 'archipelagic State' as 'a State constituted wholly by one or more archipelagos and may include other islands' and thus, an Article 46 archipelagic State is distinguished from archipelagos that are part of a continental State. According to the *travaux préparatoires* and commentaries on Article 46, it turned out that a number of States with dependent archipelagos, such as Ecuador for the Galapagos, sought to have them included. Competing versions appeared in the texts that were considered during the 1974 and 1975 sessions of the Third Conference. But the relevant proposal did not achieve consensus, and was dropped in the version considered at the fourth session in 1976, the RSNT, and did not reappear subsequently.

Therefore, the fact that neither Article 5 on the normal baseline nor Article 7 on straight baselines explicitly precludes their use to offshore archipelagos, makes it possible to apply the last preambular paragraph of the LOSC, which states that 'matters not regulated by the Convention continue to be regulated by the rules and principles of general international law'.[64]

It is necessary to examine the *Anglo-Norwegian Fisheries* case carefully and identify the factors regarded by the ICJ as fundamental for justifying the establishment of straight baselines. In this case, the ICJ identified 'certain basic considerations inherent in the nature of the territorial sea':

> Another fundamental consideration, of particular importance in this case, is the more or less close relationship existing between certain sea areas and the land formations which divide or surround them ...
>
> Finally, there is one consideration not to be overlooked, the scope of which extends beyond purely geographical factors: that of certain economic interest peculiar to a region, the reality and importance of which are clearly evidenced by a long usage.[65]

Obviously, the considerations on the adoption of straight baselines include not only pure geographical factors, but also social, economic and historical factors. This is the case to justify the reason why China established straight baselines to enclose the Xisha Islands.[66]

Furthermore, there are more than ten dependent archipelagos worldwide that have been enclosed with straight baselines: the *Faroes* (Denmark), *Svalbard* (Norway), the *Canary* Islands (Spain), the *Azores* (Portugal), *Kerguelen* Islands (France), *Galapagos* (Ecuador), the *Bijagos* Archipelago (Guinea-Bissau), the *Arctic* archipelago (Canada), *Co Co* and *Preparis* Islands (Myanmar).

Even though this state practice over the decades cannot be deemed as a rule of customary international law since there are a few oppositions which prevented the development of a uniform and widely accepted practice, it is unreasonable to conclude that the use of straight baselines to enclose dependent archipelagos is contrary to the Convention or customary international law.

Entitlement of Territorial Sea in the Nansha Islands (Spratly Islands)

The Meiji Jiao (Mischief Reef), which was involved in the USS Dewey, USS John S. McCain and USS Mustin Incidents, is taken by the US as a low-tide elevation (LTE). An LTE, according to Article 13 of the Convention, does not have territorial sea of its own unless it is wholly situated at a distance within the breadth of the territorial sea from the mainland or an island.[67] In other words, an LTE may be used as a basepoint in drawing a baseline to 'bump out' the territorial sea, which makes it different from mid-ocean LTE or non-offshore LTE such as the Meiji Jiao. This position is also supported by the Award in the *South China Sea Arbitration* case.[68] Thus, the USS Dewey, according to a report, was 'engaged in normal operations by conducting a maneuvering drill inside 12 nautical miles of Mischief Reef'.[69] Article 19 of the Convention provides that 'innocent passage' shall be continuous and expeditious; and shall not engage in certain activities, including 'any exercise or practice with weapons of any kind', or 'the launching, landing or taking on board of any aircraft'. The US destroyer conducted a 'man overboard' exercise, specifically to show that its passage within 12 nautical miles was not innocent passage; and this action 'demonstrated that Mischief Reef is not entitled to its own territorial sea regardless of whether an artificial island has been built on top of it'.[70]

However, China has long reiterated the position that it enjoys sovereignty, sovereign rights and maritime jurisdiction over the Nansha Islands *in its entirety*, rather than a single island or reef or LTE. On 4 September 1958, the Chinese government declared that,

> [t]he breadth of the territorial sea of the People's Republic of China shall be twelve nautical miles. This provision applies to all territories of the People's Republic of China including the Chinese mainland and its coastal islands, as well as Taiwan and its surrounding islands, the Penghu Islands, the Dongsha Islands, the Xisha Islands, the Zhongsha Islands, the Nansha Islands and all other islands belonging to China which are separated from the mainland and its coastal islands by the high seas.[71]

In *Note Verbale* No. CML/8/2011 of 14 April 2011 addressed to the Secretary-General of the UN, the Permanent Mission of China to the UN stated that,

> under the relevant provisions of the 1982 [LOS Convention], as well as the *Law of the People's Republic of China on the Territorial Sea and the Contiguous Zone* (1992) and the Law on the Exclusive Economic Zone and the Continental Shelf of the People's Republic of China (1998), China's Nansha Islands is fully entitled to Territorial Sea, [EEZ] and Continental Shelf.[72]

On 12 July 2016, the Chinese government reiterated that,

> China has territorial sovereignty and maritime rights and interests in the South China Sea, including, inter alia: … ii. China has internal waters, territorial sea

and contiguous zone, based on *Nanhai Zhudao*; iii. China has exclusive economic zone and continental shelf, based on *Nanhai Zhudao* ...[73]

Today however, it is not easy for China to draw such straight baselines for the Nansha Islands, as China and the ASEAN States have committed to each other under the DOC 'to exercise self-restraint in the conduct of activities that would complicate or escalate disputes'. Technically, it is also not very easy for China to find appropriate islands and reefs on the outskirts of the Nansha Islands as basepoints to draw straight lines enclosing all features of the Nansha Islands. It seems that China will not establish the baselines for Nansha Islands in the foreseeable future.

Innocent passage of warships

The Huangyan Island (Scarborough Shoal), which was involved in the USS Hopper Incident, has a territorial sea of its own with a breadth of 12 nautical miles, as determined by the 1992 Chinese Law – territorial sea must exist *ipso facto and ab initio;* the lack of publicity and non-deposition of charts or lists of geographical coordinates do not make any difference in this matter.

Upon ratification of the Convention, China reaffirmed that,

> the provisions of the [Convention] concerning innocent passage through the territorial sea shall not prejudice the right of a coastal State to request, in accordance with its laws and regulations, a foreign State to obtain advance approval from or give prior notification to the coastal State for the passage of its warships through the territorial sea of the coastal State.[74]

According to the 1992 Chinese Law, '[f]oreign ships for military purposes shall be subject to approval by the Government of [China] for entering the territorial sea of the People's Republic of China'.[75]

So far, there is no unified rule of customary international law regarding foreign warships' innocent passage. That is why, since the adoption of the LOSC in 1982, State parties have maintained a sharp difference on the issue of innocent passage of warships.[76] The Convention does not contain an explicit provision to confirm that foreign warships can enter territorial waters of costal States without prior notification or authorisation. Rather, Article 21 of the Convention confers coastal States with the right to,

> adopt laws and regulations ... relating to innocent passage through the territorial sea, in respect of all or any of the following:
>
> a   the safety of navigation and the regulation of maritime traffic;
> b   the protection of navigational aids and facilities and other facilities or installations;
> c   the protection of cables and pipelines;
> d   the conservation of the living resources of the sea;

e   the prevention of infringement of the fisheries laws and regulations of the coastal State;

f   the preservation of the environment of the coastal State and the prevention, reduction and control of pollution thereof;

g   marine scientific research and hydrographic surveys;

h   the prevention of infringement of the customs, fiscal, immigration or sanitary laws and regulations of the coastal State.[77]

This is an extensive authorisation to coastal States on the regulation of innocent passage.

At the same time, although the Convention prohibits reservation, Article 310 allows State Parties to make declarations or statements with a view to harmonising their laws and regulations with the provisions of this Convention, thus enabling auto-interpretations.[78] Article 310 was drafted and inserted, arguably, to leave space for interpretation considering that many provisions reached on the basis of consensus during the ten-year long negotiation are ambiguous. One of them is innocent passage. Pursuant to Article 310, over 25 States insisted that in order for warships to exercise passage through territorial sea, either advance approval (e.g., Iran, Oman, Yemen, China and Algeria), or prior notification (e.g., Egypt, Malta, Croatia, Finland, Sweden, Serbia and Montenegro and Bangladesh) is necessary.[79] Accordingly, their domestic laws and regulations regarding innocent passage will not change even after the ratification of the Convention.

In conclusion, while the US has believed that its FONOPs are to enforce rule of law at sea, legal analysis better supports China's position that the US FONOPs in the South China Sea are offensive to its sovereignty. Moreover, the adverse effect of the FONOPs to the process of peaceful settlement of territorial issues and maritime disputes as well as to the security of SLOCs in the South China Sea region cannot be ignored.

Conclusion

We have reason to believe that the prospects of the Belt and Road Initiative should be optimistic, and all parties who participate in the cooperation should hope that the MSR will be an opportunity to gather momentum for common development and to deliver tangible outcomes. Nevertheless, we cannot ignore the important role of the South China Sea region and the safety of navigation in this region for the future success of the MSR Cooperation.

It is worth noting that we are in a period of reassessment and transition regarding how to strike the balance between navigational freedoms and the right of coastal States to limit navigation for self-protection. The Law of the Sea has always been created through the give-and-take process of states making conflicting claims, which are ultimately resolved through negotiation, a decision rendered by a tribunal or international organisation, military force, or a pattern of practice that emerges and is accepted as obligatory by those concerned about the issue.[80] We are in a particularly active law-making period at present regarding navigational rights and responsibilities, and it appears that the law that will emerge will be different from the law that had existed previously.[81] The freedom of navigation that has dominated the Law of the Sea during the past several centuries are diminishing in the face of competing considerations for environmental protection and security needs. All States should carefully exercise such freedom in accordance with international law without jeopardising the legitimate rights and interests of coastal States, including peace and security.

Notes

1 Cui Hongjian, The Belt and Road Initiative and Its Impact on Asia–Europe Connectivity, *ASEF Outlook Report 2016/2017: Connectivity: Facts and Perspectives, Volume II: Connecting Asia and Europe* (Asia–Europe Foundation, June 2016), p. 161.
2 Para. 53 in *Resolution adopted by the General Assembly on 17 November 2016* reads:

> Welcomes and urges further efforts to strengthen the process of regional economic cooperation, including measures to facilitate regional connectivity, trade and transit, including through regional development initiatives such as the Silk Road Economic Belt and the 21st-Century Maritime Silk Road (the Belt and Road) Initiative …

> See: Resolution No. A/RES/71/9, Resolutions of 71st Session, www.un.org/en/ga/search/view_doc.asp?symbol=A/RES/71/9. Para. 22 in *Resolution 2274 (2016)* reads: 'Calls for strengthening the process of regional cooperation, including measures to facilitate regional trade and transit, including through regional development initiatives such as the 'Silk Road Economic Belt and 21st Century Maritime Silk Road' initiative …' See: Security Council Adopts Resolution 2274 (2016), Authorizing One-Year Mandate Extension for United Nations Assistance Mission in Afghanistan, www.un.org/press/en/2016/sc12283.doc.htm. Para. 34 in *Resolution 2344 (2017)* reads:

> Welcomes and urges further efforts to strengthen the process of regional economic cooperation, including measures to facilitate regional connectivity, trade and transit, including through regional development initiatives such as the Silk Road Economic Belt and the 21st-Century Maritime Silk Road (the Belt and Road) Initiative …

> See: Security Council Authorizes Year-Long Mandate Extension for United Nations Assistance Mission in Afghanistan, Adopting Resolution 2344 (2017), www.un.org/press/en/2017/sc12756.doc.htm.
3 Vision for Maritime Cooperation under the Belt and Road Initiative, *Xinhua Net*, http://news.xinhuanet.com/english/2017-06/20/c_136380414.htm. For details, see Chapter 3 of this book.
4 See Article 122 of the LOSC, *UN Convention on the Law of the Sea*, www.un.org/depts/los/convention_agreements/texts/unclos/unclos_e.pdf.
5 Stanley B. Weeks, Sea Lines of Communications (SLOC) Security and Access, in: Michael Stankiewicz (ed.), *Maritime Shipping in Northeast Asia: Law of the Sea, Sea Lanes, and Security*, IGCC Policy Paper No. 33 (California: Institute on Global Conflict and Co-operation, University of California, February 1998), p. 55.
6 Hal Olson, Marine Traffic in the South China Sea, *Ocean Yearbook* 12 (1996), 137.
7 China Power Team, How Much Trade Transits the South China Sea?, *CSIS Report*, 2 August, 2017; updated 27 October, 2017, https://chinapower.csis.org/much-trade-transits-south-china-sea/.

8 Vision for Maritime Cooperation under the Belt and Road Initiative, *supra* (n. 3).
9 Zou Keyuan, Navigation in the South China Sea: Why Still an Issue?, *The International Journal of Marine and Coastal Law* 32(2) (2017), 243.
10 Jon M. Van Dyke, Balancing Navigation Freedom with Environmental and Security Concerns, *15 Colorado Journal of International Environmental Law and Policy* 19(28) (2004), 25.
11 Proclamation No. 3504, 27 Fed. Reg. 10401 (Oct. 23, 1962), www.presidency.ucsb. edu/ws/index.php?pid=8987.
12 R. R. Churchill and A. V. Lowe, *The Law of the Sea*, 3rd edn. (Manchester: Juris, 1999).
13 Article 33(1), Charter of the United Nations, www.un.org/en/charter-united-nations/.
14 *Report on the Obligations of States under Article 74(3) and 83(3) of UNCLOS in respect of Undelimited Maritime Areas*, published by the British Institute of International and Comparative Law, 30 June 2016, pp. 105, 106. See also: para. 47, *Position Paper of the Government of the People's Republic of China on the Matter of Jurisdiction in the South China Sea Arbitration Initiated by the Republic of the* Philippines, 7 December 2014, www.fmprc.gov.cn/mfa_eng/zxxx_662805/t1217147.shtml.
15 China Sticks to 'Dual-Track' Approach to Solve South China Sea Issue: FM, *Xinhuanet*, 24 July 2016, www.xinhuanet.com//english/2016-07/24/c_135536484.htm.
16 See: Letter from the Philippines to the Tribunal (30 November 2015) and also: Merits Hearing Tr. (Day 4), pp. 201–205.

(9) China has unlawfully failed to prevent its nationals and vessels from exploiting the living resources in the exclusive economic zone of the Philippines;

(10) China has unlawfully prevented Philippine fishermen from pursuing their livelihoods by interfering with traditional fishing activities at Scarborough Shoal;

(11) China has violated its obligations under the Convention to protect and preserve the marine environment at Scarborough Shoal, Second Thomas Shoal, Cuarteron Reef, Fiery Cross Reef, Gaven Reef, Johnson Reef, Hughes Reef and Subi Reef;

(12) China's occupation of and construction activities on Mischief Reef

(a) violate the provisions of the Convention concerning artificial islands, installations and structures;

(b) violate China's duties to protect and preserve the marine environment under the Convention; and

(c) constitute unlawful acts of attempted appropriation in violation of the Convention;

(13) China has breached its obligations under the Convention by operating its law enforcement vessels in a dangerous manner causing serious risk of collision to Philippine vessels navigating in the vicinity of Scarborough Shoal;

(14) Since the commencement of this arbitration in January 2013, China has unlawfully aggravated and extended the dispute by, among other things:

(a) interfering with the Philippines' rights of navigation in the waters at, and adjacent to, Second Thomas Shoal;

(b) preventing the rotation and resupply of Philippine personnel stationed at Second Thomas Shoal;

(c) endangering the health and well-being of Philippine personnel stationed at Second Thomas Shoal; and

(d) conducting dredging, artificial island-building and construction activities at Mischief Reef, Cuarteron Reef, Fiery Cross Reef, Gaven Reef, Johnson Reef, Hughes Reef and Subi Reef; and

    (15) China shall respect the rights and freedoms of the Philippines under the Convention, shall comply with its duties under the Convention, including those relevant to the protection and preservation of the marine environment in the South China Sea, and shall exercise its rights and freedoms in the South China Sea with due regard to those of the Philippines under the Convention.

17 In 2006, China declared that,

the Government of the People's Republic of China does not accept any of the procedures provided for in Section 2 of Part XV of the Convention with respect to all the categories of disputes referred to in paragraph 1 (a) (b) and (c) of Article 298 of the Convention.

See: *Declarations and Statements*, Division for Ocean Affairs and the Law of the Sea, UN Website, www.un.org/depts/los/convention_agreements/convention_declarations.htm#China Upon ratification.

18 Sienho Yee, Editorial Comment: The *South China Sea Arbitration* Decisions on Jurisdiction and Rule of Law Concerns, *Chinese Journal of International Law* 15(2) (2016), 220.

19 See: *Statement of the Ministry of Foreign Affairs of the People's Republic of China on the Award of 12 July 2016 of the Arbitral Tribunal in the South China Sea Arbitration Established at the Request of the Republic of the Philippines* (2016/7/12), www.fmprc.gov.cn/nanhai/eng/snhwtlcwj_1/t1379492.htm.

20 For example, in ratifying the *International Convention on the Elimination of All Forms of Racial Discrimination* 1965 and the *Convention on the Elimination of Discrimination against Women* 1979, China submitted reservations that precluded the application both of the interstate dispute resolution provisions involving arbitration and of referrals to the ICJ.

21 *Statement of the Ministry of Foreign Affairs of the People's Republic of China on the Award of 12 July 2016 of the Arbitral Tribunal in the South China Sea Arbitration Established at the Request of the Republic of the Philippines* (2016/7/12), *supra* (n. 19).

22 *Declaration On The Conduct Of Parties In The South China Sea*, http://asean.org/?static_post=declaration-on-the-conduct-of-parties-in-the-south-china-sea-2.

23 Su Xiaohui, It's Time to Stop Political Farce in the South China Sea, *China-US-Focus*, 25 July 2016, www.chinausfocus.com/foreign-policy/its-time-to-stop-political-farce-in-the-south-china-sea.

24 China Congratulates Duterte on Taking Office, *ABS-CBN News*, 1 July 2016, http://news.abs-cbn.com/nation/06/30/16/china-congratulates-duterte-on-taking-office; Xi Jinping Meets with President Rodrigo Duterte of the Philippines, 20 November 2016, www.fmprc.gov.cn/mfa_eng/topics_665678/XJPDEGDEBLZLJXGSFWBCXZ-BLLMJXDYTJHZZDESSCLDRFZSHY/t1417419.shtml; Li Keqiang Holds Talks with President Rodrigo Duterte of the Philippines, 16 November 2017, www.fmprc.gov.cn/mfa_eng/wjdt_665385/wshd_665389/t1511465.shtml.

25 Jane Perlez, Rodrigo Duterte and Xi Jinping Agree to Reopen South China Sea Talks, *New York Times*, 20 October 2016, www.nytimes.com/2016/10/21/world/asia/rodrigo-duterte-philippines-china-xi-jinping.html?_r=1.

26 Full Text: Joint Statement of China and the Philippines, *Xinhuanet*, 21 October 2016, http://news.xinhuanet.com/english/china/2016-10/21/c_135771815.htm.

27 *Joint Statement between the Government of the People's Republic of China and the Government of the Republic of the Philippines*, 16 November 2017, Manila, website of the Ministry of Foreign Affairs of the People's Republic of China, www.fmprc.gov.cn/mfa_eng/zxxx_662805/t1511299.shtml.

28 China, Vietnam Reach Consensus on Trade, Maritime Cooperation: Joint Statement, *Xinhua*, 13 November 2017, http://news.xinhuanet.com/english/2017-11/13/c_136749356.htm.

29 Vietnam, China Issue Joint Statement, *Nhan Dan*, 13 November 2017, http://en.nhandan.com.vn/politics/external-relations/item/5641902-vietnam-china-issue-joint-statement.html.
30 *Joint Statement between the People's Republic of China and the Republic of the Philippines*, 21 November 2018, Manila. See: Full text of China-Philippines Joint Statement, *Xinhua Net*, 21 November 2018, www.xinhuanet.com/english/2018-11/21/c_137622271.htm.
31 *Ibid.*
32 *Ibid.*
33 China, Vietnam Wrap up 25th Joint Patrol in Beibu Gulf, *China Military* Online, 20 December 2018, http://eng.chinamil.com.cn/view/2018-12/20/content_9384324.htm.
34 *Joint Statement of the Foreign Ministers of ASEAN Member States and China on the Full and Effective Implementation of the Declaration on the Conduct of Parties in the South China Sea*, 24 July 2016, http://asean.org/storage/2016/07/Joint-Statement-on-the-full-and-effective-implementation-of-the-DOC-FINAL.pdf.
35 *Joint Statement on The Application of the Code for Unplanned Encounters at Sea in the South China Sea*, 7 September 2016, http://asean.org/storage/2016/09/Joint-Statement-on-the-Application-of-CUES-in-the-SCS-Final.pdf.
36 China, ASEAN Hold Joint Maritime Rescue Drill (13 October 2017), *China Military Online* (Website of the Ministry of National Defense of the People's Republic of China), http://eng.mod.gov.cn/news/2017-10/31/content_4796204.htm.
37 *Chairman's Statement of the 20th ASEAN-China Summit*, 13 November 2017, http://asean.org/storage/2017/11/FINAL-Chairmans-Statement-of-the-20th-ASEAN-China-Summit-13-Nov-2017-Manila1.pdf ; *Declaration for a Decade of Coastal and Marine Environmental Protection in the South China Sea (2017–2027)*, 13 November 2017, http://asean.org/storage/2017/11/Declaration-for-a-Decade-of-Coastal-and-Marine-Environmental-Protection-in-the-South-China-Sea-2017-2027.pdf.
38 Christian Shepherd and Manuel Mogato, ASEAN, China Adopt Framework for Crafting Code on South China Sea, *Reuters*, 6 August 2017, www.reuters.com/article/us-asean-philippines-southchinasea/asean-china-adopt-framework-for-crafting-code-on-south-china-sea-idUSKBN1AM0AY.
39 *Chairman's Statement of the 20th ASEAN-China Summit* (*supra* n. 34).
40 China, ASEAN arrive at single draft negotiating text of COC in South China Sea, Website of *China Daily*, 2 August 2018, http://global.chinadaily.com.cn/a/201808/02/WS5b62c87da3100d951b8c8460.html.
41 China, ASEAN begin joint naval drill, Website of *China Daily*, 23 October 2018, www.chinadaily.com.cn/a/201810/23/WS5bce80d7a310eff303283f68.html.
42 *Challenges to Freedom of the Seas and Maritime Rivalry in Asia*, Directorate-General for External Policies, Policy Department European Parliament, 2017, p. 10.
43 *Ibid.*, p. 1.
44 *National Security Strategy of the United States of America* (December 2017), p. 46, www.whitehouse.gov/wp-content/uploads/2017/12/NSS-Final-12-18-2017-0905.pdf.
45 Natalie Klein, *Dispute Settlement in the UN Convention on the Law of the Sea*, (Cambridge: Cambridge University Press, 2005), p. 5.
46 Zou Keyuan, Navigation in the South China Sea: Why Still an Issue? *The International Journal of Marine and Coastal Law* 32(2) (2017), 243.
47 Erik Franckx, American and Chinese Views on Navigational Rights of Warships, *10 Chinese Journal of International Law* 187, 206 (2011), 192–193.
48 See Article 21 of the LOSC *supra* (n. 4).
49 See Article 25 of the LOSC *supra* (n. 4).
50 See Article 22 of the LOSC *supra* (n. 4).
51 *Ibid.*
52 See: J. Ashley Roach, Today's Customary International Law of the Sea, *Ocean Development and International Law* 45(3) (2014), 239–252.

53 See Article 58 (3) of the LOSC *supra* (n. 4).

54 *Statement of the Government of the People's Republic of China on China's Territorial Sovereignty and Maritime Rights and Interests in the South China Sea*, 12 July 2016, www.fmprc.gov.cn/nanhai/eng/snhwtlcwj_1/t1379493.htm.

55 *China Adheres to the Position of Settling Through Negotiation the Relevant Disputes Between China and the Philippines in the South China Sea*, paras. 136–139, www.fmprc.gov.cn/nanhai/eng/snhwtlcwj_1/t1380615.htm.

56 South China Sea FONOPs (Annie Kowalewski, ed.). *Institute for China-America Studies*, https://chinaus-icas.org/research-and-publications/icas-issue-primers/south-china-sea-fonops/.

57 According to media reports, on 25 May 2017, the USS Dewey missile destroyer entered the adjacent waters of the relevant islands and reefs in China's Nansha Islands without the permission of the Chinese government; the Chinese navy legally identified and verified the US vessel and warned it to leave. On 2 July, the missile destroyer USS Stethem trespassed China's territorial waters off the Xisha Islands; China dispatched military vessels and fighter planes in response to warn off the US vessel. On 10 August, USS John S. McCain entered the neighbouring waters of relevant islands and reefs of China's Nansha Islands without the permission of the Chinese government; the Chinese armed forces immediately sent naval ships to identify and verify the US warship according to law and warn it to leave. On 10 October, the missile destroyer USS Chafee entered China's territorial sea off the Xisha Islands without China's approval; the Chinese immediately sent naval ships and fighter planes to identify and verify the US warship according to law and warn and expel it. On 17 January 2018, the USS Hopper missile destroyer sailed within 12 nautical miles off China's Huangyan Island without gaining permission from the Chinese government; the Chinese Navy carried out identification and verification procedures in accordance with law and warned the US vessel to leave. On 23 March, the USS Mustin entered the neighbouring waters of relevant islands and reefs of China's Nansha Qundao without the permission of the Chinese government; the Chinese Navy identified and verified the US warship and warned it to leave in accordance with the law. On 27 May, US Navy's warships USS Higgins and USS Antietam entered China's territorial waters off the Xisha Islands without the Chinese government's approval; the Chinese Navy conducted identification and verification of the US warships in accordance with the law, and warned them off. On 30 September, the destroyer USS Decatur sailed into waters close to China's Nansha Islands without permission from the Chinese government; the Chinese Navy identified and warned the ship to leave in accordance with laws. On 7 January, 2019, the USS McCampbell entered China's territorial seas around Xisha Islands without permission from the Chinese side; China sent military vessels and aircraft to conduct verification and identification on the US ship and warned it to leave.

58 *Annual Freedom of Navigation Report* (Fiscal Year 2017), http://policy.defense.gov/Portals/11/FY17%20DOD%20FON%20Report.pdf?ver=2018-01-19-163418-053.

59 Foreign Ministry Spokesperson Hua Chunying's Regular Press Conference, *Ministry of Foreign Affairs of China*, 11 October 2017, www.fmprc.gov.cn/mfa_eng/xwfw_665399/s2510_665401/t1500871.shtml.

60 Award, PCA Case No. 2013-19. Paras. 575–576, www.pcacases.com/web/sendAttach/2086.

61 LOSC, *supra* (n. 4).

62 See: *Law of the People's Republic of China on the Territorial Sea and the Contiguous Zone*, www.lawinfochina.com/display.aspx?lib=law&id=670.

63 Para. 575, *supra* (n. 55).

64 LOSC, *supra* (n. 4).

65 Fisheries case, Judgment of December 18th, 1951: *ICJ Reports* (1951), p. 133, www.icj-cij.org/files/case-related/5/005-19511218-JUD-01-00-EN.pdf .

66 Duan Jielong (ed.), *International Law in China: Cases and Practice* [in Chinese] (Beijing: China Law Press, 2011), pp. 84–85.

67 See Article 13 of the LOSC, *supra* (n. 4).

68 Paras. 378, 646–647, *supra* (fn. 55).

69 U.S. Warship Drill Meant to Defy China's Claim over Artificial Island: officials, *Reuters*, 25 May 2017, www.reuters.com/article/us-usa-southchinasea-navy/u-s-warship-drill-meant-to-defy-chinas-claim-over-artificial-island-officials-idUSKBN18K353.

70 *Ibid.*

71 *Declaration of the Government of the People's Republic of China on China's Territorial Sea*, 4 September 1958, www.chinausfocus.com/upload/file/2014/Annex1-4.pdf.

72 *Position Paper of the Government of the People's Republic of China on the Matter of Jurisdiction in the South China Sea Arbitration Initiated by the Republic of the Philippines.* Para. 21, 7 December 2014, *supra* (n. 14).

73 *Statement of the Government of the People's Republic of China on China's Territorial Sovereignty and Maritime Rights and Interests in the South China Sea*, 12 July 2016, *supra* (n. 49).

74 See: *Declarations and Statements*, Division for Ocean Affairs and the Law of the Sea, UN, www.un.org/depts/los/convention_agreements/convention_declarations.htm# China Upon ratification.

75 Article 6, *Law of the People's Republic of China on the Territorial Sea and the Contiguous Zone*, http://en.pkulaw.cn/display.aspx?cgid=5597&lib=law.

76 Xinjun Zhang, The Latest Developments of the US Freedom of Navigation Programs in the South China Sea: Deregulation or Re-balance, *Journal of East Asia and International Law* 9 (2016) p. 170.

77 See: Article 21 of the LOSC, *supra* (n. 4).

78 *Ibid.*, Article 310.

79 Xinjun Zhang, *supra* (n. 81), p. 170.

80 Myres S. McDougal and Norbert A. Schlei, The Hydrogen Bomb Tests in Perspective: Lawful Measures for Security, *Yale Law Journal* 64 (1955) 648, 659–660.

81 Jon M. Van Dyke, *supra* (n. 10), p. 28.

8 The Polar Code's suitability as legal protection against negative externalities in the Arctic as part of the Polar Silk Road?

Christian Frier and Kim Østergaard

Introduction

The effects of global warming have already given rise to significant climate changes in the Arctic region, as the sea ice in the Arctic Ocean is constantly diminishing.[1] Once considered a remote area and hostile environment with limited commercial interest,[2] increased access and navigability have promoted new business opportunities. This includes, *inter alia*, the utilisation of previously inaccessible living and non-living resources, as well as access to two international shipping routes, respectively termed the 'Northwest Passage across North America' and the 'Northeast Passage across Russia'.[3] The Arctic routes result in a reduction in the time of use, fuel consumption and CO_2-emission compared with the existing shipping routes,[4] thus reducing the negative externalities[5] associated with international shipping.[6] The Northeast Passage is also connected to the 'Maritime Silk Road' establishing what is commonly dubbed the 'Polar Silk Road'.[7] The possibility of navigating directly between the Polar Silk Road and the Maritime Silk Road has prompted new strategic opportunities for maritime industries. Also, Arctic shipping is not affected by political instability as it is in the Middle East or the risk of piracy in the waters off the coast of Africa.[8] Through that prism, the incentives for private actors to explore and utilise the Arctic as a viable alternative are evident. However, the positive externalities associated with commercial activities in the Arctic, shall at the same time be evaluated against the threats related to the increased accessibility,[9] thus emphasising the need to safeguard the marine environment.

Vessel-source pollution constitutes a potential negative externality,[10] which in this context, refers to environmental damage caused by either operational or accidental pollution.[11] Another concern is the maritime infrastructure or rather, the lack thereof, should an environmental damage occur. Even smaller spills might have a detrimental effect on the Arctic region's wildlife, while large scale pollution can have completely disastrous consequences for the unique and pristine habitat.[12] In addition to potential negative externalities following from the risk of environmental pollution in general, there is an increased demand within sea cruising to explore the Arctic,[13] which further reinforces the need for Search & Rescue (SAR) emergency preparedness bestowed upon the Arctic states.[14]

Taking those pointers, maritime safety and marine protection, into consideration, the International Maritime Organization's (IMO) 'International Code for Ships Operating in Polar Water' – Polar Code, has been adopted to protect the polar waters and enhance the safety of humans at sea.

The scope of this chapter is to undertake an examination of the Polar Code's impact on Arctic shipping, with a special focus on safeguarding the marine environment. It first briefly examines the legal framework governing the Arctic Ocean. This overview paves the way for a more detailed introduction to the Polar Code as a legally binding instrument, with reference to the two guidelines on which the Polar Code is formulated. This section also covers the procedural perspective, before the relevant substantive rules of the Polar Code are discussed with the purpose of evaluating its function as a stewardship tool. Understanding that compliance is not merely a question of adopting rules, but also a question of effective control and enforcement, a section of this chapter is devoted to this focus. The analysis places the Polar Code in the broader content of international law. Finally, an alternate view is presented in the context of private actors as regulators in the Arctic. The relevant question to ask in that context is whether industry self-regulation and co-regulation constitute appropriate measures to mend the gaps in the Polar Code.

The legal framework and governance of the Arctic

Despite the uncertainties that surround the future and the consequences of Arctic shipping, the legal framework pertaining to the Arctic Ocean is less ambiguous at first glance.[15] The overarching regime governing the Arctic Ocean is the UN Convention on the Law of the Sea (LOS).[16] The Arctic can be considered an enclosed or semi-enclosed sea, by the very reason of the definition set out in Article 122.[17] Except in one single article,[18] ice-covered areas are not treated any differently in the LOS Convention. Similarly, most marine and maritime treaties do not exclude particular regions or ocean spaces and can thereby be considered geographically universal in scope of application.[19] Of particular importance to the marine environment is the 1973 International Convention for the Prevention of Pollution from Ships, as modified by the Protocol of 1978 (MARPOL 73/78) and the International Convention for the Safety of Life at Sea with amendments (SOLAS). MARPOL is the foremost international convention covering prevention of pollution of the marine environment by ships from operational or accidental causes.[20] According to its preamble, the convention seeks to achieve the complete elimination of international pollution of the marine environment.[21] Another international convention of great importance is SOLAS, which defines standards pertaining to the construction, design, equipment and manning of ships (CDEM standards).[22] In addition to the international law framework, at least two other governance initiatives with influence on commercial activities in the Arctic are worth mentioning.

The 2008 Ilulissat Declaration

In 2008, the Arctic coastal states signed the Ilulissat Declaration.[23] The declaration specifies that it is the view of the signatory states that the Law of the Sea adequately serves as a basis to solve disputes, following from overlapping claims over the Arctic, thus declining the need for an 'Arctic Convention'. This soft power approach is pursued by the adoption of appropriate measures,[24] including bi- and multilateral agreements on extraction of natural resources to avoid tensions to escalate.[25] However, because of the melting ice cap, the coastal states must also take the unprecedented focus of Central Arctic Ocean (CAO) fishing into consideration.[26] Foreign-flagged fishing vessel's growing attention to accessible and cost-efficient CAO fishing presents yet another governance issue, which according to the freedom of the high seas cannot be dictated by the Arctic states.[27] The Arctic has a wide range of attractive fishing areas, including, but not limited to, North East Atlantic (Norwegian and Barents Seas), the Central North Atlantic (Iceland and Greenland), North East Canada (Newfoundland and Labrador Sea) and the North Pacific (Bering Sea). Some are home to commercially attractive species such as cod, capelin, halibut, pollock, shrimp, crab and herring.[28] In order to secure a sustainable harvesting of fish stocks in the CAO area, a regional cooperation between the Arctic five, which also includes important non-Arctic states like China and Japan, has reached out to adopt the '2018 Agreement to prevent unregulated high seas Fisheries in the Central Arctic Ocean'.[29] In spirit, the multilateral agreement supports a precautionary approach to the conservation and management of living resources. However, the ambit of the agreement is limited to fishing activities and does not set additional standards for trans-Arctic shipping.

Guidelines

Because of the navigational freedom and the rights assigned to all flag States under the LOS Convention,[30] additional legal instruments appropriate to govern Arctic shipping are required. A pivotal contributor to behaviour-related norms of formal and informal nature is the IMO.[31] As the UN's organisation with jurisdictional competence in marine and maritime affairs,[32] the IMO promotes various types of legal instruments. The IMO has for instance issued two guidelines: 'Guidelines for ships operating in arctic ice-covered waters'[33] and 'Guidelines for ships operating in polar waters'.[34] Common to both sets of guidelines is the fact that neither are mandatory, and thus characterised as 'soft law'.[35] A common feature of such instruments is that they do not have binding effect *per se* and cannot serve as a basis of enforcement or sanction within the public sphere in case of non-compliance. This is not necessarily negative, as this type of behavioural approach may be appropriate in cases where mandatory legislation cannot be achieved.[36] This interplay between formal and informal rules is a discipline that the IMO is accustomed to, as noted by F. L. Kirgis, who emphasises the organisation's ability to find ways to channel members' conduct.[37] This happens through codes and guidelines which, while not always mandatory, may have a similar effect as formal rules on the addressees.[38] Similarly, soft law is often well suited to become hard law. The adoption of the Polar Code serves as a prime example, with the initial guidelines that paved the way for the Polar Code. In summary, the regulation of Arctic Shipping is by no means a legal vacuum, but rather a complex legal setting.

The Polar Code

In recognition of the increasing need for binding and enforceable rules pertaining to Arctic shipping, Denmark, Norway and the United States pointed to the need for a mandatory code for ships to operate in polar waters.[39] According to the proposal, such an instrument should have entered into force by 2012. The ambitious time-frame was not met, however and the IMO adopted the Polar Code in the following years,[40] with subsequent dates for the Code to enter into force. In terms of source of law, the Code can be considered *lex specialis*, since the Code's geographical scope of application is limited to the two Polar regions. It is thus an addition to, rather than a replacement of, existing rules. As to the scope of the Code, it should be mentioned that it is far more exhaustive than that applicable under the two existing guidelines, from 2002 and 2010. The main difference between the guide-lines and the Code is hence not just a question of mandatory nature. The recom-mendations in the guideline from 2002 addresses issues, including, but not limited to, waste facilities, communication and environmental risks.[41] The guideline from 2010 is essentially a reproduction of the recommendations in the guideline from 2002, however as it can be deduced from the title, it also covers Antarctica.

Purpose and procedural rules

The overall purpose of the Polar Code is 'to provide for safe ship operation and the protection of the polar environment by addressing risks present in polar waters and not adequately mitigated by other instruments of the Organization'.[42] Given the dualistic focus on maritime safety and marine protection, the Polar Code was drafted by IMO's specialised agencies, the Maritime Safety Com-mittee (MSC)[43] and the Marine Environment Protection Committee (MEPC), respectively.[44] The internal structure of the Polar Code consists of two separate parts, A and B, dealing with maritime safety and pollution prevention, respec-tively. In addition, each part is divided into two separate sub-parts. The first con-tains mandatory rules (A-I and B-I), and the latter part is recommendations (A-II and B-II). It is essentially the Polar Code's mandatory parts that differentiate it from the previous guidelines. To ensure its binding effect,[45] the Code is imple-mented in SOLAS, for the part on maritime safety, and in MARPOL, for the part relating to pollution prevention.[46] The Code was adopted in accordance with IMO's tacit adoption procedure,[47] and entered into force in 2018 for ships built after the cut-off date, while ships already in service are obliged to comply with the Code upon first inspection, but no later than 2020.[48]

Safety measures

New concepts and definitions are developed within the Polar Code framework. For instance, ships are classified in one of the three nominated polar classes, A, B or C, which refers to the ice class assigned. The concept of ice classes is derived from the International Association of Classification Societies' (IACS) 'Unified Requirements for Polar Ships'.[49] Two parameters come into play when the ice class is determined. The extent of the expected activity in conjunction with risk factors. A distinction is thus made between different categories of ships. Category A is the most restrictive ice class and includes ships designed for passage in difficult ice conditions. Category B includes ships not covered by category A, but capable of navigating in ice-filled waters. Ships in category C make up the most lenient ice class and are reserved for ships operating in open water.[50] Not all ship types are included in the Polar Code. According to SOLAS Chapter 1, regulation 1 and 2 the convention applies to all ships engaged in international voyages, unless stated otherwise.[51] The exceptions with most relevance to commercial activities, are cargo ships of less than 500 gross tons and fishing vessels.

Every ship to which this Polar Code applies shall have aboard, a valid Polar Ship Certificate (PSC), which is reviewed at inspection, except for category C cargo ships where verification takes place by handing in documentation to the relevant flag State. Further rules pertaining to safety measures are contained in Chapters 2–12. Some of which relate to ship structure and stability,[52] while others concern planning and the performance of the actual voyage.[53] Not surprisingly, higher standards are expected for passenger ships and tankers. The recommendatory part on safety measures is found in I-B, which supplements the different chapters in I-A. This includes, *inter alia*, methods for determining equivalent ice class with reference to the IACS Polar Classes. Other chapters are left open. That is the case with manning and training, stating 'no additional guidance', however, part I-A contains a reference to both the Standards of Training, Certification and Watchkeeping for Seafarers (STCW) Convention[54] and the STCW Code.[55]

Pollution prevention measures

The specific provision regarding pollution prevention measures are found in part II-A, which contains the mandatory rules and part II-B on additional recommendations. The purpose of MARPOL is to prevent pollution from ship traffic, irrespective of whether the pollution occurs in connection with ship operations or as the result of an accident. MARPOL is considered among the most successful treaties in terms of international support, and some of MARPOL's annexes are ratified by 150 States[56] representing 99 per cent of the total registered world tonnage.[57] The material regulations are divided into six detailed annexes and associated appendices.[58] As opposed to the safety measures consolidated in the SOLAS convention, the MARPOL convention is amended on a thematical level for each of the relevant annexes. The Code follows the same structure of

MARPOL with categorisation of the various sources of pollution, but also contains more strict requirements for sailing in the Arctic.

The Code is relevant in relation to MARPOL's Annex I on prevention of pollution by oil; Annex II on control of pollution by noxious liquid substances in bulk; Annex IV on prevention of pollution by sewage from ships; and Annex V on prevention of pollution by garbage from ships.[59] The two annexes pertaining to Prevention of pollution by harmful substances carried by sea in packaged form or in freight containers, portable tanks, or road or rail tank wagons, Annex III, and Prevention of air pollution from ships, Annex VI, are not amended. Despite the fact that the Polar Code, with its new binding standards, contributes to protect the marine environment, the Polar Code is not exhaustive in the sense that not all sources of pollution are covered. This applies to, for example, crude oil and heavy fuel oil in addition to air pollution. These sources of pollution are instead addressed in the non-binding section, which naturally is a weakness from an environmental protection perspective.

Certification and enforcement

In continuation of the adoption of mandatory rules, the issue of oversight mechanism in the form of certification and enforcement measures are of paramount importance to ensure maritime safety and the marine environment against the many perils at sea. Compliance control and law enforcement at sea are unilateral activities performed by States, as there is no supranational agency that undertakes or coordinates the task.[60] Consequently, a structural enforcement deficit cannot be denied.[61] It is no different with the Polar Code, as the Code itself does not allocate any oversight mechanism.[62] In sum, enforcement powers rely on the equilibrium established in the LOS Convention as well as in SOLAS and MARPOL.

Flag States

As a starting point, the flag State, being the State that grants ships their nationality in accordance with the LOS Convention Art. 91, 'shall effectively exercise its jurisdiction and control in administrative, technical and social matters over ships flying its flag'.[63] Accordingly, flag State jurisdiction provides the principal way of maintaining legal order over shipping activities at sea. This means that each flag State can promote its own rules, within the boundaries of the Law of the Sea. It can be argued with some caution, however, that the significance of nationality has lessened, in tandem with the codification of international maritime and marine law.[64] Despite rule harmonisation due to the extent of international and regional regulation,[65] the integrity of the current system relies heavily on flag State jurisdiction.[66] It is a common perception that one of the fundamental concerns related to safe shipping is the ability and willingness of flag States to exercise effective control.[67] The obligations imposed on flag States are many-fold. Thus, it must be ensured that each ship is seaworthy and satisfies the CDEM standards and other requirements associated with the specific trading area. In case of prevention of vessel sources pollution, the flag State is further obliged to adopt laws which at 'least have the same effect as that of generally accepted international rules and standards'.[68] The rule of reference to international law and standards indicate the minimum threshold, which national legislation must respect. Any flag State is free to set higher standards, but States will usually refrain from doing so given the impact on competitiveness of their fleet.[69]

In shipping, it is common practice for national authorities to delegate administrative competence to private classification societies.[70] These 'recognized organizations'[71] are entrusted to undertake ship surveys and procedure reviews. The application of ROs to indirectly safeguard Arctic shipping, is not uncontroversial, especially in situations where rules give leeway to interpretation. As noted by Øystein Jensen, the goal-based approach in drafting the Polar Code has left the Code with a mixture of vague and substantive rules.[72] For ship owners to abide by the Code is costly, because of the specific measures and need of skilled seafarers. This could potentially lead to ship owners to shop between different ROs, preferring those with less stricter requirements.[73] On that background it can be argued that the application of private actors as 'State agents' in relation to securing safe shipping is commercially convenient – but doctrinally dubious.

The flag State enforcement powers over its own fleet can broadly be described as extensive. The counterpart of Art. 211 (2) follows from Art. 217 entitled 'enforcement by flag States'. The Article details the flag State's enforcement obligations with respect to the protection of the marine environment. The provision deals, among other things, with certification. Thus, it must be ensured that ships flying its flag carry mandatory certificates on board. This includes, *inter alia*, a Polar Ship Certificate. Furthermore, such compliance shall be reviewed under periodical inspections.[74] In the case where a ship fails the inspection, the flag State is obliged to ensure the ship is prohibited from sailing, irrelevant of the ship's *locus*. Measures against ships can also be initiated by requests from other States in accordance with Art. 217(6).

Coastal and port States

In case flag State enforcement fails, the question of the Arctic coastal states has the right to monitor and take enforcement actions against foreign ships arises. The LOS Convention grants separate enforcement powers over ships of other nationalities. Powers of this nature are granted to coastal and port states, depending on the *locus* of the ship.[75] Ships navigating in coastal State waters or berthed in port are thus subject to a sophisticated allocation of flag State and foreign State jurisdiction.

A coastal State is a State which has a coastline and the right to enforce international and national rules in this function. A port State is basically a coastal state, which is granted additional powers in cases where foreign ships enter port facilities or offshore terminals. This implies that enforcement powers are granted to the Arctic coastal States of Russia, United States of America, Canada, Norway and Denmark, which due to Greenland being part of the Kingdom of Denmark, is responsible for patrolling Greenlandic waters. This is a complex issue, as it depends on several factors. The answer must therefore be answered by observing which is the State – flag, coastal, or port state, that wishes to take such steps, and on what grounds. Finally, the ship's *locus* at the time of incident shall be taken into consideration.

Not surprisingly, port State jurisdiction is less complicated because foreign ships call for port or offshore terminals. In that case, mandatory certificates shall be presented upon inspection. A certificate issued under the rules of MARPOL has the same status as if the certificate had been issued by the port State itself. Accordingly, the inspection shall be confined to an examination of whether there is a valid certificate, unless there are compelling reasons that speak against the seaworthiness of the ship.[76] If the ship fails to comply with the requirements, the port State shall make sure that the ship does not leave the port facility. The effect of this provision is obviously limited in cases where the port State does not exercise any form of control. Ships not complying with the Convention would presumably seek to enter ports with no, or limited, control measures. To address the problem, several MoUs related to port State control have been adopted.[77] A similar agreement may beneficially be concluded among the Arctic port States for ensuring effective regional control and enforcement of the Polar Code. This plays into the *lex specialis* rule in Art. 218(1). Pursuant to the provision, any port State may undertake investigations and institute proceedings if necessary for any discharge that occurred on the high seas.[78]

For merchant ships transiting the exclusive economic zone (EEZ)[79] or navigation in accordance with the doctrine of innocent passage, the question of coastal State jurisdiction is relevant. The legislative jurisdiction mentioned in Art. 211(4) empowers coastal States to adopt laws to regulate vessel-source pollution in their own territorial waters. Such laws, however, must not hamper the right to innocent passage. It usually precludes rules on CDEM standards, unless they are giving effect to generally accepted international rules and standards pursuant to Art. 21(2). From the Polar Code's 'margin of appreciation' it can potentially lead to additional requirements. Furthermore, Article 234 details special powers on enforcement of non-discriminatory laws for the prevention, limitation, and control of marine pollution from vessels in ice-covered areas within the borders of the exclusive economic zone in accordance with.[80] Despite the provision, it does not provide a definition of 'ice-covered water', it is broadly accepted that the Arctic can be regarded as so.[81]

Public legal obligations or use of the contractual function as protection

Following the review of the Polar Code and its effective nature as a means of legal protection, a general comment must be addressed in relation to the distinction between public law and the contractual function (private co-regulation through contracting), as well as the applicability of the two disciplines as maritime regulatory mechanisms to prevent negative externalities in the shape of environmental damage[82] in the Arctic. In Denmark, the contractual function is already being used in a slightly broader sense than the traditional contract law-based approach, since the special marine environmental protection scheme has been in force since 2006.[83] Here, there is the possibility that people may act as guardians on a voluntary basis in return for a modest honorarium to ensure that no oil spill occurs in Danish waters. Since 2006, the number of oil spills has been reduced with more than 50 per cent in Danish waters, so the scheme that has been established between Danish public authorities, interest groups, foundations, etc., has had a fairly significant preventive effect. Thus, one could argue that the Danish scheme has been quite successful. Similar schemes may be established by the coastal States, but due to the harsher climate in the Arctic, such measures must be assumed to have a much lesser effect. The regulation of a 'new' area of law in which commercial interests are involved can be implemented through both the implementation of public law, as well as the use of the contractual function, or in a broad sense, private law. Often, there is a certain interplay between the two disciplines, so there is no dichotomous approach.

From a private law perspective, any pollution in the Arctic can be characterised as being covered by tort law. The argument for using the contractual function is the existence of well-defined rights, as pointed out by Coase. For example, in relation to emission of CO_2, which until recently was considered a public asset, an opportunity has been established to use the market and thus the contractual function to buy and sell access to the emission of CO_2 between private operators. In view of the sensitivity of the Arctic region, for that reason, the use of the contractual function upon discharge of substances covered by the Polar Code already seems ruled out. Although one could argue that the ban on discharge of substances could be defined as a well-defined right in the Coase sense – or rather, a *duty* – there will be some very special challenges in terms of with whom to contract.

The access to free passage in international waters in the Arctic and, with certain restrictions in relation to the coastal states' territory in the Arctic can be seen as a public asset or access to universally available value[84] which, among others on the basis of the Marine Environment Act and consequently, the ratification of MARPOL in Danish law, as mentioned above, implies liability on the part of the tortfeasor. This, however, presupposes that there is a legitimate tort-protected interest that impacts asset interests. Thus, based on general tort law, it is assumed that it is possible to identify whose interest is violated in connection with environmental damage. In other words, prior to, or after, the occurrence of the environmental damage, it should be possible to identify who the tortfeasor should enter into a contract with, in order for there to be an opportunity to use the contractual function as an alternative to the current public law regulation.

The risk associated with discharges of banned substances from shipping, and which constitutes environmental damage, does not appear to be directly applicable to the contractual function, which the economist, Coase, identifies as a tool for resolving tortious issues – and often with a larger economic output than a court decision would have involved. In relation to the coastal states, it will theoretically be an option, but will, in all probability, imply very high transaction costs and, in practice, would be impossible. Since the international waters of the Arctic are generally accessible, no possible co-contractor can be identified. In addition, there would be no political willingness to limit the sanction to consist solely of what in practice would be possible in private law, namely damages and perhaps remediation. Accordingly, the relevant regulation must continue to be governed by public law in the individual legal system.

The interaction between public and private law is for instance reflected in the fact that under Greenlandic law, there is an obligation to use a person with local knowledge and actual mandatory pilotage in the case of passenger ships with at least 250 passengers.[85] In practice, for ships flying a foreign flag, this implies that, as a result of public law regulation, there is a requirement to enter into a contract with a company that has local knowledge or a pilotage company when sailing with passenger ships in Greenlandic waters with a minimum of 250 passengers.[86]

Conclusion

The regulation of Arctic shipping takes place within the framework of general maritime and marine law. Within this framework, there is a need for legal instruments, which take into account the particularly sensitive, but also harsh, nature of the Arctic. The Polar Code is the latest example of a source of law of this type that relates to the commercial activities in the Arctic. In other sensitive marine areas, the challenges of the marine environment consist of repairing damaged ecosystems. In the Arctic, it is still possible to protect the region. Prevention of environmental damage is crucial in this regard. The Polar Code is an ambitious instrument aimed at raising the standard of maritime activities in the Arctic by introducing mandatory minimum requirements for the industry. The suitability of the Polar Code as legal protection, however, depends largely on the States' ability to ensure compliance and enforcement, whether it be the flag State itself or the Arctic States which have a keen interest in this matter. This will probably be a task that is imposed on the coastal States to the extent allowed in the Law of the Sea. In order to address a fragmented enforcement effort, the Arctic coastal states can adopt a holistic and common approach to control, in the form of MoUs.

Ships entering Arctic waters from the Maritime Silk Road through the Northeast Passage must comply with the Polar Code and must even comply with national law in one or more of the coastal states depending on shipping route.

The Polar Code's suitability as protection against negative externalities in the Arctic must be analysed in connection with the enforcement effort and opportunity. The contractual function is predominantly not a relevant alternative to the public law regulation in this context, as it implies both exorbitant transaction costs and insufficient legal protection to address negative externalities. If so, it must be, as discussed, that the public law regulation implies an agreement in order to do so in the territorial waters of the Arctic.

Notes

1 Paul G. Harris (ed.), Climate Change at Sea – Interactions, impacts and Governance, in: *Climate Change and Ocean Governance – Politics and Policy for Threatened Seas* (Cambridge: Cambridge University Press, 2019), p. 6.
2 Aldo Chircop, The Growth of International Shipping in the Arctic: Is A Regulatory Review Timely?, *International Journal of Marine and Coastal Law* 24 (2009), 358–361.
3 *The Kingdom of Denmark's Strategy for the Arctic 2011–2020*, p. 19.
4 See, e.g. Katerina Peterkova Mtkidis. The Role of Private Actors in Regulation of Arctic Shipping, *LMCLQ* (November 2016), pp. 544–545; W. E. Butler, Some Reflections on the Northern Sea Route in SIMPLY 2017/MarIus no. 502, pp. 178–180.
5 The concept of negative externalities does not have a clear and unambiguous meaning. It can be broadly understood as the damage caused by an act or by omission. In the eyes of the economist, R. H. Coase, who is discussed in more detail below, the principle, in its broadest sense, relates to how the contractual function can be used as a means to minimise the negative externalities and maximise the economic output, since the courts often do not come to an economically efficient result in cases of tort. The negative externalities in the are directly linked to the environmental damage in cases of operational and accidental pollution caused to the Arctic. See further in R. H. Coase, The Problem of Social Cost, *Journal of Law & Economics* III (1960), 1–44.
6 Yoshifumi Tanaka, *The International Law of the Sea* (Cambridge: Cambridge University Press, 2015), p. 271.
7 Arild Moe and Olav Schram Stokke, Asian Countries and Arctic Shipping: Policies, Interests and Footprints on Governance, *Arctic Review on Law and Politics* 10 (2019), 28.
8 Piracy is considered among the greatest maritime security threats and remains on the agenda of the MSC, see, e.g. MSC meeting summary of the 99th session (16–25 May 2018).
9 Benjamin Hofmann, Policy Responses to New Ocean Threats – Arctic Warming, Maritime Industries, and International Environmental Regulation, in: *Climate Change and Ocean Governance – Politics and Policy for Threatened Seas* (2019), pp. 215–216, *supra* (n. 1).
10 Other sources of environmental pollution, including land-based marine pollution, and pollution from seabed activities or fishing will not be examined in this chapter.
11 Donald R. Rothwell and Tim Stephens, *The International Law of the Sea* (Cambridge: Cambridge University Press, 2016), p. 376.
12 The Exxon Valdez oil spill disaster, which occurred off the coast of Alaska in 1989, triggered discussions on additional demands regarding ice-strengthened ship hulls, see IMO Doc. MSC 59/30/32.
13 Passenger ships with a capacity of over 1000 passengers are navigating the Northwest Passage. The Cruise Lines International Association (CLIA) was particularly active during the development of the Polar Code, e.g. IMO, DE 57/11/21. 'Development of a mandatory code for ships operating in polar waters – administrative procedures for application of the Polar code', submitted by CLIA.
14 Richard O. G. Wanerman, Freezing out Noncompliant Ships: Why the Arctic Council Must Enforce the Polar Code, *Case Western Reserve Journal of International Law* 47 (2015), 441–443.
15 The governance of shipping activities in the Arctic has been described as a complicated mosaic, see *Arctic Marine Shipping Assessment 2009 Report* (AMSA), p. 54.
16 1982 United Nation Convention on the Law of the Sea (LOS Convention).
17 Alfred van der Essen, The Arctic and Antarctic Regions, in: Dupuy and Vignes (eds.), *A Handbook on the New Law of the Sea* (New York: Springer, 1991), p. 525.

18 The LOS Convention contains only one article referring expressively to the polar regions, Art. 234, which places special prescriptive right to coastal States in ice-covered areas.

19 The number of subject-specific conventions with relevance to Arctic Shipping is comprehensive. A list can be found in the *ASMA 2009 Report*, p. 59–70.

20 www.imo.org/en/About/Conventions/ListOfConventions/Pages/International-Convention-for-the-Prevention-of-Pollution-from-Ships-(MARPOL).aspx (accessed 1 March 2019). MARPOL replaces the earlier 1954 International Convention for the Prevention of Pollution of the Sea by Oil (OILPOL).

21 MARPOL, Preamble, 4th Recital.

22 E. J. Molenaar, Status and Reform of International Arctic Shipping Law, *Arctic Marine Governance – Opportunities for Transatlantic Cooperation* (2013), p. 142.

23 The Ilulissat Declaration, Arctic Ocean Conference Ilulissat, Greenland, 27–29 May 2008, pp. 1–2. The Arctic coastal states include the United States, Canada, Russia, Norway and Denmark, as Greenland forms part of the Kingdom of Denmark.

24 Ilulissat Declaration (2008), p. 1.

25 See, e.g. Karen N. Scott and David L. Vanderzwaag, Polar Oceans and Law of the Sea, in: *The Oxford Handbook of the Law of the Sea* (Oxford: Oxford University Press, 2015), p. 735.

26 *Ibid.*, p. 737.

27 T. Potts, The Management of Living Marine Resources in the Polar Regions, in: Natalia Loukacheva (ed.), *Polar Law Textbook* (Copenhagen: Nordic Council of Ministers, 2010), p. 65.

28 A. van der Essen, The Arctic and Antarctic Regions, in: *A Handbook on the New Law of the Sea* (Nijhoff: Brill, 1991), p. 525.

29 EU COM (2018) 454 final.

30 LOS Convention Art. 87 entitled 'Freedom of the high sea' and to a lesser degree the regime of innocent passage (Part I, section 3) as well as regional MoUs on calling for port.

31 Elisabeth Mendenhall, The Ocean Governance Regime: International Conventions and Institutions, in: *Climate Change and Ocean Governance – Politics and Policy for Threatened Seas* (2019), pp. 29–31, *supra* (n. 1); For a more general discussion on 'legal output' from international organisations see more in Nigel D. White, *The Law of International Organisations* (2005) pp. 158–161.

32 The 1948 Convention on the International Maritime Organization (IMO Convention), Art. 1 concerning the purposes of the organisation.

33 IMO, MSC/Circ. 1056(2002) and MEPC/Circ. 399 (2002).

34 IMO, A 26/Res.1024 (2010).

35 See also H. Edwin Anderson, Polar Shipping, The Forthcoming Polar Code and Implications for the Polar Environment, *Journal of Maritime Law and Commerce* 43(1) (2012), 70–73.

36 F. L. Kirgis refers to such codes and guidelines as 'super recommendations'; see F. L. Kirgis, Specialized law-making process, *United Nations Legal Order* 1 (1995), 84.

37 F. L. Kirgis, Shipping, *United Nations Legal Order* 2 (1995), 715.

38 Aldo Chircop, The International Maritime Organization, in: Rothwell *et al.* (eds.), *The Oxford Handbook of the Law of the Sea* (Oxford: Oxford University Press, 2015), p. 420.

39 Report of the Maritime Safety Committee of the Eighty-Sixth Session, IMO Doc. MSC 86/26, 12 June 2009, para. 23.32.

40 The SOLAS amendments were adopted during the 94th session of MSC, in November 2014 and the environmental provisions in MARPOL were adopted during the 68th session of MEPC the following year in May 2015.

41 IMO, MSC/Circ. 1056, MEPC/Circ. 399 (2002), section 16.1.

42 IMO, Resolution MEPC.264(68), p. 8.

43 Maritime Safety Committee (MSC), see the IMO Convention Part VII.
44 Marine Environment Protection Committee, see the IMO Convention Part IX.
45 For a detailed exposition of the development and finalisation of the Polar Code, see further in Øystein Jensen, The international Code for Ships Operating in Polar Waters: Finalization, Adoption and the Law of the Sea, *Arctic Review on Law and Politics* 1 (2016), 61–64.
46 IMO, MEPC 68/21/Add.1.
47 J. Ashley Roach, A Note on Making the Polar Code Mandatory, *International Law and Politics of the Arctic Ocean: Essays in Honor of Donat Pharand* (2015), pp. 127–128.
48 Chapter XIV, regulation 2 (2).
49 The IACS standard are also incorporated by reference into the IMO Guidelines for Ships Operating in Arctic Ice-covered Waters.
50 For a technical clarification of terms and ice conditions, see the Polar Code (Note 10), Introduction, Section 2 Definitions.
51 General exceptions are found in Chapter 1, regulation 3 and specific exceptions are found in each of the convention's chapters.
52 Chapter 3 on 'ship structure' and Chapter 4 on 'subdivision and stability'. Chapter 5 regarding watertight and watertight integrity is also worth mentioning.
53 Example: Chapter 11 on 'voyage planning' and Chapter 12 on manning and training.
54 1978 International Convention on Standards of Training, Certification and Watch-keeping for Seafarers (STCW).
55 Chapter 12 'Manning and Training (12.3), cf. (12.2).
56 See list for ratification of the individual annexes. www.imo.org/en/About/Conventions/StatusOfConventions/Pages/Default.aspx (Status of Conventions).
57 Donald R. Rothwell and Tim Stephens, *The International Law of the Sea* (Cambridge: Cambridge University Press, 2016), p. 378.
58 Regulations for the Prevention of Pollution by Oil (Annex I); Regulations for the Control of Pollution by Noxious Liquid Substances in Bulk (Annex II); Prevention of Pollution by Harmful Substances Carried by Sea in Packaged Form (Annex III); Prevention of Pollution by Sewage from Ships (Annex IV); Prevention of Pollution by Garbage from Ships (Annex V); Prevention of Air Pollution from Ships (Annex VI).
59 Resolution MPEC.265(68) Amendments to the annex of the protocol of 1978 relating to the international convention for the prevention of pollution from ships 1973 (adopted on 15 May 2015).
60 In relation to Greenlandic waters, it is the Danish state that is responsible for this.
61 Doris König, The Enforcement of the International Law of the Sea by Coastal and Port States, *ZaöRV* 62 (2002), p. 2.
62 Richard O. G. Wanerman, Freezing out Noncompliant Ships: Why the Arctic Council Must Enforce the Polar Code, *Case Western Reserve Journal of International Law* 47 (2015), 429.
63 LOS Convention Art. 94 (1).
64 Thor Falkanger, Hans Jacob Bull and Lasse Brautaset, *Scandinavian Maritime Law – The Norwegian Perspective* (2017), p. 56.
65 Kristina Maria Siig, Private classification organisations acting on behalf of the regulatory authorities within the shipping industry, *SIMPLY* 482 (2016), 220.
66 Flag State compliance is generally considered among the main issues in shipping, often referring to the so-called 'open registers' or 'flags of convenience', that refer to flag States with much more lax, sometimes non-existent, determination to ensure compliance. A booklet is issued each year by the International Chamber of Shipping concerning flag State performance. The assessment is available at: www.ics-shipping.org.
67 Richard A. Barnes, Flag States, *The Oxford Handbook of the Law of the Sea* (Oxford: Oxford University Press, 2015), p. 304–305.

68 LOC Convention Art. 211 (2).
69 Kristin Bartenstein, Part XII. Protection and Preservation of the Marine Environment (art. 211), *United Nations Convention on the Law of the Sea – A Commentary* (2017), p. 1429 (17).
70 For information on classification societies in an EU perspective, see Vincent Power, Maritime Safety: Ship Inspection and Survey Organisations, *EU Shipping Law* (2019) Chapter 29.
71 The Code for Recognized Organizations (RO Code) by resolutions MEPC.237(65) and MSC.349(92). For specific Polar Code reference to ROs see Part I-a, Chapter 1, 1.2. 'definitions' (1.2.6).
72 Øystein Jensen, The International Code for Ships Operating in Polar Waters: Finalization, Adoption and the Law of the Sea, *Arctic Review on Law and Politics* 1 (2016), 70.
73 Regarding the possibility of 'class hopping' and the prominent example of the *Erika* case, see in Elizabeth R. DeSombre, *Flagging Standards – Globalization and Environmental, Safety and Labor Regulations at Sea* (2006), p. 183.
74 LOS Convention, Art. 217 (3).
75 Erik J. Molenaar, Port and Coastal States, *The Oxford Handbook of the Law of the Sea* (Oxford: Oxford University Press, 2015), p. 280.
76 MARPOL Art. 5 (1) and 5 (2).
77 Andrew Rakestraw, Open Oceans and Marine Debris: Solutions for the Ineffective Enforcement of MARPOL Annex V, *Hastings International and Comparative Law Review* 35(2) (2012), p. 394.
78 Kristin Bartenstein, Part XII. Protection and preservation of the marine environment (art. 218), *United Nations Convention on the Law of the Sea – A Commentary* (2017), p. 1494–1495.
79 The EEZ is considered part of the high seas, when it comes to navigational rights, see Art. 58 (1) of the LOS Convention.
80 In the case of Greenland, this involves Executive Order No. 588 of 2 June 2017 on the discharge of waste from ships in the exclusive economic zone beside Greenland and Executive Order No. 589 of 22 May 2017 on the discharge of oil in the exclusive economic zone beside Greenland.
81 Yoshifumi Tanaka, *The International Law of the Sea* (Cambridge: Cambridge University Press, 2015), p. 320.
82 See §§ 7–11 of the Environmental Damage Act. Implementing Order no. 916 of 3 July 2015. See especially § 7, subparagraph 1, item 1, where the term 'negative effect' is used directly in accordance with the somewhat vague conceptual apparatus of Coase.
83 See havmiljøvogter.dk.
84 See Peter Pagh, U.1991B.121.
85 See Executive Order no. 1697 of 11 December 2015 for Greenland on safe shipping.
86 It may be surprising that the requirement for mandatory pilotage only arises when there are at least 250 passengers on board.

Part III

Environmental security and marine resources cooperation

9 Climate law implications of the Maritime Silk Road Initiative

Lorenzo Schiano di Pepe

Development action plans

'The Belt and Road', 'One Belt, One Road' (OBOR) or 'Belt and Road Initiative' (BRI) is a development action plan, a strategy and a framework led by the People's Republic of China (PRC) and involving other Asian, European and, to a lesser extent, African countries. It is aimed at strengthening China's role in the global economy while having also a geopolitical dimension. It was unveiled by PRC President Xi Jinping in 2013 and consists of two main elements: the land-based 'Silk Road Economic Belt' and the seagoing 21st Century 'Maritime Silk Road' (MSR).

An 'action plan' was jointly released on 28 March 2015, by three key Chinese institutions, namely the Ministry of Foreign Affairs, the National Development and Reform Commission and the Ministry of Commerce, with a view to setting out a vision for encouraging seamless trade between China and Europe by both rail and cargo ship, based on new Chinese-built infrastructures, reduced tariffs and a simplified customs administration.[1]

The maritime component of the OBOR initiative, unlike its land counterpart, is mostly oriented towards ASEAN and its Member States and raises a number of different legal issues. Some of them are, of course, related to the fact that not all the countries involved in the 21st Century MSR are in agreement with China's policy in the region including, in particular, the South China Sea, which may render it more difficult for the overall project to receive unqualified support from key actors.

This chapter aims at focussing on an apparently indirect but undeniably very important consequence of the MSR or, rather, of its actual enforcement in due course, concerning the impact of the increased international shipping generated by it on current climate change patterns.

There are arguably two separate reasons that justify such an approach. First and foremost, once implemented, the MSR will determine a rise in maritime traffic flow. Indeed, an increase in trade streams, including maritime ones, is one of the core objectives of the overall OBOR concept. Such a trend, if not accompanied by the introduction of appropriate tools aimed at reducing the impact thereof, will augment the environmental pressure on the atmosphere and, in turn, on the Earth's climate.

Second, the growth of maritime traffic is particularly going to affect flows between China and Europe and the European Union (EU) in particular, where very different approaches exist with regard to the way in which to address international shipping's contribution to global climate change.

Research has demonstrated that international shipping significantly contributes to global climate change. This is basically due to the fact that bunker oil, in the burning process that is typical of fuel consumption, produces a number of polluting substances, including carbon dioxide (CO_2).

According to a report published in 2015 by the International Maritime Organization (IMO), after having been approved by its Marine Environment Protection Committee (MEPC), '[f]or the year 2012 … international shipping account[ed] for approximately 2.2% and 2.1% of global CO_2 and [greenhouse gas (GHG)] emissions on a CO_2 equivalent (CO_{2e}) basis, respectively'.[2] In addition, '[f]or the period 2007–2012, on average, shipping accounted for approximately 3.1% of annual global CO_2 and approximately 2.8% of annual GHGs on a CO_{2e} basis'.[3]

It is also recognised, by the same source, that '[m]aritime CO_2 emissions are projected to increase significantly in the coming decades' so that business-as-usual scenarios 'project an increase by 50% to 250% in the period by 2050'.[4] Although '[f]urther action on efficiency and emissions can mitigate the emission growth', almost all foreseeable scenarios 'project emissions in 2050 to be higher than in 2012'.[5] In this respect, the point is made by this critical IMO study that while '[e]missions projections demonstrate that improvements in efficiency are important in mitigating emissions increase … even modelled improvements with the greatest energy savings could not yield a downward trend'. Moreover, '[c]ompared to regulatory or market-driven improvements in efficiency, changes in the fuel mix have a limited impact on GHG emissions, assuming that fossil fuels remain dominant'.[6]

Among the findings of the report, it has to be noted that '[m]ost other emissions increase in parallel with CO_2 and fuel, with some notable exceptions', including methane, whose emissions 'are projected to increase rapidly (albeit from a low base) as the share of LNG in the fuel mix increases', and nitrogen oxides, projected to 'increase at a lower rate than CO_2 emissions as a result of Tier II and Tier III engines entering the fleet'.[7] 'Emissions of particulate matter', finally, 'show an absolute decrease until 2020, and sulphurous oxides continue to decline through to 2050, mainly because of MARPOL Annex VI requirements on the sulphur content of fuels'.[8]

That having been said, shipping is nonetheless usually referred to as a relatively environmentally friendly means of transport, especially considering the available alternatives. In a leaflet published by the International Chamber of Shipping (ICS) on the basis of the IMO Study above, the point is made that, in terms of grams of CO_2 per tonne/km, a very large container vessel will produce 3.0, an oil tanker 5.9 and a bulk carrier 7.9, while the production from an equivalent number of trucks will be 80 and from typical cargo planes (such as B747) 435.[9]

Relevant normative framework

The way in which international climate law developed since the adoption of the United Nations Framework Convention on Climate Change (UNFCCC) in 1992 is well known and has been the subject of countless publications.[10] While it is obviously not possible to give a full account of such developments in the context of the present contribution, it is important to recall here that, when the UNFCCC was concluded, it basically consisted of a series of principles and procedural obligations, according to the typical format of a 'framework' convention, but fell short of providing a body of coercive obligations and a set of precise deadlines. The objective that the UNCCC intended and still intends to achieve is, nonetheless, straightforward: to stabilise GHGs in the atmosphere at a level that would prevent dangerous anthropogenic interference with the climate system.[11]

It was only five years later, with the adoption of the Kyoto Protocol (KP) in 1997, that an international agreement was arrived at, as to the allocation of legally binding commitments (entailing emission reductions or controlled increases of six different types of GHGs) for a number of industrialised States.[12] In short, parties to the KP decided that developed countries listed in Annex B to the KP would release into the atmosphere, in the five-year commitment period 2008–2012, a limited quantity of GHGs expressed as a percentage of the same States' emissions as achieved in 1990. The overall objective of a 5 per cent reduction of GHG emissions globally was to be obtained as a result of differentiated commitments undertaken by the States concerned, ranging from reductions pledged by the EU (–6 per cent); USA (–7 per cent); and Canada (–6 per cent) to the controlled increases of Norway (+1 per cent); Australia (+8 per cent); and Iceland (+10 per cent).

Crucially, for the purpose of the present reflections, Article 2(2) of the KP made it clear that shipping as an activity was not to be covered thereby, since 'Parties included in Annex I' to the UNFCCC were required to 'pursue limitation or reduction of emissions of greenhouse gases not controlled by the Montreal Protocol from aviation and marine bunker fuels, working through the International Civil Aviation Organization and the International Maritime Organization, respectively'.

Much has been written on the limited success of the KP and on the possible reasons for it, including its delayed entry into force (in 2005) and the lack of ratification by some of the key players and major emitters listed in its Annex B, such as the United States of America (USA). Be as it may, the KP was always intended to have a limited temporal scope of application. This is why the need to adopt a new international instrument has been under discussion since 2009 and in particular since when, at the (in)famous Copenhagen Conference (7–18 December 2009), States parties to the UNFCCC were only able to reach a political 'accord', with no legal effect, on how to follow-up to the KP with a view to achieving the UNCCC's objectives.[13]

A potentially significant move occurred three years after the Copenhagen Conference, in Doha, when an agreement on a series of amendments to the KP was adopted, including the establishment of a new eight-year commitment period starting with 2014, a revised list of GHGs to be covered and the upgrade and strengthening of the applicable reduction targets. The so-called 'Doha Agreement', however, failed to achieve the required number of ratifications required for its entry into force.

The 2015 Paris Agreement and the way forward

The most recent significant development in climate change governance is undoubtedly represented by the so-called 'Paris Agreement' (PA), adopted in connection with the meeting of the Conference of the Parties (CoP) to the UNFCCC held from 30 November to 11 December 2015. The PA, which is firmly based on the principles of equity and common but differentiated responsibilities and capabilities,[14] can be broadly said to be founded on five main pillars: adaptation, financial assistance, technology development and transfer, capacity building and transparency.

There are differing views as to the merits and flaws of such an outcome and it is clearly not possible in this context to examine it fully, let alone in detail. For the purposes of the present discussion, however, it is important to note that the PA is a legally binding instrument, a result that was not to be given for granted until the very last stages of the negotiations. It entered into force on 5 October 2016, i.e. on the 30th day after the date of the 55th ratification by a State party to the UNFCCC, determining the coverage of at least 55 per cent of total global GHG emissions. As of December 2018, there are 184 parties to the PA out of the 197 parties to the UNFCCC.

Admittedly, though, in contrast with previous achievements (namely, the KP), no firm reduction or limited increase obligations is set forth, not even for industrialised countries. Instead, a long-term commitment has been subscribed to, aiming at holding the increase in global average temperature 'well below 2°C above pre-industrial levels' and at 'pursuing efforts to limit the temperature increase to 1.5°C above pre-industrial levels, recognizing that this would significantly reduce the risks and impacts of climate change'.[15]

Considering the approach taken, it is clear that a key role in the successful enforcement of the PA will be played by nationally determined contributions that individual States will (voluntarily) pledge to.[16] Bearing in mind that the relevant plans will have to be submitted by each party every five years,[17] one has also to note that, as a requirement, each contracting State's successive nationally determined contribution shall 'represent a progression beyond the Party's then current nationally determined contribution and reflect its highest possible ambition, reflecting its common but differentiated responsibilities and respective capabilities, in the light of different national circumstances'.[18] It remains to be seen to what extent this will actually ensure a progressive increase in the level of the commitments successively undertaken by individual States rather than an incentive, for some States at least, to act somewhat unambitiously in the early phases of implementation of the Agreement.

The absence of firm commitments is coherent with the style of many of the provisions contained in the PA, which, despite its formally legally binding nature, is often worded in hortatory form. Reference can be made, by way of an example, to the fact that in the context of Article 4, where the intention of reaching the 'global peaking of greenhouse gas emissions as soon as possible' is spelled out as a cornerstone of the overall agreement, paragraph 4 makes it very clear that, on the one hand, '[d]eveloped country Parties *should* continue taking the lead by undertaking economy-wide absolute emission reduction targets' and, on the other hand, '[d]eveloping countries *should* continue enhancing their mitigation efforts, and *are encouraged to* move over time towards economy-wide emission reduction or limitations targets in the light of different national circumstances'.[19]

Against such a relatively weak legal background, at least from the standpoint of the substantive obligations adhered to by the contracting parties to the PA, one might have expected negotiators to be able to introduce stricter monitoring (and related procedural) requirements, with a view to verifying in a timely fashion the actual progress towards the agreed global targets referred to above.

Regrettably, however, the only two clear deadlines that can be traced in the PA and its accompanying documents are set at 2018, when the International Panel on Climate Change (IPCC) will be required to provide a 'special report … on the impacts of global warming of 1.5°C above pre-industrial levels and related global greenhouse gas emission pathways',[20] and 2023, when the UNFCCC CoP, serving as the meeting of the parties to the PA 'shall undertake its first global stocktake', which means that stock will have to be taken (in 2023 and not before) 'of the implementation of [the] Agreement and its long-term goals'. As to the outcome of this stocktaking process, this appears to be – by and large – of merely informative character, since it is primarily aimed at 'updating and enhancing, in a nationally determined manner, [the parties'] actions and support in accordance with the relevant provision of [the] Agreement, as well as … enhancing international cooperation for climate action'.[21]

The system was put to the test for the first time on the occasion of CoP 24, held in Katowice, in December 2018. Although no meaningful new substantive commitment was subscribed to in Poland, parties were able to agree (with some difficulty) on a set of rules designed to ensure the workability of the PA, including those relating to measurement and reporting of national pledges.[22] It remains to be seen whether future meetings in 2019 and 2020 will be able to yield new emission targets as invoked by some State parties and environmental groups in line with the recent findings of the Intergovernmental Panel on Climate Change (IPCC).

Of particular interest for the scope of this chapter, is the fact that, despite requests coming from certain States and the 'open' attitude of significant segments of the industry, shipping (as well as aviation) was, in the end, not specifically covered by the PA, notwithstanding the declared ambition of the negotiators to approach the climate change problem by adopting an 'economy-wide' approach with regard to both absolute emission reduction and limitation targets. Yet, in contrast with the KP's Article 2(2), no explicit exclusion of the shipping sector is present in the text of the PA, nor is there a reference to the work and competence of the IMO (or the ICAO) in this area. Such exclusions have attracted the criticism of environmental NGOs[23] as well as, more surprisingly, of selected business actors.[24]

In a line of continuity with the KP, obligations under the PA are assigned as a matter of principle to contracting States, notwithstanding the existence in the PA itself of multiple references to the role of the private sector. This, as it shall be seen, represents one of the major difficulties in developing a proper legal regime applicable to GHG emissions by ships, due to the 'mobile' nature of the sources of the emissions and the likely absence of any substantive link between a State and ships flying its flag. While the question will be taken up below in some more detail, before moving on, it is appropriate to refer to Article 6(4) of the PA, where an indication is given of the establishment of a mechanism intended to 'contribute to the mitigation of greenhouse gas emissions and support sustainable development'. Such a mechanism shall aim, *inter alia*, '[t]o incentivize and facilitate participation in the mitigation of greenhouse gas emissions by public and private entities authorized by a Party'. Although the provision is placed in a context where voluntary cooperative approaches are dealt with, the possibility should not be excluded to rely on such a mechanism for the purpose of addressing some of the peculiarities posed by the direct involvement of the maritime industry in the always-developing climate change regime.

The global, sector-based approach and the role of the International Maritime Organization

The United Nations Convention on the Law of the Sea (UNCLOS) requires contracting parties 'to protect and preserve the marine environment'.[25] It further specifies that States 'shall take, individually or jointly as appropriate, all measures consistent with [the] Convention that are necessary to prevent, reduce and control pollution of the marine environment *from any source*',[26] thus including also – at least in principle – the emission of GHGs. It will be in fact assumed, for the purpose of the present discussion, that the release of GHGs into the atmosphere by a ship is liable to determine the introduction of

> substances or energy into the marine environment … which results or is likely to result in such deleterious effects as harm to living resources and marine life, hazards to human health, hindrance to marine activities, including fishing and other legitimate uses of the sea, impairment of quality for use of sea water and reduction of amenities[27]

That is, what amounts to 'pollution of the marine environment' according to Article 1(4) of UNCLOS.

UNCLOS contains a number of provisions that are relevant to atmospheric pollution. Reference has primarily to be made, in this respect, to Articles 212 and 222, dealing, respectively, with legislative and enforcement jurisdiction. According to Article 212, in particular:

> States shall adopt laws and regulations to prevent, reduce and control pollution of the marine environment from or through the atmosphere, applicable to the air space under their sovereignty and to vessels flying their flag or vessels or aircraft of their registry.

In conducting their legislative action, States are required to *take into account* 'internationally agreed rules, standards and recommended practices and procedures and the safety of air navigation'.[28]

A key role is attributed to 'competent international organizations' and diplomatic conferences, through which States are expected to 'establish global and regional rules, standards and recommended practices and procedures to prevent, reduce and control such pollution'.[29] The IMO is universally considered to be the international organisation that this, as well as other provisions of UNCLOS, refer to, when dealing with vessel-source pollution prevention, including atmospheric pollution.[30]

It emerges from the succinct account that has just been given, that the IMO's mandate to govern GHG emissions from ships can said to be based on at least two different sets of sources: the UNFCCC system and, in particular, the KP, on the one hand, with specific reference to its Article 2(2), as briefly mentioned above, and UNCLOS, on the other hand, to be combined of course with the Convention establishing the IMO.[31]

The most important IMO achievement in the field of atmospheric pollution is undoubtedly represented by the adoption and entry into force of Annex VI to the International Convention for the Prevention of Pollution from Ships (MARPOL), entitled 'Regulations for the Prevention of Air Pollution from Ships'.[32] MARPOL Annex VI, in its original version, set limits on sulphur oxide and nitrogen oxide emissions from ship exhausts and prohibited deliberate emissions of ozone depleting substances. The Annex also designated emission control areas and introduced more stringent standards for sulphur and nitrogen oxide and particulate matter. It was not meant, however, to cover also the emission of GHGs from ships.

Although the IMO started working on possible GHG standards after the adoption of the UNFCCC and more or less simultaneously to the adoption of the KP, it was only in 2011 that a new Chapter 4 was adopted, introducing a series of amendments to MARPOL Annex VI and expressly dealing with 'Regulations on Energy Efficiency for Ships'. Such amendments, which entered into force on 1 January 2013, were intended to optimise the energy efficiency of ships and reduce emissions caused by fuel oil through the use of technical standards and operational measures *without necessarily requiring ships to be fitted with new technologies or to respect new designs*, let alone introducing emission reduction (or limited increase) targets.

Two mandatory tools were specifically put in place by the new Chapter 4: namely, an Energy Efficiency Design Index (EEDI) and a Ship Energy Efficiency Management Plan (SEEMP).

The EEDI is basically intended to measure the quantity of CO_2 emitted by a ship per unit of transport. Only new ships of 400 gross tonnes and above are subject to EEDI. A ship will be considered 'new' for the purpose of EEDI rules, when the relevant building contract has been placed on or after 1 January 2013, its keel has been laid on or after 1 July 2013 or its delivery occurs on or after 1 July 2015. The possibility of a waiver exists, but only for a limited period of time and subject to the relevant contract, keel or delivery being, respectively placed, laid or foreseen by certain set dates. Two additional features of the EEDI are worth mentioning in the present context: first, the wide (but not general) scope of application of the system as far as the types of ships covered are concerned (while these range from tankers to bulk carriers, gas carriers and cargo ships and although some of the originally excluded ships have subsequently been included,[33] a significant percentage of global emissions is still left out of the system). Second, an International Energy Efficiency Certificate has been introduced, to be issued to ships whose emissions, after a survey, are confirmed to be in accordance with the Chapter 4.

In contrast to the EEDI, the SEEMP applies to all ships and is designed as a mechanism to improve the energy efficiency thereof. A series of guidelines have been adopted by the IMO's MEPC in recent years for the purpose of facilitating the implementation of such management plans and incentivising adherence to measures relating, for example to voyage planning, speed optimisation and weather routeing. Specific directions are given with regard to hull maintenance and, in particular, to the use of new technologies in coating, as well as to the proper maintenance of the machinery also through adequate training of crew members and other staff.[34]

The controversial stance of the European Union and the adoption of regulation (EU) 2015/757

In its communication entitled 'Blue Growth: Opportunities for Marine and Maritime Sustainable Growth' of 2012, the European Commission noted *inter alia* that,

> the need to reduce greenhouse gas emissions has not only driven the deployment of offshore renewable energy installations, but has also provided a further impetus for energy savings and an additional reason to favour seaborne transport over land transport due to its lower emissions per tonne-kilometre.[35]

Hence, if, on the one hand, maritime transport is expected to play a greater and greater role in the years to come, in light of its reduced environmental impact compared with other means of transport, on the other hand, a situation must be avoided whereby emissions from the shipping sector are not subject to a proper regulatory framework.

When Directive 2009/29/EC of the European Parliament and of the Council of 23 April 2009 was adopted, amending Directive 2003/87/EC 'so as to improve and extend the greenhouse gas emission allowance trading scheme of the Community',[36] it was made clear in its recital no. 3 that, had no international agreement including international maritime emissions in its reduction targets been adopted by 31 December 2011, the Commission would have made a proposal 'to include international maritime emissions according to harmonised modality in the [EU] reduction commitment, with the aim of the proposed act entering into force by 2013'.[37]

It is against this backdrop that, in the absence of an agreement adopted through the IMO or the UNFCCC, Regulation (EU) 2015/757 'on the monitoring, reporting and verification of carbon dioxide emissions from maritime transport and amending Directive 2009/16/EC' was adopted by the European Parliament and the Council on 29 April 2015, following a proposal by the European Commission.[38] A few features of the recently adopted Regulation, which has attracted significant criticism from the industry,[39] appear of particular interest and shall therefore provide the main focus of the reflections contained in the remaining part of the present section.

First of all, it is important to observe that the scope of application of the Regulation is reasonably wide. All ships above 5000 gross tonnes are in fact covered, with the exception of warships, naval auxiliaries, fishing vessels, wooden ships of a primitive build, ships not propelled by mechanical means and government ships used for non-commercial purposes. Ships are subject to the Regulation on a 'per voyage' basis, as long as they are engaged in a voyage to a port located under the jurisdiction of a Member State or from a port located under the jurisdiction of a Member State. In line with the indications contained in recital no. 20, however, only CO_2 emissions are taken into account, being this 'the most relevant greenhouse gas emitted by maritime transport', bearing in mind, on the one hand, the need to 'reduce the administrative burden for shipowners and operators' and, on the other, the fact that '[i]n the light of the rapidly developing scientific understanding of the impact of non-CO_2 related emissions from maritime transport on the global climate', 'an updated assessment should be carried out regularly in the context of [the] Regulation' and 'the Commission should analyse the implications for policies and measures, in order to reduce such emissions'.[40]

Second, and moving to the normative approach endorsed by the Regulation, it has to be noted that the European legislators have aimed at introducing in the shipping sector a 'monitoring and reporting' system. As far as the precise method to be used for this purpose, the Regulation, far from imposing a single option, lists no less than four different alternatives (including 'Bunker Fuel Delivery Note', 'Bunker fuel tank monitoring on board', 'Flow meters for applicable combustion processes' and 'Direct CO_2 emissions measurements') so as to allow fleets to take advantage of requirements and data 'already available on board ships'. Interestingly, although no greenhouse gas emission reduction commitment is presently implied by the Regulation, it is made very clear that the Regulation itself represents the 'first step' of a 'staged approach' towards 'the inclusion of maritime transport emissions in the Union's greenhouse gas reduction commitment, alongside emissions from other sectors that are already contributing to that commitment'.[41]

A third aspect of the Regulation that is worth addressing relates to the timeline that has been devised for ensuring its full entry into operation. In fact, although the Regulation entered into force on 1 July 2015, the first monitoring plans by the concerned companies was to be submitted to accredited verifiers only by 31 August 2017. As to the actual monitoring activities, these were set to start on 1 January 2018, since from this day 'companies shall, based on the monitoring plan assessed … monitor CO_2 emissions for each ship on a per-voyage and an annual basis'.[42] From 2019, in turn, on 28 April of each year,

> companies shall submit to the Commission and to the authorities of the flag States concerned … an emission report concerning the CO_2 emissions and other relevant information for the entire reporting period for each ship under their responsibility, which has been verified as satisfactory by a verifier in accordance with Article 13.[43]

That is, after a verification process has taken place intended to 'assess the conformity of the monitoring plan with the requirements laid down in Articles 6 and 7'.[44]

One cannot exclude as a possible reason for adopting the staged approach that has just been described, alongside the technical difficulties that are typical of the sector, the intent to favour (or at least to prepare the ground for) the attainment of meaningful developments at the international level. A crucial provision in this respect is represented by Article 22(3) of the Regulation. The Commission is in fact thereby called to review the Regulation in order to ensure its alignment with any international agreement or global 'monitoring, reporting and verification system for greenhouse emissions' or 'global measures to reduce greenhouse emissions from maritime transport' if and when such a result is reached.

After all, in a study prepared by the European Parliament's Policy Department A on 'Economic and Scientific Policy' for the Committee on the Environment, Public Health and Food Safety, and whose manuscript was completed in November 2015 (and therefore after the adoption of Regulation 757), the point was made that '[e]stablishing reduction targets for [the aviation and maritime] sectors would provide clear signals for all actors in these sectors and thus contribute to improving investment perspectives in both sectors with their long investment cycles'.[45] The study further noted that 'potential targets range from a somewhat reduced increase of future emissions over a stabilization at 2020 levels to a full decarbonisation of those sectors by 2050 derived from a global carbon budget approach' and concluded that 'it is important to establish targets for international aviation and maritime transport which clearly indicate that emissions cannot grow unlimited and unregulated'.[46]

Recent developments, lessons to be learned and challenges ahead

The most recent development within the IMO took place in April 2018, with the adoption by the IMO's MEPC of Resolution MEPC.304 (72) 'Initial IMO Strategy on Reduction of GHG Emissions from Ships'. The main element of the Resolution consists of a 'vision' according to how the IMO expresses its commitment to 'reducing GHG emissions from international shipping and, as a matter of urgency, aims to phase them out as soon as possible in this century'.

In addition, among the levels of ambitions declared by the IMO, particularly notable is the objective,

> to peak GHG emissions from international shipping as soon as possible by at least 50% by 2050 compared to 2008 whilst pursuing efforts towards phasing them out as called for in the Vision as a point on a pathway of CO_2 emissions reduction consistent with the [PA] temperature goals.

Far from being a stand-alone, self-sufficient instrument, the IMO Strategy provides for a policy framework for future actions. Indeed, the Strategy itself call for 'candidate' short-term, mid-term and long-term measures.

At present, when the international community may be finally prepared to move towards a set of coherent and comprehensive rules governing the contribution of international shipping to climate change, a few remarks seem particularly appropriate on what has been learned so far in this respect and what lies ahead in terms of challenges, based on the assumption that the sector may witness new developments at the international as well as at the EU law level.

A general question that has been repeatedly raised relates to the identification of the most appropriate regulatory level for addressing the subject of vessel-source GHG, and in particular CO_2, emissions. As already mentioned, the industry has questioned the decision of the EU to adopt its own monitoring, reporting and verification system on several grounds, including the possible impairment of ongoing IMO negotiations, the creation of an unnecessary administrative burden on ship operators, the risk to have commercially sensitive information transmitted to, and published by, the European Commission and the introduction of sanctions for non-compliance.

As already said, the IMO Strategy is presented as a roadmap intended to be coherent, as a matter of principle, with the PA. It is, however, not clear to what extent each and every short-, medium- and long-term measures devised thereby (and the combination thereof) will ensure consistency with the existing EU regime or, in other words, at what stage a reasonable degree of consistency between the two regimes will in fact be achieved. Until the above does not happen, the EU will be faced with the possibility of third States being unwilling to have their ships subject to the procedural requirements set out by the Regulation when visiting an EU port, as it had already occurred, in the aviation sector, as a consequence of the adoption of Directive 2008/101/EC of the European

Parliament and of the Council of 19 November 2008 'amending Directive 2003/87/EC so as to include aviation activities in the scheme for greenhouse gas emission allowance trading within the Community'.[47]

Should, however, an instrument or a set of instruments be developed equivalent to an agreement along the lines envisaged by the EU Regulation, it remains to be seen to what extent the European Commission and, in turn, the EU, will be willing to, respectively, propose and adopt 'amendments ... in order to ensure alignment with that international agreement'.[48]

In the case of aviation emissions, as it is well known, the move by the EU prompted the launch of international negotiations and, to allow time for their completion, was followed by a unilateral decision by the EU to suspend the application of its Emission Trading Scheme (ETS) requirements, in 2012, to flights to and from non-EU countries. With effect from 2013 to 2016, an amendment was introduced to the effect that only emissions from flights within the European Economic Area (EEA) would be subject to the EU ETS in view of a global market-based mechanism addressing international aviation emissions being developed within the ICAO framework by 2016. Admittedly, the point could be made in support of the similar measure recently adopted with regard to emissions by shipping, that the EU may, in so doing, be able to trigger (or to 'force') a negotiating process at the international level, as it did in the aviation sector. There are, however, additional obstacles in the maritime field that Regulation No 2015/757 may not be able to easily overcome, as shall briefly be discussed later on.

A different, although somewhat related point that has to be made, concerns the actual consequences of a failure to comply with the monitoring and reporting obligations set out by the Regulation for two or more consecutive reporting periods in case 'other enforcement measures have failed to ensure compliance'.[49] Under such circumstances, in fact, 'the competent authority of the Member State of the port of entry may issue an expulsion order which shall be notified to the Commission, the European Maritime Safety Authority (EMSA), the other Member States and the flag State concerned', so that 'every Member State shall refuse entry of the ship concerned into any of its ports until the company fulfils its monitoring and reporting obligations'. The fact that this 'shall be without prejudice to international maritime rules applicable to ships in distress' and that a 'right to an effective remedy before a court' shall be assured to the ship-owner or operator of the ship or its representative in the Member State does not seem enough to avoid and contrast possible challenges concerning the compatibility of such a provision, not only with several Law of the Sea rules (including, for example those set in bilateral treaties providing for a right of access to foreign ports), but also with general principles of EU law including certainty of law and proportionality.

In light of the recent developments at the IMO, in the medium term, the adoption of an international agreement on a 'global monitoring, reporting and verification system for greenhouse gas emissions' remains possible and, in any event, certainly much more so than one on 'global measures to reduce greenhouse emissions from maritime transport'. In order for such a result to be achieved, however, a political compromise will have to be found on the respective roles to be played by industrialised and developing countries, bearing in mind the respective weights of the two 'groups' when it comes to the percentage of world tonnage represented and, thus, the need to have on board developing nations' fleets too.

In this respect, the claim is often made that, in order to comply with one of the UNFCCC's (as well as the PA's) founding principles, developing nations should be put in a position to benefit from a treatment reflecting their differentiated responsibilities ad capabilities even when it comes to regulating GHGs emitted from ships and even when what is at stake is the establishment of a monitoring and reporting system rather than the introduction of emission targets.[50] To support such a position, it is usually maintained that the alignment to whatever procedure embodied in an international instrument entails a cost to be borne by the States that are parties to that instrument.

An alternative (but not necessarily conflicting) view could be one trying to interpret the principle of common but differentiated responsibilities and capabilities in perspective, considering that the fact that a ship flies a certain flag does not necessarily represent an indication of the existence of a substantive link between that ship and a given national community. Having said that, the point could also be made that, as a consequence, an individual ship and a whole fleet may be considered to represent only in part the developmental conditions of the State whose flag they fly. In this respect, while it is true that an element of differentiation will have to be introduced as a component of any future regime, this will have to be designed – along the lines of principles and detailed provisions that are already contained in the UNFCCC and the KP – having as a core concept the idea to provide the necessary technical assistance to parties in need, i.e. to provide additional rights to such parties rather than to subject them to lighter obligations.[51]

This appears indeed the direction that the IMO is taking. In the 2018 Strategy, in fact, mention is made of the 'special needs' of developing countries 'with regard to capacity-building and technical co-operation'. More specifically, and of course subject to the actual content of the various measures that will be taken in due course, the possibility is envisaged of the MEPC assisting 'the efforts to promote low-carbon technologies by facilitating public partnerships and information exchange' and, even more importantly, 'providing mechanisms for facilitating information sharing, technology transfer, capacity building and technical cooperation'.

Notes

1 *Vision and Actions on Jointly Building Silk Road Economic Belt and 21st-Century Maritime Silk Road*, http://en.ndrc.gov.cn/newsrelease/201503/t20150330_669367. html (accessed 3 December 2018).
2 T. W. P. Smith, J. P. Jalkanen and B. A. Anderson *et al.*, *Third IMO GHG Study 2014*; International Maritime Organization (IMO), London, UK, April 2015, p. 1.

3 *Ibid.*

4 *Ibid.*, p. 4.

5 *Ibid.*

6 *Ibid.*

7 *Ibid.*

8 *Ibid.*

9 *Delivering CO$_2$ Emission Reductions: International Shipping is Part of the Solution,* published in 2015 by the International Chamber of Shipping, www.ics-shipping.org/docs/default-source/resources/environmental-protection/shipsandco2-cop21.pdf?sfvrsn =16 (last visited 3 December 2018).

10 The contribution of academic legal literature on the international climate change regime is incredibly vast. On the UNFCCC in general, see the timely reflections of D. Bodansky, The United Nations Framework Convention on Climate Change, *Yale Journal of International Law* (1993), 518; and D. Goldberg, As the World Burns: Negotiating the Framework Convention on Climate Change, *American Journal of International Law* (1993), 239. For a more recent (and critical) analysis of the role of the UNFCCC, see S. W. Scott, Does the UNFCC Fulfil the Functions Required of a Framework Convention? Why Abandoning the United Nations Framework Convention on Climate Change Might Constitute a Long Overdue Step Forward, *Journal of Environmental Law* (2015), 69.

11 Article 2.

12 See, for example, C. Breidenich, D. Magraw, A. Rowley and J. W. Rubin, The Kyoto Protocol to the United Nations Framework on Climate Change, *American Journal of International Law* (1998), 315.

13 See, for example, D. Bodansky, The Copenhagen Climate Change Conference: A Postmortem, *American Journal of International Law* (2010), 230.

14 For an appraisal of this principle in the climate change context, see T. Honkonen, The Principle of Common But Differentiated Responsibilities in Post-2012 Climate Negotiations, *Review of European Community and International Environmental Law* (2009), 257; more, in general, L. Rajamani, *Differential Treatment in International Environmental Law* (Oxford: n.p., 2006).

15 Article 2(1)(a).

16 Article 2(2).

17 Article 2(9).

18 Article 4(3).

19 Emphasis added.

20 Document FCCC/CP/2015/L.9/Rev.1, par. 21.

21 Article 14.

22 To know more, refer to the dedicated website at https://unfccc.int/event/cop-24 (accessed 21 December 2018).

23 See, in the press, Shipping Dropped from Paris Climate Deal, http://worldmaritime news.com/archives/178438/shipping-dropped-from-paris-climate-deal/ (accessed 3 December 2018).

24 See, in the press, Maersk 'Disappointed' in Shipping's Exclusion from Paris Climate Deal, http://gcaptain.com/maersk-disappointed-by-shippings-omission-from-paris-climate-deal/ (accessed 3 December 2018).

25 Article 192.

26 Article 194(1).

27 Article 1(1)(4).

28 Article 212(1).

29 Article 212(3).

30 T. Treves, La participation de 'l'organisation internationale compétente' aux decisions de l'état côtier dans le nouveau droit de la mer, in: *Le droit intérnational à l'heure de sa codification. études en l'honneur de Roberto Ago,* (n.p.: Milano, 1987), vol. II, p. 473. See also, more recently, C. Pisani, Fair at Sea: The Design of a Future

Legal Instrument on Marine Bunker Fuels Emission within the Climate Change Regime, *Ocean Development and International Law* (2002), 57.

31 For a detailed analysis of some of the implications of these multiple sources of authority, see Y. Shi, Greenhouse Gas Emissions from International Shipping: The Response from China's Shipping Industry to the Regulatory Initiatives of the International Maritime Organization, *International Journal of Marine and Coastal Law* (2015), 77.

32 X. Hinrichs Oyarce, Greenhouse Gas Emissions from Ships and Technology Transfer, in: A. Kirchner and I. Kirchner Freis, *Green Innovations and IPR Management* (n.p.: Alphen aan den Rijn, 2013), p. 215; S. Karim and S. Alam, Climate Change and Reduction of Emissions of Greenhouse Gases from Ships: An Appraisal, *Asian Journal of International Law* (2011), 131. For a domestic perspective see also R. Hildreth and A. Torbitt, International Treaties and U.S. Laws as Tools to Regulate the Greenhouse Gas Emissions from Ships and Ports, *International Journal of Marine and Coastal Law* (2010), 347.

33 MEPC, at its 66th session in 2014, adopted amendments to MARPOL Annex VI, with a view to extend the application of EEDI also to LNG carriers, ro-ro cargo ships, ro-ro passenger ships and cruise passenger ships with non-conventional propulsion.

34 Y. Shi (n. 31), p. 92.

35 European Commission, Blue Growth: Opportunities for Marine and Maritime Sustainable Growth, COM (2012) 494 final, 13 September 2012.

36 OJEU, 5 June 2009, L 140, p. 63.

37 K. Kulovesi, Addressing Sectoral Emissions outside the United Nations Framework Convention on Climate Change: What Roles for Multilateralism, Minilateralism and Unilateralism?, *Review of European Community and International Environmental Law* (2012), 193. On the aviation sector, see also, recently, B. Martinez Romera and H. van Asselt, The International Regulation of Aviation Emissions: Putting Differential Treatment into Practice, *Journal of Environmental Law* (2015), 259.

38 OJEU, 19 May 2015, L 123, p. 55.

39 According to a joint statement of ICS, BIMCO and INTERCARGO,

> [t]here is a real danger that the EU initiative will be seen by non-EU states as an attempt to present them with a fait accompli which includes controversial elements, such as the publication of individual ship efficiency data, which had previously been rejected by the majority of IMO governments during a meeting of the MEPC in October 2014.

www.bimco.org/news/priority-news/20150428_ep_vote_on_regional_co2_measures (accessed 3 December 2018).

40 Recital no. 4.

41 Recital 10.

42 Article 8.

43 Article 11.

44 Article 13(1).

45 European Parliament's Directorate-General for Internal Policies, Policy Department A – Economic and Scientific Policy, Emission Reduction Targets for International Aviation and Shipping, 2015, www.europarl.europa.eu/RegData/etudes/STUD/2015/569964/IPOL_STU(2015)569964_EN.pdf (accessed 18 March 2016).

46 OJEU 2009, L 8, p. 3.

47 L. Schiano di Pepe, European Union Climate Law at the End of the Kyoto Era: Unilateralism, Extraterritoriality and the Future of Global Climate Governance, in: R. V. Percival, J. Lin and W. Piermattei, *Global Environmental Law at a Crossroads* (Cheltenham-Northampton: n.p., 2014), p. 279.

48 Article 22(3).

49 Article 20(3).

50 See, also for further references, Y. Shi (n. 31).

51 X. Hinrichs Oyarce (n. 32), p. 229.

10 Environmental security in the South China Sea region

Cooperation and challenges under the Maritime Silk Road Initiative

Lei Zhang

Introduction

The South China Sea is one of the world busiest and most volatile maritime areas connecting China and Southeast Asia. It is the second most frequently used sea lane in the world, and while in terms of world annual merchant fleet tonnage, over 50 per cent passes through the Strait of Malacca, the Sunda Strait and the Lombok Strait.[1] This sea area is also the global centre of shallow water tropical marine biological diversity.[2] However, the South China Sea is experiencing profound environmental changes, such as serious environmental pollution, increasing scarcity of natural resources, the loss of biodiversity, etc. The First Assessment of the Intergovernmental Panel on Climate Change (IPCC) anticipated that the South China Sea would experience significant climate and ecological change to the detriment of the region's coastal inhabitants, ecosystems and economies, among others.[3] Climate change and its adverse impact made the environmental conditions there even worse.

The environmental challenges have no national boundaries, and any individual country cannot respond alone. Over the past years, there has been a growing sense of urgency in the need to take action in environmental cooperation among South China Sea countries, and they do manage some achievements. For example, ASEAN members have put their priority on environmental cooperation since the Association's 1994 Strategic Plan highlighting the importance of conserving the region's natural resources, protecting its environment and noting the need for greater collective awareness of environmental interconnectedness, for cooperative efforts to be successful.[4] Furthermore, ASEAN and China agreed on a Plan of Action to Implement the Joint Declaration on ASEAN-China Strategic Partnership for Peace and Prosperity for every five-year period and establish the China-ASEAN Environmental Cooperation Centre (CAEC) in Beijing, which opened in May 2011 as the main agency for technical support and implementation of relevant projects.[5] In addition, there are other multilateral and inter-regional environmental cooperations in the South China Sea region. However, there still lacks a consensus on 'environmental security' among the South China Sea countries, that is to say, some countries are reluctant to treat the environmental challenges as important as the security issue, which leads some environmental protection policies to stay just 'on paper'.

In 2013, Chinese President Xi Jinping stated that China hoped to 'vigorously develop a maritime partnership with ASEAN in a joint effort to build the 21st-Century Maritime Silk Road'.[6] This will play a key role in sustainable development and the prospects for a community of common destiny of China and ASEAN States. In 2015, the National Development and Reform Commission, Ministry of Foreign Affairs, and Ministry of Commerce of China, with State Council authorisation, issued the 'Vision and Actions on Jointly Building Silk Road Economic Belt and 21st-Century Maritime Silk Road'.[7] This document mentioned it would: 'Deepen cooperation in environmental protection industries' and 'increase cooperation in conserving eco-environment, protecting biodiversity, and tackling climate change'. This could indicate that environmental cooperation is an important aspect of the One Belt One Road Initiative. Against this background, the 'Maritime Silk Road' could be regarded as a new chance for China and ASEAN states to deepen China-ASEAN environmental cooperation.

Environmental issues as a complex non-traditional threat to the security of the South China Sea region

Non-traditional security challenges are defined as challenges to the survival and well-being of peoples and states that arise primarily out of non-military sources.[8] Environmental issues such as climate change and natural disasters belong to the non-traditional security category.[9] These challenges share common characteristics: they cannot be prevented entirely, but can be mitigated through coping mechanisms.[10] National solutions are often inadequate, and thus regional and international cooperation is essential. In addition, security no longer only concerns the state, state sovereignty or territorial integrity, but the people's survival and well-being at both individual and societal levels.[11] The South China Sea is a major crossroads in the world economy and is also a repository of valuable natural resources; but the region's great natural wealth is now being affected by a number of marine uses, expanding populations, and economic activity and climate change makes the condition worse. The potential collapse of the ecological systems and the serious degradation of natural resources which support human life poses an obvious security threat.

More than half of the world's oil tanker traffic passes through the South China Sea. Over half of the world's merchant fleet (by tonnage) sails through the South China Sea every year.[12] Pollution of the marine environment from vessels is a serious issue in the South China Sea, especially when large volumes are released such as during major oil spills, and which are significant in areas such as the Straits of Malacca, where substantial volumes of shipping are concentrated during their passage from the Indian Ocean to the South China Sea.[13] In addition to ship-sourced pollution, there is also sedimentation and extensive pollution from land-based activities, much of which has resulted from rapid industrialisation and urbanisation of coastlines, agriculture and aquaculture.[14] The South China Sea States are some of the most densely populated, with the fastest growing economies in the world.[15] Land-based activities are therefore one of the main sources of contaminants and pollutants in coastal waters, including agricultural and urban run-off, industrial discharges and discharges from ports and harbours.[16] The pollutants, including suspended solids or oil, and heavy metals and persistent organic elements, etc., pose an immediate threat to both living resources and marine ecosystems of the South China Sea.[17] Based on several studies, it has been found that concentrations of heavy metals such as mercury (Hg), Arsenic (As) and lead (Pb) have increased over the past two decades.[18] These heavy metals have potential negative impacts on the health of marine living resources and humans who consume seafood products.

Despite marine environmental pollution, climate change is the other undeniable threat to the marine ecosystem that should be particularly worrisome for South China Sea states. The rising sea levels caused by global warming could physically alter the coastlines and small islands or rocks would disappear from the higher sea-level, which will have significant repercussions for the maritime disputes. As coastlines change, there might be demands to alter the boundaries between coastal States traditionally measured from baselines, and the positions taken by states in maritime delimitation negotiations with opposites or adjacent states may fluctuate. There are several unsolved maritime disputes over islands and maritime boundaries in the South China Sea, and the impacts of climate change will further complicate the settlement of the multi-party disputes there. The South China Sea has abundant levels of biodiversity and moderately high productivity.[19] The higher ocean temperature will result in the timing and success of fish migrations, spawning, sex ratios and peak abundance, with the potential loss of shifts in composition for some species.[20] In addition to sea-level rise and the changes of the marine environment, the increased frequency and severity of weather-related disasters linked to climate change is likely to lead to the loss of dwellings and the spread of disease in the South China Sea region.

Environmental challenges and environmental security (low level–high level)

Whether marine environmental pollution or climate change, both will cause a threat to the security of South China Sea States. The serious degradation of fisheries and marine biodiversity associated with marine environmental pollution, climate change and human activities such as overfishing and bycatch, could trigger socioeconomic and food security issues along with traditional security issues. The fisheries are the main food sources and mainstay of economy for South China Sea States. The reduction in basic food supplies derived from fisheries as a consequence of pollution and climate change could be a contributing factor in destabilising the societies and fuel social tension in the region.[21] The prospect of dwindling fisheries in the South China Sea heightens the potential for fisheries disputes and illegal fishing, which will inevitably lead to tension between SCS States with the accompanying negative consequences for regional security.[22] In addition, the sea-level rise will 'swallow' small islands or rocks and alter coastlines, and the coastal cities and towns will also confront the risk of the uninhabitable housing and infrastructure, which means there will be a great number of environmental refugees seeking shelter and economic viability within, and even beyond, their own States.[23] This will put greater public pressure on governments to tighten border security and devote their efforts into more law enforcement and immigration resources.[24]

These brief examples of a possible relationship between environmental deterioration and security in the South China Sea region are presented to illustrate the necessity to apply the environmental security concept if the problems of the region are to be valued and solved. There is no general agreement about a clear causal relationship between environmental challenges on the one hand and violent conflict on the other.[25] What is more generally accepted is that environmental factors interact with each other and traditional security issues, prompting intra- or international conflict.[26] The environmental issues are the common threat that South China Sea States have to face, which creates a strong driving force for South China Sea States' cooperation in order to not only protect the common interests but also maintain regional peace and stability.

Collaborative mechanisms to combat the adverse environmental impacts in the South China Sea region

Global and regional legal frameworks

Most South China Sea States are parties to the most important global international environmental law instruments relevant for environmental protection, such as the United Nations Convention on the Law of the Sea (LOSC), the Convention on Biological Diversity (CBD), United Nations Framework Convention on Climate Change (UNFCCC) and its Kyoto Protocol, Paris Agreement, etc.

All South China Sea States, except Cambodia (Cambodia has signed the Convention but have not ratified it), are parties to the 1982 LOSC, which provides a framework for individual and cooperative action for the protection and preservation of the marine environment.[27] The LOSC has equipped coastal states with comprehensive maritime zones with the authority necessary to exercise jurisdiction over the marine environment. According to the definition provided by the LOSC, the South China Sea is a semi-enclosed sea. Article 123 of the LOSC provides that States bordering an enclosed or semi-enclosed sea should cooperate with each other to:

1   Coordinate the management, conservation, exploration and exploitation of the living resources of the sea. In particular, states bordering the semi-enclosed SCS have a responsibility to cooperate
2   Coordinate the implementation of their rights and duties with respect to the protection and preservation of the marine environment
3   Coordinate their scientific research policies and undertake, where appropriate, joint programmes of scientific research in the area

4   Invite, as appropriate, other interested states or international organisations to cooperate with them in furtherance of the provisions of this Article.[28]

These undertakings cover the full range of actions that South China Sea States would need to take in cooperating on marine conservation. The UNEP, the United Nations Development Program (UNDP) and IUCN have provided assistance to facilitate cooperative marine conservation.

All the South China Sea States are parties to the CBD[29] and the global instruments relevant to climate change.[30] The 2015 Paris Agreement achieved a universal agreement on the intended nationally determined contributions (INDCs), and that means not only developed states but also developing countries should take action to reach the 1.5–2°C target.[31] Each South China Sea State has submitted the INDCs to the Secretariat of the Conference of the Parties to the UNFCCC and has specific GHG emissions reduction commitment.[32] South China Sea States have the consensus on coping with climate change, and cooperation of, e.g. information sharing, technology support, infrastructure construction is vital in order to achieve the INDCs target. The CBD is also an important instrument for the South China Sea States' cooperation: 'Each Contracting Party shall … cooperate with other Contracting Parties, directly or where appropriate, through competent international organizations … for the conservation and sustainable use of biological diversity'.[33]

As for the regional level, the Declaration on the Conduct of Parties in the South China Sea (DOC) provides a legal framework for China and the ASEAN States to conduct cooperation on environmental issues. In 2002, China and ASEAN countries signed the DOC, which agrees in principle, to promote five kinds of cooperative activities, including: marine environmental protection, marine scientific research, search and rescue operations, etc.[34] China and ASEAN states also agreed that, pending the settlement of the SCS disputes, they may explore or undertake cooperative activities, including marine environmental protection.[35]

Cooperation in the South China Sea region

To avert some of the worst impacts of environmental degradation and to realise sustainable development in the South China Sea region, cooperation among the countries of the region, extra-regional partners and some organisations is already occurring in this region. Although there is no marine environmental regime focused on the South China Sea, there are bilateral, regional or inter-regional programmes with a wider coverage of the East Asia seas, including the South China Sea.

One of these programmes is the 'Coordinating Body of the Seas of East Asia' (COBSEA), which was established in 1994. The member States include Cambodia, China, Indonesia, South Korea, Malaysia, the Philippines, Singapore, Thailand and Vietnam.[36] According to its East Asian Seas Action Plan 1994, COBSEA is designed to assess the effects of human activities on the marine environment, to control coastal pollution, to protect mangroves, sea grasses and coral reefs and to manage wastes.[37] Its current activities aim to implement the New Strategic Direction of COBSEA (2008–2012) and to focus on marine and land-based pollution, coastal and marine habitat conservation and management and response to coastal disasters.[38] COBSEA has been instrumental in the initiation of several projects in the region, the most notable one being the 'UNEP/GEF project on Reversing Environmental Degradation Trends in the South China Sea and Gulf of Thailand'.[39]

Another regional environmental programme, involving both China and ASEAN States, is the Regional Programme on Partnerships in Environmental Management for the Seas of East Asia (PEMSEA), jointly sponsored by the International Maritime Organization (IMO), the United Nations Development Programme (UNDP), the Global Environmental Facility (GEF) and the World Bank, with the mission to foster and sustain healthy and resilient coasts and oceans, communities and economies across the Seas of East Asia, through integrated management solutions and partnerships.[40] This regional programme has country partners, including Cambodia, China, Indonesia, Japan, North Korea, Laos, the Philippines, South Korea, Singapore, Timor-Leste and Vietnam. The programme launched the Marine Pollution Monitoring and Information Management Network to help build linkages with participating countries to notify each of the status of the marine environment in the East Asian seas.[41] The latest Sustainable Development Strategy for Seas of East Asia (SDS-SEA) was adopted in 2015. It has been updated to address the changing context in ocean governance, in light of new or amended international and regional agreements, including the UNFCCC, the Rio+20 'The Future We Want', etc.[42] The SDS-SEA 2015 provides a framework for policy and programme development and implementation at the regional, national and local levels for achieving the goals and targets set by these various global instruments.[43]

The two regional programmes above are mostly designed to protect the marine environment and to prevent and control marine pollution, but sustainable management of marine natural resources is not covered. Unlike some other regions, in which regional fisheries management organisations (RFMO) have a mandate for fisheries management and the introduction of fisheries conservation measures, the South China Sea does not have an RFMO arrangement. Rather, the South China Sea falls within the larger geographical mandate of the Asia-Pacific Fishery Commission, which includes most South China Sea States among its membership, namely: Cambodia, China, Indonesia, Malaysia, the Philippines, Thailand and Vietnam.[44] With its current orientation towards sustainable fisheries management, the Commission has the potential to play an important role in advocating conservation measures among its membership.[45]

At the sub-regional level, threats to the Coral Triangle region reflect many of those relevant issues to the South China Sea region, including overfishing, destructive fisheries activities, land-based sources of marine pollution and the ravages of climate change.[46] In 2007, the Coral Triangle Initiative on Coral Reefs, Fisheries, and Food Security (CTI-CFF) was established as a multilateral partnership of six countries working together to sustain extraordinary marine and coastal resources by addressing crucial issues such as food security, climate change and marine biodiversity.[47] The Member States include: Indonesia, Malaysia, Papua New Guinea, the Philippines, Solomon Islands and Timor-Leste.[48] The Member States have committed to guiding principles, including the recognition of the transboundary nature of important marine resources and the need to align their activities with existing international law instruments such as the LOSC, CBD and UNFCCC.[49]

Challenges

Difference in the awareness of environmental security

A considerable degree of political will seems to be a necessary driving force in the cooperation process. The stronger political will for cooperation the States have, the easier cooperation can be reached, and *vice-versa*. This political will is usually related to high political considerations. High politics is politics that concern vital national interests, which the political actors regard as sensitive to the State and should be dealt with by the highest authorities of the State.[50] Hence the cooperation objective must be related to the general perceptions of the politicians. The political actors must recognise and perceive the link between their high politics concern and international/regional cooperation.[51]

According to this theory, if the political actors address serious environmental problems as security matters, they are more likely to put them at the top of the agenda and deal with them in a satisfactory manner, i.e. to cooperate and find solutions that are acceptable to all parties involved.[52] While among the South China Sea States, maximising national economic growth is the principal goal of state-led industrialisation, environmental protection is not considered a priority for national policies.[53] For example, Indonesia, one of the biggest palm oil producers in the world, in order to maximise the profits, the plantation owners slash and burn existing vegetation to clear the way for more and more palm lands.[54] These agriculture fires in Indonesia have resulted in a smoky haze blanketing the South East Asia States, including Malaysia, Singapore, the south of Thailand and the Philippines, which cause a significant deterioration in air quality.[55] In addition, the environment essentially belongs to the 'public good', which means if this public good, i.e. sustainable environment and resources, is provided, every State in the region can enjoy it, even if the country has not contributed to producing it.[56] Hence, there is an incentive to free ride – to wait until others have provided the good and then consume it.

Maritime disputes

There has been a complex set of maritime boundary and sovereignty disputes in the South China Sea region.[57] Some bilateral disputes have been resolved through negotiation or third-party assistance but others remain intractable.[58] The

South China Sea issue might become one of the obstacles to the cooperation of China and ASEAN States. At the bilateral level, the Philippines has strengthened security cooperation with the United States in the past. However, although the new President Rodrigo Duterte announced his 'separation' from the United States and showed his willingness to set aside the Philippines *v.* China arbitral award to improve Manila's relationship with Beijing, it is still unknown whether his policy will be strong and consistent. At the multilateral level, the South China Sea issue may weaken the mutual trust between China and some ASEAN countries in politics and security, especially those that have sovereignty and maritime delimitation disputes with China. As mentioned above, the marine environmental issue in the South China Sea is a transboundary issue; hence the need for all the regional States to take action. The problem for the protection of the marine environment in this region is that all the States involved in the South China Sea must tackle the crucial and thorny sovereignty issue.[59] Any unilateral effort to deal with marine pollution in disputed areas might be considered by other parties to be sovereign action.[60] For example, when China adopted its Law on Islands Protection in 2009, Vietnam protested China's application of this legal instrument to the South China Sea.

The concept of 'setting aside dispute and pursuing joint development' advanced by Deng Xiaoping, provides a method of cooperation in the disputed waters, through which conditions for the eventual resolution of territorial disputes might be created.[61] In state practice, the State-owned oil companies of China, the Philippines and Vietnam did sign an agreement on joint seismic exploration in a designated area of the South China Sea in 2005.[62] But after the first stage of the joint seismic survey, there has been no follow-up activity sponsored by the three countries.[63] The reasons for the failure might be distrust and conflict tensions. Compared with the joint development for oil and gas resources, the cooperation for marine environmental protection belongs to a 'low political sensitivity' area, and thus it might be easier to build mutual trust at this level.

Trust deficit

There is historical animosity among the Southeast Asian countries, as well as between China and some of these countries.[64] However, because of the end of the Cold War and the increasing economic interactions in the South China Sea region, this animosity has declined. China though, emerging as a global power, presents both opportunities and difficulties for ASEAN countries, resulting in these countries' ambivalent feeling about China's rise.[65] China became a full ASEAN dialogue partner in 1996 and China adopted a doctrine compatible with ASEAN's concept of resilience, called the 'New Security Concept'.[66] After that, China and ASEAN signed the DOC in 2002, and both sides signed the Joint Declaration on Strategic Partnership for Peace and Prosperity in the following year, which was meant to mark the China and ASEAN 'Strategic Partnership'. China-ASEAN cooperation follows the ASEAN Way,[67] and China uses its superior resources and political entrepreneurship to lead.[68] Generally speaking,

ASEAN's attitude towards China's rise is complicated. On the one hand, China's economic development and trade both offer economic opportunities for ASEAN States; on the other hand, the rise of Chinese power makes comparatively smaller ASEAN States feel threatened.[69] Because of the 'China threat' theory, some ASEAN countries have long-standing suspicions towards China, which is an obstacle to China and the ASEAN States' cooperation.

Prospects

First, common environmental issues need to be considered within the context of common security in order to heighten the level of cooperation. To a large degree, security questions have been a driving force for continued regional integration in Southeast Asia.[70] In the future, questions of environmental security may be playing the same role.[71] There are two aspects related to environmental issues: one is risk sharing, the other is resource sharing, both of which attract concern among the South China Sea States.[72] Moreover, the international community's increasing concern with the adverse impacts of climate change and the vulnerability of the South China Sea draws more attention from South China Sea States to environmental security. This positive momentum of development should make the potential cooperative interests grow.

Second, the 'Maritime Silk Road' will act as a new driving force for China-ASEAN cooperation. The ancient Maritime Silk Road was developed under political and economic backgrounds and was the result of cooperative efforts from the ancestors of both the East and the West. China's proposal to build the '21st-Century Maritime Silk Road' is aimed at exploring the unique values and concepts of the ancient road, enriching it with new meaning for the present era and actively developing economic partnerships with countries situated along the road.[73] Southeast Asia has become an important hub for the MSR and China seems willing to enhance maritime cooperation with ASEAN countries, and boost maritime partnerships.[74] The MSR is a new chance for China and ASEAN States to build common development strategy, and a chance to deepen China-ASEAN environmental cooperation. In 2011, China established the China-ASEAN Maritime Cooperation Fund valued at RMB3-billion, pushing maritime cooperation to new heights.[75] In 2014, China set-up the $40-billion Silk Road Fund to 'promote common development and prosperity of China and other countries and regions involved in the Belt and Road Initiative'.[76] Strengthening China-ASEAN maritime cooperation will benefit both sides. These efforts have offered long-term and stable fund guarantees for connectivity between China and ASEAN, especially regarding maritime connectivity. This cooperation should also help to realise maritime peace and stability in the South China Sea region.

Last but not least, does 'setting aside dispute and pursuing joint protection' work for the dispute areas? The South China Sea dispute is probably the most difficult maritime dispute in the world, due to the nature of overlapping claims and interests underlying the sovereignty issues. The complex nature of the dispute is exacerbated by the important security and economic interests at stake in the region.[77] Though initiatives towards a legal resolution have been taken, these disputes will not likely be resolved in the near future.[78] For regional cooperation purposes, joint development for oil and gas resources in the disputed maritime zones has been proposed by China,[79] but the actual effect is not as expected. However, joint development can still be used as a means of diffusing tensions and enhancing regional cooperation.[80] The most optimal option for the South China Sea countries to consider is the joint protection, instead of joint development. From a political point of view, cooperation to protect the marine environment in a disputed area might be accepted by relevant claimants more easily than joint development of resources, because environmental protection is a non-exploitative undertaking.[81] Unlike joint development for oil and gas or joint use of fisheries, cooperation to protect the marine environment does not require any type of commercial extraction or sharing of marine resources. Therefore, countries could participate in relevant initiatives in disputed areas without having to worry about seeing their potential resources exploited 'unfairly' by others.

The marine protected areas (MPAs) is a tool of environmental protection and biodiversity conservation, expanding fast both in the areas within national jurisdiction and increasingly on the high seas. At present, most of the marine areas under protection fall within undisputed waters. What is missing is a network of existing MPAs as well as cooperation to pursue the common conservation interest in disputed waters.[82] In this context, MPAs and a network of MPAs offer a political opportunity to maintain a peaceful, cooperative and stable environment in the South China Sea. Traditionally, MPAs are considered to have several major functions, such as to provide protection for the marine ecosystem by protecting habitats and sites that are important for marine biodiversity,[83] safeguarding life-support processes of the sea and preserving sites from human impacts, to enable them to recover from stresses.[84] In addition, another role of MPAs is to help ease conflicts and maintain peace between States. In fact, where there is a history of rivalry or conflict between adjacent nations, the conservation of a shared resource can be an important step in building mutual understanding and cooperation.[85] Therefore, the development of a regional network of MPAs in the South China Sea with marine peace parks as components, might contribute to easing the tension and enhancing cooperation between States in dispute.

Conclusion

The environmental issues are a common threat to South China Sea States, which creates a driving force for the South China Sea States' cooperation in order to not only protect the common interests, but also maintain regional peace and stability. Although efforts are made at bilateral, regional and inter-regional levels, environmental cooperation still needs to be more effective to achieve a balance between the environment and economic development without being tilted towards fast economic growth. Only if the political leaders address environmental problems as security matters, environmental conservation will be at the top of a country's agenda and they might have a stronger willingness to enhance environmental cooperation. The MSR is a chance for China and ASEAN States to deepen trust and strengthen the foundation for cooperation, which will be a new driving force for environmental cooperation in the South China Sea region. In addition, not only joint development but also joint protection in the disputed areas might be a better choice for the States in dispute.

Notes

1 A. Handa, *China's Geo-Strategy and International Behaviour* (India: Vij Books India Pvt Ltd., 2014), p. 26.
2 UN Environment, *South China Sea Countries to Cooperation on Integrating Fisheries and Marine Ecosystem Management*, 2016, www.rona.unep.org/news/2016/south-china-sea-countries-cooperate-integrating-fisheries-and-marine-ecosystem-management.
3 IPCC Working Groups II to the Fifth Assessment Report, *Climate Change 2014: Impacts, Adaptation, and Vulnerability* (Cambridge: Cambridge University Press, 2014) p. 1334.
4 Koh Kheng-Lian, ASEAN Strategic Plan of Action on the Environment, in: *ASEAN Environmental Law, Policy and Governance: Selected Documents (Volume I)* (2009), 413–468.
5 ASEAN Secretariat, *ASEAN and China Officially Launch the Establishment of the China–ASEAN Environmental Cooperation Centre.* 2011, http://asean.org/asean-and-china-officially-launch-the-establishment-of-the-china-asean-environmental-cooperation-centre/.
6 The National Development and Reform Commission, Ministry of Foreign Affairs, and Ministry of Commerce of the People's Republic of China, Vision and Actions on Jointly Building Silk Road Economic Belt and 21st-Century Maritime Silk Road, http://en.ndrc.gov.cn/newsrelease/201503/t20150330_669367.html.
7 *Ibid.*
8 Consortium of Non-Traditional Security Studies in Asia, http://rsis-ntsasia.org/about-nts-asia/; M. Caballero-Anthony (ed.), *An Introduction to Non-Traditional Security Studies – A Transnational Approach* (London: Sage Publications, 2015).
9 *Ibid.*
10 *Ibid.*
11 *Ibid.*
12 Teshu Singh, South China Sea: Emerging Security Architecture, *Institute of Peace and Conflict Studies Special Report* (2012), 132.
13 N. Liu, Prevention of Vessel-Source Pollution in the South China Sea: What Role Can China Play?, *Asia Pacific Journal of Environmental Law* 15(1) (2013), 147–166.
14 UNEP, *Land-Based Pollution in the South China Sea*, UNEP/GEF/SCS Technical Publication No. 10, 2007.
15 Asian Development Bank, The Economics of Climate Change in Southeast Asia: A Regional Review, *Environmental Policy Collection* 71(1) (2009), 13, www.adb.org/sites/default/files/publication/29657/economics-climate-change-se-asia.pdf.
16 UNEP, *supra* (n. 14).
17 *Ibid.*
18 *Ibid.*
19 Yann-huei Song, A Marine Biodiversity Project in the South China Sea: Joint Efforts Made in the SCS Workshop Process, *International Journal of Marine and Coastal Law* 26 (2011), 121.
20 World Fish Center. *The Threat to Fisheries and Aquaculture from Climate Change*, http://pubs.iclarm.net/resource_centre/ClimateChange2.pdf.

21 *USA National Intelligence Council Conference Report*, 'Southeast Asia: The Impact of Climate Change to 2030: Geopolitical Implications', 2010, p. 17.

22 Robin Warner, The Portents of Changing Climate: Maritime Security Implications for the South China Sea, in: S. Wu and K. Zou (eds.), *Non-Traditional Security Issues and the South China Sea: Shaping a New Framework for Cooperation* (Farnham: Ashgate Publishing, 2014), pp. 241–256.

23 A study of the Asian Development Bank (ADB) showed that with a sea-level rise of 0.25 cm per year, 40 km^2 of the total land area of north Jakarta in Indonesia is expected to be inundated by 2050, with faster increases if land subsidence continues; *supra* (n. 15).

24 J. Barnett and W. N. Adger, Climate Change, Human Security and Violent Conflict, *Political Geography* 26(6) (2007), 649.

25 K. Dokken, Environment, Security and Regionalism in the Asia-Pacific: Is Environmental Security a Useful Concept?, *The Pacific Review* 14(4) (2001), 509–530.

26 *Ibid.*

27 Table Recapitulating the Status of the Convention and of the Related Agreements, www.un.org/Depts/los/reference_files/status2018.pdf.

28 United Nations Convention on the Law of the Sea, Article 123.

29 List of Parties of the Convention on Biological Diversity, www.cbd.int/information/parties.shtml.

30 UNFCCC Process, https://unfccc.int/process.

31 Paris Agreement, Articles 15, 17 and 18.

32 Intended Nationally Determined Contributions (INDCs) as communicated by Parties, www4.unfccc.int/submissions/indc/Submission%20Pages/submissions.aspx.

33 Convention on Biological Diversity, Article 5.

34 The Declaration on the Conduct of Parties in the South China Sea, Article 6.

35 *Ibid.*

36 Coordinating Body of the Seas of East Asia, www.cobsea.org/index.html.

37 *Ibid.*

38 *Ibid.*

39 Current Projects, www.cobsea.org/projects/index.html.

40 About PEMSEA, see www.pemsea.org/about-pemsea.

41 PEMSEA, *Pollution and Waste Management*, www.pemsea.org/our-work/pollution-and-waste-management.

42 PEMSEA, *Sustainable Development Strategy for the Seas of East Asia (SDS-SEA)* (Quezon City, Philippines: PEMSEA, 2015), p. 40.

43 *Ibid.*, p. 14.

44 Asia-Pacific Fishery Commission, www.fao.org/apfic/background/about-asia-pacific-fishery-commission/membership/en/.

45 *Ibid.*

46 *Regional Plan of Action: Coral Triangle Initiative on Coral Reefs, Fisheries and Food Security (CTI-CFF)* (Indonesia: CTI-CFF Regional Secretariat, 2016), p. 2.

47 The Coral Triangle Initiative on Coral Reefs, Fisheries, and Food Security (CTI-CFF), www.coraltriangleinitiative.org/countries.

48 *Ibid.*

49 *Ibid.*

50 Dokken, *supra* (n. 25), p. 521.

51 *Ibid.*, p. 522.

52 *Ibid.*

53 Nong Hong, Exploring A Pragmatic Settlement Regime for the SCS Dispute, *Asia Pacific Security and Maritime Affairs* 1 (2017), 21.

54 Christopher L. Atkinson, Deforestation and Transboundary Haze in Indonesia: Path Dependence and Elite Influences, *Environment & Urbanization Asia* 5(2) (2014), 253.

55 *Ibid.*

56 David W. Pearce and Jeremy J. Warford, *World without End: Economic, Environment, and Sustainable Development* (Washington, DC: World Bank, 1993), pp. 18, 36.

57 There are many discussions about the maritime disputes in the South China Sea, such as, Robert C. Beckman, The Philippines v. China, Case and the South China Sea Disputes, in: J. Huang and A. Billo (eds.), *Territorial Disputes in the South China Sea* (Basingstoke: Palgrave Macmillan, 2015), pp. 54–65; Keyuan, Zou, *et al.*, South China Sea Arbitration Case and China's Entitled Historic Rights in the South China Sea, *Southeast Asian Studies* 4 (2017), 92–113 (in Chinese); *The South China Sea Dispute: A Brief History*, www.lawfareblog.com/south-china-sea-dispute-brief-history, etc.

58 Aldo Chircop, Regional Cooperation in Marine Environmental Protection in the South China Sea: A Reflection on New Direction for Marine Conservation, *Ocean Development & International Law* 41 (2010), 334.

59 Peter Kien-Hong Yu, Setting up International (Adversary) Regimes in the South China Sea: Analyzing the Obstacles from a Chinese Perspective, *Ocean Development & International Law* 38(1–2) (2007), 147–156.

60 Liu, *supra* (n. 13), p. 149.

61 For details, see Keyuan Zou, Joint Development in the South China Sea: A New Approach, *The International Journal of Marine and Coastal Law* 21(1) (2006), 83–109.

62 *Oil Companies of China, the Philippines and Vietnam Signed Agreement on South China Sea Cooperation*, www.fmprc.gov.cn/ce/ceph/eng/zt/nhwt/t187333.htm.

63 Zou, *supra* (n. 61), p. 104.

64 S. Chen, Environmental Cooperation in the South China Sea: Factors, Actors and Mechanisms, *Ocean & Coastal Management* 85 (2013), 131–140.

65 Rommel C. Banlaoi, Southeast Asian Perspectives on the Rise of China: Regional Security after 9/11, *Parameters* (2003), 98–107.

66 China's Position Paper on the New Security Concept, www.china-un.org/eng/xw/t27742.htm.

67 Kuik Cheng-Chwee, Multilateralism in China's ASEAN Policy: Its Evolution, Characteristics, and Aspirations, *Contemporary Southeast Asia: A Journal of International and Strategic Affairs* 27(1) (April 2005), 102–122.

68 D. Arase, Non-traditional Security in China-ASEAN Cooperation: The Institutionalization of Regional Security Cooperation and the Evolution of East Asian Regionalism, *Asian Survey* 50(4) (2010), 852.

69 *Ibid.*

70 Dokken, *supra* (n. 25), p. 509.

71 *Ibid.*

72 Hong, *supra* (n. 53), p. 22.

73 Vision and Actions on Jointly Building Silk Road Economic Belt and 21st-Century Maritime Silk Road, *supra* (n. 6).

74 *Ibid.*

75 Penghong Cai, China-ASEAN Maritime Cooperation: Process, Motivation, and Prospects, *China International Studies* 4 (2015), 31.

76 *Ibid.*

77 V. H. Dang, *Marine Protected Areas Network in the South China Sea: Charting a Course for Future Cooperation* (Leiden: Martinus Nijhoff Publishers, 2014).

78 *Ibid.*

79 Zou, *supra* (n. 61).

80 Keyuan Zou, Realizing Sustainability in the South China Sea, in: Shicun Wu and Keyuan Zou (eds.), *Non-Traditional Security Issues and the South China Sea: Shaping a New Framework for Cooperation* (London: Routledge, 2014).

81 Dang, *supra* (n. 77), p. 132.
82 N. T. A. Hu and T. L. McDorman, *Maritime Issues in the South China Sea: Troubled Waters or a Sea of Opportunity* (London: Routledge, 2013), p. 102.
83 Such as mangrove areas, kelp forest, seagrass beds, coral reefs and seamounts. See, for example: Ant Maddock, *UK Biodiversity Action Plan Priority Habitat Descriptions* (updated July 2010), Joint Nature Conservation Committee, http://jncc.defra.gov.uk/page-5711.
84 IUCN, *Establishing Resilient Marine Protected Area Networks – Making it Happen* (Washington, DC: IUCN-WCPA, 2008).
85 C. Toropova *et al.* (eds.), *Global Ocean Protection: Present Status and Future Possibilities*, 2010, p. 21, https://pipap.sprep.org/content/ocean-protection-present-status-and-future-possibilities.

11 Protection and preservation of the marine environment in the South China Sea in the aftermath of the Philippines/China arbitration

Sophia Kopela

Introduction

The South China Sea (SCS) is one of the most biodiverse semi-enclosed seas in the world but is also increasingly threatened by human activities, including pollution, overfishing, destructive fishing, land reclamation and island construction. The South China Sea disputes and consequent tensions in the area have also exacerbated the threats and risks to the marine environment. The *South China Sea Arbitration* between the Philippines and China highlighted the need and urgency to address the risks to the environment by human activities in the area. The Tribunal examined the status of the environment and the environmental risks and threats in the Spratly Islands, and clarified the scope and content of state obligations under the Law of the Sea Convention (LOSC) and other international agreements (i.e. Convention for the International Trade of Endangered Species, CITES) in areas within and beyond national jurisdiction.

Despite the fact that there is no legally-binding regional agreement for the protection of the marine environment or the preservation of marine living resources, including fisheries in the SCS, there have been various collaborative initiatives and projects either for the wider area of East Asia or more specifically for the SCS. Various proposals have also been made for actions and mechanisms to enhance cooperation and to protect the marine environment. Most of them aim to disassociate the protection and preservation of the environment from the sovereignty and maritime delimitation disputes, and stress the need for the prioritisation of the collective interests of all littoral states to achieve the shared aims of sustainable development and effective management of this fragile, diverse and unique environment.

The South China Sea is an important segment of the 21st Century Maritime Silk Road, which includes two routes: the first through the South China Sea and the Indian Ocean to Europe, and the second through the South China Sea to the South Pacific.[1] The key values underpinning the 21st Century Maritime Silk Road Initiative are, according to China, 'peace and cooperation, openness and inclusiveness, mutual learning and mutual benefit'. Reflecting on these values, the objective of this initiative is to promote 'practical cooperation in all fields' and to 'build a community of shared interests, destiny and responsibility featuring mutual political trust, economic integration and cultural inclusiveness'.[2] The conflicts and tension created by the South China Sea disputes and the resulting environmental degradation, including fisheries depletion, are obstructing regional stability[3] but also hampering the materialisation of the objectives of the 21st Century Maritime Silk Road Initiative.

The aim of this chapter is to examine the legal framework for the protection and preservation of the marine environment in the South China Sea, in the aftermath of the Philippines/China arbitration. The chapter examines the key findings of the Tribunal with respect to the environmental obligations of States, and then reviews the existing initiatives for the protection of the marine environment in the South China Sea. It finally makes some suggestions for collaborative action for the protection of the marine environment and preservation of biodiversity in the South China Sea, in the light of the findings of the Tribunal in the Philippines/China arbitration and the 21st Century Maritime Silk Road Initiative.

Environmental obligations of States in the SCS and findings of the Tribunal in the Philippines/China arbitration

The Philippines requested the Tribunal to declare that 'China has violated its obligations under the Convention to protect and preserve the marine environment at Scarborough Shoal, Second Thomas Shoal, Cuarteron Reef, Fiery Cross Reef, Gaven Reef, Johnson Reef, Hughes Reef and Subi Reef' (Submission 11) – and that 'China's occupation of and construction activities on Mischief Reef violate China's duties to protect and preserve the marine environment under the Convention' (Submission 12 (b)).[4] These submissions referred to two types of activities: harmful fishing practice and harmful construction activities.[5] Harmful fishing practices concerned use of cyanide and explosives, harvesting of endangered species such as giant clams, sea turtles, giant oysters and harvesting of coral. Construction activities concerned land reclamation and construction of artificial islands, installations and structures on certain maritime features. The arbitration assessed the scope and extent of destruction of the marine environment through the reports submitted by the Philippines (Carpenter Reports) and the independent report commissioned by the Tribunal (Ferse Report), and identified the activities which contributed to this destruction, by examining reports, reviewing satellite imagery, photographic and video evidence, contemporaneous press reports, scientific studies and the materials from the two reports submitted by the Philippines and the expert report commissioned by the Tribunal.[6]

Relying on recent case law by international courts and tribunals, the SCS Tribunal clarified the scope and content of the environmental obligations States have by virtue of Part XII LOSC and other international environmental agreements. The Tribunal stressed that the Part XII obligations to protect and preserve the marine environment apply to all States in all maritime areas both within and beyond national jurisdiction,[7] but also in areas of disputed jurisdiction. Questions of sovereignty or maritime entitlement are irrelevant to the application and compliance of these obligations; these obligations apply regardless of which State has sovereign rights/jurisdiction over a maritime area.

The Tribunal found that Article 192 LOSC, despite its general wording and scope, poses both a positive obligation to 'take active measures to protect and preserve the marine environment' and a negative one 'not to degrade the marine environment'.[8] These obligations relate to protection of the environment from future damage but also 'maintaining or improving its present condition'.[9] The content of the general obligation to protect and preserve the marine environment is specified in other provisions of the LOSC (i.e. Article 194–195) but also in other international agreements to which the LOSC refers (Article 237). The Tribunal specifically referred to CITES as 'the subject of nearly universal adherence' and 'part of the general corpus of international law that informs the content of Article 192 and 194 (5) of the Convention'.[10] It also confirmed the findings of the Tribunal in the *Chagos Marine Protection Area* case that Part XII is 'not limited to measures aimed strictly at controlling marine pollution',[11] and the Tribunal's conclusion in the *Southern Bluefin tuna* arbitration that 'the conservation of living resources of the sea is an element in the protection and preservation of the marine environment',[12] and concluded that Article 192 'includes a due diligence obligation to prevent the harvesting of species that are recognised internationally as being at risk of extinction and requiring international protection'.[13] Apart from species-related protection,[14] the Tribunal also found that Article 192 'imposes a due diligence obligation to take those measures "necessary to protect and preserve rare or fragile ecosystems as well as the habitat of depleted, threatened or endangered species and other forms of marine life"'.[15] These comments also demonstrate the complementarity between the LOSC and other international agreements and its dynamic and evolutionary character and scope, which allows its interpretation and application in line with developments of international rules on environmental protection.

With respect to the scope of these obligations, the Tribunal found that they relate to activities undertaken by the state itself through its organs or agents but they also entail a due diligence obligation of conduct in 'relation to ensuring activities within their jurisdiction and control do not harm the marine environment'.[16] In areas of contested sovereignty and jurisdiction, the role of the flag state is important. The Tribunal relied on the ICJ judgement in the *Pulp Mills case*, the *Seabed Disputes Chamber Advisory Opinion* and *ITLOS Fisheries Advisory Opinion* and quoted the latter to stress the scope of this due diligence obligation of the flag State as entailing not only the adoption of appropriate rules and measures but also a 'certain level of vigilance of their enforcement and the exercise of administrative control'.[17]

The Tribunal also referred to the obligations of States to cooperate based on Articles 197 and 123 LOSC (for semi-enclosed seas). The Tribunal highlighted the link between cooperation and managing and preventing the risk of damage to the marine environment.[18] This relates to engagement in activities (such as construction on maritime features) that may have adverse impact on the environment. The Tribunal also stressed the obligation to monitor and evaluate the risks to the marine environment of activities, which are 'likely to pollute the marine environment' (Article 204 LOSC), which include the obligation to conduct an Environmental Impact Assessment (EIA) both as a 'direct obligation under the Convention and a general obligation under customary international law'.[19] The importance of the obligation to communicate the results of reports of activities, which 'may case substantial pollution of or significant and harmful changes to the marine environment' was also highlighted with reference to Article 206 LOSC: 'while the terms "reasonable" and "as far as practicable" contain an element of discretion for the State concerned, the obligation to communicate reports of the results of the assessments is absolute'.[20]

China was found to be in violation of its LOSC obligations (Article 192 and 194 LOSC) for 'harvesting of endangered species from the fragile ecosystems at Scarborough Shoal and Second Thomas Shoal',[21] 'its toleration and protection of the harvesting of giant clams by the propeller chopping method',[22] 'artificial island-building activities',[23] 'dredging in such a way as to pollute the marine environment with sediment'[24] and the obligation to communicate reports on the adverse impacts of its activities or EIA as enshrined in article 206 LOSC. The Tribunal rejected the Philippines' submission with respect to use of explosives and cyanide, as there was no evidence in that respect.[25]

Despite the fact that the questions before the Tribunal referred to activities by China and China's violation of its obligations to protect and preserve the marine environment, the Tribunal's findings are important, as they concern obligations of all the littoral states in the South China Sea and they also provide a legal framework for the conduct of States, while the dispute is pending but also regardless of the dispute. The Tribunal noted the destruction caused on the coral reefs by construction activities on the maritime features by all States (even by the more modest pre-2013 activities), as demonstrated in the expert report submitted by the Philippines (Carpenter report).[26] The Ferse Report commissioned by the Tribunal also noted that the area 'had already been affected by the impacts of human activity, such as overfishing and destructive fishing, construction activities and human habitation for several decades prior to commencement of large-scale construction in 2013'.[27] Both reports however noted that China's post-2013 activities led to much more extensive damage to the marine environment.[28] What can also be concluded from the arbitration is that the sovereignty and maritime entitlements/delimitation disputes and ensuing tensions have led to environmental harm and damage. The construction activities have been undertaken by States as a means of strengthening and enhancing the sovereignty claims and the maritime entitlements of the relevant features. Fishermen are also used as an extension of the sovereign power to solidify and consolidate the presence of a State in the area with respect to maritime entitlements.[29]

Existing mechanisms and initiatives for regional cooperation to protect and preserve the marine environment in the South China Sea

There are no legally-binding regional agreements or mechanisms for the protection of the marine environment or for the preservation of living resources including fisheries in the South China Sea. However, there have been various collaborative initiatives and projects either for the more general area of East Asia or more specifically for the SCS, which aim at enhancing cooperation for protecting the environment, but also provide an informal framework for cooperation for the resolution of other aspects of the SCS disputes.

One of the key mechanisms for the protection of the environment in the East Asia area, which also includes the SCS, is the UNEP Regional Sea Coordinating Body on the Seas of East Asia (COBSEA), which was established in 1994.[30] According to its Strategic Direction for 2008–2012, the key objectives focus on marine and land-based pollution, coastal and marine habitat conservation and management and response to coastal disasters; these objectives are to be achieved via four interlinked strategies of information management, national capacity building to facilitate the implementation of international environmental agreements and obligations, assisting states with strategic and emerging issues and enhancing regional cooperation through partnerships.[31] Despite the fact that COBSEA has promoted a number of projects concerning various activities in the area to raise awareness and to involve various stakeholders in protection and conservation of the marine environment, including coral reefs, its impact has been restricted, due to inadequate interest by the Member States to participate actively and to cooperate more assertively.[32] Other reasons that have been suggested for its limited impact is funding and staff deficiencies and weak mandate of the Regional Coordinating Unit (EAS/RCU), its broad and diverse geographical scope, lack of political commitment and support, and lack of country ownership of the EAS Action Plan.[33]

A number of projects/programmes have been adopted and implemented in the East Asia Seas Region, most of them funded by GEF and coordinated by UNEP and/or UNDP promoting capacity-building, exchange of information, demonstration projects and research programmes.[34] The most influential with direct relevance for the SCS was a UNEP/GEF Project entitled 'Reversing Environmental Degradation Trends in the South China Sea and Gulf of Thailand' in partnership with seven riparian states bordering the South China Sea (Cambodia, China, Indonesia, Malaysia, Philippines, Thailand and Vietnam).[35] A key objective of this project was to enhance cooperation and integration both within and between participating countries.[36] The two main outcomes of the project was a Transboundary Diagnostic Analysis, which assessed key features of the marine ecosystems and the issues and problems in the area regarding degradation of the environment and a Strategic Action Programme (SAP) for the South China Sea, which was endorsed by the 13th intergovernmental meeting of COBSEA in 2008.[37] The suggested framework for the management of the marine environment of the South China Sea included the following components: a Memorandum of Understanding to be adopted by environment ministers as a political instrument for the implementation of the SAP,[38] Regional Strategic Action Programme as the basis for action, sub-regional and bilateral agreements and enhancement of the existing National Action Plans.[39] It is noted in the SAP that research by the Regional task force on Legal matters concluded that there is preference for a non-legally binding document.[40] The Plan also includes a cost and benefit analysis of the regional actions proposed, which is based on the determination of detailed economic values for coastal habitat goods and services. The analysis and strategic priority actions refer to various aspects of the environment of the SCS, including mangroves, coral reefs, seagrass, coastal wetlands bordering the SCS, fish habitats and fish stocks and land-based pollution.

This project has contributed to regional cooperation and confidence- and trust-building, and has strengthened collaboration between states and other stakeholders. A key element was the separation of policy and scientific aspects of the project and relevant discussions at both national and regional levels.[41] It has been suggested that 'the SCS regional SPA and NAPs developed under this project must be seen as the starting point for strengthening the consensus and cooperation in the region'.[42] However, the negotiations and discussions for the adoption of the project with the participation of all regional states demonstrate the difficulties caused by the SCS dispute. The Chinese Ministry of Foreign Affairs raised concerns about the sovereignty dispute in the SCS and about the internationalisation of the SCS. China posed six conditions for its participation in the project, which included exclusion of disputed areas, exclusion of multilateral fisheries cooperation, and involvement of only UNEP, COBSEA and relevant countries and not external actors. The sovereignty concerns were addressed by adding an explicit statement that 'the term SCS is used in its geographic sense and does not imply recognition of any territorial claims within the area' and by excluding activities under the project in disputed areas. It was also clarified that 'issues of sovereignty shall not be addressed directly or indirectly through project activities'.[43] Fisheries, apart from the Gulf of Thailand, were excluded from the scope of the project, as were non-oceanic coral reefs. International organisations apart from UNEP were also excluded.[44] Despite initial hesitation, China participated in the project (with the above conditions accepted) and it was noted that this was due to the fact that 'Chinese non-participation in such a forum would place it in a disadvantageous position by missing information and losing the opportunity to influence the agenda'.[45]

A further regional programme jointly sponsored by the IMO, UNDP, GEF and WB is the Partnerships in Environmental Management for the Seas of East Asia (PEMSEA).[46] The key objective of PEMSEA is to formulate and adopt integrated approaches to managing land and water uses in order to tackle challenges such as climate change, loss of biodiversity, depleting fisheries and marine resources and to 'foster and sustain healthy and resilient oceans, coasts, communities and economies across the region', through intergovernmental, interagency and multisectoral partnerships.[47] A Sustainable Development Strategy for Seas of East Asia (SDS-SEA) was adopted under the auspices of PEMSEA, which provides for a policy framework for achieving the goals and targets of sustainable development as enshrined in various global instruments, complying with international obligations enshrined in international instruments and enhancing cooperation among PEMSEA parties and other stakeholders.[48] Establishing and developing collaboration and partnerships between key stakeholders and various interest groups, including NGOs, scientific institutions and communities are key issues in PEMSEA's activities.[49] It has been noted that, despite the fact the SDS-SEA is not legally binding, 'many national efforts related to coasts and oceans are in line with the visions and objectives of the marine strategy', and that it 'has proven to be a useful regional ocean governance framework in the implementation of relevant provisions of Agenda 21 and the plan of actions of the WSSD'.[50] PEMSEA's role in the implementation of the SDS-SEA is instrumental, especially following the Haikou Partnership Agreement (signed by 11 countries) in which PEMSEA was formally recognised as the coordinating mechanism for the implementation of the SDS-SEA and was 'transformed' from a 'regional project-based arrangement to a self-sustained and effective regional collaborative mechanism with a mandate to pursue the implementation of the SDS-SEA through collaborative, synergistic and responsible actions'.[51] However, PEMSEA's geographical scope is very broad, including six large marine ecosystems (one of which is the SCS) and 12 countries,[52] and thus lacks focus on the SCS and its ecological and political circumstances.

ASEAN has also initiated and endorsed a Strategic Action Plan on the Environment, a sub-regional Environmental Programme, and the ASEAN Senior Officials on Environment,[53] The ASEAN Working group on coastal and marine environment has been established to 'promote a coordinated and harmonised approach to the establishment and management of marine protected areas networks in the region'.[54] The Asia-Pacific Economic Council (APEC) has also established a marine resources conservation working group and has adopted an Action Plan for the Sustainability of the marine environment (1994).

With respect to fisheries' management, apart from various bilateral agreements signed by littoral states,[55] two regional fisheries bodies/arrangements, namely the Asia-Pacific Fishery Commission and Southeast Asian Fisheries Development Centre (SEAFDEC),[56] are relevant for the SCS, but these bodies only have advisory and not decision making or management mandates and cover the broader area and not specifically the SCS.[57] What is more, China is not a party to SEAFDEC. Under the auspices of the SEAFDEC, whose aim is to collaborate with government and communities to 'integrate habitat and biodiversity conservation considerations into fishery management and practices',[58] the South China Sea Fisheries Refugia Initiative was adopted (financed by GEF and implemented by UNEP). This initiative is part of the Strategic Action Programme for South China Sea and aims at achieving fisheries targets.[59]

Cooperation for the protection of the marine environment in the SCS has also been suggested as a means of facilitating conflict management and de-escalation of tensions in the South China Sea, and contributing to the peaceful resolution of the SCS disputes. The 2002 Declaration on the Conduct of Parties in the South China Sea adopted by China and ASEAN was the first regional document regulating the conduct of parties in the South China Sea. According to this non-legally binding declaration, the parties to the dispute committed themselves to 'exercise self-restraint in the conduct of activities that would complicate or escalate disputes and affect peace and stability'.[60] The parties also agreed to 'explore ways for building trust and confidence' and 'intensify efforts' and to do so by cooperative activities, including marine environmental protection, marine scientific research, safety of navigation and communication at sea, search and rescue operations and combating transnational crime such as piracy. Further mechanisms and instruments have been adopted to complement and facilitate the implementation of the Declaration: the ASEAN-China Senior Official Meeting on the implementation of the DOC; the ASEAN-China joint working group on the implementation of the DOC; and the 2011 Guidelines for the implementation of the DOC; the latter aimed at promoting possible joint cooperative activities, measures and projects. Cooperation for the protection of the marine environment has been suggested as an effective mechanism for confidence and trust-building and, as noted by Hong 'marine environmental protection has been identified by the informal SCS working group as a priority area for regional cooperation'.[61] The Informal Workshops on Managing Potential Conflicts in the SCS initiated by Indonesia in 1991 also attempted to explore cooperation regarding preservation and protection of the marine environment and marine scientific research as tools to enhance cooperation and avoid tension in the area and various projects were explored and carried out.[62]

All the above programmes and initiatives have had some success as a means of enhancing cooperation and understanding the causes of environmental risks, but also as tools for confidence- and trust-building engaging with all relevant stakeholders, but have not led to effective cooperative measures for tackling environmental risks and threats. Even though progress has been made especially with the two GEF-funded projects and the more enhanced role played by COBSEA,[63] the existence of many different instruments and projects with overlapping scopes and limited coordination has been criticised as leading to 'waste of resources on duplication of effort and gaps in habitat and species protection'.[64] The link between the political disputes and environmental protection has not been addressed, but on the contrary, the aim has been to disassociate one from the other and present environmental protection as a neutral cooperative initiative especially under the mediatory role of UNEP to 'forge and broker environment protection and depoliticise environmental cooperation'.[65]

Developing a legal framework for collaboration for the protection and preservation of the marine environment in the SCS

Various obstacles have been identified for the lack of a coherent and legally-binding framework for environmental cooperation and protection in the SCS, e.g. financial constraints, lack of understanding of the root causes and impacts of regional marine environmental problems, lack of understanding of the benefits of regional cooperation and lack of political will.[66] A key hindrance to developing a regional legal environmental framework is the sovereignty and territorial disputes and the ensuing lack of trust between some of the littoral states.[67] Bai and Hu observe that 'these issues were bound together and used as political tools in the ongoing sovereignty, delimitation or sovereign rights disputes'.[68] Whereas the various initiatives to address environmental protection, including involvement of communities and other stakeholders have enhanced the cooperative spirit, the SCS disputes continue to pose an important obstacle to environmental cooperation but also a source of environmental damage, as noted by the Tribunal.

Suggestions have been made to strengthen and coordinate the existing initiatives with the adoption of a legally binding framework (Framework Agreements and Protocols in other regional seas).[69] Nevertheless, the adoption of such a legal framework would be ineffective in the disputed areas in the SCS due to the sovereignty and maritime delimitation disputes especially related to the implementation and enforcement of the agreed framework in these areas. The concerns raised during the adoption of the GEF/UNEP SCS project and the limitations to avoid inclusion of the disputed areas in the scope of the project demonstrate the negative impact of the disputes on the adoption of cooperative, integrated and coherent protective measures and their implementation.

Existing initiatives rely on and aim at the disassociation of the disputes (sovereignty/maritime delimitation) from environmental protection, the 'depoliticisation of environmental cooperation in the SCS' and the enhancement of trust- and confidence-building, which will contribute to the peaceful settlement of the dispute and the de-escalation of tension.[70] Whereas it is true that environmental protection reflects common interests and collective interests and responsibilities, it is not disassociated from the core disputes regarding sovereignty and maritime delimitation. The activities found by the Tribunal to be in violation of the LOSC and other international environmental obligations are connected with the claims in the SCS, as some of the activities performed by the states in the region to assert their claims (either sovereignty or maritime entitlements/maritime delimitation) have an adverse impact upon the marine environment. Environmental protection should therefore form part of the discussions for conflict management in the area.

Code of conduct and obligations to protect and preserve the marine environment

As mentioned above, the DOC encourages the states to 'explore or undertake cooperative activities' for marine environmental protection. It has generally been suggested that these activities, due to the 'neutral' scope and weak political sensitiveness could lead to confidence and trust-building and develop mechanisms for dialogue for the settlement of other more politically-sensitive aspects of the disputes.[71] Discussions and negotiations have been ongoing at ASEAN for many years for the adoption of a legally-binding instrument, a code of conduct (CoC), which would pose legally-binding obligations upon the parties to the dispute and facilitate conflict management and the peaceful settlement of the dispute. ASEAN and China have adopted a framework to 'facilitate the work for the conclusion of an effective CoC on a mutually-agreed timeline' in the South China Sea.[72] The framework has not been made public, but concerns have been raised about its weak content, especially its lack of endorsement of legally binding obligations and a dispute settlement mechanism.[73]

The CoC should also refer to environmental protection, not solely as a confidence-building activity, but also as an important aspect of the conduct of states. This is in line with suggestions to consider environmental problems as security concerns and prioritising protection and preservation of the marine environment as part of, as Hong notes, 'securitising' the marine environment in the SCS.[74] Specifically, the CoC should incorporate the existing obligations of states to protect the environment as enshrined in the LOSC and multilateral environmental agreements. As noted by the Tribunal, these should include the negative obligation to abstain from actions which cause harm and damage to the marine environment, and positive obligations to take measures to ensure that actions within their jurisdiction, including vessels flying their flags, do not harm the environment, to monitor and assess the risks and threats on the environment of activities, to communicate this information to other states, and to cooperate and/or set up a collaborative framework for the protection of the marine environment. These are not new obligations for the states; states are already bound by international instruments establishing these obligations, i.e. the LOSC, CITES, CBD, and by customary international law. With respect to undelimited and disputed areas, states also have the obligation 'not to jeopardize or hamper the reaching of the final [delimitation] agreement', by virtue of Articles 74 (3) and 83 (3) LOSC. This obligation has been found to entail activities that cause permanent physical impact and damage to the marine environment.[75] It has been suggested that the 'no harm principle', as established in customary international law is relevant in this framework; as noted by a BIICL study,

> this would imply that a state should exercise caution when conducting activities in the undelimited area, on the basis that such activities may cause harm to the environment in the maritime zones of a neighbouring state, which may prove to extent further than anticipated.[76]

Legal framework for a cooperative regime to protect and preserve the marine environment in the SCS

A legal framework for environmental protection in the SCS (such as those adopted in other regional seas, i.e. Framework Agreement and protocols) may not be effective without either the resolution of the disputes or a temporary freezing of the claims. The uncertainty with respect to the status and regime of parts of the SCS would create implications for the enforcement of any protective legal regime. States would also be reluctant to include disputed areas in any framework for the protection of the marine environment due to fears that this may prejudice their claims. The difficulties in resolving these complex political disputes and the ensuing attempts of states to assert and strengthen their position by engaging in activities such construction of islands, extraction of resources, etc. may demonstrate that the most appropriate mechanism for the South China

Sea is a joint-protection/management regime. These suggestions are not new. The establishment of a Marine Peace Park for the Spratly Islands[77] and the adoption of transboundary MPAs or a network of MPAs have been suggested[78] and the benefits of joint-protection have been highlighted. Some states have discussed and spoken favourably about these initiatives.[79] This joint-protection/ management regime would ensure that no state would have to renounce their claims but only freeze them for the benefit of protecting collective interests and achieving sustainable development and peace and stability in the area. Some of the findings of the Tribunal in the SCS arbitration are pertinent for the establishment of this multilateral cooperative joint-protection/management framework.

This regime should be based on an ecosystem approach and provide a coherent and integrated framework for environmental protection, including both marine pollution and preservation of marine resources. Management of fisheries cannot be disassociated from protection of the marine environment as the threats and risks are interrelated and management measures need to take into account these risks. Joint mechanisms for the continuous monitoring of the status of the environment should also be adopted.[80] This would include projects to enhance scientific knowledge and understanding of environmental risks and threats. This should also include assessment of the environmental impact of activities in the area and exchange of information on these EIAs. As noted by the Tribunal, states have the obligation, both in international law and in the LOSC, to conduct EIAs and communicate this information to other states. Furthermore, the Tribunal referred to the extent of the existing damage to the coral reefs and biodiversity including fish stocks in the South China Sea. It also noted that the obligations include not only prevention of damage but also 'improving its present condition'; this necessitates that states need to collaborate to restore and rehabilitate the marine environment especially in areas which have suffered extensive damage.

The establishment of such a joint-management/protection regime would require the freezing of the maritime claims and the collaborative management of the designated areas. The Tribunal found that the maritime features in the Spratly Islands have the status of Article 121 (3) rocks and cannot therefore generate EEZ/CS.[81] It also found that the historic rights claim advanced by China has no validity in international law.[82] This would mean that apart from the territorial seas around some of the maritime features of the Spratlys, the rest of the waters would be CS/EEZ generated by the mainland of the littoral states and parts of the high seas. China has stated that 'the award is null and void and has no binding force. China neither accepts nor recognizes it'.[83] The award is legally binding on both parties despite China's non-participation.[84] However, the Philippines have not, at least for now, appeared willing to enforce the award. The parties to this arbitration could ignore its findings with respect to the entitlement of the maritime features in their bilateral relationships and proceed to delimit their maritime zones accordingly. The decision of the littoral states to allow the maritime features to generate full maritime zones can be disputed by third states, to the extent that this would include areas which would otherwise be high seas/

Area, but not if these areas would be included in the maritime zones of the littoral states generated by the mainlands, as states have the right to delimit their overlapping maritime zones in whichever way they think is appropriate and equitable. The award is binding upon the parties but not upon third states,[85] but third states may invoke it to demonstrate the validity of their arguments. This however should not be seen as a restriction to the establishment of a joint-protection/management regime, based on concepts of stewardship for the protect collective interests. Marine Protected Areas have been established on the high seas with the view to protecting the marine environment; similarly, RFMOs can have mandates to protect and manage fisheries in areas of high seas adjacent to the EEZ of their member states.

The joint-protection/management regime should not however, hinder freedom of navigation. States in the region have acknowledged navigation and overflight and have declared their commitment to these freedoms in the South China Sea. Nonetheless, protection of the marine environment from risks related to navigation should also be included in the joint-protective regime. In this respect, the establishment of a Particularly Sea Sensitive Area by the IMO can offer an effective collaborative action to protect the environment.[86]

Finally, with respect to the enforcement of obligations, emphasis should be placed on flag state jurisdiction. For the effective implementation of the regime, however, coordination and exchange of information would be required with respect to violations and enforcement actions, and a monitoring body on compliance by flag states could be established to coordinate action and ensure effective implementation of the protective regime. The findings of the Tribunal with respect to the scope of flag state jurisdiction especially related to due diligence obligations are important in this respect.

Conclusions

The 21st Century Maritime Silk Road Initiative aims at promoting cooperation and peace, but also sustainability and sustainable development. It is also about uniting and expanding common interests and achieving mutual benefits between China and other littoral states.[87] It has also been suggested that this road needs to be 'green' based on 'marine ecological partnerships' and regional environmental protection.[88] For the Maritime Silk Road Initiative to achieve its objectives, the South China Sea (SCS), an important segment of this road, needs to reflect the same principles, namely sustainable development, protection of the environment, peace and cooperation. The SCS disputes deprive the area of achieving its sustainable development goals. In this respect, 'marine environmental cooperation is needed not only for environmental cooperation, but also for achievement of the region's economic prosperity and peace'.[89] The establishment of a joint protection/management regime for the protection of the marine environment in the disputed areas of the SCS and the freezing of the sovereignty and maritime entitlement claims, would reflect these principles and facilitate the promotion of the objectives of the Maritime Silk Road.

Protection of the marine environment in the South China Sea requires urgency, ambition and innovative perspectives. As noted by the Tribunal in the SCS arbitration, the states are already bound by international obligations to protect the environment and to cooperate as enshrined in international instruments such as the LOSC and other international environmental agreements, and customary international law. These obligations apply both within and beyond national jurisdiction but also regardless of which state has sovereign rights and jurisdiction in these maritime areas. Joint management/protection solutions reflect the ecosystem approach, which does not recognise maritime boundaries and different types of maritime jurisdiction, but also the history of the South China Sea as an area of long coexistence and interaction of nations. This communal regime beyond sovereignty claims can be re-established with an emphasis on sustainable management and protection of the South China Sea. An innovative joint-management regime would demonstrate leadership and ambition to create a pioneering prototype of sustainable management of the seas with people and the marine environment in its centre. Any such solution would require strong political will, reconsideration of foreign and national policy and progressive and innovative thinking, but it might be the only solution for the creation of a peaceful sea of harmonious coexistence and collaboration, and effective management which would implement and facilitate the Maritime Silk Road initiative.

Notes

1 *Vision and Actions on Jointly Building Silk Road Economic Belt and 21st-Century Maritime Silk Road*, issued by the National Development and Reform Commission, Ministry of Foreign Affairs, and Ministry of Commerce of the People's Republic of China, with State Council authorization (March 2015), http://en.ndrc.gov.cn/news release/201503/t20150330_669367.html.
2 *Ibid.*
3 J. W. McManus, Offshore coral reef damage, overfishing and paths to peace in the South China Sea 32(2) (2017), *IJMCL,* 233.
4 *The Republic of the Philippines v the People's Republic of China,* PCA Case N° 2013-19 in the Matter of the South China Arbitration, Award of 12 July 2016 (Merits), paras. 815–816.
5 *Ibid.,* para. 817.
6 *Ibid.,* para. 955.
7 *Ibid.,* para. 940.
8 *Ibid.,* para. 941.
9 *Ibid.,* para. 941.
10 *Ibid.,* para. 956.
11 *Ibid.,* para. 945.
12 *Southern Bluefin Tuna (New Zealand v. Japan; Australia v. Japan), Provisional Measures,* Order of 27 August 1999, ITLOS Reports 1999, p. 280, at p. 295, para. 70.
13 *South China Sea Arbitration* award (Merits), *supra* (n. 4), para. 956.
14 *Ibid.,* para. 957.
15 *Ibid.,* para. 959.
16 *Ibid.,* para. 944.
17 *Ibid.,* para. 944; *Request for an Advisory Opinion Submitted by the Sub-Regional Fisheries Commission,* Advisory Opinion of 2 April 2015, ITLOS Reports 2015, para.118–136.
18 *Ibid.,* para. 985.

19 Responsibilities and Obligations of States with respect to Activities in the Area, Advisory Opinion, 1 February 2011, *ITLOS Reports 2011*, p. 10, at p. 50, para. 145. *South China Sea Arbitration* award (Merits), para. 948.
20 *South China Sea Arbitration award* (Merits), *supra* (n. 4), para. 948.
21 *Ibid.*, para. 964.
22 *Ibid.*, para. 966.
23 *Ibid.*, para. 983.
24 *Ibid.*
25 *Ibid.*, para. 975.
26 *Ibid.*, para 977; *Second Carpenter Report*, p. 6,

> he opined in his first report that the earlier generation of concrete structures (including those built) by other states) reduced the coral reefs on which they were installed, displaced the organisms that inhabited them and made the reefs' structural integrity vulnerable to wave action and storm.

27 *Ibid.*, para. 977.
28 *Ibid.*, para. 977; The Carpenter Report referred to pre-2013 construction activities as being 'limited to building discrete structures with a minimal footprint on the natural form and structure of existing coral reefs' (*Second Carpenter Report*, p. 6); *Ferse Report*, p. 59: 'the scale of these previous impacts generally cannot be compared with the environmental harm caused by the construction activities, both in terms of spatial extent and duration'.
29 On this point, see J. W. McManus, *supra* (n. 3), p. 207.
30 See Action Plan for the Protection and Sustainable Development of the marine and coastal areas of the East Asian Region, UNPE(OCA)EAS IG5/6 Annex IV, www.cobsea.org/documents/action_plan/ActionPlan1994.pdf.
31 UNEP/DEPI/COBSEA, IGM 21/INF.5 (22 January 2013) New Strategic Directions for COBSEA 2008–2012, pp. 5–14. See also www.cobsea.org/activities/current_activities.html.
32 H. Kirkman, The East Asian Seas UNEP Regional Seas Programme, *International Environmental Agreements* 6 (2006), 310.
33 S. M. Lexmond, Review of Instruments and Mechanisms for Strengthening Marine Environmental Cooperation in the South China Sea, *UNEP/GEF/SCS Technical Publication* 17 (2008), 24.
34 See T-E. Chua, Coastal and Ocean Governance in the Seas of East Asia: PEMSEA's Experience, *Ocean and Coastal Management* 41(2) (2013), 102, for a list of major projects in the region.
35 See www.unepscs.org/.
36 H. Kirkman, *supra* (n. 32), p. 314.
37 UNEP, Strategic Action Programme for the South China Sea, *UNEP/GEF/SCS Technical Publication* 16 (2008), 1.
38 M. N. Basiron and S. M. Lexmond, Review of the Legal Aspects of Environmental Management in the South China Sea and Gulf of Thailand, *Ocean and Coastal Management* 85 (2013), 266: 'Although the countries participating in the project agreed on the wording and content of the MOU, there was no opportunity for arranging signatures with all ministers present prior to the closure of the UNEP/GEF SCS project'.
39 UNEP Strategic Action Plan for the SCS, *supra* (n. 37).
40 *Ibid*, p. 62. See comments by M. M. Basiron and S. M. Lexmond, *supra* (n. 38), p. 265:

> a majority agreed that a legally-binding agreement was appropriate to strengthen regional cooperation. However, only a few countries supported pursuing a legally-binding agreement at that time. In keeping with the majority view, the RTFL proposed a co-operative management framework with a non-legally binding umbrella instrument.

Chircop also notes that 'treaty-based regional environmental regimes appear to generate antipathy in the region' and he is suggesting a voluntary Memorandum of Understanding on the basis of consensus; A. Chircop, Regional Cooperation in Marine Environmental Protection in the South China Sea: A Reflection on New Directions for Marine Conservation, *ODIL* 41 (2010), 349.

41 V. S. Tuan and J. Pernetta, The UNEP/GEF South China Sea Project: Lessons Learnt in Regional Cooperation, *Ocean and Coastal Management* 53 (2010), 595.

42 *Ibid.*

43 S. Chen, Environmental Cooperation in the South China Sea: Factors, Actors and Mechanisms, *Ocean and Coastal Management* 85 (2013), 136.

44 *Ibid.*

45 *Ibid*, p. 139.

46 See www.pemsea.org/.

47 See www.pemsea.org/about-PEMSEA.

48 See www.pemsea.org/our-work/regional-marine-strategy; Sustainable Development Strategy for the Seas of East Asia Strategy GEF/UNDP/PEMSEA (2015) www.pemsea.org/sites/default/files/SDS-SEA%202015%20FINAL%2011272015%20FULL%20rev_1.pdf.

49 See T-E. Chua, *supra* (n. 34), p. 113.

50 *Ibid*, p. 112.

51 See   www.pemsea.org/publications/agreements-and-declarations/haikou-partnership-agreement-implementation-sustainable.

52 Lexmond, *supra* (n. 33), p. 27.

53 See K. Kheng-Lian and N. A. Robinson, Strengthening Sustainable Development in Regional Intergovernmental Governance: Lessons from the 'ASEAN Way', *Singapore Journal of International and Comparative Law* 6 (2002), 640–682.

54 See http://environment.asean.org/46-2/.

55 See, for example the 2002 Sino-Vietnamese Fishery Agreement in the Gulf of Tonkin.

56 See www.seafdec.org/about/.

57 See M. George, Fisheries Protections in the Context of the Geo-Political Tensions in the South China Sea, *Journal of Maritime Law and Commerce* 43(1) (2012), 86–100.

58 On fisheries refugia and their application in the SCS, see C. J. Paterson *et al.*, Fisheries Refugia: A Novel Approach to Integrating Fisheries and Habitat Management in the Context of Small-Scale Fishing Pressure, *Ocean and Coastal Management* 85 (2013), 214–229. Fisheries refugia were 'developed as a novel approach to the identification and designation of priority areas in which to integrate fisheries and habitat management'.

59 https://fisheries-refugia.org/.

60 Declaration of the Conduct of Parties in the South China Sea, http://asean.org/?static_post=declaration-on-the-conduct-of-parties-in-the-south-china-sea-2.

61 N. Hong, *UNCLOS and Ocean Dispute Settlement: Law and Politics in the South China Sea* (London: Routledge, 2012), p. 179.

62 Y-H. Song, A Marine Biodiversity Project in the South China Sea: Joint Efforts Made in the SCS Workshop Process, *IJMCL* 26 (2011), 122.

63 *Ibid.*, p. 29.

64 S. M. Lexmond, *supra* (n. 33), p. 29.

65 S. Chen, *supra* (n. 43), p. 139.

66 Strategic Action plan, *supra* (n. 37), p. 61. See also S. M. Lexmond, *supra* (n. 33), p. 19, who refers to challenges to mindset, institutional challenges, functional challenges (including processes and mechanisms for cooperation) and ecological and scientific challenges.

67 M. J. Valencia, Regional maritime regime building: prospects in Northeast and Southeast Asia, *ODIL* 31 (2000), 240.

68 J. Bai and H. Hu, Transcending Divisions and Harmonising Interests: How the Arctic Council Experience Can Inform Regional Cooperation on Environmental Protection in the SCS, *Chinese Journal of International Law* 15 (2016), 940.

69 See S-M. Kao *et al.*, Regional Cooperation in the South China Sea: Analysis of Existing Practices and Prospects, *ODIL* 43 (2012), 283–295.

70 N. Hong, *supra* (n. 61), p. 178.

71 *Ibid.*, pp. 178–180.

72 Joint Communique of the 50th ASEAN Foreign Ministers' Meeting (Philippines, 5 August 2017), http://asean.org/storage/2017/08/Joint-Communique-of-the-50th-AMM_FINAL.pdf.

73 See www.cnbc.com/2017/08/06/asean-china-adopt-framework-for-crafting-code-on-south-china-sea.html and www.reuters.com/article/us-asean-philippines-south chinasea/asean-china-adopt-framework-for-crafting-code-on-south-china-sea-idUSK BN1AM0AY.

74 N. Hong, *supra* (n. 61), 216–220.

75 *Ibid.*, para. 87.

76 BIICL, *Report on the Obligations of States under Articles 74 (3) and 83 (3) of UNCLOS in Respect of Undelimited Maritime Areas* (BIICL, 2016), para. 67. The BIICL Report argues that Articles 73/84 and the obligation 'not to jeopardize or hamper the reaching of the final agreement' also applies in instances where the maritime area is also subject to disputes over sovereignty or disputes related to the status of maritime features; see paras. 112–119, but there are limitations with respect to what activities are covered by the restraint obligations especially in instances where sovereignty issues are involved (as the activities may also relate to strengthening their sovereignty claims); there is also some uncertainty concerning whether Articles 74 (3) and 83 (3) are applicable in instances where states disagree whether there is a maritime boundary between them.

77 J. W. McManus, Toward Establishing a Spratly Islands International Marine Peace Park: Ecological Importance and Supportive Collaborative Activities with an Emphasis on the Role of Taiwan, *ODIL* 41 (2010), 270–280; J. W. McManus, The Spratly Islands: A Marine Park Alternative, *Naga, The ICLARM Quarterly* (1992), 4–8. See also J. W. McManus, *supra* (n. 3), pp. 207–210, for an overview of these suggestions.

78 V. Hai Dang, Marine Protected Areas Network in the South China Sea: Charting a Course for Future Cooperation (Leiden: M. Nijhoff/Brill, 2014), p. 237 *et. seq.* A. Chircop, Regional Cooperation in Marine Environmental Protection in the South China Sea: A Reflection on New Directions for Marine Conservation, *ODIL* 41 (2010), 346, 349–350.

79 McManus, *supra* (n. 3), pp. 209–210 referring to the Philippines and Vietnam.

80 See McManus who refers to the establishment of 'a regional body to oversee resources' including 'cutting-edge fisheries analysis and careful selection of management protocols', 'environmental impact analysis and mitigation procedures', *supra* (n. 3), p. 234.

81 *South China Sea Arbitration award* (Merits), *supra* (n. 4), para. 643–648.

82 *Ibid.*, para. 276–278.

83 Statement of the Ministry of Foreign Affairs of the People's Republic of China on the Award of 12 July 2016 of the Arbitral Tribunal in the *South China Sea Arbitration* Established at the Request of the Republic of the Philippines (13 July 2016), www.fmprc.gov.cn/mfa_eng/zxxx_662805/t1379492.shtml.

84 Article 296 (1) LOSC, which provides that 'Any decision rendered by a court or tribunal having jurisdiction under this section shall be final and shall be complied with by all the parties to the dispute'.

85 Article 296 (2) LOSC: 'Any such decision shall have no binding force except between the parties and in respect of that particular dispute'.

86 R. Beckman and L. Bernard, The Use of PSSAs in the South China Sea, Conference paper, Cooperation for the safety of navigation in East Asia: Legal arrangements and

political implications, organised by the National Institute for South China Sea Studies (2011), www.cil.nus.edu.sg/wp/wp-content/uploads/2009/09/Beckman-Hainan-SCS-Nov-2011-rev.pdf.; A. Chircop, *supra* (n. 4078), pp. 347–348.

87 Liu Cigui, *Reflections on Maritime Partnership: Building the 21st Century Maritime Silk Road*, China Institute of International Studies (2014), www.ciis.org.cn/english/2014-09/15/content_7231376.htm.

88 *Ibid.*

89 N. Hong, *supra* (n. 61), p. 172.

12 Conciliation for marine transboundary energy resources

A law and economics approach

Volker Röben and Rafael Emmanuel Macatangay

Introduction

Within the cosmos of risks to marine security, high-end security challenges remain as acute as ever in history. Such challenges pitch States against each other, and their actual or potential conflict often relate to valuable marine energy resources, fossil as well as renewables. Such resources may be known, or merely suspected.

The 1982 UN Convention on the Law of the Sea ('the Convention' or 'UNCLOS'), the universally applicable codification of international law, assigns the right to exploit marine resources exclusively to one or another coastal state. It relies on two concepts enabling the exploitation activities of a coastal state: a continental shelf for seabed resources and an exclusive economic zone ('EEZ') for resources in the water column. However, much of the world's marine energy resources, such as oil, gas and renewables, typically straddle jurisdictional lines. The exploitation activity of one coastal state, depending on how it does so, likely has an undue impact on that of another. In other words, there is a huge risk to the efficient, equitable, or legally certain exploitation of marine transboundary energy resources. The peril arising from the national assignment of the exclusive right to exploit such resources is pervasive, yet remains barely discussed methodically in the literature on the law of sea, international economic law or cognate disciplines.

To help fill this gap, and drawing on the insights of the law and economics literature, this chapter proposes a conciliatory approach that considers a marine transboundary energy resource as a whole, an undivided unit abutting the disputing states, in order to maximise aggregate social welfare. It aims to move beyond the concept of 'joint development', whose presuppositions about sovereignty are obscuring the view on the objective of reaching an efficient outcome that maximises the social welfare of all states concerned. The objective of this chapter is to characterise axioms of rationality underpinning international conciliation for the governance of marine transboundary energy resources. The analytical foundations of this chapter are the advance of social welfare, the instrumentality of treaty-as-contract, and the integration of legal concepts and economic analysis.

This chapter then argues that an axiomatic assembly of instruments, bringing the explanatory and predictive powers of contract theory and allied concepts to bear upon an international setting, can serve as a tool for states wishing to reach an agreement through compulsory or voluntary conciliation, in order to achieve efficient, equitable, and legally certain outcomes for exploiting undisputed or disputed marine transboundary energy resources.

The chapter makes this argument in three steps. The first step is to discuss the positive outcome of the first ever international conciliation under UNCLOS, the Maritime Boundaries Treaty signed on 6 March 2018 between Timor-Leste and Australia ('the Treaty'), containing a special regime for the Greater Sunrise Field in the Timor Sea ('special regime'). The second step is to investigate conciliation in general and assess how the design of international conciliation proceedings under the Convention assists states in reaching a specific type of agreement on marine transboundary energy resources in particular, a so-called unitisation agreement. Finally, the third step is to identify general contractual principles (primitives), the fundamental elements motivating conciliation in an international setting, such as the features of the marine transboundary energy resource, the profile of the disputing states, and the nature of their decisions.

The findings of this chapter produce interdisciplinary insights for the formulation of general principles guiding future efforts at international conciliation over disputed marine areas rich in energy resources.

The rest of this chapter proceeds accordingly. Section two gives a background on and analyses the Maritime Boundaries Treaty between Timor-Leste and Australia and the Special Regime for the Greater Sunrise Area that it sets up, in essence, the outcomes of the conciliation between the two parties. Section three positions this chapter in the literature and defines its philosophical premises on the function of international conciliation and unitisation agreements. Section four is an analysis of contractual primitives potentially inspiring international conciliation amongst disputing states. Section five offers conclusions, indicates possible practical application of the findings, and suggests areas for further interdisciplinary research in marine energy resources.

The Maritime Boundaries Treaty between Timor-Leste and Australia

The Timor Sea is located between Australia and Timor-Leste and Indonesia to the north. It contains rich deposits of natural gas and oil. It is less than 200 nm wide, and so the maritime entitlements of the riparian states to an EEZ and a Continental Shelf (CS) necessarily overlap. Prior to Timor-Leste's regained independence,[1] Australia and the United Nations Transitional Administration in East Timor (UNTAET) had negotiated a non-binding agreement for the joint development of an area of the Timor Sea.[2] In 2002, Timor-Leste and Australia concluded the Timor Sea Treaty.[3] That treaty provided for the application of Timor-Sea Arrangement as between the parties.

The maritime boundaries between Timor-Leste and Australia were never settled. Negotiations were started but unsuccessful. In 2016, Timor-Leste commenced conciliation proceedings, given that Australia has made use of the opt-out option under Article 298 UNCLOS. The Conciliation Commission proceedings conducted under the auspices of the Permanent Court of Arbitration[4] resulted in a report with recommendations and annexes.[5] Importantly, however, the proceedings had an iterative character, comprising milestones. In August 2017, the Commission presented a comprehensive package and a relating work plan to the parties that those accepted.[6] On 6 March 2018, Timor-Leste and Australia signed a new Maritime Boundaries Treaty, constituting the culmination of proceedings. The new Maritime Boundaries Treaty delimits the maritime boundary between Timor-Leste and Australia in the Timor Sea.[7] But the Treaty separately addresses the legal status of the Greater Sunrise gas field. This gas field straddles the new jurisdictional lines of the EEZs of both parties. Annex B of the Treaty establishes a Special Regime for Greater Sunrise. The Annex innovates by providing that the parties will be jointly exercising their jurisdiction as per Article 77 UNCLOS.[8] But most importantly for the present purpose, that regime determines a pathway to the development of the resource by the parties.

This pathway has a number of features. It establishes an institutional set-up in the shape of a two-tiered regulatory structure for the regulation and administration of the Greater Sunrise Special Regime, consisting of a Designated Authority and a Governance Board and a Dispute Resolution Committee.[9] It also requires the drawing up of a Development Plan for the Greater Sunrise Fields. Production of Petroleum from the Greater Sunrise Fields shall not commence until a Development Plan has been submitted by the Greater Sunrise Contractor in accordance with the Greater Sunrise Production Sharing Contract and been approved.[10] As soon as practicable, the Designated Authority shall enter into the Production Sharing Contract under conditions equivalent to those in the existing licences issued under Article 22 of the Timor Sea Treaty and Article 27 of the Unitisation Agreement.[11] It also indicates two options for how upstream revenue from Greater Sunrise will be shared 70/30 in Timor-Leste's favour if the field is developed by a pipeline to Timor-Leste, or 80/20 in Timor-Leste's favour if the field is developed by a pipeline to Australia.

Furthermore, there is a process being put in place that is to assist the parties in concretising Annex B of the Treaty. In its Report, the Commission identifies a process by which it remains at the disposition of the parties beyond the formal end of the conciliation. It sets out the relevant items for discussion in a series of annexes on specific issues of the regime.[12]

How to conceptualise this regime? Under the general normative-legal understanding, a regime is series of international rules that belong together, and which must be accepted together.[13] From an economic point of view, this regime forms a unitisation agreement for a transboundary marine energy resource. The successful first ever conciliation under UNCLOS proves that the mechanism for the design of such agreed regimes exists.

Conciliation and unitisation agreements under the Convention

International conciliation is a long-standing mechanism in third party dispute settlement.[14] Although not much used by states in the more recent past, its features are well accepted. In contradistinction from the adjudication and arbitration, conciliation does not lead to a binding outcome, but to a proposal. Other than that, the procedure and competence is not too well defined, and it may well resemble arbitration or adjudication.

One of the important innovations of UNCLOS is that it formalises conciliation as a general mechanism of third party settlement of disputes concerning the Convention. Annex V deals with Conciliation. Where parties have agreed to conciliation of a dispute relating to the Convention pursuant to Article 284 UNCLOS, any party may institute such proceedings.[15] Section 1 then determines rules for the constitution, the procedure, and the functions of a commission, and the report. Annex V can, of course, be used generally, for all disputes concerning the interpretation or application of the Convention.

Annex V, Section 2 innovates, referring to the compulsory conciliation of delimitation disputes pursuant to Section 3 of Part XV of the Convention. The Convention provides for principles of a high level of abstraction on the delimitation of the EEZ and CS of states with opposite coasts (Articles 74 and 83).[16] These principles are underpinned by dispute settlement. According to Article 288 UNCLOS, there is compulsory adjudication, unless one of the parties has made a declaration under Article 298(1)(a) UNCLOS to opt out. In that case, either party can refer the dispute to conciliation pursuant to Annex V of the Convention. Article 298 then provides that the parties shall negotiate an agreement on the basis of the report of the conciliation commission. The provision's wording is not entirely clear, but it is generally interpreted to mean that there is no obligation to submit to binding adjudication if these attempts are not successful.

Such conciliation by an independent third party, rather than adversarial arbitration and adjudication, can assist States to reach agreement on the governance of transboundary resources. In the Law of the Sea literature, such governance has been discussed under the label of joint development.[17] This may have been helpful at some point, but it now comes with a baggage of presuppositions and assumptions about sovereignty that are in danger of obscuring the view on the underlying principles. This chapter, therefore, takes a step back, and does not use the term. It rather seeks to clear the perspective on the underlying idea of establishing an overall efficient (optimal) approach to the management of the resource that benefits all.

In what follows, the rationale for a particular type of such agreement, a unitisation agreement, is discussed. It is optimal to consider a shared resource, such as an oil or gas reservoir, as an undivided unit to maximise aggregate social welfare. This is well understood for resources under the jurisdiction of one sovereign. Garcia Sanchez and McLaughlin[18] show that, based on technical criteria, the optimal approach to the unit exploitation of a reservoir shared by several parties includes not only the estimated number, location, and timing of the wells, but also a process for making subsequent changes to such estimates. Wiggins and Libecap[19] expound on the concept of unitisation. Property rights to the oil are typically assigned only upon its extraction, but the oil itself is migratory, freely flowing about, whilst in a common pool or reservoir. If multiple firms have fragmented access to the reservoir, they each compete to drill for and extract the oil. Uncoordinated drilling or extraction by one firm increases its share of total output, but increases marginal extraction costs and reduces total oil recovery. The reason is that sub-surface pressure around the wells may fall, and the natural gas throughout the reservoir could be depleted. As a result, the oil risks becoming increasingly viscous, the costly injection of natural gas and water is likely required to raise the pressure, and, as natural gas escapes, oil could be permanently trapped in pockets. By contrast, under the unitisation agreement, a single firm is selected to develop the reservoir, and all firms share in the net returns.

The fundamental purpose of all regulatory policy is arguably to promote social welfare suitably defined.[20] A traditional measure of social welfare is the sum of consumer surplus and producer surplus. A unitisation agreement achieves the social welfare optimum. Unitisation is a contractual solution to rent dissipation, the undue loss of social welfare. Clearly, rent dissipation is a major concern from a functionalist welfare perspective. In the context of transboundary resources, social welfare it is the aggregate welfare of all concerned states interested in the resource and hence their populations. A treaty containing an international unitisation agreement between these states maximises their welfare and is the contractual solution to any rent dissipation. It bears pointing out that this rationale for a unitisation agreement applies to all resources that are transboundary, in the formal the sense that they are not under the undisputed exclusive jurisdiction of one state. In other words, it fits all resources that straddle accepted marine boundaries, or resources that are in parts of the sea that do not have clear boundaries and where claims of states intersect or overlap.

A unitisation agreement achieves Pareto efficiency if it is perfect.[21] In that respect, if not in other normative respects, the agreement between states can be equated to a contract. Contract is one of the 'master institutions' of society.[22] Indeed international law, Posner and Sykes explain,[23] is an explicit contract (e.g. a treaty) or an implicit contract (e.g. customary international law). A role for international law is to enable states to move from an inefficient, non-cooperative equilibrium to an efficient, cooperative equilibrium. In the absence of a world government, the benefits from cooperation are obtained through the establishment of a self-enforcing treaty in which the strategy profile with a superior payoff is a Nash equilibrium.[24] 'Properly conceived, the best way to understand international law is as a Nash Equilibrium – a focal point that states gravitate toward as they make rational decisions regarding strategy in light of strategies selected by other states'.[25] Without a third-party enforcer, '... nations will tend to comply with international law only if compliance is in their self-interest'.[26]

There are parallels with other shared natural resources. In the context of transboundary watercourses, Macatangay and Rieu-Clarke[27] pioneer the concept of an optimal treaty. In the quest for the social welfare ideal, the conceptualisation of international law as a contract, explicitly as a treaty or implicitly as a norm, brings forth a set of market-based mechanisms for the continuous estimation of optimal water allocations among riparians. A unified modelling framework, articulating the promotion of social welfare, the estimation of impartial transfers, and their use as monetary damages or non-monetary inducements, offers a coherent set of analytical devices enabling states to move from an inefficient, non-cooperative equilibrium to an efficient, cooperative equilibrium.[28] Solving for a dominant strategy and Pareto-superior Nash equilibrium, it serves as a common language for riparians contemplating the optimisation of their water allocations in the context of treaty formation or execution. A treaty is to be optimised through a continuous cycle of efforts to perfect or complete it.

This section closes with an inference that international conciliation under the auspices of a third party, such as a commission under Annex V, Section 1 or 2, is uniquely placed to assist the parties in reaching unitisation agreements amongst themselves that cannot be imposed externally. For it provides a collaborative process for disputing states to arrive at a non-binding agreement bringing a resolution or facilitating its discovery. Unpacking this rich concept, the following three key features enable a commission to fulfil this function.

First, the conciliation commission hears the arguments of disputing states and makes proposals in order for them to reach an amicable settlement. In other words, it does not impose a decision, as a court or regulator would, from above. The collaboration intrinsic in the process not only gives birth to a natural agreement arising spontaneously from the proceedings, but also fosters a sense of ownership of the resolution. It thus enhances the prospects of compliance. The non-binding nature of the agreement both respects the sovereignty of the disputing states and relies on their gains from compliance as the inherent incentives to adhere to the agreement. The agreement is essentially a self-enforcing contract, a key mechanism for discipline in a transboundary setting, in which there is no global police.

Second, the conciliation commission has an opportunity to establish a special regime, as it were, a customised organisation, for the efficient, equitable, and legally certain governance of the resource. This is fundamentally a form of law creation, which a court or regulator cannot do. It is legitimate for the commission to do so precisely because of its function to develop and submit proposals that the parties are free to accept or reject. Conciliation becomes a process of law-making in which the proposal of the third party it absorbed into the authoritative consensual treaty-making by the parties.

Third, the natural agreement emerging from international conciliation remains intact and indeed the foundation of ongoing transboundary discourse, even if the disputing states then proceed to grant it the legally binding status of a formal treaty. As a highly desirable result, therefore, the compelling logic constituting the cornerstone of the conciliation proceeding would have been explicitly formalised as international law. This chapter, in effect, incubates a collection of analytical prototypes helping explain or predict the propensity for international conciliation in disputes involving marine transboundary energy resources. The next section expatiates that the three contractual primitives become maxims for the design of international conciliation on transboundary resources, paving the way for the generalisability of treaty optimisation concepts.

Contractual primitives

Conciliation between two or more states with marine resource entitlement under the Convention is a general mechanism to arrive at agreed outcome. It is, by law of the Convention and by default, available to either party to a maritime delimitation dispute in the technical sense. It is also available to the parties to broader disputes relating to marine resources, by their consent (Article 284 UNCLOS). After reviewing both the first ever UNCLOS-conciliation and theoretical foundations, this section develops three contractual primitives at the heart of international conciliation for the governance of marine transboundary energy resources: the features of the resource, the profile of the disputing states, and the nature of their decisions. The following discusses each of them in turn.

The first contractual primitive enshrines that marine transboundary energy resources are exploited in merit order (i.e. starting with the lowest risk-adjusted and geology-informed cost). This is hardly a controversial matter. As discussed above, in the quest for social welfare, there is an optimal approach, based on commercial and technical standards, to the exploitation of the resource. In the absence of an approach considering the resource as an undivided whole, there is a tendency for undesirable rent dissipation that reduces overall social welfare.

If the natural agreement emerging from international conciliation is a perfect contract, facilitating the merit order exploitation of a marine transboundary energy resource, the outcome is Pareto efficiency. Yet it is obvious that few contracts, if any, attain perfection. Various sources of contractual failure, such as irrationality, coercion, externalities, lack of or asymmetric information, high transaction costs, or market power, may give rise to contractual imperfection. In the context of energy resources, there are often deep roots of contractual failure hindering merit order exploitation, such as pride of ownership and operational control, loss of operating experience, strategically holding out for an increase in shares or due to a structural advantage, ignorance, mistrust, communication difficulties, anxiety from reduced current income, fear of violating antitrust laws, or the presence of two reservoir substances (i.e. oil and gas, rather than oil or gas only) with varying levels of uncertainty.[29] In the context of oil, Wiggins and Libecap identify two principal problems of contractual failure: hold-out strategies of firms seeking to enlarge their share of rents, and imperfect or asymmetric information preventing agreement on lease values.[30] The problem of hold-out strategies concerns the readiness of actors, varying systematically due to structural conditions, to join the unitisation agreement, either early even before production starts or late in the life of the reservoir. The information problem pertains to disputes over subjective opinions or ad hoc approaches of engineers or geologists in the estimation of future reservoir production.

How germane are these two problems in a transboundary setting? On one hand, the problem of hold-out strategies speaks to the inclination of disputing states to participate in neighbourly conversations. The rights and responsibilities of coastal states, as sovereigns, under the Convention, are obviously different to those of profit-maximising firms. On the other hand, the information problem highlights the non-trivial risk that disputing states may simply doubt each other's facts or figures. For this or other reasons, disputing states may dither in their declarations of support for international dialogue. Thus, the problems of hold-out strategies or imperfect or asymmetric information expose the difficulties associated with how the number or distribution of the coastal states involved, or how their relationships with each other, may influence their individual or joint decision-making processes.

This leads to the second contractual primitive, the profile of the disputing states, affirming that the sovereignty of each of them is respected. In principle, a coastal state participating in a conciliation proceeding is a self-determining agent. The key implication is that a coastal state remains free to make decisions, such as the award of operating licenses, on its side of the border. There is, nevertheless, an innate incentive to select operators, ideally through an auction,[31] on the basis of capability (rather than capricious criteria). 'Protecting the unity of deposit through cooperative measures such as joint development or transboundary unitization agreements', Garcia Sanchez and McLaughlin explain, 'balances the sovereign rights of nations to exploit natural resources within their territory as they see fit with the ability to engage in the efficient extraction of hydrocarbon resources'.[32] Indeed a coastal state seriously pursuing social welfare is unlikely to make a knowingly imprudent commercial decision. Thus, an affirmation of sovereignty is not as deal-breaking as it may appear at first blush.

What could be efficiency-reducing is an inconsiderate unilateralism, a misplaced assertiveness, dimming the prospects of contractual success. The hazard of inconsiderate unilateralism is ubiquitous. One of the lessons from unitisation efforts within US territory is that the transaction costs of having a large number of parties may erode the gains.[33] Indeed, many small interests could delay or threaten unitisation. In order to determine the efficacy of private contracting, it is vital to investigate the impact of transactions costs on production or exchange problems. Mohan and Goorha show that, rather than a tragedy of the commons (i.e. the overuse of a resource which nobody owns), there is an analogous tragedy of the anticommons (i.e. the under-use of a resource which has many owners).[34] For example, a piece of land owned by tens of thousands of entities, each having a tiny slice, may hardly be put to any use if the multitude of owners is required to reach an agreement. The resulting under-use of the land is probably not as noticeable as its over-use, but would still have adverse effects on social welfare.

A smaller number of players in oil exploration or production reduces the risk of high transaction costs. This is also likely the case in a transboundary setting involving a limited number of states. Yet, in the absence of a self-enforcing mechanism, such as international conciliation, the efficiency or equity of outcomes depends precariously on not much more than the agency of disputing states. In a vivid display of inconsiderate unilateralism, a coastal state is free not to participate in, or other coastal states are likewise free to plot its outright exclusion from, the transboundary discourse, even for the smallest of reasons. The inclusion of an irrelevant coastal state, or the inadvertent exclusion of a pertinent one, could block the benefits from merit order exploitation. The tendency for international contractual failure, therefore, is a function of whether or not the appropriate states somehow find themselves sat around the table, seriously considering, as a whole, the marine transboundary energy resource they happen to abut. Why, for instance, is Indonesia not a party to the Maritime Boundaries Treaty signed on 6 March 2018 between Timor-Leste and Australia? The historical hurts suffered in the Timor Sea,[35] from an economics perspective, are sunk. How significant, then, is the risk of economic damage in the Greater Sunrise gas field, if only Timor-Leste and Australia are involved in its development?

International contractual outcomes could be inefficient if the structure fails to incorporate both the rights of use and exclusion. If the rights of use and exclusion are unified under single ownership, the unitary owner has the ability not only to use the asset optimally, but also to preclude others from using it. Otherwise, fragmented owners fail to internalise the externality of over-use arising from the exercise of their rights to use (i.e. the tragedy of the commons), or the externality of under-use arising from the exercise of their rights to exclude (i.e. the tragedy of the anti-commons). We claim that international conciliation, through its property of self-enforcement, practically re-structures the property rights of disputing states in order to incorporate and unify their rights of use and exclusion over the marine transboundary energy resource.

In the international context, notwithstanding the number or distribution of the coastal states involved, or their relationships with each other, including the burdens of history, international conciliation serves to guard against the contractual vulnerabilities associated not only with a tragedy of the commons or anti-commons, but also with a misplaced assertiveness. It prompts the decision-making processes of disputing states, within the fullness of their sovereignty, towards the pursuit of aggregate social welfare.

Finally, the third contractual primitive, the nature of the decision-making of disputing states, maintains that international conciliation institutionalises the opportunity for them to choose the optimisation of their aggregate social welfare. This, in principle and practice, is intimately linked to the first and second contractual primitives. Under international conciliation, the agreement proposed by the commission is non-binding, a decision is not imposed on disputing states, and the disputing states freely enter into a self-enforcing contract in which the benefits from concurrence with merit order exploitation motivate compliance. The key implication is that a joint regulatory agency, if disputing states elect to create one, is suitably positioned to actualise the monetisation of the marine transboundary energy resource in an efficient, equitable, and legally certain manner. Such a joint regulatory agency, offering 'a time and place to talk', is in the tradition of an entity typically provided by unitisation agreements, the special regime established under the Maritime Boundaries Treaty between Timor-Leste and Australia, or a joint commission overseeing transboundary watercourses.

The work of the joint regulatory agency inevitably relates to matters of law and economics. For example, as discussed above, the violation of merit order exploitation, perhaps due to uncoordinated drilling or extraction, could reduce total oil recovery or raise marginal extraction costs and consequently harm aggregate social welfare. In the unlikely event of illicit deviations from Pareto optimality, the joint regulatory agency could determine not only the optimal allocations, but also the compensation for the victim (and the penalty for the perpetrator). Moreover, similar to the continuous portfolio optimisation of transboundary watercourse assets, it is highly desirable to grow the value of the constituent goods or services of a marine transboundary energy resource. The portfolio of assets in a marine transboundary energy resource, including but not limited to the substances or commodities in the shared reservoir, the technologies deployed for their exploitation, or the surrounding infrastructure, is large and diverse, and their valuations, individually or in combination, in light of their risks, are always evolving. Thus, through a process of continuous portfolio optimisation, the job of the joint regulatory agency, in the face of uncertainty, is to enhance the market worth of the marine transboundary energy resource on behalf of disputing states.

The joint regulatory agency might have to address the neutrality of the fiscal regimes of disputing states. It is vital to determine if the design or implementation of their fiscal regimes somehow serves as a disincentive for them to participate in an international conciliation proceeding or to support the establishment of a joint regulatory agency. As an illustration, in the context of unitisation negotiations, a coastal state with a royalty rate that changes with the oil price would likely have a different strategy to one with a royalty rate that does not. The challenge for international conciliation or the joint regulatory agency resulting from it is to remind states of the favourable implications of the harmonisation of their fiscal regimes. If fiscal regimes fragmented across disputing states threaten the merit order exploitation of the resource as a whole, then aggregate social welfare is at risk.

Overall, the approach of the joint regulatory agency to transboundary regulation ought to be transparent and flexible. As to transparency, Littlechild[36] shows that, in the context of regulated utilities in the United States and Canada, the underlying philosophy of the regulator, rather than to make all the decisions itself, is to establish an open environment empowering the parties to the proceedings to become active participants. This enables 'good liquidity and price discovery', a multiplicity of views arriving at a level-headed consensus, akin to what might prevail in well-functioning markets. Recent decisions of the US Supreme Court, recognising the technical or institutional complexity of energy markets, rest on whether or not the lower courts have made decisions on the basis of the record, including a variety of expert testimony.[37] This is consistent with the concept of prudence in economic regulation. Indeed transparency or openness in regulatory proceedings, in essence, discussions expressed in general terms accessible to non-specialists, helps avoid regulatory capture. Potentially resulting in inefficiency and inequity at once, regulatory capture concerns the phenomenon of a private interest conquering the public interest.[38] Under a situation of capture, a private actor commandeers legislative or regulatory processes for its benefit at the expense of society as a whole. A misalignment between a private interest and the public interest provides a motive for a private actor to allow or encourage the faulty formulation or untidy execution of legal instruments deemed to bring it disproportionate advantages.

In the context of international conciliation, the legitimacy of a special regime or a joint regulatory agency rests crucially on the healthy flow of appropriate information and support from multiple stakeholders, including the disputing states, but especially an assortment of private actors, such as consultants, service providers, or manufacturers of equipment or machinery. One of the chief determinants of regulatory capture is the information asymmetry between regulators and private actors, in essence, an imbalance in their access to, or their ability to digest, voluminous technical material. It is thus crucial that the participation of private actors in international conciliation or joint regulatory proceedings neither harms the integrity of legal frameworks or the pursuit of justice, nor slows the continuous delivery of ideas or cooperation crucial to the freely expressed goal of disputing states (i.e. efficiency, equity, and legal certainty in the governance of their marine transboundary energy resource).

International conciliation provides the institutionalised opportunity for disputing states to freely make flexible, optimal choices for their portfolio of assets in their marine transboundary energy resource. Thus, the Commission responsible for the international conciliation yielding the Maritime Boundaries Treaty recognises that there are two competing development concepts for the Greater Sunrise gas field: a pipeline to Darwin, Australia ('Darwin LNG'), or a pipeline to Beaço on the south coast of Timor-Leste ('Timor LNG'). Proponents of Darwin LNG claim that the contemporaneous development of a related asset, available only for a limited time period, could enhance the overall value of the Greater Sunrise gas field. Proponents of Timor LNG claim that its features were not given a fair hearing. The Commission encourages the parties to continue their discussions in order to reach an agreement on the development concept. The parties probably have reasonable differences in opinion, especially over the real option seemingly embedded in Darwin LNG. This is an excellent opportunity for the special regime to organise transparent regulatory proceedings for the analysis of competing development concepts *vis-à-vis* the continuous portfolio optimisation, a hallmark of flexibility, of the Greater Sunrise gas field.

Conclusion

The Special Regime for the Greater Sunrise Field, which straddles the new maritime boundary in the Timor Sea, agreed between the parties to the new treaty, can be conceptualised as a unitisation agreement striving at the optimal exploitation of this transboundary marine energy resource for both. More generally, such unitisation agreements are supported by principles of social welfare maximisation, and are achievable under international law through the mechanism of conciliation. That is due to the unique properties of conciliation, which has a law-creating capacity and permits parties to reach a natural agreement that can then be formalised as treaty.

The agreement being optimal for all parties, compliance with it lies in the interest of each. Such agreements becoming self-enforcing, needing no external surveillance or intervention. They defuse tensions and misunderstanding between the parties, enhancing high-end marine security.

This chapter has used analytical prototypes to deploy conciliation maxims supporting treaty optimisation concepts for the governance of marine transboundary energy resources, to be arrived at by means of international conciliation under the Convention. These maxims are generalisable. They can be applied to a relatively straightforward scenario such as the Timor Sea. In such a scenario, two or more states have agreed or determined marine boundaries, straddled by a known resource. But they can also be applied to more complex scenarios. Such a scenario would involve a number of riparian states, with undetermined/contested boundaries, marine spaces both under national jurisdiction and beyond national jurisdiction. And it would involve both known and merely suspected resources. Unitisation through (voluntary) conciliation would prove particularly useful there to arrive at an efficient, equitable and legally certain solution. The South China Sea, among others, may turn out to be a case in point.

Notes

1 Timor-Leste acceded to the Convention, with effect as from 7 February 2013.
2 On 5 July 2001, Australia and UNTAET concluded a Memorandum of Understanding of Timor Sea Arrangement (the 'Timor Sea Arrangement'). The Timor Sea Arrangement established a Joint Petroleum Development Area (the 'JPDA').
3 Timor Sea Treaty between the Government of East Timor and the Government of Australia, East Timor-Australia, signed 20 May 2002 and entered into force 2 April 2003, 2258 UNTS 3. In Annex E, the parties agreed,

> to unitise the Sunrise and Troubadour deposits (collectively known as 'Greater Sunrise') on the basis that 20.1% of Greater Sunrise lies within the JPDA. Production from Greater Sunrise shall be distributed on the basis that 20.1% is attributed to the JPDA and 79.9% is attributed to Australia.

> Timor-Leste and Australia then signed an Agreement relating to the Unitisation of the Sunrise and Troubadour Fields with respect to Greater Sunrise, which entered into force on 23 February 2007.

4 PCA Case N° 2016-10, In the Matter of the Maritime Boundary Between Timor-Leste and Australia (The Democratic Republic of Timor-Leste – and – the Commonwealth of Australia) (The 'Timor Sea Conciliation').
5 Report and Recommendations of the Compulsory Conciliation Commission Between Timor-Leste and Australia on the Timor Sea, 9 May 2018, https://pcacases.com/web/sendAttach/2327.

6 These are contained in annexes to the final report of the Commission. Annex 21: Comprehensive Package Agreement of 30 August 2017 and Annex 22: Protocol to meet the Commission's Action Plan of 25 September 2017.

7 The Treaty signed by the Parties on 6 March 2018 is contained in Annex 28 to the report. It has not yet been ratified by either party.

8 Article 16.

9 Article 5–8.

10 Article 9.

11 Article 4.

12 Annex 23, Exchange of Correspondence between Australia and Timor-Leste on Transitional Arrangements for Bayu-Undan and Kitan; Annex 25, Exchange of Letters between the Commission and the Parties on the interpretation of the treaty provisions relating to the fiscal regime for Greater Sunrise; Annex 26, Supplemental Action Plan of 23 December 2017; Annex 27, Commission Paper on the Comparative Benefits of Timor LNG and Darwin LNG & Condensed Comparative Analysis of Alternative Development Concepts.

13 Territorial and Maritime Dispute (*Nicaragua v. Colombia*), [2012], *ICJ Reports* 2012, pp. 137–139.

14 James Crawford *Brownlie's Principles of International Law*, 8th edn (Oxford: Oxford University Press, 2016). See the discussion and references in the Commission Report, at para 52.

15 Note that the prior conditions set forth in Articles 281–283 UNCLOS, as discussed comprehensively in the *South China Sea Arbitration*, apply. See Conciliation Commission, 19 September 2016, Decision on Competence, reproduced as Annex 9 to the Commission Report.

16 Both provisions call for delimitation to 'be effected by agreement on the basis of international law, as referred to in Article 38 of the Statute of the International Court of Justice, in order to achieve an equitable solution'.

17 David Ong, Joint Development of International Common Offshore Oil and Gas Deposits: 'Mere' State Practice or Customary International Law? *American Journal of International Law* 93 (1999), 771–804.

18 G. Garcia Sanchez and R. McLaughlin, The 2012 Agreement on the Exploitation of Transboundary Hydrocarbon Resources in the Gulf of Mexico: Confirmation of the Rule or Emergence of a New Practice? *Houston Journal of International Law* 37 (2015), 681–792.

19 S. Wiggins and G. Libecap, Oil Field Unitization: Contractual Failure in the Presence of Imperfect Information *American Economic Review* 75 (1985), 368–385.

20 C. Sunstein, Cost-Benefit Analysis and Arbitrariness Review, *Harvard Environmental Law Review* 41 (2017), 1–41.

21 R. Cooter and T. Ulen, *Law and Economics* (Harlow: Pearson, 2014).

22 T. Rakoff, The Five Justices of Contract Law, *Wisconsin Law Review* (2016), 733–796.

23 E. Posner and A. Sykes, Efficient Breach of International Law: Optimal Remedies, Legalized Noncompliance, and Related Issues, *Michigan Law Review* 110 (2011), 243–294.

24 P. Dutta and R. Radner, Self-enforcing climate-change treaties, *PNAS* 101(14) (2004), 5174–5179.

25 J. Ohlin, Nash equilibrium and international law, *Cornell Law Review* 96 (2011), 869–899.

26 E. Posner and A. Sykes, *supra* (n. 23), p. 254.

27 R. Macatangay and A. Rieu-Clarke, The Role of Valuation and Bargaining in Optimising Transboundary Watercourse Treaty Regimes, *International Environmental Agreements: Politics, Law and Economics* (2018), https://doi.org/10.1007/s10784-018-9396-y.

28 A. Rieu-Clarke and R. Macatangay, Towards Optimal Treaties for Transboundary Watercourse Management, presentation at the 36th USAEE/IAEE Conference, September 2018, Washington DC.
29 V. Mohan and P. Goorha 2008 *infra* (n. 34); G. Libecap and J. Smith, Regulatory Remedies to the Common Pool: The Limits to Oil Field Unitization, *The Energy Journal* 22 (2001), 1–26.
30 S. Wiggins and G. Libecap, Oil Field Unitization: Contractual Failure in the Presence of Imperfect Information, *American Economic Review* 75 (1985), 368–385.
31 P. Daniel, M. Keen and C. McPherson, *The Taxation of Petroleum and Minerals (Principles, Problems and Practice)* (New York: Routledge, 2010).
32 G. Garcia Sanchez and R. McLaughlin, *supra* (n. 18), p. 692.
33 G. Libecap and S. Wiggins, Contractual Responses to the Common Pool: Prorationing of Crude Oil Production, *American Economic Review* 74 (1984), 87–98.
34 V. Mohan and P. Goorha, Competition and Unitization in Oil Extraction: A Tale of Two Tragedies, *Review of Law and Economics* 4 (2008), 519–561.
35 For a historical account, see the Memorial of the Democratic Republic of Timor-Leste in the ICJ Case *Questions Relating to the Seizure and Detention of Certain Documents and Data (Timor-Leste v Australia)*, www.icj-cij.org/files/case-related/156/18698.pdf.
36 S. Littlechild, Regulation and Customer Engagement, *Economics of Energy & Environmental Policy* 1 (2012), 1.
37 M. Willrich, *Modernizing America's Electricity Infrastructure* (Cambridge, MA: MIT Press, 2017).
38 C. Devaux, Towards a legal theory of capture, *European Law Journal* (2018), https://doi.org/10.1111/eulj.12217.

13 Cooperation on fisheries management in the South China Sea

Lingqun Li

Introduction

With the Code of Conduct framework agreement recently concluded, the region now finds renewed interests in promoting maritime cooperation among littoral countries in the South China Sea. What are the challenges and obstacles facing the region with regard to maritime cooperation? Of all the major issues that need to be tackled, which one should be started with? What form or structure of cooperative mechanisms is preferable? This chapter attempts to provide insights to these critical questions by looking at two clusters of marine cooperative practices in the area of fisheries management. One cluster consists of past practices of fisheries cooperation between China and its maritime neighbours, the other rich experience of cooperative fisheries management in the Mediterranean Sea. In these practices, the chapter identifies a number of useful elements, which can be applied to establish and promote cooperative mechanisms for fisheries management in the South China Sea.

Fisheries in the South China Sea – prioritising a bilateral approach

The South China Sea (SCS) is usually defined as encompassing a portion of the Pacific Ocean extending from the Strait of Malacca in the southwest to the Taiwan Strait in the northeast. This area includes more than 200 small islands, rocks and reefs used to bolster claims to the surrounding sea and its resources. Over 500 million people in mainland China, Taiwan, the Philippines, Malaysia, Brunei, Indonesia, Singapore, Cambodia, Thailand and Vietnam live within 100 miles of the coastlines.

The SCS is an integrated ecosystem with remarkable biological diversity. It is one of the richest seas in the world in terms of marine flora and fauna, coral reefs, mangroves, sea grass beds and, consequently, fisheries. It supports over 30 per cent of the world's coral reefs, where part of the Coral Triangle is located.[1] According to UN Food and Agriculture Organization (FAO) statistics, of 23 major producer countries/parties in 2015, eight come from the South China Sea region, China (no. 1), Indonesia (no. 2), Vietnam (no. 8), the Philippines (no. 10),

Thailand (no. 13), Malaysia (no. 14), Myanmar (no. 18) and Taiwan (19). Total fisheries' catch of these eight parties constitutes 37 per cent of global marine catch production.[2]

While millions of people rely on fisheries in the SCS for daily consumption of protein and other nutrients, fisheries resources in the SCS are diminishing at a quick pace, threatening to place this important marine area and a huge population in jeopardy.[3] There are a number of reasons for this. These include environment degradation as a result of pollution and other human activities; unsustainable fishing such as overexploitation, now a global phenomenon; destructive fishing using large-size net, poisons or dynamites; IUU fishing; climate change and natural disasters.

Many scholars have pointed out the vulnerability and transnational nature shared by fisheries management in semi-enclosed seas worldwide.[4] It is for this concern that Article 123 of the UN Convention on the Law of the Sea (UNCLOS) specifically calls on countries bordering semi-enclosed seas to cooperate with each other and,

> endeavour, directly or through an appropriate regional organization, to (a) coordinate the management, conservation, exploration and exploitation of the living resources of the sea and (b) to coordinate the implementation of their rights and duties with respect to the protection and preservation of the marine environment.

The SCS is a typical semi-enclosed sea where many highly migratory and other transboundary fisheries inhabit, which are vulnerable to human activities from the vast and populated coastal areas. Both the sources and the impact of threat to fisheries resources identified above exceed the limit of national jurisdiction, which means close cooperation among littoral countries is critical to successful management of fisheries resources in the SCS.

China's practices in cooperative fisheries management

Over the past six decades, China has participated in a number of formal and informal, inter-governmental and non-governmental cooperative fisheries management in its bordering waters (see Table 13.1). China and Japan cooperated through three fisheries arrangements in the Yellow Sea and the East China Sea; China and South Korea entered into one inter-governmental fisheries agreement in the Yellow Sea and the East China Sea; China and Vietnam worked together to manage fisheries in the Gulf of Tonkin (Beibu Bay in Chinese) through three official agreements. There are also bilateral and trilateral mechanisms working at non-governmental level between China, Japan and South Korea. More recently, an informal arrangement between China and the Philippines was established in the Scarborough Shoal area. Overall, as the analysis shows below, these cooperative efforts share some important characteristics. They were all undergirded by pragmatic approaches and together demonstrate great policy flexibility

Table 13.1 Cooperative arrangements between China and its maritime neighbours

Cooperative arrangements		Bilateral	Trilateral
Formal	Inter-governmental	Sino-Japanese Fisheries Agreement (1955, 1975, 1997); Sino-South Korean Fisheries Agreement 2000; Sino-Vietnamese Fisheries Agreement in the Gulf of Tonkin (1957, 1963, 2000)	
	Non-governmental	Bilateral annual meeting between CFA and KFA since 2010; Bilateral meeting between CFA and JFA in 2008	Trilateral annual meeting of CFA, KFA and JFA
Informal		Sino-Filipino informal arrangement of fisheries in the Scarborough Shoal area	

by the relevant parties in terms of the form of cooperation. In the meantime, these arrangements differ greatly from case to case in terms of the drivers and outcomes.

Formal inter-governmental agreements

China and Japan

The need for fisheries management in a cooperative manner began to emerge in waters surrounding China as early on as in the 1950s. At that time, Japanese fishing boats, equipped with distant fishing technology, engaged in large-scale fishing exploitation near Chinese shores and often caused frictions with Chinese fishermen and coastguards. To solve this problem, the governments of China and Japan started to engage each other in 1953, seeking for a framework regulating Japanese fishing activities in waters close to Chinese coastlines bordering the Yellow Sea and the East China Sea. Due to diplomatic constraints, negotiations between the two countries were represented by non-governmental entities – China Fisheries Association and Japan–China Fisheries Council. These two fisheries entities concluded an agreement on fisheries in the Yellow Sea and the East China Sea in 1955 (the 1955 Agreement), marking China's first bilateral arrangement on fisheries management. The agreement was renewed several times in the following years, but the main goal of such arrangement as envisaged in the agreement remained the same, that is, to reduce conflicts of fishing activities through better regulation.[5]

Soon after China and Japan established official diplomatic relations, the two governments entered into a second cooperative arrangement in 1975 –*Fisheries Agreement between the Government of the People's Republic of China and the Government of Japan* (the 1975 Agreement). Compared with the 1955 Agreement, the 1975 Agreement applied stricter rules and new measurements, such as moratorium and fisheries protection zone, for the purpose of fisheries conservation. A Joint Fisheries Committee was established under the new Agreement, which was the first institutional cooperative mechanism specialised in fisheries management in China's surrounding waters.[6]

The latest fisheries cooperative management effort between China and Japan took place in the 1990s. With the 1982 UNCLOS scheduled to enter into force, China and Japan started to negotiate on a new framework to bring fisheries activities of both sides in line with the implementation of the Exclusive Economic Zone regime in the Yellow Sea and the East China Sea. The two countries concluded the 1997 Fisheries Agreement, which entered into force in 2000.[7] The two countries agreed to set aside the thorny issue of maritime delimitation and cooperate through a provisional arrangement to manage fisheries resources in the two seas. Compared with previous Sino-Japanese fisheries agreements, the latest one was primarily driven by the need and rising awareness of conserving the rich, transboundary, yet quickly depleting, fisheries resources shared by the two countries.

China and South Korea

In 1993, China and South Korea started to work on an official agreement managing fisheries activities in the Yellow Sea and the East China Sea. Both countries ratified the UNCLOS in 1996 and were determined to implement the UNCLOS in their maritime governance. After nearly 30 rounds of negotiation over 7 years, the two sides finally reached an agreement on 3 August 2000 in which a cooperative framework was established to manage the shared fisheries resources in the two seas.[8] Again, like the 1997 agreement between China and Japan, the Sino-South Korean fisheries agreement was intended to be a provisional arrangement pending the final resolution of maritime delimitation.

China and Vietnam

Similar to Sino-Japanese fisheries management, China and Vietnam cooperatively arranged fisheries activities in the Gulf of Tonkin for more than half a century. China and Vietnam signed two fisheries agreements in 1957 and 1963, respectively.[9] These two agreements recognised exclusive fishing rights in each other's territorial seas. It is worth noting that these two agreements timely reflected changes in the legal regime governing territorial seas. The 1957 agreement restricted Chinese fishing activities in a belt of six nautical miles seaward from Vietnamese coast and vice versa. In 1963, the length was extended to 12 nautical miles, reflecting the trend of growing acceptance of 12 nautical miles of territorial seas.[10]

More importantly, China and Vietnam managed to reach a package deal that simultaneously resolved dispute over maritime boundary and arranged for a framework of fisheries cooperation. This process started in 1991 and after rounds of painstaking negotiations, the two countries signed two agreements in December 2000, one on maritime delimitation in the Gulf of Tonkin and the other fisheries cooperation in the Gulf of Tonkin.[11]

Non-governmental mechanisms of fisheries cooperation among China, South Korea and Japan

In addition to inter-governmental cooperation on fisheries management, there have been several fisheries cooperative mechanisms working at non-governmental level, mainly through national fisheries associations from China, South Korea and Japan, to supplement and meet the challenges of fisheries management in shared seas. Their presence in the fisheries regime between China and its neighbours helped to reduce accidents and frictions caused by competition over fisheries in provisional measures zones (joint fishing zones) and enhanced the effective management of fishing activities.[12]

The entry into force of Sino-Japanese fisheries agreement and Sino-South Korean fisheries agreement in 2000 and 2001 respective introduced significant changes to traditional fishing activities in the Yellow and the East China Sea and consequently, the area witnessed increasing fishing disputes. Moreover, the issue of managing fisheries in overlapping areas to which all three countries claimed put another challenge before fisheries regulators in the three countries. In view of these challenges, non-governmental fisheries entities – Chinese Fisheries Association (CFA), Japan Fisheries Association (JFA) and the Korea Fisheries Association (KFA) engaged with each other through a trilateral mechanism to help coordinate and facilitate the handling of disputes between fishermen from the three countries.[13] This mechanism has proved to be quite productive, emanating the establishment of a trilateral annual meeting, a series of fisheries-related documents such as the Initiative on Safeguarding Fisheries Operation at Sea and two Protocols on the safety of fishing operations between China and South Korea in 2004 and China and Japan in 2007, respectively, as well as a number of seminars related to maritime safety and the management of fisheries disputes and accidents. On a bilateral level, there have been annual meetings between CFA and KFA since 2010 and non-governmental meeting are convened between CFA and JFA on need-based.[14]

Informal fishing arrangements between China and the Philippines

Unlike the aforementioned arrangements, which are all guided by publicised written agreements, the fishing arrangement between China and the Philippines in the Scarborough Shoal is more of a tacit consensus between the top leaders from the two countries following the Filipino President Duterte's state visit to China in consideration of the high sensitivity of the Scarborough Shoal.[15] This arrangement allows Filipino fishermen to enter the lagoon area of the Scarborough Shoal to operate fishing activities. Subsequently, the two governments agreed to reactivate the joint fisheries committee, which was originally established in 2004 but ceased to function since the first meeting in 2005. The annual meeting of the Sino-Filipino joint fisheries committee was resumed in April 2017 in Manila. The two sides decided to deepen cooperation in several areas including fisheries technology transfer, capacity building and assistance, training and exchanges, product import and joint ventures.[16]

The aforementioned cooperative efforts on fisheries management between China and its maritime neighbours share a few important features. First, these arrangements were largely driven by rising demand to regulate competition over fisheries resources. It is known that for centuries, fishermen from bordering countries have been operating in the Yellow Sea, the East China Sea and the South China Sea (including the Gulf of Tonkin). Thanks to the abundance of resources and limited fishing technology, peaceful coexistence dominated the pattern of these fishing practices for most of the time. However, starting from the 1950s, this situation began to alter, when technical advancement enabled large-scale operations and overexploitation of fisheries and greatly intensified competition among fishermen from littoral countries in these regional seas. The tension was further fuelled by the implementation of EEZ in the 1990s. This is the background from which the need for cooperation on fisheries management emerged.

Second, these arrangements, accordingly, responded to the gradual transition in the governance of world's oceans from a regime of limited regulation to a more sophisticated and comprehensive maritime order, reflecting the acute awareness on the part of China of the development of the Law of the Sea. One example, as mentioned earlier, is the extension of territorial sea from 6 NM in the 1957 Sino-Vietnamese fishery agreement to 12 NM in the 1963 agreement, a timely adjustment to the 12 NM standard for territorial seas as codified in the 1958 Convention on the Territorial Sea and the Contiguous Zone. The other example is the three latest bilateral agreements that China concluded with Japan, South Korea and Vietnam, behind which the consideration of implementing EEZ regime served as the main driver.

Third, these cooperative efforts, in particular the latest three official agreements, highlight a considerable degree of policy flexibility and pragmatism of China and its neighbours in an effort to implement modern international Law of the Sea. Table 13.2 illustrates the designation of different zones established under the latest three official agreements, which shows that each cooperation is tailored to cope with existing practices and suit the special circumstances in each case.

Table 13.2 Zoning of the Fisheries Agreements between China and Japan, South Korea and Vietnam

Zones Agreements	Provisional measures zone	Joint fishing zone	Transitional zone	Status quo zone	Special zone
1997 China–Japan Agreement	X			X	X (longline squid zone)
2000 China–South Korea	X		X	X	
2000 China–Vietnam		X	X		X (buffer zone for artisanal fishing)

In the 1997 Sino-Japanese agreement, pending the final resolution of EEZ, a large Provisional Measures Zone (PMZ) was established, between the near-coast EEZs of the two countries, to promote management and conservation of fisheries resources; a Status Quo Zone (SQZ) was designated to maintain existing fishing activities; and a Special Zone (SZ) was preserved for traditional longline squid catch by Chinese fishermen. Cooperation of management and conservation was established in four major aspects: (1) a joint fisheries committee recommending fisheries quota, other regulation measures and proposals of marine cooperation; (2) obligation of joint scientific research and conservation of living resources; (3) rights in the PMZ to report unlawful activities to the flag state of fishing boats under its administration; (4) mutual assistance to fishing boats and crew members in distress.

In the 2000 Sino-South Korean agreement, three types of zones were established: a PMZ and a SQZ, both similar to the Sino-Japanese PMZ and SQZ, and two transitional zones, which were EEZ in nature to allow fishing operations from the other side to gradually phase out (see Figure 13.1). Cooperation was arranged in five areas: (1) a joint fisheries committee recommending fisheries quota, other regulation measures and proposals of marine cooperation; (2) obligation of joint scientific research on the conservation of living resources and exchange information; (3) rights in the PMZ to report unlawful activities to the flag state of fishing boats under its administration; (4) mutual assistance to fishing boats and crew members in distress; (5) joint law enforcement activities such as joint patrols, joint boarding and joint inspection in transitional zones. As of 2011, China and South Korea had conducted 14 joint inspections in transitional zones, five switch boarding of surveillance vessels and quite a few mutual visits of law enforcement officers. Over the years, practice of these cooperative arrangement have yielded a regular and stable mechanism of communication and mutual assistance between Chinese law enforcement authority and the South Korean counterpart.[17]

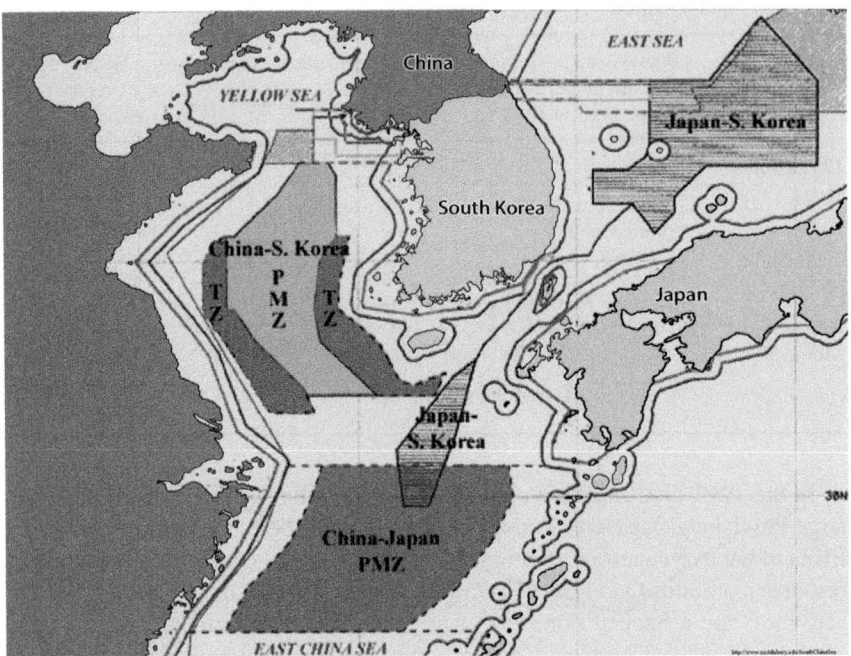

Figure 13.1 Different fishing zones in the Yellow Sea and the East China Sea.

Source: David Rosenberg, Japan China Korea TZs & PMZs, www.southchinasea.org/files/2011/08/Japan-China-Korea-TZs-PMZs.jpg.

In the 2000 Sino-Vietnamese agreement (see Figure 13.2), three zones were set up: a joint fisheries zone (JFZ), a transitional zone, which later divided into two EEZs, and a buffer zone for small-scale artisanal fishing. This agreement envisaged long-term fisheries cooperation in the JFZ, including (1) a joint fisheries committee establishing regulation measures and determining fishing capacity in the JFZ based on regular joint scientific survey on fisheries resources; (2) jointly establishing measures for conservation and sustainable use of the living resources in the JFZ; (3) joint surveillance and inspection in the JFZ. Other cooperation included managing fishing disputes in buffer zone through joint fisheries committee and mutual assistance to fishing boats and crew members in distress.

In comparison, there are three major differences worth noting in these three agreements. First, while all the three agreements were originally negotiated to implement the EEZ, only the Sino-Vietnamese agreement achieved complete success. The Sino-Japanese and Sino-South Korean agreements are essentially provisional arrangements of a practical nature pending the final agreement. Second, the Sino-Japanese PMZ is larger than the Sino-Korean PMZ, this is mainly because the disputed area between China and Japan includes the Diaoyu

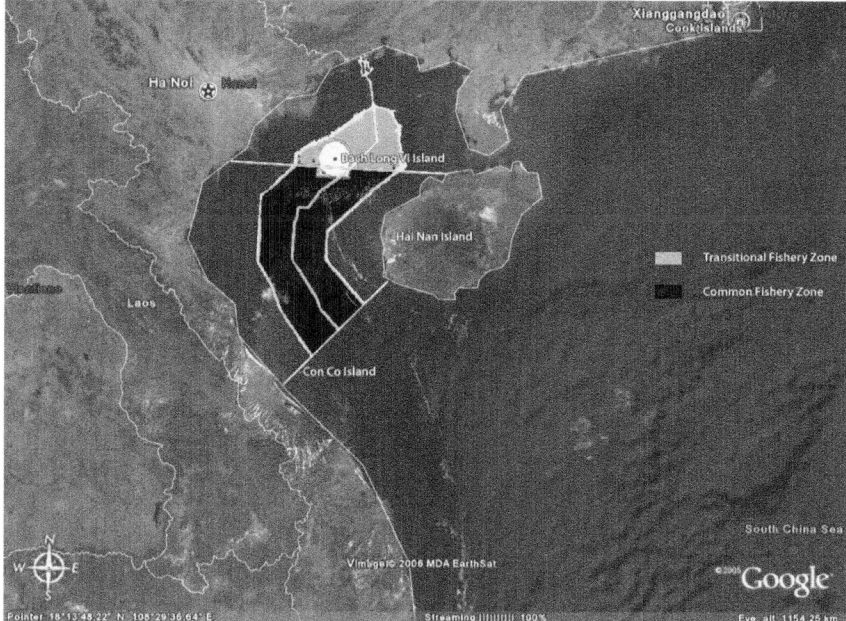

Figure 13.2 Maritime delimitation and fishing zones in the Tonkin Gulf.

Source: David Rosenberg, Tonkin Gulf JRMZ, http://www.southchinasea.org/files/2011/08/Tonkin-Gulf-JRMZ.jpg.

Islands and hence is bigger in size than the area under dispute between China and South Korea. The third difference is that, the Sino-Vietnamese JFC is more powerful and has more authority in fisheries management than the Sino-Japanese and Sino-South Korean counterparts. The Sino-Vietnamese JFC is designed to conduct regular scientific survey, determine fishing capacity and other regulations in the JFZ, and resolve fishing disputes in the buffer zone, while the main duty of the other two JFCs is advisory, that is, making policy recommendations for governments.

Finally, the fact that all the official fisheries agreements China concluded so far are bilateral, seems to suggest that for fisheries cooperation, due to its often sensitive and highly complicated nature, bilateral negotiation may be the first step to start with. As evidenced in the trilateral mechanism set up by non-governmental fisheries organisations, once cooperation is placed on the ground, its functioning will spin off new demand for more sophisticated multilateral mechanism and help to roll in diversified stakeholders and participants.

Fisheries cooperation in the Mediterranean Sea – prioritising a regional framework

The European region has been *avant-garde* in the development of the Law of the Sea regime. There are four regional seas in Europe, the Mediterranean Sea, the Black Sea, the Baltic Sea and the North Sea. Since the end of the Second World War, regional seas in Europe have engaged in quite sophisticated and fruitful cooperation in marine fisheries management. Of these four regional seas, the Mediterranean Sea is most similar to the South China Sea in terms of the reality and challenges the region faces in the area of fisheries cooperation.

The Mediterranean Sea and the South China Sea share some important characteristics. Article 122 of the UNCLOS defines 'enclosed or semi-enclosed sea' as

> a gulf, basin or sea surrounded by two or more States and connected to another sea or the ocean by a narrow outlet or consisting entirely or primarily of the territorial seas and exclusive economic zones of two or more coastal States.

According to this definition, both the Mediterranean Sea and the South China Sea are typical semi-enclosed seas. The two seas are hot spots for navigation, both in strategic and economic terms. Like the South China Sea, the Mediterranean Sea is also rich in biodiversity. Occupying only 0.8 per cent of the world oceans in terms of geography, the Mediterranean Sea contains 10 per cent of the world marine biodiversity.[18] Both are surrounded by many countries, most of which are developing countries, which means economic development takes priority in fisheries management. The Mediterranean Sea is bordered by 22 countries, while the South China Sea has seven bordering countries.[19]

Moreover, these two regional seas are overshadowed by sovereign and maritime disputes that sometime threaten regional peace and stability. In the Mediterranean Sea, the codification of additional maritime entitlements through the 1982 UNCLOS, such as the Exclusive Economic Zone and Continental Shelf, has created a handful of disputes concerning maritime delimitation of these entitlements among littoral states. As Tullio Scovazzi pointed out, if full-size 200 NM exclusive economic zones were to be proclaimed by all its coastal states, no areas of high seas would be left, as no point in the Mediterranean Sea is located at a distance exceeding 200 NM from the nearest land or island.[20] In particular, maritime disputes between Greece and Turkey have been a sore spot in their diplomatic relations and sometimes even involved use of force. In the 1970s and 1980s, the two countries engaged in military build-up due to Turkish exploration activities in contested Continental Shelf in the Aegean Sea, which almost led to open military conflict. In 1996, a military crisis between Greece and Turkey over two small islets in the Aegean Sea caused the death of three Greek officers. Tensions between the two countries have remained to-date.

Despite these similarities, however, the Mediterranean Sea region is much more advanced than the South China Sea region in terms of fishery co-management and maritime cooperation in general. Cooperation in fisheries management in the Mediterranean Sea started as early as in 1949, when a regional conference was held to conclude the Agreement for the establishment of a General Fisheries Council for the Mediterranean (GFCM). The 1949 GFCM agreement was approved by the FAO and entered into force in 1952. At that time, not all bordering countries in the Mediterranean Sea were parties to the GFCM. Only France, Greece, Italy, Lebanon, Turkey, the UK and Yugoslavia were contracting states to the 1949 GFCM agreement.[21] Over the course of nearly seven decades, fishery co-management in the Mediterranean has developed into a systematic, legalised and highly institutionalised management regime.

First, as the most overarching RFMO in the Mediterranean, the GFCM is well-structured and quite powerful. As mentioned earlier, the GFCM has only seven founding countries. Today, the GFCM has 24 contracting parties, including 23 states and the European Union. The GFCM has experienced several major reforms in 1963, 1976, 1997 and 2011. The most important reform took place in 1997, when the General Fisheries Council for the Mediterranean was replaced by a General Fisheries Commission for the Mediterranean. Compared to the Council, the new Commission was more powerful as it acquired legal personality and was able to issue legally binding policy decisions and recommendations.[22]

The GFCM plays a central role in promoting effective functioning of the regional fisheries management regime. It divides the Mediterranean Sea into 27 geographical subareas. Under the GFCM framework, there are delegation meetings, subcommittees and working groups focusing on specific tasks. More importantly, the GFCM has regular connections with other inter-governmental bodies such as the FAO and the EU and non-governmental organisations. This complicated internal structure and external linkages allows the GFCM to play an effective role in coordinating works of major actors in regional fisheries management.

Second, cooperation of fisheries management in the Mediterranean Sea is highly sophisticated. In the beginning, the GFCM was the only regional fisheries management organisation (RFMO) in the Mediterranean. Over the years, more and more organisations and institutions were developed and joined in. Today, the cooperative fisheries management regime in the Mediterranean Sea is composed of a diversified range of governing entities, each with specific mission, authority, geographical focus and targeted species. For example, there is the International Commission for the Conservation of Atlantic Tunas (ICCAT). The ICCAT, established in 1966, is a regional fisheries management organisation responsible for the management of tuna, swordfish, and other large pelagic fish. This includes responsibility for allocating available quotas of these fish stocks among Commission members. The ICCAT has been given exclusive authority in overseeing tuna species and undertaking the range of work required for the study and management of tunas and tuna-like fishes in the entire Atlantic including the

Mediterranean sea.[23] Besides the GFCM and ICCAT, there also exist a number of scientific advisory entities and non-government organisations, which participate in regional fisheries co-management, such as the International Council for the Scientific Exploration of the Mediterranean (ICSEM), World Wildlife Fund (WWF) and International Union for Conservation of Nature (IUCN) and Green Peace. Some of these organisations supplement the operation of fisheries management works through their own projects, others provide scientific information and policy recommendations for major fisheries management organisations as well as coastal government agencies responsible for fisheries management. For example, the IUCN conducted regular reports on the conservation status of fishing stocks in the Mediterranean, which help the EU with the design of fisheries policy.[24] The Green Peace, a well-funded NGO, makes regular dispatches of vessels to visit fishing grounds, harbours and airports in the Mediterranean sea region, obtaining timely information of fisheries-related activities and reporting illegal fishing.[25] Meanwhile, very specific measures have been developed to better manage fishing activities in the region. Two control systems have been in implementation, one on quota control and the other fishing capacity. These measures cover different aspects of fisheries activities including artisanal fishing, commercial fishing, marine production market, marine aquaculture and other related activities.

Third, cooperative management of fisheries in the Mediterranean has turned out to be quite effective in ensuring a stable environment for fisheries development in the region, thanks to decades of smooth functioning of the GFCM and the implementation of common fisheries policy (CFP) of the European Economic Community/European Union, which highlights the principle of stable development in fisheries management. In the meantime, however, emphasis on stable fisheries development has left the issue of overexploitation of fisheries largely unattended and, as a result, the Mediterranean region left far behind other regional seas in Europe in terms of the fisheries preservation and conservation. In recent years, to respond to the urgent need to alter the trend of quick depletion of fish stocks in the Mediterranean Sea, focus has shifted from regulating fishing activities to cooperation on fisheries conservation/sustainable fisheries management. The Mediterranean nations signed a declaration in Venice in 2003 that laid the foundation to improve scientific research, protect vulnerable areas and limit fishing capacity, and EU member states agreed to reduce their fleets in an effort to ensure sustainable fishing. In 2017, the European Union launched a new initiative called 'MedFish4ever' in 2017, in an effort to mobilise Mediterranean states in particular the southern and eastern countries to commit political will to determined action using a comprehensive approach to improve the state of the fishing stocks.[26]

A number of factors have been identified as conducive to those remarkable achievements outlined above with respect to cooperative fisheries management in the Mediterranean region. Peter M. Hass long ago pointed out that the active presence of epistemic community, comprised of ecologist, marine scientists and informed government officials, played a constructive role in raising awareness of marine protection and facilitating cooperation among bordering states in the Mediterranean region.[27] Contribution from the EEC and later on the EU was believed to be critical in promoting continual region cooperation in managing marine environment and the fisheries resources. The EEC/EU has long been an active member in major fisheries management mechanisms such as the GFCM and the ICCAT. One of the effective tools the EU employs to shape regional fisheries management is its CFP. The CFP guides and coordinates fisheries activities of all EU member states in the Mediterranean. In recent years, a series of fisheries-related policy initiatives under the EU framework have been introduced into the Mediterranean Sea. These include Multi-annual Guidance Programs, IIU Regulations, Marine Strategy framework Directive, Integrated Marine Policy, and others. Through the implementation of these policy, this powerful and ambitious inter-government organisation steers regional cooperation in fisheries governance in the Mediterranean Sea.

More importantly, from a practical perspective, the design of a regional framework, that is, a top-down approach, a key in facilitating the formulation and fruitful development of regional cooperation in fisheries management in the Mediterranean Sea. Marine cooperation in the Mediterranean Sea is featured by being bracketed in an overarching regional framework. Marine environmental protection in the Mediterranean has been operating for nearly four decades under the Mediterranean Action Plan (Med Plan), a region-wide regime for marine pollution control in the Mediterranean Sea. Hailed as a model framework for regional marine protection, the design of the Med Plan was promulgated worldwide through the UNEP Regional Seas programme. Cooperative fisheries management in the Mediterranean, as illustrated earlier, also started under a regional overarching mechanism – the GFCM – and achieved distinctive success compared with other semi-enclosed sea regions. What these two arenas of marine governance in the Mediterranean share in common is that from the very beginning, UN organs served as the leading actor instituting a regional overarching framework. The Med Plan was designed, funded and implemented by the UNEP through the Regional Seas programme, while the GFCM was initiated by and put under the FAO as part of the latter's effort to establish regional fisheries management organisations across the world.

In the meantime, the EEC/EU through its active presence has provided strong support, both politically and financially, and propelled the deepening and coordination of regional efforts in fisheries co-management under an overarching regional framework. This is done in three dimensions. First, with regard to financial support, the EU is a major donor for the new GFCM. It also provides generous financial assistance for regional fisheries management through a series of funding programmes, major ones including Financial Instrument for Fisheries Guidance, European Fisheries Fund and European Marine Fisheries Fund.[28]

Second, the EU plays a steering role in setting the agenda, guiding the direction, and promoting specific approaches of regional fisheries cooperation. Since the 1990s, the EU organised ministerial meetings and special seminars on fisheries management to enhance interaction and communication among fisheries departments of Mediterranean countries. In 1991, the EU convened a conference 'Fisheries in the 1990s' in Spain, in which it proposed closer cooperation between Mediterranean states and distant fishing states operating in the region in efforts to implement comprehensive fisheries management policy. It also called for setting up regular meetings at the ministerial levels to bring together government officials from across the region to cooperate and coordinate their fisheries policy. The EU closely followed the latest development in international fisheries management regime and actively introduced new principles and approaches in Mediterranean fisheries management. For example, the concept of sustainable development was widely promulgated in the Rio earth summit in 1992.[29] The EU introduced this concept in fisheries management in the Mediterranean in the Mediterranean Ministerial meeting in 1994 and launched a range of programs such as Community Action Plan for the conservation and sustainable exploitation of fisheries resources in the Mediterranean Sea to implement the principle of responsible and sustainable fishing.[30] For this purpose, Medisamak – a trans-Mediterranean association of fisheries organisation was established in 2003, bringing together both EU and non-EU states bordering the Mediterranean Sea to promote better coordination and implementation of sustainable fishing in the region.

The third dimension is the broad political environment. The EEC/EU has for decades been promoting political integration and unity of the Mediterranean region, thus creating an amicable atmosphere of trust and confidence conducive to regional cooperation. The Mediterranean Sea region traditionally has close bond with Europe. Political, economic and cultural exchanges and interactions date back centuries between the European and non-European countries in the Mediterranean Sea and between the Mediterranean area and the European continent more generally. Given the traditional linkage and the need to expand its influence, the EEC/EU started to strengthen ties with Maghreb and Mashreq countries by offering trade opportunities as well as financial support to assist environment and fisheries management in the Mediterranean as early as in the 1960s. This trend continued with a greater effort in the post-Cold war era, as the EU attempted to fill in the power vacuum left out by the Soviet Union's retreat and counter the diffusion of terrorism in this region. This led to the Barcelona Declaration in 1995, which launched the so-called 'Barcelona Process', an initiative aimed at promoting regional political integration among the 15 EU member states and 12 non-EU states surrounding the Mediterranean Sea. A comprehensive Euro-Mediterranean partnership was established as a major fruit emanated from the Barcelona Process, covering cooperation on a diversified range of issue-arenas including marine governance, of which marine fisheries management is a major element.[31] After ten years of Barcelona Process, France proposed the idea of Union for the Mediterranean (UFM) in 2007, an upgraded version of the Euro-Mediterranean partnership designed to further boost integration and cooperation of the pan-Mediterranean region. As a result, the first Mediterranean Summit was convened in July 2008 during which the UFM was officially established. The UFM members include the 28 Member States of the European Union and 15 Mediterranean partner countries from North Africa, the Middle East and Southeast Europe. One of the six priority areas for action highlighted by the UFM – water and environment – is closely related to marine fisheries management as part of regional cooperative efforts on marine environment protection and sustainability of biodiversity and natural resources.[32]

To sum up, cooperative fisheries management in Mediterranean Sea has achieved distinctive success. It started from a very basic framework seven decades ago and developed into a comprehensive and vibrant regime of management. From a practical perspective, this achievement hinges upon a well-designed regional framework implemented and supported by strong and powerful organisations – in particular the FAO and the EEC/EU. The institutional, financial and political resources provided by these organisations directed regional efforts to the adherence to, and smooth operation of, the regional framework of cooperation.

Fisheries cooperation in the South China Sea: useful elements

Practices of fisheries cooperation in the Mediterranean Sea have yielded rich experience from which decision makers in the SCS can draw to push forward fisheries cooperation in the SCS region. An important lesson identified in the Mediterranean experience is that a regional framework could be quite conducive to forging regional cooperation. In the SCS, a regional framework is both desirable and feasible for orchestrating regional efforts in fisheries management. A regional framework for fisheries cooperation could serve as a basic platform providing venues where regional countries can sit side by side to discuss about fisheries issues and share concerns. Such a framework can start with a general and simple design, and, as shown in the Mediterranean case, once placed on the ground, it will gradually expand to become more sophisticated and enrol in more and more stakeholders and relevant parties. The region has developed a solid foundation upon which such a regional framework could be established – that is, the DOC implementation mechanism between China and ASEAN. The 2002 DOC stipulated that 'pending a comprehensive and durable settlement of the disputes, the Parties concerned may explore or undertake cooperative activities'. Of the five areas listed in the DOC as priority areas for parties to engage in cooperative activities, two were related to fisheries management: (1) marine environmental protection and (2) marine scientific research.[33] The China-ASEAN DOC implementation mechanism emanated a number of cooperative projects and initiatives relating to fisheries management and the management of marine living resources more generally. A number of seminars on issues related to regional marine studies and marine ecology and biodiversity in the SCS have been organised.

Furthermore, the past few years witnessed the accumulation of political momentum concerning the progress of DOC implementation. Negotiation on the implementation of DOC China and ASEAN are conducted through two interlinked venues: one is China-ASEAN Joint Working Group (JWG on DOC), the other China-ASEAN Senior Officials' Meeting on the implementation of the DOC (SOM on DOC). As illustrated in Table 13.3 and Table 13.4, negotiation on the implementation of the DOC between China and ASEAN accelerated in the post-2013 period. The first China-ASEAN Senior Officials' Meeting on the implementation of the DOC was convened in 2004. Between 2004 and 2012, there were only five SOM on DOC meetings. In contrast, from 2013 to 2017, China and ASEAN convened nine SOM on DOC meetings, three taking place in the year 2016.

A similar pattern is identified in the China-ASEAN Joint Working Group meetings (see Table 13.4). The first JWG on DOC meetings was held in 2005. Of all 21 JWG on DOC meetings, 13 meetings were convened in post-2013 period.

In 2017, the DOC process achieved a major breakthrough as China and ASEAN agreed on a framework text of the Code of Conduct in the SCS (the COC).[34] The COC was often seen as the most controversial and sensitive part in the implementation of the DOC. The speed-up of negotiation on a legally binding COC issue will not only help to stabilise the region but also boost parties' interests in cooperative efforts in less difficult areas such as fisheries management and environment protection. Therefore, China and ASEAN could use the mechanism of JWG and the SOM on DOC to work on drafting a regional framework on fisheries management as part of the DOC implementation process.

As regards the form of such a regional framework, the Mediterranean region began with a general council, composing of a convention outlining the scope and basic function of the council and member states. In the SCS, compared with a general council under a legally binding convention, an advisory body or a multilateral consulting mechanism between China and ASEAN may be more practical so as to serve as a regular venue for parties to consult fisheries-related issues and share concerns.

Meanwhile, under this regional mechanism, bilateral approaches could also be employed in concrete cooperative programmes. It has been discussed earlier that pragmatism was a key element in past experiences of fisheries cooperation between China and its maritime neighbours. It is also highlighted that bilateral approach is the first choice when it comes to fostering fisheries cooperation in the SCS. So far, fisheries cooperation between China and other bordering states in the SCS is largely bilateral. There has been bilateral exchanges and technology transfer between China and Malaysia. There is a joint fisheries committee between China and the Philippines which was originally set up in 2005 and resumed in 2017. These cooperative efforts used to be sporadic and the content varied case by case. Under a new regional mechanism, they could be merged into a more systematic and routinised framework that may expand into trilateral or multilateral in the future.

Table 13.3 Chronology of meetings of SOM on DOC

Year	SOM on DOC	Location
2004	1st SOM	Malaysia
2007	2nd SOM	China
2011	3rd SOM	Indonesia
2012	4th SOM (January); 5th SOM (June)	China; Vietnam
2013	6th SOM	China
2014	7th SOM (April); 8th SOM (October)	Thailand; Thailand
2015	9th SOM (July); 10th SOM (October)	China; China
2016	11th SOM (April); 12th SOM (June); 13th SOM (August)	Singapore; Vietnam; China
2017	14th SOM	China

Table 13.4 Chronology of meetings of JWG on DOC

Year	JWG on DOC	Location
2005–2011	1st–5th JWG	
2011	6th JWG	Indonesia
2012	7th JWG (January); 8th JWG (June)	China; Vietnam
2013	9th JWG	China
2014	10th JWG (March); 11th JWG (June); 12th JWG (October)	Singapore; Indonesia; Thailand
2015	13th JWG (March); 14th JWG (July); 15th JWG (October)	Cambodia; Malaysia; China
2016	16th JWG (March); 17th JWG (June); 18th JWG (August)	Philippines; Vietnam; China
2017	19th JWG (February) 20th JWG (March) 21st JWG (May)	Indonesia; Cambodia; China

Conclusion

Fisheries cooperation in the SCS is in urgent need as the region is facing serious challenges of marine environmental degradation and overexploitation of fisheries resources. Hundreds of millions of people in the SCS region depends on the SCS for a living. It is the responsibility of littoral states to take care of the well-being of their people and take on the challenge of promoting cooperation in fisheries management in the SCS.

The analysis above has identified two useful elements for decision makers to consider when formulating fisheries cooperation in the SCS. First, as reviewed in this chapter, a bilateral approach is the dominant approach in existing cooperative efforts in fisheries management between China and its maritime neighbours. A bilateral approach is pragmatic to lower the threshold of negotiation. It also helps to reduce sensitivity and complexity of the issues in question.

The second element is drawn from the Mediterranean experience is the establishment of a regional framework or mechanism which as a basic regular venue pulls together all parties in the region to consult with each other and share concerns with regard to fisheries management. In the Mediterranean Sea, a general fisheries council was established in the 1950s to promote fisheries cooperation among states bordering the Mediterranean. Today, it has developed into a multi-layered well-funded organisation with the authority to formulate legally binding fisheries policies and coordinate a diverse range of fisheries-related activities in the Mediterranean area. A regional framework or mechanism, once installed in the SCS, will certainly create new opportunities for fisheries cooperation and help coordinate regional efforts in fisheries management. Cooperative programmes, while still on a bilateral basis, will be more coordinated and regularised under a regional mechanism.

In the Mediterranean case, there is a powerful and ambitious actor – the EU – whose active presence has played an indispensable role in fostering regional cooperation in fisheries management. Although not as powerful as the EU in terms of the influence in shaping member states' policy, the ASEAN in the South China Sea has been quite active and this organisation also intends to take a central role in managing the South China Sea issue. The ASEAN's importance in the SCS issue has been recognised by China in the latter's proposal of dual-track approach, which envisioned (1) relevant disputes being addressed by countries directly concerned through friendly consultations and negotiations in a peaceful way, and (2) peace and stability in the South China Sea being jointly maintained by China and ASEAN countries.[35] With the DOC implementation process progressing smoothly and China and ASEAN are making a major breakthrough on the issue of a legally binding COC, the ASEAN is granting the opportunity and responsibility to take the lead in promoting concrete cooperation in regional fisheries co-management and regional marine governance in general.

Notes

1 The Coral Triangle is a marine area located in the western Pacific Ocean. It includes the waters of Indonesia, Malaysia, the Philippines, Papua New Guinea, Timor Leste and the Solomon Islands.
2 FAO, FAO Global Capture Summary Information 2015, www.fao.org/3/a-br186e.pdf (accessed 20 April 2017).
3 Ju Hailong, Studies on the Decrement of Fishery Resource in the South China Sea, *Southeast Asian Studies* 6 (2012), 51–55 [in Chinese].
4 For example, see D. A. Russell and D. L. VanderZwaag (eds.), *Recasting Transboundary Fisheries Management Arrangements in Light of Sustainability Principles: Canadian and International Perspectives* (Leiden: Martinus Nijhoff Publishers, 2010); M. J. Valencia, The Yellow Sea: Transnational Marine Resources Management Issues, *Marine Policy* 12(4) (1988), 382–395; Guifang Xue, *China and International Fisheries Law and Policy* (Leiden: Martinus Nijhoff Publishers, 2005).
5 For an overview of the Sino-Japan fisheries agreements, see Guifang Xue, *China and International Fisheries Law and Policy, ibid.*, pp. 175–181.
6 For full text of the 1955 and 1975 Sino-Japanese fisheries agreements and their revisions, see *Fisheries Bureau of Chinese Ministry of Agriculture, Laws and Regulations on Fisheries of the People's Republic of China* (Beijing: Law Press, 2006).
7 Chinese Foreign Ministry, *China–Japan Fisheries Agreement 1997*, www.fmprc.gov.cn/web/ziliao_674904/tytj_674911/tyfg_674913/t556672.shtml (accessed 20 April 2017).
8 Chinese Foreign Ministry, *China–South Korea Fisheries Agreement 2000*, www.fmprc.gov.cn/web/ziliao_674904/tytj_674911/tyfg_674913/t556669.shtml (accessed 20 April 2017). The agreement was concluded in 1998 and formally signed in 2000.
9 In 1961, the two governments signed a supplement agreement, which introduced a few changes to the 1957 agreement.
10 China promulgated the *Declaration on Territorial Seas 1958* in which it recognised the water of 12 nautical miles (NM) seaward from the baseline as territorial sea.
11 Chinese Foreign Ministry, *Agreement between the People's Republic of China and the Socialist Republic of Vietnam on Fishery Cooperation in Beibu Bay 2000*, www.fmprc.gov.cn/web/ziliao_674904/tytj_674911/tyfg_674913/t556668.shtml (accessed 20 April 2017).
12 The Committee on Economic works of Shanghai, China–Japan–South Korea Seminar on Management of Fisheries Incidents and Working Level Talk Held in Shanghai, 29 February 2008, www.shzgh.org/renda/node9708/node9720/userobject1ai1474252.html, accessed 20 August 2017.
13 Chinese Ministry of Commerce, South Korea Proposed Trilateral Non-Governmental Fisheries Cooperation Mechanism, 14 December 2011, www.mofcom.gov.cn/aarticle/i/jyjl/j/201112/20111207879027.html (accessed 20 August 2017).
14 See, e.g. China Aquaculture, China Fisheries Association and Korean Fisheries Association Held Coordinating Meeting in Beijing, 7 December 2011, www.shuichan.cc/news_view-69701.html (accessed 20 August 2017).
15 This arrangement was confirmed by the Chinese Foreign Ministry during a press conference on 31 October, see Chinese Foreign Ministry, Foreign Ministry Spokesperson Hua Chunying's Regular Press Conference on 31 October 2016, www.fmprc.gov.cn/web/wjdt_674879/fyrbt_674889/t1411616.shtml (accessed 20 August 2017).
16 Second Sino-Filipino Joint Fisheries Committee Meeting Held in Manila, *Xinhua News*, 28 April 2017, http://news.xinhuanet.com/politics/2017-04/28/c_129580527.htm (accessed 30 August 2017).
17 Tenth Anniversary of the Implementation of China–South Korea Fisheries Agreement, *China News*, 9 April 2011, www.chinanews.com/cj/2011/04-09/2961235.shtml (accessed 20 August 2017).

18 R. Margalef, Introduction to the Mediterranean, in: R. Margalef (ed.), *Western Medi-terranean* (Oxford: Pergamon Press, 1985), p. 1.

19 Countries bordering the Mediterranean Sea include Spain, France, Monaco, Italy, Malta, Slovenia, Croatia, Bosnia and Herzegovina, Montenegro, Albania, Greece, Turkey, Syria, Cyprus, Lebanon, Israel, Egypt, Libya, Tunisia, Algeria, Morocco and Britain.

20 Tullio Scovazzi, The Mediterranean Sea Maritime Boundaries, in: Jonathan I. Charney *et al.* (eds.), *International Maritime Boundaries, Vol. 5* (The American Society of International Law/Nijhoff, 2005), p. 3477.

21 FAO, *Agreement for the Establishment of a General Fisheries Commission for the Mediterranean*, www.fao.org/fileadmin/user_upload/legal/docs/003s-e.pdf (accessed 20 April 2017).

22 FAO, *Amendments to the Agreement and Rules of Procedure of GFCM*, GFCM Twenty-second Session, Rome, Italy, 13–16 October 1997, www.fao.org/docrep/MEETING/005/W6063E.HTM (accessed 20 April 2017).

23 *ICCAT*, Introduction, www.iccat.es/en/introduction.htm (accessed 20 April 2017).

24 For example, see IUCN, *Overview of the Conservation Status of the Marine Fishes of the Mediterranean Sea 2008*, http://cmsdata.iucn.org/downloads/overview_of_the_conservation_status_of_the_marine_fishes_of_the_mediterranean_sea_rep.pdf (accessed 20 August 2017).

25 Green Peace, Mediterranean Countries Fail Again to Protect Bluefin Tuna, 21 June 2017, www.greenpeace.org/international/en/press/releases/2007/mediterranean-countries-fail-a/ (accessed 20 April 2017).

26 European Commission, MEDFISH4EVER, https://ec.europa.eu/fisheries/inseparable/en/medfish4ever (accessed 20 August 2017).

27 Peter M. Haas, Do Regimes Matter? Epistemic Communities and Mediterranean Pol-lution Control, *International Organization* 43(3) (1989), 377–403.

28 These funding resources supplement each other and all were designed to promote the effective implementation of fisheries policies of the EU.

29 The 1992 Earth Summit produced the *Rio Declaration on Environment and Develop-ment*, a set of 27 principles designed to commit governments to global collaboration on environmental protection and the implementation of sustainable development throughout the world. Full text is available on the UN website, www.un.org/documents/ga/conf151/aconf15126-1annex1.htm (accessed 12 February 2017).

30 For more information on the Community Action Plan for the conservation and sus-tainable exploitation of fisheries resources, see European Commission, Commission Proposes Action for Sustainable Fisheries in the Mediterranean, 9 October 2003, http://europa.eu/rapid/press-release_IP-03-1361_en.htm (accessed 12 February 2017).

31 The Barcelona Process encouraged deepening fisheries cooperation between the EU and non-EU countries in the Mediterranean Sea. In 2001, the European Commission president paid a special visit to Morocco in efforts to eliminate obstacles facing fish-eries cooperation in the Mediterranean region. See European Commission,'First Offi-cial Visit by a Commission President to the Maghreb Countries Boosts Barcelona Process, 8 January 2001, http://europa.eu/rapid/press-release_IP-01-6_en.htm (accessed 10 June 2017).

32 For the list of six priority areas, see Union for the Mediterranean, Priority Areas, http://ufmsecretariat.org/priority-areas/ (accessed 10 June 2017).

33 For the full text of the 2002 DOC, see ASEAN, Declaration on the Conduct of Parties in the South China Sea, http://asean.org/?static_post=declaration-on-the-conduct-of-parties-in-the-south-china-sea-2 (accessed 10 June 2017).

34 China, ASEAN Countries Agree on COC Framework, *Xinhua News*, 18 May 2017, http://news.xinhuanet.com/english/2017-05/18/c_136295814.htm (accessed 31 July 2017).

35 Chinese Foreign Ministry, Wang Yi: Handle the South China Sea Issue through the 'Dual-track' Approach, 9 August 2014, www.fmprc.gov.cn/mfa_eng/zxxx_662805/t1181523.shtml (accessed 31 July 2017).

Part IV

Handling financial and trade issues

14 Prospects for the integration of environmental, social and cultural sustainability within the Belt and Road Initiative

Case study of the Duqm Port Development Project in Oman

David M. Ong

Introduction

China's President Xi Jinping first raised the initiative of jointly building the Silk Road Economic Belt and the 21st Century Maritime Silk Road in 2013. According to Manuel, the maritime road aspect of this Initiative 'will include perhaps a dozen ports from Asia to Africa and the Mediterranean'.[1] Now that the Belt and Road Initiative (BRI) is moving from its initial *conception/ideational* phase, through its *institutional* phase, and towards its *operational* phase, additional considerations arise regarding its prospects for successful implementation. Among the most pressing of these considerations are the environmental, social and cultural impacts of the infrastructure projects proposed by the BRI within the individual countries that lie on the pathways of both the land and maritime routes of this Initiative. While the longer-term economic benefits of the BRI are arguably undeniable, the challenge is to ensure that these benefits are fairly distributed among and within the societies of the many countries lying along these BRI routes. Moreover, environmental concerns, as well as social and cultural sensitivities, must be addressed to ensure complete sustainability is achieved.

This chapter examines current efforts at the inter-State/governmental level and within international institutions (e.g. through the Asian Infrastructure Investment Bank, AIIB), as well as domestic/Chinese institutions, to ensure that such social, cultural and environmental concerns are being actively considered in BRI project implementation, especially along the Maritime Silk Road aspect of the BRI. These two agencies, namely, the AIIB and the Maritime Silk Road, are then brought together in a case study on the AIIB's support for the Duqm Port Development project in Oman, to assess how environmental, social and cultural risks were considered in the AIIB decision-making process for supporting this project, as well as the AIIB response to calls for its accountability over concerns for migrant labour within this project.

From Western *ecological modernisation* to Chinese *ecological civilisation*: the environmental, social and cultural dimensions of sustainability

The BRI is undoubtedly a significant Chinese national policy in terms of its numbers: the total capital investments, size and number of infrastructure projects, as well as individual amounts of investment per project are truly awe-inspiring. A recent advertisement by a major international bank envisages that the BRI 'will connect nearly two-thirds of the world's population', as well as become 'one of the largest platforms for economic co-operation on earth, improving land and sea routes across Asia, Europe, the Middle East and Africa'.[2] Away from these impressive headline facts and figures, however, it is possible to discern a paradigm shift in the Chinese approach towards its national, as well as international, development policy. This paradigm shift attempts to move away from the mainly neoliberal economic thinking that underpins Western-style infrastructure development strategies, to an approach that (re-)places important sociocultural elements at the heart of sustainable development.

This attitude shift is arguably encapsulated by the Chinese notion of ecological 'civilisation', as opposed to the more well-known Western concept of ecological 'modernisation'.[3] This Chinese emphasis on ecological 'civilisation', rather than (ecological) 'modernisation', taps into and reflects both a formative as well as ingrained Chinese attitude towards the notion of 'Chinese civilisation' itself – whereby 'Chinese civilisation' is presented historically as a form of continuous sociocultural development, aimed at ultimately achieving the highest level of aesthetic form known to humankind. According to Oswald, for example,

> (f)or the Chinese leadership, the term 'Civilisation' meant a model life to which people must aspire. It was also supposed to distinguish China's model of modernisation from that of the West, notwithstanding the fact that China's 'modernisation' was often associated with 'Westernisation'.[4]

Thus, Chinese scholars and officials looked at the examples of Japan and Singapore as two well-developed Asian economies with high levels of civilisation that had not lost their unique cultural identities and argued that China should similarly seek to achieve economic success while maintaining and developing its cultural heritage.[5]

As a renascent (rather than simply emerging) world power, this elevated notion of 'Chinese civilisation' had hitherto not been emphasised in the post-Mao period and certainly not during the reformist Deng Xiaoping era in which the dominant feature of Chinese political discourse was one that prioritised economic development, arguably at the expense of environmental, social, and cultural concerns. Once Deng's exhortation to China to 'hide its brightness/ capabilities and bide its time' had allowed China to effect at least a partial return to its former prowess, at least in raw economic terms, then the search began for a new form of narrative to guide a renascent China into the 21st century. In 2012, at the Seventeenth National Congress of the Communist Party of China (CCP), the then Party General Secretary Hu Jintao, announced a proposed change in China's model of economic growth. As Oswald observes, '(t)hus began the incorporation of the expression "Ecological Civilisation" into the official discourse as a new model of growth to replace the old unsustainable model'.[6] Under President Xi Jinping, 'ecological civilisation' has become the central concept of this discourse. In fact, according to Oswald, 'ecological civilisation' is the fourth in the official series of China's civilisation or civilising slogans, coming after Deng Xiaoping's/Ye Jianying/Hu Yaobang's concurrently pronounced Spiritual Civilisation and Material Civilisation and Jiang Zemin's Political Civilisation.[7] Oswald then notes that the Chinese scholar Ma Jun introduced this term – Ecological Civilisation – into the Western lexicon in 2007 shortly after the Seventeenth Party Congress.[8]

At almost the same time, however, the Chinese State was issuing a study on ecological 'modernisation',[9] thereby raising uncertainty as to whether initial Chinese conceptions of ecological 'civilisation' really differed all that much from Western conceptions of ecological 'modernisation'. Indeed, Chinese scholars still freely draw from the ecological 'modernisation' perspective and apply its perceived methodology to domestic Chinese policies. Yu Zhou for example applies the ecological modernisation framework to analyse China's green building programme on the basis that ecological 'modernisation' embodies the effective institutionalisation of environmental objectives into respective political and economic systems, and thus provides valuable insights into the roles of the state and other stake holders in environmental regulation.[10] As Yu Zhou notes,

> Since the mid-2000s, the Chinese government green building campaign, which is distinguished by its speed, scale, and evolution from one of voluntary participation to a top-down implementation through administrative hierarchies. While this has resulted in a remarkable growth of green building projects, questions remain about the effectiveness and sustainability of such a State-centered approach.[11]

Yu Zhou concludes that the Chinese State 'must embrace reform to build flexible and collaborative processes with other parties with strong public participation. China's ecological modernization process may feature a stronger state and faster changes, but it is not exempted from the need of political modernization.'[12]

On the other hand, Oswald has expressed scepticism about efforts by both Chinese scholars and their Western counterparts suggesting that the West and China are proposing similarly ecologically friendly models of development. Instead, he notes that they stem from very different perspectives, with the almost post-industrial, post-modern Western approach standing in stark contrast to the rapidly industrialising Chinese economy. Western approximations of 'ecological civilisation' to such Western-originating concepts as 'ecological modernisation' are also criticised by Oswald, as amounting to little more than an embellishment to the Western response to global environmental issues. Acknowledging for example that Magdoff had conducted the most thorough examination of the term 'Ecological Civilisation' to date,[13] Oswald nevertheless points out that Magdoff does not discuss how such 'ecological civilisation' would benefit a developing economy like China, with its large population, the majority of whom are unlikely to achieve the standard of living in developed economies in their lifetime.[14]

Two inter-connected issues arise at this stage: first, what exactly does China mean by the concept: 'ecological civilisation'; and second, how far is this concept (and its application) different from those that have emerged in Western environmental policy such as 'ecological modernisation' and more generally, 'sustainable development' itself? As Oswald notes, 'Chinese scholars explain and elaborate on the concept of "Eco-civilisation" very differently. Some writers take the term to mean the next link in the chain of human civilisations'.[15] In summary, these 'civilisations' range from 'original civilisation', incorporating the hunter/gatherer lifestyle; followed by 'agricultural civilisation' and culminating with 'industrial civilisation'.[16] Thus, as Oswald observes, '(i)f industrial civilisation highlights the human/nature binary, the Chinese literature argues that "Eco-(logical) civilisation" – as the next stage – represents the transformation of society from mindless and destructive industrial progress toward ecological mindfulness'.

In brief, 'Eco-civilisation involves shifting human society away from the destructive consequences of human attempts at mastering nature and seeks instead to nurture an interdependence between people and nature, and among people in society'.[17] Oswald continues:

> 'Eco-civilisation' as discussed in China is very much a China-focused strategy. The term is treated as a guiding principle for China's sustainable development and attentive to local Chinese situations. The advocates of 'Eco-(logical) civilisation' see it as a necessary measure for achieving a 'Moderately Well-off Society'. The primary aim of 'Eco-(logical) civilisation', they argue, is to ameliorate the damage already done to the environment while reducing further damage. The educational aspect of 'Eco-civilisation' is to promote a healthy relationship between humans and nature, and to reintegrate humankind and the natural environment. Despite the domestic focus, the term has also been used to discuss the global nature of environmental issues. In this broader use, 'Eco-(logical) civilisation' serves as a critique of Western-style industrialisation.[18]

Staying at the domestic (Chinese) level, 'ecological civilisation' has been promoted since the Third Plenary Session of the Eighteenth CCP Central Committee as a commitment to be enshrined in law and policy. However, according to Zhang *et al.*, '(t)his Chinese interpretation of ecological modernisation is thus primarily limited to the technological-economic dimensions of sustainable development, without entering too much into relations with equity, equality, citizen empowerment and the like'.[19]

At the international level, according to Parr and Henry, 'ecological civilisation' not only means a brighter future for the Chinese environment, but also new policy and diplomatic opportunities for China,[20] as well as Chinese investments abroad through the BRI and the AIIB. According to Xi Jinping in his report to the 19th National Congress of the Communist Party,[21] among several achievements in the five years since the 18th National Congress, *inter alia*, as follows:

> We have made notable progress in building an ecological civilization. We have devoted serious energy to ecological conservation. As a result, the entire Party and the whole country have become more purposeful and active in pursuing green development, and there has been a clear shift away from the tendency to neglect ecological and environmental protection. Efforts to develop a system for building an ecological civilization have been accelerated; the system of functional zoning has been steadily improved; and progress has been made in piloting the national park system. Across-the-board efforts to conserve resources have seen encouraging progress; the intensity of energy and resource consumption has been significantly reduced. Smooth progress has been made in major ecological conservation and restoration projects; and forest coverage has been increased. Ecological and environmental governance has been significantly strengthened, leading to marked improvements in the environment. Taking a driving seat in international cooperation to respond to climate change, China has become an important participant, contributor, and torchbearer in the global endeavor for ecological civilization.[22]

The relationship between the BRI and the AIIB

Given the fact that the BRI and AIIB are the two main Chinese international policy and institutional development initiatives in the second decade of the 21st century, a preliminary analysis of their relationship in furthering China's foreign policy goals must be undertaken to contextualise their separate, yet related efforts to integrate all the political, economic, social, cultural and environmental issues arising from these international development initiatives. Manuel first observes that the BRI will be implemented over the course of several decades so that, '(n)o one knows quite how much this will cost',[23] before asserting that BRI projects 'will be funded through a number of vehicles, most importantly through the [AIIB] with its US$100 billion in initial capital, and though the separate US$40 billion New Silk Road Fund'.[24] Enlarging on this relationship between the BRI and AIIB, Yu notes that,

> [t]he 2013 'One Belt, One Road' initiatives form the centrepiece of the Chinese leadership's new foreign policy. Developing inter-connectivity of infrastructure development forms a central part of China's OBOR initiatives. The [AIIB] aims to facilitate and accelerate infrastructure improvement in the region by providing capital loans and technical services. The

AIIB will serve as the spearhead of China's OBOR initiatives. The AIIB and OBOR initiatives have put China at the centre of geo-economics and geopolitics in the region and beyond, a position from which it hopes to strengthen its economic ties with other Asian countries. The new Silk Road initiatives also provide a channel for Chinese companies and capital to invest in other countries by leveraging China's strengths in infrastructure development, financial power and manufacturing capacity. The OBOR initiatives and the AIIB could change the economic and political landscape of Asia, the most dynamic and economically vibrant region of the twenty-first century. However, China faces serious challenges, both internally and externally, in implementing these initiatives.[25]

On the external/international front, Yu postulates further that: 'the OBOR initiatives are a reflection of China's ascendance in the global arena, economically, politically, and strategically'.[26] This perception of Chinese ascendancy has brought this (BRI) Initiative to the negative attention of both global (USA) and regional (India) powers, respectively. As Callaghan and Hubbard note,

the English-language media coverage of the Asian Infrastructure Investment Bank (AIIB) was also framed initially in terms of strategic rivalry between China and the United States. Having turned the AIIB into a battle for global influence, it was the United States, not China, that lost this battle when key allies such as the UK, France, Germany and Australia, joined the Bank.[27]

Perhaps more significantly, they then characterise the establishment of the AIIB as symptomatic of China's frustration with slow reform to existing multilateral development banks (MDBs).[28] Given China's patchy investment record, especially in Africa, which has generated criticism due to, *inter alia*, its perceived 'high-handed' nature, Callaghan and Hubbard insightfully postulate that:

China had a positive agenda for establishing the AIIB, particularly as part of its flagship 'one belt, one road' regional initiative. By establishing a multilateral lender for Asian infrastructure, China can de-politicize what can be fraught bilateral financing deals as well as boost its image in the region.[29]

However, as they then go on to note:

This requires the AIIB being a truly multilateral institution. The AIIB will have to meet the standards of other MDBs, particularly for safeguards, procurement and transparency. The bank will be under international scrutiny and AIIB shareholders should build the bank cautiously, initially focusing on co-financing with other MDBs. The AIIB need not mirror existing lenders, but can learn from their experience and improve on their efficiency. The AIIB will be a learning experience for China and could boost its credentials for future multilateral leadership.[30]

The Belt and Road Initiative: addressing environmental, social and cultural impacts?

There is no doubt that: 'China's ambitious Belt and Road Initiative, which seeks to expand the ancient land routes that connect China to the Mediterranean Sea and corresponding ocean-based routes, is expanding global cooperation with profound socioeconomic and ecological implications'.[31] As a recent Press Release from the Belt and Road Green Development Partnership Programme states:

> Given the large scale of the Initiative and the environmentally-fragile region which it covers, the attitude of the international community towards BRI remains cautious, with concerns that China is shifting its outdated and excess industrial capacity abroad. There is also apprehension over the potential environmental impacts of investments going into countries with weak environmental laws and governance. To alleviate these concerns, China has been using domestic and international dialogue platforms and cooperation mechanisms to reaffirm its intention to work with the international community to strive towards a 'green, healthy, intelligent, and peaceful' Belt and Road.[32]

As China and associated countries are developing specific policies to implement the BRI, it is important to integrate several major challenges facing the Belt and Road region: complex natural features, mismatched resources, shared ecological issues, and diverse socioeconomic conditions. To meet these challenges, Yang *et al.* apply the integrated framework of telecoupling (socioeconomic and environmental interactions over distances) and propose to enhance infrastructure connection, transboundary actions, scientific and cultural exchanges, and institutional innovations within the Belt and Road region; as well as collaborate with more international organisations and countries beyond the Belt and Road region for a prosperous and sustainable world.[33] Following The Leaders Roundtable of the Belt and Road Forum for International Cooperation held in Beijing on 15 May 2017,[34] a joint communique was issued, the salient points of which are, *inter alia*, as follows:

> Co-operation Objectives
> …
> 12. We are determined to protect the planet from degradation, including through taking urgent action on climate change and encouraging all parties which have ratified it to fully implement the Paris Agreement, managing the natural resources in an equitable and sustainable manner, conserving and sustainably using oceans and seas, freshwater resources, as well as forests, mountains and drylands, protecting biodiversity, ecosystems and wildlife, combating desertification and land degradation so as to achieving sustainable development in its three dimensions in a balanced and integrated manner.
> …

Cooperation Principles

14. We uphold the spirit of peace, cooperation, openness, transparency, inclusiveness, equality, mutual learning, mutual benefit and mutual respect by strengthening cooperation on the basis of extensive consultation and the rule of law, joint efforts, shared benefits and equal opportunities for all. In this context we highlight the following principles guiding our cooperation, in accordance with our respective national laws and policies:

a) Consultation on an equal footing: Honoring the purposes and principles of the UN Charter and international law including respecting the sovereignty and territorial integrity of countries; formulating cooperation plans and advancing cooperation projects through consultation.

b) Mutual benefit: Seeking convergence of interests and the broadest common ground for cooperation, taking into account the perspectives of different stakeholders.

c) Harmony and inclusiveness: Acknowledging the natural and cultural diversity of the world and recognizing that all cultures and civilizations can contribute to sustainable development.

d) Market-based operation: Recognizing the role of the market and that of business as key players, while ensuring that the government performs its proper role and highlighting the importance of open, transparent, and non-discriminatory procurement procedures.

e) Balance and sustainability: Emphasizing the importance of economic, social, fiscal, financial and environmental sustainability of projects, and of promoting high environmental standards, while striking a good balance among economic growth, social progress and environmental protection.

Cooperation Measures

15. We affirm the need to prioritize policy consultation, trade promotion, infrastructure connectivity, financial cooperation and people-to-people exchanges, and we highlight concrete actions, in accordance with our national laws and regulations and international obligations where applicable, such as:

a) Pursuing dialogue and consultation in order to build synergies in development strategies among participating countries, noting the efforts to strengthen cooperation in coordinating development of the Belt and Road Initiative with other plans and initiatives as mentioned in Paragraph 6 and to promote partnerships among Europe, Asia, South America, Africa and other regions.

b) Conducting in-depth consultation on macroeconomic issues by optimizing the existing multilateral and bilateral cooperation and dialogue mechanisms, so as to provide robust policy support for practical cooperation and the implementation of major projects.

c) Strengthening cooperation on innovation, by supporting innovation action plans for e-commerce, digital economy, smart cities and science and technology parks, and by encouraging greater exchanges on innovation and business startup models in the Internet age in respect of intellectual property rights.

d) Promoting practical cooperation on roads, railways, ports, maritime and inland water transport, aviation, energy pipelines, electricity, fiber optic including trans-oceanic cable, telecommunications and information and communication technology, and welcoming the development of interconnected multimodal corridors, such us a new Eurasian Land Bridge, Northern Sea Route, the East-West Middle Corridor etc., and major trunk lines to put in place an international infrastructure network over time.

e) Maximizing synergies in infrastructure planning and development by taking into account international standards where applicable, and by aiming at harmonizing rules and technological standards when necessary; fostering a favorable environment and predictability for infrastructure investment by private capital; promoting public-private partnership in areas that create more jobs and generate greater efficiency; welcoming international financial institutions to increase support and investment for infrastructure development.[35]

These international and regionally-oriented undertakings by China in relation to BRI projects have been buttressed at the national level by domestic Chinese government policy guidance initiated by the Communist Party of China (CPC) Central Committee and the State Council.[36] This domestic policy guidance is concerned, to mainstream ecological civilization in the BRI and promote a 'green' Belt and Road, *inter alia*, i) to share the ecological civilization philosophy and achieve sustainable development; ii) to participate in global environmental governance and promote green development concept; iii) to serve and forge communities of shared interests, common responsibility and common destiny; and iv) to conducting pragmatic cooperation, promoting green investment, green trade and green financial systems, achieving a win-win situation for economic growth and environmental protection, and building communities of shared interests, common responsibility and common destiny. ...[37]

Shifting attention to the overtly maritime-related aspects of the BRI, on 20 June 2017, the Chinese National Development and Reform Commission (NDRC) and the State Oceanic Administration (SOA) released a further policy document entitled: *Vision for Maritime Cooperation under the Belt and Road Initiative*.[38] This 'Vision' built on an earlier 2015 version, entitled: 'The Vision and Actions on Jointly Building the Silk Road Economic Belt and the 21st Century Maritime Silk Road', which promotes policy coordination, connectivity of infrastructure and facilities, unimpeded trade, financial integration and people-to-people bonds, adhering to the principle of achieving shared growth through discussion and collaboration in propelling the Belt and Road construction. The 2017 Vision is intended to synchronise development plans and promote joint actions among countries along the 21st Century Maritime Silk Road. The underlying Principles of this 2017 Chinese 'Vision' for cooperation along the maritime aspects of the BRI are then provided as follows:

II. Principles

Shelving differences and building consensus. We call for efforts to uphold the existing international ocean order, and to respect diversified concepts of ocean development in the countries along the Road. Concerns of all parties involved will be accommodated, differences bridged, common ground sought and consensus achieved.

Openness, cooperation and inclusive development. We advocate further opening up the market, improving the investment environment, eliminating trade barriers and facilitating trade and investment. Mutual political trust will be sought, inter-civilizational dialogue strengthened, and inclusive development and harmonious coexistence promoted.

Market-based operation and multi-stakeholder participation. We abide by market rules and international norms, giving play to the primary role of enterprises. We encourage the creation of stakeholder partnerships and promote the broad participation of governments, international organizations, civil society, and industrial and commercial sectors in ocean cooperation.

Joint development and benefits sharing. We respect the will of the countries along the Road, take into account the interests of all parties and give play to the comparative strengths of each. We will plan together, develop together and share the fruits of cooperation. Together, we will help developing countries eradicate poverty and foster a community of shared interests.[39]

These Principles are to be applied within the following overarching 'Framework', as follows:

III. Framework

...

In line with the priorities of the 21st Century Maritime Silk Road, China will deepen ocean cooperation by fostering closer ties with countries along the Road, supported by the coastal economic belt in China. Ocean cooperation will focus on building the China-Indian Ocean-Africa-Mediterranean Sea Blue Economic Passage, by linking the China-Indochina Peninsula Economic Corridor, running westward from the South China Sea to the Indian Ocean, and connecting the China-Pakistan Economic Corridor (CPEC) and the Bangladesh-China-India-Myanmar Economic Corridor (BCIM-EC). Efforts will also be made to jointly build the Blue Economic Passage of China-Oceania-South Pacific, travelling southward from the South China Sea into the Pacific Ocean. Another Blue Economic Passage is also envisioned leading up to Europe via the Arctic Ocean.[40]

Finally, China has followed up the articulation of the aims, principles, and framework for the implementation of the regional maritime aspects of the BRI with concrete action, summarised as follows:

> *High-level guidance and facilitation.* With the leaders of relevant states bearing witness, China has signed intergovernmental agreements, MOUs and joint statements for ocean cooperation with countries such as Thailand, Malaysia, Cambodia, India, Pakistan, the Maldives and South Africa. We have made efforts in synching strategies and building extensive partnerships with countries along the Road.

> *Boosting the role of cooperation platforms.* Under mechanisms such as APEC, the East Asian Leaders' Meetings, and the China-ASEAN Cooperation Framework, we have launched consultations on maritime affairs and established dialogue and cooperation platforms including the Blue Economy Forum, the Seminar on Marine Environmental Protection, the Ocean Cooperation Forum, the China-ASEAN Marine Cooperation Center, and the East Asian Ocean Cooperation Platform. A series of Maritime Silk Road related activities, including the 21st Century Maritime Silk Road Expo, the Maritime Silk Road International Art Festival and the Global Matsu Maritime Culture Forum, have been held in succession, thereby promoting understanding, building consensus and enhancing ocean cooperation.

> *Increasing financial investment.* The Chinese government has mobilized domestic resources and set up the China-ASEAN Maritime Cooperation Fund and the China-Indonesia Maritime Cooperation Fund. We have also implemented The Framework Plan for International Cooperation for the South China Sea and its Adjacent Oceans. Meanwhile, the Asian Infrastructure Investment Bank and the Silk Road Fund have provided capital support for major ocean cooperation programs.
>
> …
>
> *IBR projects being implemented.* Progress has been achieved in implementing a series of programs and projects, including the Malaysia Malacca Seaside Industrial Park, the Pakistan Gwadar Port, the port+industrial park+city mode of integrated development of the Kyaukpyu port in Myanmar, the Colombo Port City and the Phase II Hambantota Port Project in Sri Lanka, the railway linking Ethiopia and Djibouti, the railway between Mombasa and Nairobi in Kenya, and the Piraeus port in Greece. China is collaborating with the Netherlands in developing offshore wind power generation and with Indonesia, Kazakhstan and Iran in implementing seawater desalination projects. The connectivity of submarine communication has been remarkably enhanced and the Asia-Pacific Gateway (APG) submarine optical fiber cable is officially up and running. The industrial parks in China's Qinzhou and Malaysia's Kuantan, the Sihanoukville Special Economic Zone in Cambodia and the Suez Economic and Trade Cooperative Zone in Egypt, are currently under construction, and have achieved remarkable progress.[41]

AIIB: leading the way on integration of environmental, social and cultural sustainability issues in the BRI?

Hanlon has offered three arguments outlining the AIIB's significance in relation to BRI-related projects to help policy planners navigate the complex relationship between China, the Bank and themes of sustainability. According to him,

> [f]irst, there is little uncertainty that China is serious about development and sustainability. The [AIIB] is but one extension of China's increasing commitment to sustainability and should therefore be embraced by development stakeholders. Second, the Asian Infrastructure Investment Bank's commitment to infrastructure development complements other multilateral development banks and should not be considered a challenger to the existing order of development lending practices. Rather, China's interest in establishing the [AIIB] points to competitive pluralism and poses no threat to the existing international order. Finally, the [AIIB]'s sustainability guidelines are not unique and fall in line with similar policy of other large development banks. The [AIIB] therefore reinforces sustainability norms while posturing itself as a partner for development.[42]

To begin with, Article 13(1) of the Charter establishing AIIB provides that when making financing decisions, the Bank will be guided by 'sound banking principles in its operations'. The Bank has also undertaken to ensure that each of its operations complies with its environmental and social policies. Specifically, the Bank shall ensure that each of its operations complies with the Bank's operational and financial policies, including without limitation, policies addressing environmental and social impacts.[43] These policies are in turn subject to approval by the Board of Directors in accordance with Article 26 and will be based on international best practices.[44] Within this context, one of the main concerns raised by international civil society/non-governmental organisations (NGOs) over the streamlined decision-making systems and procedures for AIIB lending relates to the potentially reduced oversight role that these procedures may provide over social and environmental impacts of the approved infrastructure development projects funded by the new Bank. In recognition of these concerns, the Board of Directors of the AIIB committed to the establishment of environmental and social policies for the Bank, resulting in the adoption of an Environmental and Social Framework in February 2016.[45]

This was followed by the promulgation of a further Risk Assessment Framework in November 2017. Buttressing both these Frameworks, the AIIB has also adopted a Directive on Environmental and Social Policy on 4 December 2017, which has just one overriding objective, namely,

> to facilitate the implementation of the Bank's *Environmental and Social Policy*, including the Environmental and Social Standards and Environmental

and Social Exclusion List (Policy). The Policy derives directly from the requirement in the Bank's Articles of Agreement that '[t]he Bank shall ensure that each of its operations complies with the Bank's operational and financial policies, including without limitation, policies addressing environmental and social impacts'. The Policy constitutes one of the major policies of the Bank, and is central to the design and implementation of Projects supported by the Bank's Financing.[46]

AIIB Environmental and Social Framework, and AIIB Risk Framework

This Environmental and Social Framework was developed through a consultative process with AIIB's Founding Members and other stakeholders.[47] In this regard, the overall Framework is composed *inter alia* of an Environmental and Social Policy (ESP) comprising mandatory environmental and social requirements for each project that the Bank finances, as well as Environmental and Social Standards (ESSs) comprising three associated mandatory sets of environmental and social standards, which in turn establish more detailed environmental and social requirements.[48] Within this Environmental and Social Framework, the first *Environmental and Social Standard* (ESS 1), entitled: 'Environmental and Social Assessment and Management' provides, *inter alia*, for the

> [c]onduct an environmental and social assessment for the proposed Project to identify direct, indirect, cumulative and induced risks and impacts to physical, biological, socioeconomic and cultural resources in the Project's area of influence; these include impacts on air and water quality, including environmental health; natural resources, including land, water and ecosystems; livelihoods; vulnerable groups; gender; worker and community health and safety; and cultural resources; …

Among the substantive goals/objectives that these environmental and social assessments need to strive for are, *inter alia*, 'conserving biodiversity'[49] and conserving 'cultural resources'.[50]

A further, important aspect of this Environmental and Social Framework is that of 'Stakeholder Engagement', which is described, *inter alia*, as transparency and 'meaningful consultation' that is essential for the design and implementation of a Project. 'Meaningful consultation' is further elaborated as a process that begins early and is ongoing throughout the Project, and which is inclusive, accessible, timely and undertaken in an open manner. Such 'meaningful consultation' conveys adequate information that is understandable and readily accessible to stakeholders in a *culturally* appropriate manner and in turn, enables the consideration of stakeholders' views as part of decision-making. Stakeholder engagement is conducted in a manner commensurate with the risks to, and impacts on, those affected by the Project.[51] 'Consultation' itself is conceived by the AIIB as a proportionate exercise dependent on the prior assessed environmental and social risk levels, as well as impacts of the proposed Project. 'Consultation' covers Project design, mitigation and monitoring measures, sharing of development benefits and opportunities on a Project-specific basis, and with stakeholders during the Project's preparation and implementation phases, in a manner commensurate with the risks to, and impacts on, those affected by the Project.

> Consultation is required for each Category A Project, and for each Category B Project, proportionate to its risks and impacts. Consultation for a Category A Project is normally more elaborate than consultation for a Category B Project. For each Project with: (a) significant adverse environmental and social impacts; (b) Involuntary Resettlement; or (c) impacts on Indigenous Peoples, the Bank may participate in consultation activities to understand the concerns of the affected people and to ensure that the Client addresses such concerns in the Project's design and ESMP or ESMPF (as applicable). The Bank ensures that the Client includes a record of the consultations and list of participants in the environmental and social assessment documentation.[52]

However, even prior to the publication of this Framework and its associated Policy and Standards, specific concerns had already been raised regarding both the consultation and implementation of these standards for AIIB-supported projects.[53] As Kim notes, no one can be certain of the extent of the AIIB commitment to environmental and social sustainability until more detailed information on how the new Bank decides which projects it will fund is known.[54] On the other hand, discernible institutional differences are already emerging between the AIIB and other Multilateral Development Banks (MDBs) such as the World Bank-related International Finance Institutions (IFIs) and this may lead to different outcomes in practice. For example, the AIIB aims to have a simpler internal review and risk assessment system for projects compared with its peers in order to hold down costs and cut red tape. Thus, the AIIB followed-up promulgation of its Environmental and Social Risk Framework, with a general Risk Assessment Framework, established in November, 2016,[55] whose risk philosophy aims to be the foundational pillar of the Bank's risk management and the guiding basis for the entire risk governance framework.[56] The AIIB's high-level, overarching philosophy of its 'risk management' function is constituted by the following three aims in its 'Mission Statement':

1   Enable the Bank to fulfil its mandate to promote infrastructure and other productive sectors;
2   Ensure the stability and financial continuity of the Bank through efficient capital allocation and utilisation, and comprehensively manage risks and reputational consequences;
3   And foster strong risk culture by embedding risk accountability in the Bank.[57]

The AIIB Risk Assessment Framework then elaborates on the last of these aims with the following statement: 'As an integral part of the institution's operations, AIIB takes *extra precaution* in appropriately managing its risks, and will only aim to take risks which it understands thoroughly and can adequately manage'[58] [emphasis added].

According to paragraph 3 of this Risk Management Framework, it is 'aimed at providing the coherent foundation for such effective risk management by outlining an overarching methodology and guideline for governing the key risks that the Bank faces'. It is notable that there is no explicit mention of environmental and social sustainability risks here, at least until these risks are defined in paragraph 26 of the AIIB Risk Framework by direct cross-reference to its Environmental and Social Framework, as follows: 'Environmental and Social Risk is the risk of breaching any environmental and social rules and commitments as covered in the Bank's Environmental and Social Framework'.[59] The AIIB's Risk Framework then builds on this cross-reference in the following way:

> Integrity, Environmental & Social, and Reputational Risks management and mitigation comprises the identification of the most relevant risks for the Bank along with their accompanying impact assessment; mitigation and crisis management; reporting and monitoring; as well as developing an action plan. With respect to projects, such risks are managed through the applicable Bank operational policies and directives and their application in the preparation and implementation of projects, including the corresponding policy assurance.[60]

While it is possible to conclude from these provisions that environmental and social sustainability considerations are now included within the AIIB decision-making criteria, and thereby also integrated into the AIIB project decision-making process; the fact remains that the AIIB is not expected to unnecessarily delay project approvals to allow all parties to do due diligence. Such delays are a common feature at the World Bank and other MDBs as they have become more risk-averse over time but this has in turn led to criticism that these MDBs have become slow and bureaucratic. Notwithstanding the optimal outcomes these different institutional priorities and practices might stimulate through competition between MDBs for prime international development finance projects, the advent of the AIIB has already prompted other MDBs to review how they work. Such MDB competition to finance major projects can be to the potential benefit of prospective borrowers, but also to the possible detriment of social and environmental sustainability in relation to these projects.

Moreover, the simplification of due diligence, particularly when combined with the less-risk averse loan/investment decision-making procedures that the AIIB has already trailed as one of its operational efficiency aims, does not augur well for the last of the three strictures that the AIIB has bound itself to uphold, namely, international best practice in the application of social and environmental standards. This issue is especially pertinent when we consider that one of the stated aims of the AIIB is to focus on major infrastructure development projects. Such major projects almost inevitably result in equally significant social and environmental impacts, thereby necessitating more, not less, due diligence on the part of institutional lenders such as the AIIB.

Initial assessments of the AIIB environmental and social framework have yielded a mixed bag of results. A World Resources Institute comment observed that:

> On some issues, the AIIB has embraced more progressive positions than some of its peers. For example, the AIIB excludes financing for commercial logging operations in tropical or old-growth forests, which goes beyond the current commitment made by the World Bank. On other subjects, the AIIB's commitments are not quite as strong. For example, the AIIB has not followed the lead of the Asian Development Bank (ADB) or International Finance Corporation (IFC) in giving Indigenous Peoples the right to consent to activities taking place on their lands.[61]

Indigenous peoples. The Bank screens each Project to determine whether or not it would have impacts on Indigenous Peoples. In conducting this screening, the Bank seeks the technical judgement of qualified social scientists with expertise on the social and cultural groups in the Project area. The Bank also consults the Indigenous Peoples concerned and the Client. If the Project would have impacts on Indigenous Peoples, the Bank requires the Client to prepare an Indigenous Peoples plan or IPPF (Indigenous Peoples Planning Framework). The level of detail and comprehensiveness of the IPPF is to be proportionate to the degree of the impacts.[62]

Moreover, since Indigenous Peoples may be particularly vulnerable to the loss of, alienation from, or exploitation of their land and access to natural and cultural resources, the Bank requires the Client to engage in Free, Prior and Informed Consultation (FPICon) with the affected Indigenous Peoples if activities under the Project would: (a) have impacts on land and natural resources subject to traditional ownership or under customary occupation or use; (b) cause relocation of Indigenous Peoples from land and natural resources subject to traditional ownership or under customary occupation or use; or (c) have significant impacts on Indigenous Peoples' cultural heritage. In these circumstances, the Bank requires the Client to engage suitably qualified and experienced independent experts to assist in the identification of these activities' risks to and impacts on Indigenous Peoples.[63]

According to Kim, many environmental provisions of the AIIB Standards are on par with that of the IFC Performance Standards on Environmental and Social Sustainability.[64] For instance, in its pollution prevention section, the AIIB cites the World Bank Group's Environmental, Health and Safety Guidelines (EHSGs) and ensures that its projects will follow these EHSGs. On the other hand, the AIIB Standards lack detail or are different in ways that may lead to arbitrary outcomes. Kim has outlined a few examples of these discrepancies, as follows:

1 The IFC Performance Standards provide more detailed requirements on how adverse environmental effects should be mitigated, applying specific terms such as 'no net loss' of biodiversity and 'set-aside' areas of significant biodiversity value.[65] By contrast, the corresponding AIIB requirement appears to be merely to 'avoid adverse Project impacts on biodiversity. When avoidance of adverse impacts is not possible, implement measures to minimize adverse impacts and restore biodiversity, including, as a last resort, biodiversity offsets.'[66] The AIIB requirements are therefore not as detailed as the IFC's, *inter alia* providing that any conversion or degradation of natural habitats is appropriately mitigated through 'measures acceptable to the Bank'.[67] According to Kim, if the AIIB is not rigorous in its evaluation of mitigation measures, recipients of funding may be able to escape with implementing measures that are superficial, cheap, and ineffective.[68]

2 For projects located in natural habitats, the AIIB requires a cost–benefit analysis of the proposed project to be undertaken, to ensure that, *inter alia*, the Project's overall benefits 'substantially outweigh' the environmental costs.[69] As the IFC Standards do not have a similar requirement, the IFC may finance projects even if the overall economic benefits are deemed not to 'substantially outweigh' the environmental costs. Nevertheless, Kim cautions that such cost-benefit analysis will not always lead to wise decisions, because it is unclear *how* the AIIB will conduct cost–benefit analyses, so the ultimate decision could be arbitrary. Indeed, the AIIB may allow projects that significantly destroy natural habitats by simply concluding that the overall benefit of the Project does in fact 'substantially outweigh' the cost. Thus, the cost–benefit analysis might be used to justify or defend AIIB's decisions to value economic gain over environmental protection.[70]

3 Finally, when critical habitats of high biodiversity value are involved, the IFC will not implement any project activities unless several imperative criteria are met. These criteria include the fact that there will be no measurable adverse impacts on this biodiversity and the ecological processes supporting this biodiversity, as well as no net reduction in global, regional or national populations of endangered species in these critical habitats. By contrast, while there appears to be a similar, initial presumption that AIIB-sponsored 'Project activities in areas of critical habitats are prohibited', the AIIB then focuses on whether any adverse impacts impair the habitat's 'ability to function'.[71]

Based on the different wording and emphasis in these separate texts, Kim postulates that the AIIB may ultimately allow a project by determining that a habitat may be able to function even if many of its biodiversity values are lost, whereas the IFC would not allow a project that would reduce biodiversity values, even if the habitat were able to function.[72]

AIIB individual project-level grievance mechanism and institutional-level complaints handling mechanism

At the individual project level, the Environmental and Social Framework requires that AIIB borrowers establish a suitable project-level grievance mechanism in accordance with AIIB's Environment and Social Policy (ESP) and applicable Environmental and Social Standards (ESS), and inform affected people of the project-level grievance mechanism's availability.[73] According to the Framework, this grievance mechanism may utilise existing formal or informal procedures, provided that they are properly designed and implemented, and deemed by the Bank to be suitable for the individual project. In other words, each project-level grievance mechanism needs to be scaled to the risks and impacts of the Project.[74] There is also provision for the grievance mechanism to address affected people's concerns and complaints promptly, using an understandable and transparent process that is gender-sensitive, culturally appropriate and readily accessible to all affected people.[75] The Framework includes provisions to protect any complainants using the project-specific grievance mechanism from retaliation and to remain anonymous, if requested.[76] Finally, the grievance mechanism also provides for maintenance of a publicly accessible case register, and reports on grievance redress and outcomes, which are disclosed in accordance with the applicable Environmental and Social Standards (ESS).[77]

In addition to such individual project-based grievance mechanisms, the AIIB has also pledged to establish its own (AIIB) bank oversight mechanism for people who believe they have been or are likely to be adversely affected by a failure of the Bank to implement the Environmental and Social Policy (ESP).[78] This the AIIB has now done in the form of an independent Compliance, Effectiveness and Integrity Unit (CEIU) that exercises oversight in these three areas. The CEIU is also mandated to receive complaints about AIIB operations. The CEIU is independent of AIIB Management and its Director General reports directly to the AIIB Board of Directors.[79] The CIEU of the AIIB is now working to establish an institutional (as opposed to individual project-based) AIIB complaints handling mechanism. The proposed mechanism will allow people who feel they are harmed, or could be harmed, by an AIIB-funded project to voice their concerns to AIIB regarding AIIB's non-compliance with its own environmental and social safeguards, as well as seek help for resolution of related problems. The initial Call for Public Consultation for this proposed AIIB Complaints Handling Mechanism, commenced from 27 April 2017 and ended on 30 September 2017. By December 2017, the AIIB Board of Directors had considered the final draft of the proposed Project-affected People's Mechanism (PPM). The AIIB then launched a 60-day second phase of public consultation for its project complaints handling mechanism on 26 January 2018, welcoming comments and suggestions on the above draft Mechanism by 26 March 2018. A summary of the continuing issues of concern raise by the first phase of consultation on this draft Mechanism is as follows:

1   Project-affected People's Mechanism (PPM) and Compliance, Effectiveness and Integrity Unit (CEIU) independence: particularly from Management, and in CEIU staff selection to avoid conflict of interest and ensure expertise;

2   PPM and CEIU outreach and site visits: including for local awareness-raising about the PPM and for monitoring purposes;

3   Complaint handling process: taking an early and pre-emptory approach; allowing a complaint from even one to two complainants; allowing complainants to move flexibly between complaint channels; and using clear, easy, timely and transparent processes that are culturally sensitive and in appropriate languages;

4   Complainant protection: against retaliation and through anonymity;

5   Remedial actions: including a PPM role to propose and design actions; suspension; remedy funding and PPM monitoring of remedial action plans;

6   Learning: for policy improvement (including the Environmental and Social Framework) and documentation to improve practice.[80]

Case study of 21st Century Maritime Silk Road-related AIIB-funded projects: the Duqm Port Development Project in Oman

Introduction to the Duqm project and the role of AIIB

To understand the link between the integration of environmental, social and cultural considerations through the AIIB Environmental and Social, as well as Risk Assessment Frameworks and their application to an AIIB-financially assisted project that is part of the BRI, a case study in the form of the Duqm Port Commercial Terminal and Operational Zone Development Project in the Sultanate of Oman (hereinafter, 'the Duqm Port Development Project'),[81] will be undertaken. Although an oil-dependent economy, Oman is in the process of economic diversification from petroleum and has undertaken two initiatives to guide this policy, as follows: (1) TANFEEDH – National Program for Enhancing Economic Diversification;[82] and (2) ITHRAA – Oman's inward investment and export development agency.[83] As may be surmised from this case study of the Duqm Port Development Project, this economic diversification programme is at least in part focussed on infrastructure investment, and can be summarised in the following paragraphs.

   The Duqm Port Development Project is managed by the Special Economic Zone Authority (SEZAD) and is being supported both financially and technically by the AIIB. The Duqm project is the larger of two projects that the AIIB's Board of Directors have approved loans for, totalling US$301 million to finance two transport sector projects in the Sultanate of Oman, the Bank's first in the Arabian Peninsula. The Bank's support comprises US$265 million towards Oman's maritime infrastructure at Duqm Port and US$36 million to prepare the country's first railway system. Upon successful completion, the projects are expected to enhance economic prospects in Oman and provide more efficient and effective maritime trade links to other Bank members, both in the Persian/Arabian Gulf and further afield. Duqm Port is strategically located with the potential to become a regional logistics hub with an economic footprint far beyond Oman's borders.[84]

The objective of this Project is to achieve the potential economic benefits from Duqm port development through improved transport efficiency, strengthened logistics, facilitated mineral exports, and reduced supply chain delivery time and costs for the wide spectrum of industries in the new Duqm Special Economic Zone. The Project will mainly include the civil works for the construction of port related infrastructure including port access roads, cargo storage, Terminal buildings, and Operational Zone's facilities buildings. The Project is estimated to be implemented over a period of 3.5 years from January 2017 to June 2020. A Special Economic Zone Authority Duqm (SEZAD) will execute the Project. The Project will mainly include the civil works for the construction of port related infrastructure including port access roads, cargo storage, Terminal buildings, and Operational Zone's facilities buildings. The Project is estimated to be implemented over a period of 3.5 years from January 2017 to June 2020. The total Project cost is estimated at US$353.33 million, for which SEZAD has requested a loan of US$265 million from AIIB to help finance the Project. SEZAD will provide the counterpart funding of US$88.33 million.[85]

Have the environmental and social risks of the Duqm Project been adequately addressed by the AIIB?

The Duqm Project has been placed in Category B under the provisions of AIIB's Environmental and Social Policy (ESP). The potential risks and impacts, which will occur primarily during the construction period, are limited and localised, and concentrated within the existing port area, at commercial quays that are already built. A Preliminary Environmental Impact Assessment (PEIA) has been prepared to meet the requirements of the national legislation of Oman and a Preliminary Environmental Permit has been issued by the Oman Ministry of Environment and Climate Affairs (MECA). The PEIA addresses the provisions of AIIB's ESS 1 – Environmental and Social Assessment and Management, which is applicable to the Project. The Special Economic Zone Authority Duqm (SEZAD) disclosed the Preliminary Environmental Impact Assessment (PEIA) on its website on 6 November 2016. However, it is notable that, despite the promulgation of both environmental and social (E&S), as well as risk frameworks and, moreover, their inclusion within the ultimate finance decision-making procedure for such projects by the AIIB, the relevant PEIA exercise was undertaken according to national Omani domestic laws. This is undoubtedly due to the continuing lack of precise international environmental, social and cultural *standards* within the current AIIB Environmental and Social, as well as Risk Assessment Frameworks. Such precise standards are prevalent within more well-established Multilateral Development Banks (MDBs) such as the World Bank (including the International Finance Corporation, IFC) and its regional, sister MDB, namely, the Asian Development Bank (ADB). For example, the World Bank has recently (as of 1 October, 2018) adopted a revised Environmental and Social Framework (ESF).[86] The World Bank's ESF consists of:

- The World Bank's Vision for Sustainable Development
- The World Bank's Environmental and Social Policy for Investment Project Financing (IPF), which sets out the requirements that apply to the Bank
- The ten Environmental and Social Standards (ESS), which set out the requirements that apply to the Borrowers
- The Bank Directive on Addressing Risks and Impacts on Disadvantaged or Vulnerable Individuals or Groups.[87]

Meanwhile, the IFC has also updated its *Sustainability Framework* – effective from 1 January, 2012, to reflect the evolution in good practice for sustainability and risk mitigation over the past five years. The IFC's Sustainability Framework incorporates modifications on challenging issues that are increasingly important to sustainable businesses, including supply-chain management, resource efficiency and climate change and business and human rights.[88] The IFC's 2012 Sustainability Framework consists of its Policy on Environmental and Social Sustainability,[89] which defines IFC's commitments to environmental and social sustainability; the IFC Performance Standards,[90] which define clients' responsibilities for managing their environmental and social risks; and its Access to Information Policy,[91] which articulates the IFC's commitment to transparency.

This raises the question, *inter alia*, as to whether there is a need for a Generally Applicable International Rules and Standards (GAIRS) provision for application in AIIB-supported projects, as well as BRI projects generally, and 21st Century Maritime Silk Road projects, specifically. For example, under the UN Convention on the Law of the Sea (UNCLOS) Article 211(2) on Flag State Jurisdiction over vessel-source pollution provides that: 'Such (national/domestic) laws and regulations *shall at least have the same effect* as that of generally accepted international rules and standards established through the competent international organization or general diplomatic conference', [emphasis added]. A similar type of provision could be inserted/included within all AIIB-supported and BRI individual Project requirements.

Moving on from the environmental and social risks to the cultural risk aspects of the Duqm Project, the CEMP further provides as follows:

> Should cultural heritage be identified during the project, work shall cease in the location and the Ministry of Heritage and Culture shall be notified immediately. Cultural heritage in this context would include archaeological, historical and/or sacred sites or materials, including graves. While this is not expected to be a concern at the main construction site (reclaimed land), it could become one during the construction of the IP2 construction camp or in borrow pits that may be required during the construction of the works. (The Omani) Ministry of Heritage and Culture (MHC) had conducted a

survey in the SEZ area to identify cultural and archaeological evidences including graves and has documented the same in a report with the location co-ordinates, description, photographs and archaeological evaluation. Since this is unlikely to be an issue at the main site, it is not a primary focus area of this CEMP. However a 'Chance-find' procedure has been developed (Appendix J) and will be communicated to all contractors working on the site so that action could be taken in case of observations on any archaeological or cultural findings during construction phase.[92]

Concerns have also been raised by an international civil society group/non-governmental organisation (NGO) – the Business and Human Rights Resource Center (hereinafter the Center) – over the use of migrant workers in this Project by SEZAD.[93] In its initial submission, to the AIIB, the Center noted, *inter alia*, that the AIIB's Environmental and Social Framework (ESF) stipulates that, as part of its due diligence, the Bank is required to determine whether 'all key potential environmental and social risks and impacts of the Project have been identified'[94] and whether 'effective measures to avoid, minimize, mitigate, offset or compensate for the adverse impacts are incorporated into the Project's design and ESMP'.[95] Specifically,

> Environmental and Social Standard 1 (ESS 1) requires the Client to 'assess labor and working conditions of project workers' and 'ensure that, in connection with the Project, there is no work or service not voluntarily performed that is exacted from an individual under threat of force or penalty (including any kind of forced or compulsory labor, such as indentured labor, bonded labor or similar labor-contracting arrangements, or labor by trafficked persons)'.[96]

In its initial submission on this issue, the Center (NGO) stated that:

> in our view, the Preliminary Environmental Impact Assessment should be revised to identify and address the social risks attached to the employment of migrant construction labor on the Project … [And] address the risk of use of forced labor in a manner that is consistent with international guidelines for construction projects in the Gulf region.[97]

The final AIIB response to this submission, noted, *inter alia*, as follows:

> In the near future, the Special Economic Zone Authority at Duqm (SEZAD) will be posting a revised version of the Construction Environmental Management Plan (CEMP), that has been expanded to include coverage of how health, safety and labor issues will be addressed in the implementation of the project. The revised draft CEMP provides an overview of measures being taken to address labor conditions under the project, consistent with Omani Regulation Royal Decree-35/2003. There are provisions in the revised draft CEMP for use of a grievance redress mechanism, which is

open to all parties, including workers, as well as an internal grievance register. Measures are planned to disseminate information on the grievance redress process to the public and to workers, both Omani and foreign. SEZAD is putting in place its project-level grievance mechanism, which is described in the CEMP. The grievance mechanism contains provisions to protect complainants from retaliation and to remain anonymous, if requested.[98]

Specifically, the Duqm Project's Construction Environmental Management Plan (CEMP) provides as follows:

SEZAD has prepared and approved a Grievance Redress Mechanism (GRM) that is now operational. The intention of this mechanism is to enable anyone within DUQM; to be able to have access to a complaint process that can be used, without risk of retaliation, by individuals, workers, communities and/or civil society organisations that are being affected by business activities and operations within the special economic zone authority. The Grievance Redress Service (GRS) being handled by the Partnership and Development Department (CSR Section) ensures that complaints are promptly reviewed, addressed and responded within a certain time frame by the department within the Special Economic Zone Authority of SEZAD. The intention of this procedure is to validate the importance of having SEZAD more accessible to its communities and to help ensure faster and better resolution related to any grievance or service issues. Participation in the GRS is voluntary, anonymous (when requested) and without charge. The GRS is open to all however does not relate the same with regard to lands as this is handled by the Ministry of Housing, all enquiries received with regard to this will be advised of whom to contact at the Ministry of Housing as well as the dedicated person.[99]

Final observations on AIIB support for the Duqm Port Development Project

Oman's economic diversification strategy will require investment in capital, technology and technical human resources from foreign sources. However, the influx of such foreign investment within diverse economic sectors such as manufacturing, mining, as well as transport links and logistical infrastructure has the potential to generate *environmental, social and cultural concerns (especially in the form religious issues)*. Thus, Oman needs to focus not only in creating *optimal economic conditions* for investment to assist its diversification strategy, but also to ensure that Oman has the legal means to uphold its unique social and cultural characteristics/qualities. Fortunately, 'international best practice' in both international development finance law and international investment law is increasingly providing for such concerns to be addressed by both MDBs as well as Omani laws regulating foreign investment. This case study of AIIB support for the Duqm Port Development Project is therefore an example of the progressive, if not quite comprehensive, integration of these environmental, social and cultural/religious risks within the former legal field.

Conclusions

Both the BRI-related and especially, 21st Century Maritime Silk Road projects need to (and arguably do) proactively take environmental, social and cultural considerations into account in their construction as well as operational phases. In this regard, where such BRI/Maritime Silk Road projects are reliant on Asian Infrastructure Investment Bank support, then it can be seen that environmental, social and cultural considerations have been integrated into the AIIB decision-making process through the Environmental and Social Framework, Risk Assessment Framework, and Operational Policy on Financing, as well as being rendered accountable against individual project operators through the establishment of local Grievance Redress Mechanisms. However, an institutional-level Complaints Handling Mechanism against the AIIB itself is yet to be established.

Moreover, it remains to be seen whether AIIB can provide 'international best practice' for BRI-related projects, especially Maritime Silk Road projects, with regard to these three – environmental, social and cultural – sustainability concerns. To the extent that the AIIB does so, it is currently proving helpful for the AIIB to be aligned with several other more-established MDBs for many of its projects. According to a recent *Financial Times* (UK) newspaper report, for example, 'so far, 18 of the 25 projects financed by the Beijing-based bank have involved co-lending with the World Bank, Asian Development Bank (ADB), European Bank for Reconstruction and Development (EBRD), European Investment Bank and Islamic Development Bank',[100] with the remaining seven financed solely by the AIIB. These issues are growing in topicality given the AIIB's reported extension of its financing operations to Latin America and Africa following agreements with the two regions' MDBs, namely, the African Development Bank (AfDB) and Inter-American Development Bank (IADB).[101] Finally, since not all Maritime Silk Road projects are AIIB-related, such 'international best practice' also needs further institutionalisation, for example, within the Silk Road Fund lending and investment decision-making processes.

Notes

1 Anja Manuel, *This Brave New World: India, China and the United States*, (New York: Simon & Schuster, 2016), p. 218.
2 See: Hong Kong & Shanghai Banking Corporation (HSBC) Advertisement, *Financial Times* (UK) (2018).
3 For an account of the theoretical evolution of the 'Ecological Modernization' concept and the debate it has engendered, see Arthur P. J. Mol and Gert Spaargaren, Ecological Modernisation Theory in Debate: A Review, *Environmental Politics: Special Issue on Ecological Modernisation Around the World: Perspectives and Critical Debates* 9(1) (2000), 17–49. For a more recent critical account of this concept, see Jeffrey A. Ewing, Hollow Ecology: Ecological Modernization Theory and the Death of Nature', *Journal of World-Systems Research* 23(1) (2017), 126–155.

4 James P. F. Oswald, What Does Eco-civilization Mean?, The China Story, Australian Centre on China in the World, posted on 4 September 2014, citing Nicholas Dynon, 'Four Civilizations' and the Evolution of Post-Mao Chinese Socialist Ideology, *China Journal* 60 (2008), 106; Luo Rongqu (ed.), *From Westernisation to Modernisation* (2008) [in Chinese], www.thechina.story.org/2014/09/.

5 Oswald (2014) *ibid.*, citing A. Anagnost, Constructing the Civilized Community, in: Theodore Huters, Roy Bin Wong and Pauline Yu (eds.), *Culture & State in Chinese History: Conventions, Accommodations, and Critiques* (Stanford, CA: Stanford University Press, 1997), p. 359.

6 *Ibid.*

7 *Ibid.* citing Dynon (2008), *supra* (n. 4).

8 *Ibid.* citing Ma Jun, Ecological Civilization Is the Way Forward, *China Dialogue*, 31 October 2007. www.chinadialogue.net/article/1440-Ecological-civilisation-is-the-way-forward.

9 The China Modernization Report 2007: Study on Ecological Modernization (China Centre for Modernisation Research, 2007) Officially released in Beijing, 27 January 2007.

10 Yu Zhou, State Power and Environmental Initiatives in China: Analyzing China's Green Building Program through an Ecological Modernization Perspective, *Geoforum* 61 (2015), 1–12.

11 *Ibid.*

12 *Ibid.*

13 Oswald (2014) *supra* (n. 4), citing Fred Magdoff, Ecological Civilization, *Monthly Review* 62(8) (2011), http://monthlyreview.org/2011/01/01/ecological-civilization.

14 Oswald (2014) *Ibid.*

15 Oswald, *supra* (n. 4), citing Yan Geng and Yang Zhihua, *Constructing a Theory and System of Ecological Civilisation* (2009); He Aiguo, *Contemporary China's Road to Eco-Civilisation* (2012) [in Chinese].

16 Oswald, *Ibid.*

17 *Ibid.*

18 *Ibid.*

19 Lei Zhang, Arthur P. J. Mol and David A. Sonnenfeld, the Interpretation of Ecological Modernisation in China, *Environmental Politics* 16(4) (2007), 659–668, www.uio.no/studier/emner/annet/sum/SUM1000/h08/Zhang.pdf.

20 Ben Parr and Don Henry, China Moves Towards Ecological Civilisation, *Australian Outlook*, Australian Institute for International Affairs, 24 August 2016, www.inter nationalaffairs.org.au/australianoutlook/china-moves-towards-ecological-civilisation/.

21 See: 'Secure a Decisive Victory in Building a Moderately Prosperous Society in All Respects and Strive for the Great Success of Socialism with Chinese Characteristics for a New Era, Report by Xi Jinping, delivered at the 19th National Congress of the Communist Party of China (CPC), 18 October 2017, 65, p. 4. www.xinhuanet.com/english/download/Xi_Jinping%27s_report_at_19th_CPC_National_Congress.pdf.

22 *Ibid.*

23 Manuel (2016) *supra* (n. 1), p. 218.

24 *Ibid.*

25 Hong Yu, Motivation behind China's 'One Belt, One Road' Initiatives and Establishment of the Asian Infrastructure Investment Bank, *Journal of Contemporary China* 26(105) (2017), 353–368.

26 *Ibid.*

27 Mike Callaghan and Paul Hubbard, AIIB: Multilaterism on the Silk Road, *China Economic Journal* 9(2) (2016), 116–139.

28 *Ibid.*

29 *Ibid.*

30 *Ibid.*

31 D. Yang, *et al*., New Road for Telecoupling Global Prosperity and Ecological Sustainability, *Ecosystem Health and Sustainability* 2(10) (2016), Article e01242, www. ecohealthsustain.org.

32 See, Green Development under Belt and Road Initiative: Pushing Forward the Global Implementation of the Paris Agreement, Belt & Road Green Development Partnership, Press Release, 11 November 2017, Bonn, Germany. Media Contact Person: Xiulan Li, Researcher, Global Green Leadership Research Center, https://cop23. unfccc.int/sites/default/files/resource/Press%20Release-Green%20Development%20 Under%20the%20BRI-Phusing%20Forward%20the%20Global%20Implementation %20of%20the%20Paris%20Agreement-20171108.pdf.

33 Yang *et al*., *supra* (n. 31).

34 Joint Communique of the Leaders Roundtable of the Belt and Road Forum for International Cooperation, Source: Xinhua News Agency, Yamei (ed.), 15 May 2017, www.xinhuanet.com/english/2017-05/15/c_136286378.htm.

35 *Ibid.*

36 Domestic Chinese Government Guidance on Promoting Green Belt and Road, issued on 10 May 2017, https://eng.yidaiyilu.gov.cn/zchj/qwfb/12479.htm.

37 *Ibid.*

38 Published by *Xinhua* news agency, 20 June 2017, http://english.gov.cn/archive/ publications/2017/06/20/content_281475691873460.htm.

39 *Ibid.*

40 *Ibid.*

41 *Ibid.*

42 Robert J. Hanlon, Thinking about the Asian Infrastructure Investment Bank: Can a China-Led Development Bank Improve Sustainability in Asia?, *Asia & the Pacific Policy Studies* 4(3) (2019), 541–554.

43 Article 13(4) of the AIIB Charter.

44 See Report on the Articles of Agreement of the AIIB, by the Chief Negotiators for Establishing the AIIB, Singapore, 22 May 2015. p. 3, www.aiib.org/en/about-aiib/ basic-documents/_download/articles-of-agreement/basic_document_report_on_the_ articles_of_agreement.pdf.

45 See the AIIB website, www.aiib.org/en/policies-strategies/operational-policies/ environmental-social-framework.html.

46 See AIIB Directive on Environmental and Social Policy, para. 1.1, www.aiib.org/en/ policies-strategies/_download/environment-framework/environmental-and-social-directive.pdf.

47 See AIIB, Environmental and Social Framework, February 2016, www.aiib.org/en/ policies-strategies/_download/environment-framework/20160226043633542.pdf.

48 See AIIB, Environmental and Social Framework, February 2016, *Ibid.*

49 AIIB, Environmental and Social Framework, *Ibid.*, para.17.

50 *Ibid.*

51 *Ibid.*, para. 13.

52 *Ibid.*, para. 59.

53 Felix Preston, Rob Bailey and Sian Bradley (from Chatham House) and Dr Wei Jigang and Dr Zhao Changwen of the Development Research Center (DRC) of the Chinese State Council, *Navigating the New Normal: China and Global Resource Governance*, Joint DRC and Chatham House report, 16 January, 2016, p. 31, www. chathamhouse.org/sites/files/chathamhouse/publications/research/2016-01-27-china-global-resource-governance-preston-bailey-bradley-wei-zhao-final.pdf.

54 Jisan Kim, Regulating Economic Development: Environmental and Social Standards of the AIIB and the IFC, *Harvard Journal of International Law* 21 (April 2016), www.harvardilj.org/2016/04/regulating-economic-development-environmental-and-social-standards-of-the-aiib-and-the-ifc/.

55 AIIB Risk Assessment Framework, November, 2016, www.aiib.org/en/policies-strategies/_download/risk-management-framework/AIIB-Risk-Management-Framework-final-14Nov-clean.pdf.
56 *Ibid.*, para. 7.
57 *Ibid.*, para. 8.
58 *Ibid.*, para. 8.1.1.
59 *Ibid.*, para. 26.
60 *Ibid.*, para. 31.
61 Gaia Larsen and Sean Gilbert, Asian Infrastructure Investment Bank Releases New Environmental and Social Standards: How Do They Stack Up?, World Resources Institute Blog Post, 4 March 2016, www.wri.org/blog/2016/03/asian-infrastructure-investment-bank-releases-new-environmental-and-social-standards.
62 AIIB, Environmental and Social Framework, *supra* (n. 48), para.33.
63 *Ibid.*, at para. 60.
64 Kim (2016), *supra* (n. 54). The latest version of the IFC Performance Standards was adopted on 1 January 2012, www.ifc.org/wps/wcm/connect/c8f524004a73dae ca09afdf998895a12/IFC_Performance_Standards.pdf?MOD=AJPERES.
65 See, for example, paragraph 15 under IFC Performance Standard 6 on Biodiversity Conservation and Sustainable Management of Living Natural Resources.
66 See, B. Environmental Coverage, in: AIIB Environmental and Social Standard 1: Environmental and Social Assessment and Management.
67 *Ibid.*
68 See Kim (2016), *supra* (n. 54).
69 AIIB Environmental and Social Standard 1, *supra* (n. 66).
70 Kim (2016), *supra* (n. 54).
71 AIIB Environmental and Social Standard 1, *supra* (n. 66).
72 Kim (2016), *supra* (n. 54).
73 Environmental & Social Framework, *supra* (n. 47), para. 63.
74 *Ibid.*
75 *Ibid.*
76 *Ibid.*
77 *Ibid.*
78 *Ibid.*, para. 64.
79 See AIIB organizational chart, www.aiib.org/en/about-aiib/governance/_common/_download/AIIB_organizational_structure.pdf.
80 See, AIIB Launches Second Phase of Public Consultation on Draft Complaints Handling Mechanism, www.aiib.org/en/policies-strategies/operational-policies/public-consultation-phase2/index.html.
81 AIIB Project No. 000013, www.aiib.org/en/projects/approved/2016/duqm-port-commercial-terminal.html.
82 See www.tanfeedh.gov.om/en/.
83 See www.ithraa.om.
84 Asian Infrastructure Investment Bank Breaks New Ground Approving Two Projects in Oman, AIIB Press Release, Beijing, 9 December 2016, www.aiib.org/en/news-events/news/2016/20161209_001.html.
85 AIIB Project Document, para. 20.
86 See World Bank Environmental and Social Sustainability Framework, www.world bank.org/en/projects-operations/environmental-and-social-framework.
87 *Ibid.*
88 IFC Sustainability Framework, www.ifc.org/wps/wcm/connect/topics_ext_content/ifc_external_corporate_site/sustainability-at-ifc/policies-standards/sustainability+framework.
89 IFC Policy on Sustainability, www.ifc.org/wps/wcm/connect/topics_ext_content/ifc_external_corporate_site/sustainability-at-ifc/policies-standards/sustainability-policy/sustainability-policy.

90 IFC Performance Standards, www.ifc.org/wps/wcm/connect/topics_ext_content/ifc_external_corporate_site/sustainability-at-ifc/policies-standards/performance-standards.

91 IFC Access to Information Policy, https://disclosures.ifc.org/#/accessInfoPolicy.

92 See Construction of Roads, Infrastructure & Buildings at the Commercial Terminal & Operational Zone Areas, Port of Duqm – IP2, CEMP (2017), para. 7.7, p. 72–73, www.aiib.org/en/projects/approved/2016/_download/duqm-port-commercial/final-construction-environmental-management-plan.pdf.

93 See Oman: AIIB and Construction Joint Venture Respond to Concerns Over Labour Safeguards for Migrant Workers on Port Project, Business & Human Rights Center website, https://business-humanrights.org/en/oman-joint-submission-to-aiib-expresses-concerns-makes-recommendations-for-the-protection-of-migrant-construction-workers-on-port-project.

94 AIIB Environmental and Social Framework (2016), *supra* (n. 45), para. 17.

95 *Ibid.*

96 AIIB Environmental and Social Standard (ESS) 1, *supra* (n. 66).

97 Business & Human Rights Center, Initial Submission on 1 May 2017, *supra* (n. 93).

98 AIIB response (on 25 August 2017) to this initial submission, following an initial response and a rejoinder (on 20 July, 2017) by the Business & Human Rights Center (NGO).

99 Duqm Port Development Project, CEMP (2017), para. 4.7, p. 54.

100 See James Kynge, China-led bank: AIIB looks to invest in Latin America and Africa, *Financial Times*, 6 May 2018, p. 7.

101 *Ibid.*

15 The new Maritime Silk Road and WTO law

Road to harmony or conflict?

Henrik Andersen

Introduction

Debates on geopolitical strategies concerning China's Maritime Silk Road (MSR) have raged for a while.[1] Where focus in literature has been on geopolitical strategies and security, there is a gap in research concerning international economic law and the 'One Belt, One Road' (OBOR) Initiative and the MSR. After the failed Doha Negotiations of the World Trade Organization (WTO), OBOR might seem as a welcoming complement to global trade. Where the Doha agenda had attempted to amend WTO agreements – and to reach new agreements – concerning *inter alia* agriculture, services, market access for non-agricultural products, intellectual property rights, relationship between trade and investment, relationship between trade and competition, relationship between trade and environment, and dispute settlement,[2] the outcome was reduced to trade facilitation and a few decisions in respect of agriculture and intellectual property rights. OBOR moves beyond the trade confines of the WTO. OBOR is a set of investment strategies to enhance trade in general, cultural exchange and education, but the heavy investments in infrastructure to reduce trade costs seem to match the trade facilitation dimension of the WTO. While OBOR strategies aim at free trade, based on market economy principles, the question is to what extent they are compatible with the market economy principles and rules of the WTO.

The aim of this chapter is to identify areas where OBOR overlaps with WTO law and to assess the extent of conformity of OBOR with WTO law. It takes a WTO law perspective and is delimited to maritime issues with focus on the market. The reason for choosing a WTO law perspective is that the WTO system already exists and OBOR comes to complement it by facilitating trade on an interregional scale. The chapter claims that the OBOR trade facilitation, which can be in line with WTO law, potentially can lead to increased use of unfair trading rules of the WTO. The chapter must be read with some reservations, as OBOR is still in its infancy and thus only provides limited materials to analyse the OBOR-WTO relationship.

The following part discusses the overall aims and principles of OBOR and the WTO constitutional setting. Then the chapter more specifically discusses

WTO law and regional trade agreements (RTA), as well as specific WTO law concerning maritime services. Finally, it discusses trade facilitation and competition issues resulting from improved trading facilities along the MSR in the context of WTO law.

Overall principles of OBOR

'One Belt One Road' refers to the dual overland 'belt' and the maritime 'road' projects. It is an initiative proposed by President Xi Jinping in 2013. The maritime road is inspired by the old Maritime Silk Road and is called the 21st Century Maritime Silk Road. It connects the East coast of China to the ports in Sri Lanka and Pakistan and crosses over the Indian Ocean and the Red Sea to connect with the port in Pireaus, Greece and continuing on to Venice in Italy.[3]

The OBOR initiative aims at encouraging countries along the belt and road to: 'achieve economic policy coordination and carry out broader and more in-depth regional cooperation of higher standards; and jointly creating an open, inclusive and balanced regional economic cooperation architecture that benefits all'.[4]

OBOR is still in its infancy. There are visions and overall principles guiding OBOR but it has not reached a substantive institutionalisation through rules or practices on an overall level although with a few exceptions. For example, the Asian Infrastructure Investment Bank (AIIB), where China is a major investor, is engaged with OBOR projects. Also, the Silk Road Fund, which is a state owned investment fund, has been established. Its purpose is to provide investment and financing support for trade and economic cooperation and connectivity in OBOR and to promote common development and prosperity in China and other countries and regions involved with OBOR.[5]

There are a number of states involved with OBOR investments. It is, in line with the WTO, open to all States regardless of their compliance with the UN Charter. For example, the government of Venezuela, which currently violates national constitutional law and its international human rights obligations,[6] was accepted as prospective member of the AIIB on 21 March 2017.[7]

The MSR has not reached the same level of maturity as the 'belt', which may be a result of the disputes in the South China Sea.[8] The MSR raises a number of security issues and disputes over territory in the South China Sea as well as the East China Sea between China and Japan and China and South Korea. An escalation of the disputes – and with the current US rhetoric – can potentially lead to questions about national security and thus be an issue to be balanced in the trade relationships which are governed under WTO law.

From an economic perspective, the main aim of the MSR is to improve port, transport and transit facilities between China and countries along the MSR. Improved conditions for ship transport can improve the volume of goods shipped between China and Europe and can reduce transaction costs benefitting the market actors with increased and easier flow of trade in goods. Through the OBOR initiative, China has, for example, invested in the port of Piraeus, Greece through the State-owned enterprises (SOE) Chinese Ocean Shipping and

COSCO Pacific. The port is now one of the fastest growing container ports in the world.[9] It opens up for a faster process of transport of products from China and other states along the MSR destined for Europe.

The economic aims are reflected in the OBOR principles but they are not detached from their legal environment of rights and obligations under international law as well as Chinese holistic and harmonious approaches to relations. The core principles of OBOR have been issued by China's National Development and Reform Commission, Ministry of Foreign Affairs, and Ministry of Commerce of the People's Republic of China. They are also reflected in the policies and purposes of the AIIB and the Silk Road Fund. The principles are:

- To be in line with the purposes and principles of the UN Charter and upholding the Five Principles of Peaceful Coexistence
- Openness for cooperation for countries and international and regional organisations
- Inclusiveness and harmony with tolerance among civilisations and respect of respective countries' development and supporting dialogue between different civilisations where common ground is to be sought in order to be in peace for common prosperity
- Abiding market rules and international norms where market will have a decisive role in allocation of resources with a primary role of enterprises and where governments perform their due functions
- Seeking mutual benefits for all parties involved.[10]

The principles are manifested through development of infrastructure, trade liberalisation, financial integration, policy coordination and people-to-people ties. The principles will be discussed in the following sub-parts.

Purposes and principles of the UN Charter and the Five Principles of Peaceful Coexistence

By referring to the principles of the UN Charter, China shows that OBOR strategies will follow principles of international rules of law. For example, the UN Charter provides in its preamble that the purpose of the UN is 'to establish conditions under which justice and respect for the obligations arising from treaties and other sources of international law can be maintained'.[11] There are some reservations to be taken here as OBOR does not exclude participation of states which violate their international human rights obligations, as mentioned above.

The reference to the UN Charter is in line with the reference to the Five Principles of Peaceful Coexistence.[12] They have achieved international recognition in UN instruments. In 1970, the UN General Assembly, after years of considerations of form and content, adopted the *Declaration on Principles of International Law concerning Friendly Relations and Co-operation among States in accordance with the Charter of the United Nations,* which reflects the Five Principles of Peaceful Coexistence.[13]

The Five Principles must be understood in the context of China's overall strategic approaches in international relations; soft and hard approaches. Where the Five Principles form a hard core, i.e. cannot be derogated from,[14] they serve as basis of the soft approaches and strategies, like flexibility in the types of OBOR agreements made across the regions instead of an overall, multilateral treaty, and Chinese investments beyond its own borders and the focus on mutual development.[15]

It should be made clear that, even though the Five Principles form a hard core of China's strategies in international relations, there is some flexibility *around* the principles themselves. For example, China's increasing involvement with international dispute settlement bodies, like the WTO Dispute Settlement Body (DSB), is a changed strategy compared to pre-2001 where China mainly would seek resolution of disputes through diplomacy. The softer approach towards international courts indicates that China wants to honour its international obligations and uphold the international rule of law,[16] in particular in the context of the WTO where it is a legal obligation to comply with decisions from the WTO judiciaries.

Cooperating with other countries and international organisations

The soft framework of OBOR with only principled institutional structures makes the line between on the one side OBOR participants and OBOR institutions and on the other side non-participants rather aqueous. For example, there are states, which are not geographically on the OBOR lines, like Denmark and Venezuela, which are members or prospective members of the AIIB. However, it demonstrates the inclusiveness of OBOR.

There are several regional trade agreements (RTA) that are relevant in an OBOR context. For example, the Association of Southeast Asian Nations (ASEAN) works towards integrated markets and facilitating trade. China has a free trade agreement with ASEAN, the ASEAN–China Free Trade Area, which reduces tariffs between the Members. They can be important actors in the OBOR initiative by working towards trade facilitation by reducing trade barriers, like tariffs and quantitative restrictions. See more below about the relationship between free trade agreements and the WTO.

Inclusiveness, harmony and dialogue-based approaches

The inclusive approach and the soft institutional framework open up for participation of countries which are not geographically on the OBOR routes as mentioned above. The harmonious and dialogue-based approach between the states seems to be a good starting point to handle potential conflicts between OBOR participants. However, there can be risks of uneven negotiation power between states in disputes and it might affect investors. In order to attract investors, OBOR should provide a clearer dispute settlement system or overall frameworks to ensure predictability and transparency within the OBOR framework.[17] From a market economy perspective, rule of law is essential for investors and the markets. It provides the certainty that in case of negligence or fraudulent behaviour by market participants, the investors can within their contractual arrangement claim damages. In addition, such a system will penalise criminal activities. For example, insider dealing and money laundering are activities which create market uncertainty by increasing risks on investors.[18]

In line with the UN Charter and the Five Principles of Peaceful Coexistence, disputes must be solved peacefully. The starting position will be through diplomatic means. In case of WTO disputes, it is administrated by the WTO DSB. But in other areas of disputes, there are still no clearly defined institutional bodies with authority to handle OBOR disputes. It has been suggested by the Malaysian Prime Minister, Ong Ka Ting, that the Kuala Lumpur Regional Center for Arbitration (KLRCA) and the China Economic and Trade Arbitration Commission (CIETAC) can cooperate in the relationship between Malaysia and China in OBOR issues. Prime Minister Ong also suggested that arbitration rules among the OBOR states should be harmonised to provide a uniform and consistent mechanism for the enforcement of awards.[19]

Abiding market rules and international norms

The concept of the 'market' is not defined. A market economy can have a low or high level of governmental interference and still be considered as a market economy. For example, it has for a long time been debated whether antidumping rules are protecting importing states from unfair competition or whether they serve as protectionist tools.[20] However, they are part of the market economy system of the WTO and is from that perspective considered as essential for the market economy.

China has faced overcapacity in its production industries and can through OBOR to access new markets in Europe.[21] With the MSR it is expected that shipping times between China and Europe can be reduced with 10 days. The reduced transport time will increase the Chinese competitiveness on European markets.[22] However, many Chinese companies are SOEs. There are economic challenges in respect of the global competition and SOEs. The problem is if the state can decide prices of the SOEs' products and if their financial connections are opaque thus potentially concealing state subsidies. That will be unfair competition against private and public companies where shares are sold on the open market and where the investors will require transparency in order to make informed decisions before making the investment.[23] In addition, state subsidies can be a problem from a market economy perspective as they can make competition on the global market uneven. State subsidies should only apply if they counter negative externalities, like combatting pollution.[24]

Seeking mutual benefits for all parties involved

The investments in infrastructure to facilitate trade should benefit all parties involved. It is not only for increasing the export of Chinese products to Europe but also products from Europe to China and between all other participants.[25]

The question is what 'mutual benefits' implies and how it will be formalised. For example, the flexibility of OBOR seems to fit a model with bilateral agreements between the states along the MSR where states can discuss their respective benefit they seek through the agreements. However, there is uneven negotiation power among the states along the MSR. The question is how China will exercise its strong negotiation power in bilateral negotiations.

Where the principles of OBOR are based on flexibility, inclusiveness, harmony, market economy, diplomacy, and mutual benefit, they might to some extent overlap with the principles of the WTO, which will be discussed in the next part. In that respect, the different levels of negotiation powers between the various OBOR participants may to some extent be caught by WTO law, which will provide a minimum level of trade rights and obligations, which cannot easily be exempted.

WTO constitutional dimension and core principles

The WTO administrates a number of multilateral and plurilateral trade treaties between its 164 members. It serves as a forum for trade negotiations and as a dispute settlement organ in trade disputes concerning the WTO treaties. The WTO covers three areas: trade in goods; trade in services; and intellectual property rights.

The aims of the WTO are mostly of economic character. Market economy principles, like allocation of resources to their best use, are central to the WTO system and are reflected in WTO law. The market economy aims of the WTO are clearer formulated than the market economy principles of the OBOR initiative. However, the stronger institutional structure of the WTO as well as its long time practice of exercising the market economy principles reflected in the WTO treaties provide a clearer picture of the scope and content of the market economy principles of the WTO compared to the OBOR initiative.

The market economy aims are reflected in the WTO core principles. They are:

- *Non-discrimination*, which is reflected in the *most favoured nation principle*, where a WTO Member must not discriminate between its trading partners, and the *national treatment principle*, where a WTO Member must provide the same treatment to foreign products as provided to national products after the foreign product has passed the custom zone;
- *Market access,* which is reflected in the continuous work on lowering tariffs and eliminating trade barriers like quotas;
- *Transparency* which is required in national legal systems that exporters can see through the custom and other import procedures which the product will face once it enters the foreign markets;

- *Fair markets* in order to keep a certain level of fairness on the markets, investors and producers can expect that certain conduct, like dumped prices, is condemned in the WTO and with rights of the importing state to impose antidumping duties. Furthermore, some subsidies are prohibited and can be countered with countervailing duties;
- *Protection of the environment and health* are principles which are attaining stronger hold in WTO law. From an economic perspective, damage to environment and health can be seen as negative externalities, which can be reduced by allowing WTO members to use environmental and health considerations as rights to restrict trade. Such rights are reflected in most of the WTO treaties, like Article XX of the General Agreement on Tariffs and Trade (GATT) 1994.

Besides the overall principles of WTO law, the WTO provides a dispute settlement system which is based on rule of law principles. The rule of law principles are balanced with the basic assumption of state sovereignty of public international law.[26] A WTO member can make a complaint over another WTO Member for violation of WTO law. In the initial phase, negotiations take place between the disputing states. The dialogue-based approach is in line with the overall OBOR principles. However, if the disputing parties cannot reach a solution, the case will be handled by a panel, which will interpret the WTO treaties and reach a binding decision.[27] That decision can be appealed to the Appellate Body (AB), which has authority to overrule the panel. One difference between the WTO dispute settlement, in particular the role of the AB, and the principles of OBOR, is the authority of a non-state actor to provide decisions with *stare decisis*-like characteristics. The authority of the states is clear in Article IX of the WTO Agreement, where it is the Ministerial Conference and the General Council, both represented by the WTO Members, who have final authorities to interpret the WTO treaties. Thus the dispute settlement institutions of the WTO cannot make decisions which will bind in future cases. However, even though the dispute settlement institutions cannot provide decisions that will be binding in future cases *de jure*, they do *de facto* provide binding decisions. Article 3.2, the Dispute Settlement Understanding (DSU), provides that panels and AB cannot add to or diminish the rights and obligations provided in the WTO treaties but must at the same time provide predictability and security into the WTO system. It has been established in WTO case law to mean that panels must follow previous AB decisions unless there are cogent reasons to depart from established practice.[28] Furthermore, there is in theory support of the view that the AB takes upon it some functions like a constitutional court by, for example, reviewing national law.[29]

The WTO has clear institutional and jurisdictional limits. It is confined to the rules and principles of the WTO treaties. Where OBOR provides soft regulation with no bindings on any state – apart from the commitments that states make as members of the AIIB, the Silk Road Fund or the contractual obligations in case of loans provided by the AIIB, etc., WTO law has binding laws, which states must comply with. Lack of compliance with WTO law can result in cases before the WTO dispute settlement system with centralised judiciaries providing *de facto* precedents which the states must follow.

Relationship between the WTO and other trade agreements

The strategies of the MSR will involve investments in projects, which will facilitate regional trade and which potentially will open up for bilateral and multilateral trade agreements between MSR participants. The MSR investments are not a problem from a WTO perspective, but reduced tariffs between MSR participants in various types of free trade agreements can be. There are already a number of RTAs in place between MSR states, like the ASEAN Free Trade Area,[30] and ASEAN – China,[31] which are relevant for the MSR as they reduce tariffs and facilitate market access between their members. This part will address how the WTO approaches RTAs and custom unions. There are potential conflicts between on one hand providing favourable trade conditions to members within a RTA/custom union and on the other hand the most favoured nation principle of the WTO.

WTO law allows RTAs and custom unions. In a recent speech the WTO Director-General Roberto Azevêdo stated: 'Indeed, our analysis of regional agreements shows that they all have WTO DNA. And in the areas where they overlap with WTO rules we have found no obvious conflicts'.[32]

Even though RTAs/custom unions are not obvious problems in the context of the WTO, there have been some issues leading to conflicts about RTAs and WTO law. In order to make RTAs and custom unions, Article XXIV of GATT 1994 provides that custom duties must be eliminated on substantially all trade between the members of the RTA/custom union, and in respect of a custom union there must be use of the same external custom duties towards third countries. Furthermore, they must not put third countries in a disadvantageous position, and the general rules of GATT 1994 must be complied with unless the formation of a RTA/custom union would otherwise be prevented.[33] There is in this respect, a principle of proportionality that must be taken into account. If measures are used, which otherwise would violate GATT 1994, they must not be more trade restrictive than necessary in order to ensure the function of the custom union. In *Turkey – Textiles,*[34] India made a complaint against Turkey for applying quantitative restrictions on textiles from India. Article XI of GATT 1994 prohibits quantitative restrictions which India also referred to. The Turkish restrictions were allegedly a result of its custom union with the EU, which otherwise would be prevented if Turkey did not impose the quantitative restrictions on textile from India. The argument by Turkey was rejected by both the panel and the AB as there were less trade restrictive alternatives available to Turkey, which should have been applied instead of the quantitative restrictions. In the context of the OBOR principles, an argument similar to the one posed by Turkey could be seen as reducing certain OBOR participants' access to the market in violation of the principle of mutual benefits and the inclusiveness principle.

The AB has also dealt with issues which can question whether there is a hierarchical structure between the WTO and RTA/custom unions. *Brazil – Retreaded Tyres*[35] concerned a potential conflict between WTO law and the *Mercado Común del Sur* (MERCOSUR). Brazil had imposed a general ban on the import of retreaded tyres. The ban was found by the MERCOSUR Tribunal to violate MERCOSUR law. In order to comply with the decision from the MERCOSUR Tribunal, Brazil eliminated the ban on the import of retreaded tyres from MERCOSUR Members only but kept the ban in respect of all other non-MERCOSUR states. In the WTO, Brazil was found to violate the most favoured nation principle and the question was whether Brazil had a legitimate exception to the most favoured nation principle by claiming that it had to discriminate between MERCOSUR and non-MERCOSUR states in order to comply with the decision from the MERCOSUR Tribunal. In addition, Brazil referred to Article XX(b) of GATT 1994 about exemptions necessary to protect human health as retreaded tyres carried mosquitoes which could increase the risks of malaria. The AB rejected the claim by Brazil as there was unjustifiable discrimination between MERCOSUR and non-MERCOSUR states. The AB was not persuaded by the health argument either as Brazil had not used that argument before the MERCOSUR Tribunal.

The problem that the AB faced was one about the relationship between the WTO judiciaries and the MERCOSUR Tribunal. The AB does not have jurisdiction over MERCOSUR matters and is not a higher ranking court in the relationship with other international courts. The question was whether the AB indirectly claimed priority over decisions made by the MERCOSUR Tribunal as the AB stated that compliance with a decision from the MERCOSUR Tribunal is not a legitimate basis for applying the exceptions of WTO law. The AB stated that it did not find any conflict between the MERCOSUR Tribunal and the WTO as Brazil had not in the case before the MERCOSUR Tribunal referred to Article 50(d) of the Treaty of Montevideo which has similar protection of human, animal, and plant life and health as Article XX of GATT 1994.[36] Thus, different arguments were forwarded by Brazil before the MERCOSUR Tribunal and the WTO judiciaries.

Even though there is no conflict between the WTO and the MERCOSUR in the specific case, a WTO Member must – regardless of its membership with other trade organisations and their specific rules – comply with its obligations under WTO law in good faith. Treaty compliance in good faith is a fundamental principle of international law and enshrined in the preamble to the UN Charter and codified in the Vienna Convention on the Law of Treaties.[37] Regardless of the soft or hard law and institutional arrangements along the MSR, if it is within the jurisdiction of WTO law, the WTO legal obligations must be honoured. Full compliance with WTO law would also be in line with the principles of OBOR with reference to both the principles of the UN Charter and the Five Principles of Peaceful Coexistence. Should there as a result of OBOR be established custom unions or RTAs, with the aim of reducing tariffs and facilitating market access for goods, the requirements of Article XXIV of GATT 1994 must be met by those participants who are also members of the WTO. Regardless of the internal rules of such RTAs/custom unions and their common external approaches, they cannot deprive the rights which third states have under WTO law.

The WTO and maritime trade facilitation

The WTO does, only to a limited extent, provide rules specific for maritime trade. There are however, some specific rules concerning maritime trade in the General Agreement on Trade in Services (GATS). WTO Members can individually commit to allowing market access and national treatment to foreign service suppliers in the shipping industry. Each WTO Member has its own schedule of commitments to market access and national treatment. For example, in China's Service Schedule under GATS, China has committed to allow foreign ships arriving at ports in China.[38] However, according to China's commitments there are limitations on foreign investment and presence in the Chinese shipping industry:

• Foreign service suppliers are permitted to establish joint venture shipping companies.
• Foreign investment shall not exceed 49 per cent of the total registered capital of the joint venture.
• The chairman of board of directors and the general manager of the joint venture shall be appointed by the Chinese side.[39]

China has only agreed to allow joint ventures between Chinese and foreign companies but with the majority of registered capital in favour of China and with requirement of the chairman of the board of directors as well as the general manager being appointed by China. China is not bound under WTO law in respect of any other type of commercial presence by foreign companies. Internal waterways transport is also limited. Only international shipping in ports open to foreign vessels is permitted.

In respect of the MSR, it is necessary to consult each potential MSR partner's GATS Schedule of Commitments. Where China has made commitments in respect of foreign service suppliers to arrive at port in China, India, for example, has not made any of such commitments.[40] If a WTO Member, who is also an MSR participant, in order to facilitate the trade relationship with other MSR participants provides more favourable shipping terms than the terms provided in the Schedule of Commitments towards other MSR participants, it is a violation of the most favoured nation principle of the WTO. Only by granting similar conditions to all WTO members, or by establishing an RTA/custom union, can an MSR participant provide better shipping conditions than those in the Schedule of Commitment of GATS.

Trade facilitation and competition

Where maritime services are only regulated to a limited extent in the WTO, the picture is different when it comes to general rules on market access of goods.

The OBOR investments in improved ports and general infrastructure along the MSR are aiming towards facilitating trade and reducing the trade costs of the transport of goods from China and other MSR states. Trade costs can be defined as 'all costs apart from the cost of production incurred in getting a good from the producer to the final consumer'.[41] That will include:

> transportation costs, tariffs and non-tariff measures, information costs, customs fees and charges, the cost of time, etc. Some trade costs are easy to measure (e.g. fees and charges for customs processing) but others are more difficult (e.g. the cost of delays in customs clearance).[42]

According to the WTO, trade costs in developing countries can amount to as much as 219 per cent *ad valorem* tariff.[43] From a WTO perspective, trade facilitation and reduced trade costs are important for the growth of the world markets. In the World Trade Report of 2015, it is stated:

> In today's interconnected global economy, efforts to streamline, speed up and coordinate trade procedures, as much as efforts to further liberalize trade policies, will drive the expansion of world trade and help countries to integrate into an increasingly globalized production system, rather than being left on the margins of world trade.[44]

WTO law provides a number of trade facilitation rules. For example, tariffs are regulated in GATT 1994, Art. II, and are provided in each WTO Members' Tariff Schedule, where the aim has been to reduce tariffs over the years. However, MSR participants cannot eliminate tariffs for only MSR participants without violating the most favoured nations principle against other WTO members. Only by establishing an RTA or a custom union in accordance with Article XXIV of GATT 1994 can MSR members eliminate tariffs for other MSR participants.

Furthermore, GATT 1994 provides rules about WTO Members' obligations to provide transparency into their trading systems and rules about goods in transit. Article V of GATT 1994 provides freedom of goods in transit which includes freedom from transit duties. Article VIII of GATT 1994 provides that fees connected with import and export must be limited and that WTO members must minimise formalities in respect of import and export of goods. Article X of GATT 1994 provides that a WTO Member must publish trade regulations and decisions from courts in a timely manner so traders can become associated with them. To strengthening the trade facilitation rules of GATT 1994, one of the few successful outcomes of the Doha Round was the Trade Facilitation Agreement (TFA), which was adopted at the Bali Round in 2013. The TFA aims at reducing trade costs by requiring WTO Members to provide increased transparency in respect of custom procedures, custom duties, fees, and informing about procedures for importation, exportation and transit.

The MSR investments complement WTO law. The improved port infrastructural facilities can reduce time of transportation and thus reduce trade costs. A product produced in China can reach the destinations faster than before by the easier access to port and by improved container facilities, etc. As mentioned above, the port of Piraeus is an example of improved trade facilitation as a result of the MSR investments. Others are the building of a deep-sea port in Kyaukphyu in Myanmar, tow port projects in Sri Lanka, and a deep-sea port at Sonadia Island, Bangladesh.[45] The infrastructural element is outside the scope of WTO law.[46] WTO law provides rules on fees, tariffs, authorities' administration of and procedures related to imported goods, etc. whereas the MSR initiative provides the financial conditions necessary to improve infrastructure as well as opening up for various private, public, and public-private partnerships to bid into the infrastructural projects.

Competition on the markets

Where the MSR investments and strategies seem to provide the necessary financial support to improve port access, terminal operation and port facilities, and seem to be in the spirit of the aims of the WTO, there are caveats to it. Where the market economy aim of the WTO concerns improving market conditions, it is resting on an assumption of fair market conduct by states and enterprises. As mentioned initially, the subjects of WTO law are states, but it does not imply that WTO law cannot provide mechanisms for states against companies acting against fairness on the market.[47]

The overcapacity of Chinese production being shipped to Europe is not in itself subject to the challenge. As promoting market access and aiming towards efficient allocation of resources, it must generally be accepted that foreign goods can compete with domestically produced goods. After all, it can result in more efficient markets to the benefit of consumers and the overall economic welfare. Quantitative restrictions are not allowed in the WTO,[48] and WTO Members must not discriminate between the trading partners and between domestic products and foreign products as mentioned above. However, the economic rationale underlying WTO law cannot stand alone. WTO law provides exceptions to pure trade values, like protection of human, animal, or plant, life and health, protection of exhaustible resources, protection of public moral etc.[49]

Where non-economic policies can be legitimate to limit import of products, economic policies are generally not accepted as legitimate reasons for departing from WTO law. Only in special circumstances may a WTO Member use an economic rationale for imposing trade barriers to the import of products. WTO law provides a 'safeguard' mechanism if there, due to unforeseen developments, have been an increase in import which causes or threatens to cause injury to the domestic industry.[50]

If the conditions for applying the non-economic policies are not met, WTO law provides other instruments to reduce import of products. In the situation with the MSR, there are some concerns about fair competition. One is related to the nature of many Chinese enterprises which are SOEs. In addition, there are WTO rules concerning fair trade which must be considered by MSR participants, in particular China. They provide rights for WTO Members to apply measures to counter unfair market conduct. In the context of the WTO, unfair market conduct can either be conduct by a state if it subsidises its industries, or it can be conduct by enterprises if they dump the prices.

WTO law and SOEs

SOEs are regulated in WTO law. The aim is to prevent states from incorporating companies to escape their obligations under WTO law. As mentioned above, WTO law only binds on the WTO Members (states and the EU) and does not create direct obligations and rights to private parties.[51] However, there is an indirect obligation on SOEs to comply with Article XVII of GATT 1994 as a WTO Member will be held responsible for SOEs' non-compliance with WTO law.[52] Article XVII of GATT 1994 requires that an SOE:

1   complies with the general principles of non-discrimination; and
2   in its sales and purchases on the global market acts in accordance with *commercial considerations*.

The concept of 'commercial considerations' does not imply that an enterprise *must* be profit maximising. As stated by the panel in *Canada – Wheat Exports and Grain Imports*, an SOE is not necessarily established for commercial purposes,[53] and that the WTO rules:

> is simply intended to prevent [SOE]s from behaving like 'political' actors.[54]

The AB rejected the appeal concerning 'commercial considerations' as the appellant, the US, had misread the panel's argument. However, the AB found it necessary to establish that Art. XVII concerns non-discrimination and that:

> We see no basis for interpreting that provision as imposing comprehensive competition-law-type obligations on [STO]s.[55]

Thus, SOEs in the WTO are not under an obligation to act in a narrow market economy sense as a profit maximising entity on the market. However, there must be a distinction between SOEs following political requirements of the state to eliminate foreign competition and SOEs following political programmes of providing support to the public.

As China has been a transition economy, its Accession Protocol to the WTO provides special rules for Chinese SOEs in order to ensure a sufficient level of transparency concerning their import purchasing procedures and price mechanisms of exported goods.[56] China is currently reforming the rules on SOEs. The aim of the reform is to have a wider participation by private investments in SOEs by public offerings of shares; more autonomy to the Board of Directors; and SOEs will be divided into two groups; one for SOEs providing public services, and another for profit-seeking commercial operations.[57]

Nevertheless, there is the concern that Chinese SOEs have easier access to state subsidies and that such subsidies are clearly transparent. Subsidies can be considered as unfair trading practices as they create an uneven competitive environment between subsidised companies and companies which act under market conditions based on investment through market mechanisms, like the stock exchanges. The risk is that the prices of goods of subsidised SOEs can be taken down to a level where other companies cannot follow. However, it must be expected with the Chinese reforms that there will be increased transparency in the SOEs and also a wider group of stakeholders, including private investors, who will require transparency in order to be able to make informed decisions on their investments. However, the close relationship between state and SOE requires special attention in order to ensure that the SOEs compete on market-based terms with fair means on a global scale in compliance with WTO law.

Unfair trading practices

Where the SOEs can pose a challenge to the competitive environment along the MSR, the fast delivery of Chinese goods as a result of the improved trade facilitation pose another. There are in particular two issues which are of concern and which can be an obstacle to the MSR:

- Countervailing measures on subsidised products
- Antidumping duties

If the MSR initiative is a means to transport Chinese overcapacity of products to other MSR members' markets, producers of the like products in the importing states will most likely react to the potential increased import of Chinese goods and increased competition. WTO law provides for trade restrictions against two types of unfair trading practices; subsidised products and dumped products.

A subsidy is a financial contribution[58] from a public body, which is defined as an entity that possesses, exercises or is vested with governmental authority.[59] In addition, there must be a benefit conferred by the subsidy. That implies that the recipient company must be better off by the financial contribution than it otherwise would have been on the market.[60] Under WTO law, some subsidies are prohibited and some are actionable. Export subsidies and local content subsidies are examples of subsidies which are prohibited.[61] All other subsidies are allowed unless a complaining party can demonstrate that the subsidy has an adverse effect on its industries. WTO Members may use *countervailing duties* as remedy against subsidised products.

Between 1995 and 2016, the EU has imposed countervailing duties against subsidised products 37 times and is the second most user of countervailing measures after the United States.[62] China has on overall been the biggest target of countervailing measures by WTO Members in that period with 112 countervailing measures against Chinese products.[63] In particular, Chinese steel and chemicals have been subject to countervailing measures.[64] Currently, the EU has five countervailing measures in force against products from China and two cases under investigation.[65]

In light of the previous part about SOEs, it is likely that WTO Members along the MSR can apply countervailing measures against SOEs if there is no transparency in respect of their sources of income. It will otherwise be suspected to come from the state and not from the market and be considered as a subsidy, and the SOE can be seen as a public body. Thus the work towards improved transparency of SOEs in China is essential in order to reduce the risk of imposition of countervailing duties on goods from Chinese SOEs.

Chinese producers have also been heavily targeted by *antidumping duties*. Out of a total of 3316 antidumping measures reported to the WTO between 1995 and 2016, 840 have been against Chinese producers. The EU has in the period between 1995 and 2016 reported 310 antidumping measures. Currently the EU has 54 antidumping measures in force against Chinese products.[66] However, China is also a heavy user of antidumping duties and has reported 184 since it entered the WTO.

An antidumping duty may be imposed on imported products if they are dumped and they cause or threatens to cause injury to the industry of the like products in the importing state.[67] A product is dumped if the export price is lower than the normal value, i.e. the price on the domestic market. For example, if a producer sells a product on the domestic market for £3 but exports the product for £2 then the product is dumped. The antidumping rules leave wide discretion to the investigating authorities on calculation methods, and China has suffered from special non-market treatment rules by, for example, the EU. Non-market treatment means that when dumping is determined by the EU Commission, it is not based on a comparison between the Chinese producer's domestic price and export price, but based on a comparison between a price from a producer in an analogue country and the Chinese producer's export price. The non-market treatment rules should expire in 2016 but the EU is only in the process of amending its antidumping rules.[68]

The wide discretion poses risk for Chinese producers' export, in particular if it is expected that the MSR investments will reduce the trade costs of transport of products from China to states along the MSR and that there will be an increase in export of Chinese products. In addition, the antidumping rules in the WTO have several unclear provisions, which pose rule of law problems and legal uncertainty, and which leave an open door for importing states to use antidumping as a protectionist tool even though actual dumping may not occur.[69] Furthermore, as long as Chinese SOEs are not fully transparent, the link between state and SOE is regarded as a legitimate basis for other states along the MSR to apply antidumping duties. For example, the claim by the EU is that the SOEs' market conditions are not fully transparent and only if a Chinese company can demonstrate that it acts in accordance with market economy principles, where the EU Commission has wide discretion to decide whether the requirements are met, then market economy treatment will be granted.[70] In addition to the discretionary challenge with the antidumping instrument, Chinese antidumping law provides that antidumping can be applied as *retaliation* against states which impose discriminatory antidumping duties on products from China.[71] The EU is currently working towards amending its antidumping law to include antidumping as a retaliatory instrument as well.[72] The antidumping instrument is not only a tool to be used to protect national industries from allegedly dumped products, but it is also a strategic tool to be used against other states' potential application of antidumping duties.

Where OBOR investments can reduce trade costs along the MSR, the potential increase in the trade of goods between China and other OBOR participants may provide an increase in the use of unfair trading remedies. In particular China is subject to a high number of countervailing and antidumping duties. The use of unfair trading remedies is in line with WTO law but the rules, in particular the antidumping rules, leave wide discretion to the authorities in the importing states. That discretion is exercised in a manner protecting national industries from foreign competition to the detriment of the reduced trade costs.

Concluding remarks

The OBOR initiative and the WTO are not fully comparable. OBOR is an initiative with some overall market principles without a strong institutional framework and without a clear jurisdictional scope. It based on flexible frameworks with potential bilateral agreements between the various participants. The WTO on the other hand has strong institutions and a well-defined jurisdictional basis. However, both OBOR and the WTO have improved market economy as their aims and both provide directions, either through the principles of OBOR or through the binding laws of the WTO on how to reach the aims. Both work towards improving trade facilitations and OBOR complements the WTO; Where OBOR is investing in infrastructural developments of ports along the MSR, the WTO reduces tariffs, formalities and fees. Should the OBOR strategies imply that RTAs or custom unions are established along the MSR to make additional reduction of tariffs it must be in conformity with the specific WTO rules of RTAs/custom unions.

By reducing the trade costs, China might be able to deliver its overcapacity of products to other MSR participants' markets. There are challenges as China has many SOEs, which currently are being reformed in order to provide transparency. Until the reforms are fully implemented, the SOEs can be regarded as bodies of the state from a WTO perspective, and thus be under different sets of WTO law. Furthermore, an increase in export of Chinese products along the MSR can cause increased subsidy investigations and dumping investigations. The latter is a result of unclear antidumping law with wide discretion to the WTO Members and with the potential of applying antidumping as a protectionist tool. Where OBOR is in *harmony* with the aims of the WTO, increased competition may lead to unfair trading *conflicts* between the MSR participants.

Notes

1 See, for example, Klemensitz Péter, *China and the 21st Century New Maritime Silk Road*, PAGEO Geopolitical Institute, March 2017, p. 7; Christopher Len, China's 21st Century Maritime Silk Road Initiative, Energy Security and SLOC Access, *Maritime Affairs: Journal of the National Maritime Foundation of India* 11(1) (2015), 1; Gurpreet S. Khurana, China, India and 'Maritime Silk Road': Seeking a Confluence, *Maritime Affairs: Journal of the National Maritime Foundation of India* 11(1) (2015), 19; Theresa Fallon, The New Silk Road: Xi Jinping's Grand Strategy for Eurasia, *American Foreign Policy Interests* 37(3) (2015), 140.

2 Ministerial Declaration; Ministerial Conference, Fourth Session, Doha, 9 – adopted 14 November 2001, WT/MIN(01)/DEC/1, 20 November 2001.

3 Lee Hill-choi, China's One Belt, One Road Initiative Set to Transform Economy by Connecting with Trading Partners along Ancient Silk Road, *South China Morning Post*, 21 June 2016, www.scmp.com/business/china-business/article/1978450/chinas-one-belt-one-road-initiative-set-transform-economy (accessed 28 August 2017).

4 Vision and Actions on Jointly Building Silk Road Economic Belt and 21st-Century Maritime Silk Road, Issued by the National Development and Reform Commission, Ministry of Foreign Affairs, and Ministry of Commerce of the People's Republic of China, with State Council authorization, 28 March 2015, Part I: Background.

5 See the website www.silkroadfund.com.cn/enweb/23775/23767/index.html (accessed 28 August 2017).

6 See, for example statement on behalf of the UN Secretary General António Guterres; Stéphane Dujarric, Spokesman for the Secretary-General, Statement attributable to the Spokesman for the Secretary-General on Venezuela, 20 April 2017, www.un.org/sg/en/content/sg/statement/2017-04-20/statement-attributable-spokesman-secretary-general-venezuela-0 (accessed 28 August 2017).

7 See AIIB's website: www.aiib.org/en/about-aiib/governance/board-governors/index.html (accessed 28 August 2017).

8 Shannon Tiezzi, Can China Jump-Start Its Maritime Silk Road in 2016?, *The Diplomat*, 12 February, 2016, http://thediplomat.com/2016/02/can-china-jump-start-its-maritime-silk-road-in-2016/ (accessed 28 August 2017).

9 Frans-Paul van der Putten, Chinese Investment in the Port of Piraeus, Greece: The Relevance for the EU and the Netherlands, *Clingendael Report*, Netherlands Institute of International Relations, 2014.

10 Vision and Actions on Jointly Building Silk Road Economic Belt and 21st-Century Maritime Silk Road, Issued by the National Development and Reform Commission, Ministry of Foreign Affairs, and Ministry of Commerce of the People's Republic of China, with State Council authorization, Part II: Principles.

11 See also E. U. Petersmann, International Economic Law, 'Public Reason', and Multi-level Governance of Interdependent Public Goods, *Journal of International Economic Law* 14(1) (2011), 23.

12 The Five principles of peaceful co-existence are: mutual respect for each other's territorial integrity and sovereignty; mutual non-aggression; mutual non-interference in each other's internal affairs; equality and cooperation for mutual benefit; and peaceful coexistence.

13 UN General Assembly Resolution 2625(XXV) of 24 October 1970, Declaration on Principles of International Law concerning Friendly Relations and Co-operation among States in accordance with the Charter of the United Nations, A/RES/25/2625.

14 See Ella Gorian and Kristina Gorian, Chinese Conception of International Law as the Response to the challenges of Today, *Mediterranean Journal of Social Science* 6(3) (2015), 236–240.

15 Jeffrey S Payne, The G.C.C and China's One Belt, One Road: Risk or Opportunity?, Essay at the *Middle East Institute's All About China series*, 2016, www.mei.edu/content/gcc-and-china-s-one-belt-one-road-risk-or-opportunity (accessed 28 August 2017).

16 Wang Yi, China, a Staunch Defender and Builder of International Rule of Law, Ministry of Foreign Affairs of the People's Republic of China, 24 October 2014, www.fmprc.gov.cn/mfa_eng/wjb_663304/wjbz_663308/2461_663310/t1204247.shtml (accessed 28 August 2017).

17 Dominic Barton, Building the Right Silk Road – China and the 'One Belt, One Road' Initiative, *CIRSD* 4 (2015), www.cirsd.org/en/horizons/horizons-summer-2015–issue-no4/building-the-right-silk-road-–china-and-the-%E2%80%98one-belt-one-road-initiative (accessed 28 August 2017).

18 See, for example Karla Hoff and Joseph Stiglitz, After the Big Bang? – Obstacles to the Emergence of the Rule of Law in Post-Communist Societies, *American Economic Review* June (2004), 753.

19 Prashanth Parameswaran, China, Malaysia Mull Dispute Resolution for 'Belt and Road' Countries, *The Diplomat*, 2016, http://thediplomat.com/2016/09/china-malaysia-mull-dispute-resolution-for-belt-and-road-countries/ (accessed 28 August 2017).

20 See more below.

21 Junhua Zhang and Shanghai Jiao, What's Driving China's One Belt, One Road Initiative?, *EASTASIAFORUM*, September 2016; www.eastasiaforum.org/2016/09/02/whats-driving-chinas-one-belt-one-road-initiative/ (accessed 28 August 2017); Richard Ghiasy and Jiayi Zhou, The Silk Road Economic Belt – Considering Security Implications and EU-China Cooperation Prospects, *SIPRE – Stockholm International Peace Research Institute* (2017), 6.

22 Gisela Gringer of the European Parliamentary Research Service, One Belt, One Road (OBOR): China's Regional Integration Initiative, Briefing – European Parliament, July 2016, p. 10.

23 Even though private and public companies are based on open market for purchases of shares, concealing financial connections is still possible and there are numerous cases where companies have either managed to avoid taxes by transferring capital to shell companies in tax havens, or where companies have been involved in money laundering activities and thus created welfare losses on the market.

24 See, for example *Canada – Renewable Energy* and Canada – Feed-In Tariff Program, WT/DS412/AB/R and DS426/AB/R, adopted on 24 May 2013.

25 Klemensits Péter, China and the 21st Century New Maritime Silk Road, *PAGEO Geopitikai Kutatóintézet*, 2017, www.geopolitika.hu/en/2017/03/16/china-and-the-21st-century-new-maritime-silk-road/ (accessed 28 August 2017).

26 Henrik Andersen, China and the WTO Appellate Body's Rule of Law, *Global Journal of Comparative Law* 5 (2016), 146.

27 Technically the decision can be rejected by the DSB if all the WTO Members, including the disputing parties, reject it. Such rejection has never happened in the WTO.

28 See *US – Stainless Steel (Mexico)*, WT/DS344/AB/R, adopted on 20 May 2008; See also Henrik Andersen *supra* (n. 26), p. 169.

29 See, for example Alec Stone Sweet, Constitutionalism, Legal Pluralism, and International Regimes, *Indiana Journal of Global Legal Studies* 16(2) (2009), 621; and Henrik Andersen, Protection of Non-Trade Values in WTO Appellate Body Jurisprudence: Exeptions, Economic Arguments, and Eluding Questions, *Journal of International Economic Law* 18(2) (2015), 383.

30 Current signatories; Brunei Darussalam; Cambodia; Indonesia; Lao People's Democratic Republic; Malaysia; Myanmar; Philippines; Singapore; Thailand; Viet Nam.

31 Current signatories; Brunei Darussalam; Myanmar; Cambodia; Indonesia; Lao People's Democratic Republic; Malaysia; Philippines; Singapore; Viet Nam; Thailand; China.

32 WTO News: Speeches – DG Roberto Azevêdo, A Healthy Trading System Requires Progress and Engagement at all Levels, Speaking at the annual meeting of the Inter-Pacific Bar Association in Kuala Lumpur, Malaysia, on 14 April, 2016, www.wto.org/english/news_e/spra_e/spra119_e.htm – (accessed 28 August 2017).

33 Article XXIV (5) of GATT 1994 provides;

> the provisions of [GATT 1994] shall not prevent, as between the territories of contracting parties, the formation of a customs union (…); Provided that: (a) with respect to a customs union, (…) the duties and other regulations of commerce imposed at the institution of any such union (…) in respect of trade with contracting parties not parties to such union or agreement shall not on the whole be higher or more restrictive than the general incidence of the duties and regulations of commerce applicable in the constituent territories prior to the formation of such union or the adoption of such interim agreement, as the case may be.

34 *Turkey – Textiles*, WT/DS34/AB/R, report adopted by the DSB on 19 November 1999.

35 *Brazil – Retreaded Tyres*, WT/DS332/AB/R, report adopted by the DSB on 17 December 2007.

36 Treaty of Montevideo, Instrument Establishing the Latin American Integration Association (ALADI), done at Montevideo, August 1980.

37 The principle of *pacta sunt servanda* is codified in the Vienna Convention of the Law of Treaties, Article 26. See also comments by the International Law Commission, Draft Articles on the Law of Treaties with Commentaries 1966, *Yearbook of the International Law Commission* II (1966), 211.

38 That covers Central Product Classification (CPC) 7211, passenger transportation and CPC 7212, freight transportation. China has made additional commitments as certain services are made available to international maritime transport suppliers on reasonable and non-discriminatory basis: (1) Pilotage; (2) Towing and tug assistance; (3) Provisioning, fuelling and watering; (4) Garbage collecting and ballast waste disposal; (5) Port Captain's services; (6) Navigation aids; (7) Shore-based operational services essential to ship operations, including communications, water and electrical supplies; (8) Emergency repair facilities; (9) Anchorage, berth and berthing services.

39 See China's Schedule of Commitments under GATS.

40 It does not imply that foreign ships cannot access Indian ports but only that India has no legal obligation under WTO law to allow foreign ships' access to ports.

41 WTO, Speeding up trade: benefits and challenges of implementing the WTO Trade Facilitation Agreement, *World Trade Report* 2015, WTO 2015, 6.

42 *Ibid.*, 74.

43 *Ibid.*, 7.

44 *Ibid.*, 4.

45 Richard Scott, China's Maritime Silk Road project advances, *Hellenic Shipping News Worldwide*, 12 July 2016, www.hellenicshippingnews.com/chinas-maritime-silk-road-project-advances/ (accessed 28 August 2017).

46 There can be some reservations here. Construction is part of the plurilateral Government Procurement Agreement, where China is not a party but has observer status. In addition, construction services are part of GATS.

47 It should be noted that several states also have competition laws against companies' anticompetitive conduct. For example, the Treaty of the European Union, Article 101 and Article 102, and the Anti-Monopoly Law of the People's Republic of China, NPC, 30 August 2007.

48 That must also be seen with some reservations. See, for example measures that can be taken against certain Chinese products, China's Accession Protocol to the WTO.

49 Article XX of GATT 1994.

50 Article XIX of GATT 1994 and the Safeguard Agreement.

51 *Canada – Wheat Exports and Grain Imports*, WT/DS276/R, adopted by the DSB on 18 October 2004, para. 6.39.

52 *Ibid.*, para. 6.42.

53 *Ibid.*, para. 6.96.

54 *Ibid.*, para. 6.94.

55 *Canada – Wheat Exports and Grain Imports*, WT/DS276/AB/R, adopted by the DSB · on 18 October 2004, para. 145.
56 Article 6 of the Chinese Accession Protocol.
57 Gary Jefferson, State-Owned Enterprise in China: Reform, Performance, and Prospects, *Working Paper Series*, Economics Department, Brandeis University, 2016–2019, p. 12.
58 WTO law provides the following types of financial contributions: a government practice involves a direct transfer of funds (e.g. grants, loans, and equity infusion), potential direct transfers of funds or liabilities (e.g. loan guarantees); government revenue that is otherwise due is foregone or not collected (e.g. fiscal incentives such as tax credits); a government provides goods or services other than general infrastructure, or purchases goods; a government makes payments to a funding mechanism, or entrusts or directs a private body to carry out one or more of the type of functions illustrated in (i) to (iii) above which would normally be vested in the government and the practice, in no real sense, differs from practices normally followed by governments; or there is any form of income or price support in the sense of Article XVI of GATT 1994.
59 Article 1 of the SCM Agreement as clarified by the AB in *US – Anti-Dumping and Countervailing Duties (China)*, WT/DS449/AB/R, adopted by the DSB on 22 July 2014, paras 317–318.
60 *Canada – Aircraft*, WT/DS70/AB/R, adopted by the DSB on 4 August 2000, paras 157–158.
61 'Export subsidy' is a subsidy granted if certain export quotas are met. 'Local content subsidy' is a subsidy based on a requirement that the producer uses domestic products. It is regulated in The Agreement on Subsidies and Countervailing Measures and Article VI of GATT 1994.
62 The US used countervailing measures 98 times in that period.
63 The data for China only covers the period from 2001, where China entered the WTO, to 2016.
64 See statistics, www.wto.org/english/tratop_e/scm_e/scm_e.htm (accessed 28 August 2017).
65 See Semi-Annual Report under Article 25.11 of the Agreement European Union, WTO Committee on Subsidies and Countervailing Measures, G/SCM/N/313/EU, 13 April 2017.
66 Semi-Annual Report under Article 16.4 of the Agreement, European Union, WTO Committee on Anti-Dumping Practices, G/ADP/N/294/EU, 11 April 2017.
67 Antidumping is regulated in Article VI of GATT 1994 and in the WTO Antidumping Agreement.
68 China's Accession Protocol to the WTO, Article 15. The EU antidumping rules have basis in Regulation (EU) 2016/1036 of the European Parliament and of the Council of 8 June 2016 on protection against dumped imports from countries not members of the European Union.
69 See Henrik Andersen, WTO Antidumping Jurisprudence and Rule of Law Challenges, in: Pernilla Rendahl *et al.* (eds), *Festschrift in Honour of Christina Moëll* (Lund: Juristförlaget i Lund, 2017), pp. 11–33.
70 Article 2.7 of Regulation (EU) 2016/1036 of the European Parliament and of the Council of 8 June 2016 on protection against dumped imports from countries not members of the European Union. As mentioned above, the EU is in the process of amending the specific antidumping rules on Chinese producers.
71 Article 56 of the Anti-dumping Regulation of the People's Republic of China (Revised on 31 March, 2004), Decree of the state Council of the People's Republic of China No. 328.
72 Commission Staff Working Document Impact Assessment, Accompanying the document Proposal for a Regulation of the European Parliament and of The Council on the Modernisation of Trade Defence Instruments, SWD (2013) 105 final, Brussels, 10.4.2013, para. 4.3, p. 24.

Index